Database Design for Smarties

USING UML FOR DATA MODELING

Database Design for Smarties

USING UML FOR DATA MODELING

Robert J. Muller

MORGAN KAUFMANN PUBLISHERS, INC.
SAN FRANCISCO, CALIFORNIA

SENIOR EDITOR Diane D. Cerra

DIRECTOR OF PRODUCTION AND MANUFACTURING Yonie Overton

PRODUCTION EDITORS Julie Pabst and Cheri Palmer

EDITORIAL ASSISTANT Belinda Breyer

COPYEDITOR Ken DellaPenta

PROOFREADER Christine Sabooni

TEXT DESIGN Based on a design by Detta Penna, Penna Design & Production

COMPOSITION AND
TECHNICAL ILLUSTRATIONS Technologies 'N Typography

COVER DESIGN Ross Carron Design

COVER IMAGE PhotoDisc (magnifying glass)
Archive Photos (Sherlock Holmes)

INDEXER Ty Koontz

PRINTER Courier Corporation

Designations used by companies to distinguish their products are often claimed as trademarks or registered trademarks. In all instances where Morgan Kaufmann Publishers, Inc. is aware of a claim, the product names appear in initial capital or all capital letters. Readers, however, should contact the appropriate companies for more complete information regarding trademarks and registration.

MORGAN KAUFMANN PUBLISHERS, INC.
Editorial and Sales Office
340 Pine Street, Sixth Floor
San Francisco, CA 94104-3205
USA

TELEPHONE 415/392-2665
FACSIMILE 415/982-2665
EMAIL mkp@mkp.com
WWW http://www.mkp.com
ORDER TOLL FREE 800/745-7323

LIBRARY OF CONGRESS CATALOGING-IN-PUBLICATION DATA

Muller, Robert J.
     Database design for smarties : using UML for data modeling /
Robert J. Muller.
       p.   cm.
     Includes bibliographical references and index.
     ISBN 1-55860-515-0
     1. Database design. 2. UML (Computer science)   I. Title.
     QA76.9.D26 M85 1999
     005.74—dc21   98-54436
                                                CIP

To Theo,

whose database design expands every day

Chapters

Contents

Preface

This book presents a simple thesis: that you can design any kind of database with standard object-oriented design techniques. As with most things, the devil is in the details, and with database design, the details often wag the dog.

That's Not the Way We Do Things Here

The book discusses relational, object-relational (OR), and object-oriented (OO) databases. It does not, however, provide a comparative backdrop of all the database design and information modeling methods in existence. The thesis, again, is that you can pretty much dispose of most of these methods in favor of using standard OO design—whatever that might be. If you're looking for information on the right way to do IDEF1X designs, or how to use SSADM diagramming, or how to develop good designs in Oracle's Designer/2000, check out the Bibliography for the competition to this book.

I've adopted the Unified Modeling Language (UML) and its modeling methods for two reasons. First, it's an approved standard of the Object Management Group (OMG). Second, it's the culmination of years of effort by three very smart object modelers, who have come together to unify their disparate methods into a single, very capable notation standard. See Chapter 7 for details on the UML. Nevertheless, you may want to use some other object modeling method. You owe it to yourself to become familiar with the UML concepts, not least because they are a union of virtually all object-oriented method concepts that I've seen in practice. By learning UML, you learn object-oriented design concepts systematically. You can then transform the UML notation and its application in this book into whatever object-oriented notation and method you want to use.

This book is not a database theory book; it's a database practice book. Unlike some authors [Codd 1990; Date and Darwen 1998], I am not engaged in presenting a completely new way to look at databases, nor am I presenting an academic thesis. This book is about using current technologies to build valuable software systems productively. I stress the adapting of current technologies to object-oriented design, not the replacement of them by object-oriented technologies.

Finally, you will notice this book tends to use examples from the Oracle database management system. I have spent virtually my entire working life with Oracle, though I've used other databases from Sybase to Informix to SQL Server, and I use examples from all of those DBMS products. The concepts in this book are quite general. You can translate any Oracle example into an equivalent from any other DBMS, at least as far as the relational schema goes. Once you move into the realm of the object-relational DBMS or the object-oriented DBMS, however, you will find that your specific product determines much of what you can do (see Chapters 12 and 13 for details). My point: Don't be fooled into thinking the techniques in this book are any different if you use Informix or MS Access. *Design* is the point of this book, not implementation. As with UML, if you understand the concepts, you can translate the details into your chosen technology with little trouble. If you have specific questions about applying the techniques in practice, please feel free to drop me a line at *muller@computer.org,* and I'll do my best to work out the issues with you.

Data Warehousing

Aficionados of database theory will soon realize there is a big topic missing from this book: data warehousing, data marts, and star schemas. One has to draw the line somewhere in an effort of this size, and my publisher and I decided not to include the issues with data warehousing to make the scope of the book manageable.

Briefly, a key concept in data warehousing is the *dimension,* a set of information attributes related to the basic objects in the warehouse. In classic data analysis, for example, you often structure your data into multidimensional tables, with the cells being the intersection of the various dimensions or categories. These tables become the basis for analysis of variance and other statistical modeling techniques. One important organization for dimensions is the *star schema,* in which the dimension tables surround a fact table (the object) in a star configuration of one-to-many relationships. This configuration lets a data analyst look at the facts in the database (the basic objects) from the different dimensional perspectives.

In a classic OO design, the star schema is a pattern of interrelated objects that come together in a central object of some kind. The central object does not own the other objects; rather, it relates them to one another in a multidimensional framework. You implement a star schema in a relational database as a set of one-to-many tables, in an object-relational database as a set of object references, and in an object-oriented database as an object with dimensional accessors and attributes that refer to other objects.

Web Enhancement

If you're interested in learning more about database management, here are some of the prominent relational, object-relational, and object-oriented products. Go to the Web sites to find the status of the current product and any trial downloads they might have.

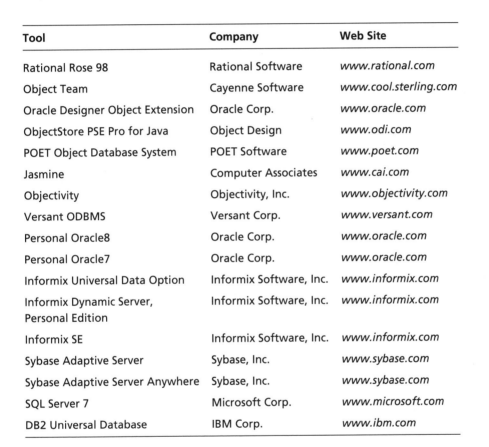

Tool	Company	Web Site
Rational Rose 98	Rational Software	*www.rational.com*
Object Team	Cayenne Software	*www.cool.sterling.com*
Oracle Designer Object Extension	Oracle Corp.	*www.oracle.com*
ObjectStore PSE Pro for Java	Object Design	*www.odi.com*
POET Object Database System	POET Software	*www.poet.com*
Jasmine	Computer Associates	*www.cai.com*
Objectivity	Objectivity, Inc.	*www.objectivity.com*
Versant ODBMS	Versant Corp.	*www.versant.com*
Personal Oracle8	Oracle Corp.	*www.oracle.com*
Personal Oracle7	Oracle Corp.	*www.oracle.com*
Informix Universal Data Option	Informix Software, Inc.	*www.informix.com*
Informix Dynamic Server, Personal Edition	Informix Software, Inc.	*www.informix.com*
Informix SE	Informix Software, Inc.	*www.informix.com*
Sybase Adaptive Server	Sybase, Inc.	*www.sybase.com*
Sybase Adaptive Server Anywhere	Sybase, Inc.	*www.sybase.com*
SQL Server 7	Microsoft Corp.	*www.microsoft.com*
DB2 Universal Database	IBM Corp.	*www.ibm.com*

The Database Life Cycle 1

For mine own part, I could be well content
To entertain the lagend of my life
With quiet hours.

Shakespeare, Henry IV Part 1, V.i.23

Databases, like every kind of software object, go through a life stressed with change. This chapter introduces you to the life cycle of databases. While database design is but one step in this life cycle, understanding the whole is definitely relevant to understanding the part. You will also find that, like honor and taxes, design pops up in the most unlikely places.

The life cycle of a database is really many smaller cycles, like most lives. Successful database design does not lumber along in a straight line, Godzilla-like, crushing everything in its path. Particularly when you start using OO techniques in design, database design is an iterative, incremental process. Each increment produces a working database; each iteration goes from modeling to design to construction and back again in whatever order makes sense. Database design, like all system design, uses a leveling process [Hohmann 1997]. *Leveling* is the cognitive equivalent of water finding its own level. When the situation changes, you move to the part of the life cycle that suits your needs at the moment. Sometimes that means you are building the physical structures; at other times, you are modeling and designing new structures.

> *Note: Beware of terminological confusion here. I've found it expedient to define my terms as I go, as there are so many different ways of describing the same thing. In particular, be aware of my use of the terms "logical" and "physical." Often, CASE vendors and others use the term "physical" design to distinguish the relational schema design from the entity-relationship data model. I call the latter process modeling and the former process logical or conceptual design, following the ANSI architectural standards that Chapter 2 discusses. Physical design is the process of setting up the physical schema, the collection of access paths and storage structures of the database.*

This is completely distinct from setting up the relational schema, though often you use similar data definition language statements in both processes. Focus on the actual purpose behind the work, not on arbitrary divisions of the work into these categories. You should also realize that these terminological distinctions are purely cultural in nature; learning them is a part of your socialization into the particular design culture in which you will work. You will need to map the actual work into your particular culture's language to communicate effectively with the locals.

Information Requirements Analysis

Databases begin with people and their needs. As you design your database, your concern should be for the needs of database users. The *end user* is the ultimate consumer of the software, the person staring at the computer screen while your queries iterate through the thousands or millions of objects in your system. The *system user* is the direct consumer of your database, which he or she uses in building the system the end user uses. The system user is the programmer who uses SQL or OQL or any other language to access the database to deliver the goods to the end user.

Both the end user and the system user have specific needs that you must know about before you can design your database. Requirements are needs that you must translate into some kind of structure in your database design. Information requirements merge almost indistinguishably into the requirements for the larger system of which the database is a part.

In a database-centric system, the data requirements are critical. For example, if the whole point of your system is to provide a persistent collection of informational objects for searching and access, you must spend a good deal of time understanding information requirements. The more usual system is one where the database supports the ongoing use of the system rather than forming a key part of its purpose. With such a database, you spend more of your time on requirements that go beyond the simple needs of the database. Using standard OO use cases and the other accouterments of OO analysis, you develop the requirements that lead to your information needs. Chapters 3 and 4 go into detail on these techniques, which permit you to resolve the ambiguities in the end users' views of the database. They also permit you to recognize the needs of the system users of your data as you recognize the things that the database will need to do. End users need objects that reflect their world; system users need structures that permit them to do their jobs effectively and productively.

One class of system user is more important than the rest: the reuser. The true benefit of OO system design is in the ability of the system user to change the use of your database. You should always design it as though there is someone looking over your shoulder who will be adding something new after you finish—maybe new database structures, connecting to other databases, or new systems that use your database. The key to understanding reuse is the combination of reuse potential and reuse certification.

Reuse potential is the degree to which a system user will be able to reuse the database in a given situation [Muller 1998]. Reuse potential measures the inherent reusability of the system, the reusability of the system in a specific domain, and the reusability of the system in an organization. As you design, you must look at each of these components of reuse potential to create an optimally reusable database.

Reuse certification, on the other hand, tells the system user what to expect from your database. Certifying the reusability of your database consists of telling system users what the level of risk is in reusing the database, what the functions of the database are, and who takes responsibility for the system.

Chapter 9 goes into detail on reuse potential and certification for databases.

Data Modeling

Given the users' needs, you now must formally model the problem. Data modeling serves several purposes. It helps you to organize your thinking about the data, clarifying its meaning and practical application. It helps you to communicate both the needs and how you intend to meet them. It provides a platform from which you can proceed to design and construction with some assurance of success.

Data modeling is the first step in database design. It provides the link between the users' needs and the software solution that meets them. It is the initial abstraction that hides the complexity of the system. The data model reduces complexity to a level that the designer can grasp and manipulate. As databases and data structures grow ever more numerous and complex, data modeling takes on more and more importance. Its contribution comes from its ability to reveal the essence of the system out of the obscurity of the physical and conceptual structures on the one hand and the multiplicity of uses on the other.

Most database data modeling currently uses some variant of entity-relationship (ER) modeling [Teorey 1999]. Such models focus on the things and the links between things (entities and relationships). Most database design tools are ER modeling tools. You can't write a book about database design without talking about ER modeling; Chapter 6 does that in this book to provide a context for Chapter 7, which proposes a change in thinking.

The next chapter (Chapter 2) proposes the idea that system architecture and database design are one and the same. ER modeling is not particularly appropriate for modeling system architecture. How can you resolve the contradiction?

You either use ER modeling as a piece of the puzzle under the assumption that database design is a puzzle, or you integrate your modeling into a unified structure that designs systems, not puzzles.

Chapter 7 introduces the basics of the UML, a modeling notation that provides tools for modeling every aspect of a software system from requirements to implementation. Object modeling with the UML takes the place of ER modeling in modern database design, or at least that's what this book proposes.

Object modeling uses standard OO concepts of data hiding and inheritance to model the system. Part of that model covers the data needs of the system. As you develop the structure of classes and objects, you model the data your system provides to its users to meet their needs.

But object modeling is about far more than modeling the static structure of a system. Object modeling covers the dynamic behavior of the system as well. Inheritance reflects the data structure of the system, but it also reflects the division of labor through behavioral inheritance and polymorphism. This dynamic character has at least two major effects on database design. First, the structure of the system reflects behavioral needs as well as data structure differences. This focus on behavior often yields a different understanding of the mapping of the design to the real world that would not be obvious from a more static data model. Second, with the increasing integration of behavior into the database through rules, triggers, stored procedures, and active objects, static methods often fail to capture a vital part of the database design. How does an ER model reflect a business rule that goes beyond the simple referential integrity foreign key constraint, for example?

Chapters 8 to 10 step back from object modeling to integrate models into a useful whole from the perspective of the user. Relating the design to requirements is a critical aspect of database design because it clarifies the reasons behind your design decisions. It also highlights the places where different parts of the system conflict, perhaps because of conflicting user expectations for the system. A key part of data modeling is the resolution of such conflicts at the highest level of the model.

The modeling process is just the start of design. Once you have a model, the next step is to relate the model back to needs, then to move forward to adding the structures that support both reuse and system functions.

Database Design and Optimization

When does design start? Design starts at whatever point in the process that you begin thinking about how things relate to one another. You iterate from modeling to design seamlessly. Adding a new entity or class is modeling; deciding how that entity or class relates to other ones is design.

Where does design start? Usually, design starts somewhere else. That is, when you start designing, you are almost always taking structures from somebody else's work, whether it's requirements analysis, a legacy database, a prior system's architecture, or whatever. The quality, or value, of the genetic material that forms the basis of your design can often determine its success. As with anything else, however, how you proceed can have as much impact on the ultimate result of your project.

You may, for example, start with a legacy system designed for a relational database that you must transform into an OO database. That legacy system may not even be in third normal form (see Chapter 11), or it may be the result of six committees over a 20-year period (like the U.S. tax code, for example). While having a decent starting system helps, where you wind up depends at least as much on how you get there as on where you start. Chapter 10 gives you some hints on how to proceed from different starting points and also discusses the cultural context in which your design happens. Organizational culture may impact design more than technology.

The nitty-gritty part of design comes when you transform your data model into a schema. Often, CASE tools provide a way to generate a relational schema directly from your data model. Until those tools catch up with current realities, however, they won't be of much help unless you are doing standard ER modeling and producing standard relational schemas. There are no tools of which I'm aware that produce OO or OR models from OO designs, for example. Chapters 11, 12, and 13 show how to produce relational, OR, and OO designs, respectively, from the OO data model. While this transformation uses variations on the standard algorithm for generating schemas from models, it differs subtly in the three different cases. As well, there are some tricks of the trade that you can use to improve your schemas during the transformation process.

Build bridges before you, and don't let them burn down behind you after you've crossed. Because database design is iterative and incremental, you cannot afford to let your model lapse. If your data model gets out of synch with your schema, you will find it more and more difficult to return to the early part of design. Again, CASE tools can help if they contain reverse-engineering tools for generating models from schemas, but again those tools won't support much of the techniques in this book. Also, since the OO model supports more than just simple schema definition, lack of maintenance of the model will spill over into the general system design, not just database design.

At some point, your design crosses from logical design to physical design. This book covers only logical design, leaving physical design to a future book. Physical design is also an iterative process, not a rigid sequence of steps. As you develop your physical schema, you will realize that certain aspects of your logical design affect the physical design in negative ways and need revision. Changes to the logical design as you iterate through requirements and modeling also require changes to physical design. For example, many database designers optimize performance by denormalizing their logical design. Denormalization is the process of combining tables or objects to promote faster access, usually through avoiding data joins. You trade off better performance for the need to do more work to maintain integrity, as data may appear in more than one place in the database. Because it has negative effects on your design, you need to consider denormalizing in an iterative process driven by requirements rather than as a standard operating procedure. Chapter 11 discusses denormalization in some detail.

Physical design mainly consists of building the access paths and storage structures in the physical model of the database. For example, in a relational database, you create indexes on sets of columns, you decide whether to use B*-trees, hash indexes, or bitmaps, or you decide whether to prejoin tables in clusters. In an OO database, you might decide to cluster certain objects together or index particular partitions of object extents. In an OR database, you might install optional storage management or access path modules for extended data types, configuring them for your particular situation, or you might partition a table across several disk drives. Going beyond this simple configuration of the physical schema, you might distribute the database over several servers, implement replication strategies, or build security systems to control access.

As you move from logical to physical design, your emphasis changes from modeling the real world to improving the system's performance—database optimization and tuning. Most aspects of physical design have a direct impact on how your database performs. In particular, you must take into consideration at this point how end users will access the data. The need to know about end user access means that you must do some physical design while incrementally designing and building the systems that use the database. It's not a bad idea to have some brainstorming sessions to predict the future of the system as well. Particularly if you are designing mission-critical decision support data warehouses or instant-response online transaction processing systems, you must have a clear idea of the performance requirements before finalizing your physical design. Also, if you are designing physical models using advanced software/hardware combinations such as symmetric multiprocessing (SMP), massively parallel processing (MPP), or clustered processors, physical design is critical to tuning your database.

> *Tip: You can benefit from the Internet in many ways as a database designer. There are many different Usenet newsgroups under the* comp.databases *interest group, such as* comp.databases .oracle.server. *There are several Web sites that specialize in vendor-specific tips and tricks; use a Web search engine to search for such sites. There are also mailing lists (email that gets sent to you automatically with discussion threads about a specific topic) such as the data modeling mail list. These lists may be more or less useful depending on the level of activity on the list server, which can vary*

*from nothing for months to hundreds of messages in a week. You
can usually find out about lists through the Usenet newsgroups relating to your specific subject area. Finally, consider joining any user
groups in your subject area such as the Oracle Developer Tools User
Group (www.odtug.com); they usually have conferences, maintain
web sites, and have mailing lists for their members.*

Your design is not complete until you consider risks to your database and
the risk management methods you can use to mitigate or avoid them. *Risk* is the
potential for an occurrence that will result in negative consequences. Risk is a
probability that you can estimate with data or with subjective opinion. In the database area, risks include such things as disasters, hardware failures, software failures and defects, accidental data corruption, and deliberate attacks on the data or
server. To deal with risk, you first determine your tolerance for risk. You then
manage risk to keep it within your tolerance. For example, if you can tolerate a
few hours of downtime every so often, you don't need to take advantage of the
many fault-tolerant features of modern DBMS products. If you don't care about
minor data problems, you can avoid the huge programming effort to catch problems at every level of data entry and modification. Your risk management methods should reflect your tolerance for risk instead of being magical rituals you perform to keep your culture safe from the database gods (see Chapter 10 on some of
the more shamanistic cultural influences on database design). Somewhere in this
process, you need to start considering that most direct of risk management techniques, testing.

Database Quality, Reviews, and Testing

Database quality comes from three sources: requirements, design, and construction. Requirements and design quality use review techniques, while construction
uses testing. Chapter 5 covers requirements and database testing, and the various
design chapters cover the issues you should raise in design reviews. Testing the
database comes in three forms: testing content, testing structure, and testing behavior. Database test plans use test models that reflect these components: the
content model, the structural model, and the design model.

Content is what database people usually call "data quality." When building
a database, you have many alternative ways to get data into the database. Many
databases come with prepackaged content, such as databases of images and text
for the Internet, search-oriented databases, or parts of databases populated with
data to reflect options and/or choices in a software product. You must develop a
model that describes what the assumptions and rules are for this data. Part of this
model comes from your data model, but no current modeling technique is completely adequate to describe all the semantics and pragmatics of database content.

Good content test plans cover the full range of content, not just the data model's limited view of it.

The data model provides part of the structure for the database, and the physical schema provides the rest. You need to verify that the database actually constructed contains the structures that the data model calls out. You must also verify that the database contains the physical structures (indexes, clusters, extended data types, object containers, character sets, security grants and roles, and so on) that your physical design specifies. Stress, performance, and configuration tests come into play here as well. There are several testing tools on the market that help you in testing the physical capabilities of the database, though most are for relational databases only.

The behavioral model comes from your design's specification of behavior related to persistent objects. You usually implement such behavior in stored procedures, triggers or rules, or server-based object methods. You use the usual procedural test modeling techniques, such as data flow modeling or state-transition modeling, to specify the test model. You then build test suites of test scripts to cover those models to your acceptable level of risk. To some extent, this overlaps with your standard object and integration testing, but often the testing techniques are different, involving exercise of program units outside your main code base.

Both structural and behavioral testing require a test bed of data in the database. Most developers seem to believe that "real" data is all the test bed you need. Unfortunately, just as with code testing, "real" data only covers a small portion of the possibilities, and it doesn't do so particularly systematically. Using your test models, you need to develop consistent, systematic collections of data that cover all the possibilities you need to test. This often requires several test beds, as the requirements result in conflicting data in the same structures. Creating a test bed is not a simple, straightforward loading of real-world data.

Your test development proceeds in parallel with your database design and construction, just as with all other types of software. You should think of your testing effort in the same way as your development effort. Use the same iterative and incremental design efforts, with reviews, that you use in development, and test your tests.

Testing results in a clear understanding of the risks of using your database. That in turn leads to the ability to communicate that risk to others who want to use it: *certification.*

Database Certification

It's very rare to find a certified database. That's a pity, because the need for such a thing is tremendous. I've encountered time and again users of database-centric systems wanting to reuse the database or its design. They are usually not able to do so, either because they have no way to figure out how it works or because the vendor of the software refuses to permit access to it out of fear of "corruption."

This kind of thing is a special case of a more general problem: the lack of reusability in software. One of the stated advantages of OO technology is increased productivity through reuse [Muller 1998]. The reality is that reuse is hard, and few projects do it well. The key to reuse comes in two pieces: design for reuse and reuse certification.

This whole book is about design for reuse. All the techniques I present have an aspect of making software and databases more reusable. A previous section in this chapter, "Information Requirements Analysis," briefly discussed the nature of reuse potential, and Chapter 9 goes into detail on both reuse potential and certification.

Certification has three parts: risk, function, and responsibility. Your reviewing and testing efforts provide data you can use to assess the risk of reusing the database and its design. The absence of risk certification leads to the reflexive reaction of most developers that the product should allow no one other than them to use the database. On the other hand, the lack of risk analysis can mislead maintainers into thinking that changes are easy or that they will have little impact on existing systems. The functional part of the certification consists of clear documentation for the conceptual and physical schemas and a clear statement of the intended goals of the database. Without understanding how it functions, no one will be able to reuse the database. Finally, a clear statement of who owns and is responsible for the maintenance of the database permits others to reuse it with little or no worries about the future. Without it, users may find it difficult to justify reusing "as is" code and design—and data. This can seriously inhibit maintenance and enhancement of the database, where most reuse occurs.

Database Maintenance and Enhancement

This book spends little time on it, but maintenance and enhancement are the final stage of the database life cycle. Once you've built the database, you're done, right? Not quite.

You often begin the design process with a database in place, either as a legacy system or by inheriting the design from a previous version of the system. Often, database design is in thrall to the logic of maintenance and enhancement. Over the years, I've heard more plaintive comments from designers on this subject than any other. The inertia of the existing system drives designers crazy. You are ready to do your best work on interesting problems, and someone has constrained your creativity by actually building a system that you must now modify. Chapter 10 goes into detail on how to best adapt your design talents to these situations.

Again, database design is an iterative, incremental process. The incremental nature does not cease with delivery of the first live database, only when the database ceases to exist. In the course of things, a database goes through many changes, never really settling down into quiet hours at the lag-end of life. The next few chapters return to the first part of the life cycle, the birth of the database as a response to user needs.

CHAPTER

System Architecture and Design 2

Works of art, in my opinion, are the only objects in the material universe to possess internal order, and that is why, though I don't believe that only art matters, I do believe in Art for Art's Sake.

E. M Forster, *Art for Art's Sake*

I s there a difference between the verbs "to design" and "to architect"? Many people think that "to architect" is one of those bastard words that become verbs by way of misguided efforts to activate nouns. Not so, in this case: the verb "to architect" has a long and distinguished history reaching back to the sixteenth century. But is there a difference?

In the modern world of databases, often it seems there is little difference in theory but much difference in practice. Database administrators and data architects "design" databases and systems, and application developers "architect" the systems that use them. You can easily distinguish the tools of database design from the tools of system architecture.

The main thesis of this book is that *there is no difference*. Designing a database using the methods in this book merges indistinguishably with architecting the overall system of which the database is a part. Architecture is multidimensional, but these dimensions interact as a complex system rather than being completely separate and distinct. Database design, like most architecture, is art, not science.

That art pursues a very practical goal: to make information available to clients of the software system. *Databases* have been around since Sumerians and Egyptians first began using cuneiform and hieroglyphics to record accounts in a form that could be preserved and reexamined on demand [Diamond 1997]. That's the essence of a database: a reasonably permanent and accessible storage mechanism for information. Designing databases before the computer age came upon us was literally an art, as examination of museum-quality Sumerian, Egyptian, Mayan, and Chinese writings will demonstrate. The computer gave us something more: the *database management system,* software that makes the database come alive in the hands of the client. Rather than a clay tablet or dusty wall, the

11

database has become an abstract collection of bits organized around data structures, operations, and constraints. The design of these software systems encompassing both data and its use is the subject of this book.

System architecture, the first dimension of database design, is the architectural abstraction you use to model your system as a whole: applications, servers, databases, and everything else that is part of the system. System architecture for database systems has followed a tortuous path in the last three decades. Early hierarchical and flat-file databases have developed into networked collections of pointers to relations to objects—and mixtures of all of these together. These data models all fit within a more slowly evolving model of database system architecture. Architectures have moved from simple internal models to the CODASYL DBTG (Conference on Data Systems Languages Data Base Task Group) network model of the late 1960s [CODASYL DBTG 1971] through the three-schema ANSI/SPARC (American National Standards Institute/Standards Planning and Requirements Committee) architecture of the 1970s [ANSI 1975] to the multitier client/server and distributed-object models of the 1980s and 1990s. And we have by no means achieved the end of history in database architecture, though what lies beyond objects hides in the mists of the future.

The *data architecture,* the architectural abstraction you use to model your persistent data, provides the second dimension to database design. Although there are other kinds of database management systems, this book focuses on the three most popular types: relational (RDBMS), object-relational (ORDBMS), and object-oriented (OODBMS). The data architecture provides not only the structures (tables, classes, types, and so on) that you use to design the database but also the language for expressing both behavior and business rules or constraints.

Modern database design not only reflects the underlying system architecture you choose, it derives its essence from your architectural choices. Making architectural decisions is as much a part of a database designer's life as drawing entities and relationships or navigating the complexities of SQL, the standardized relational database language. Thus, this book begins with architecture before getting to the issue at hand—design.

System Architectures

A *system architecture* is an abstract structure of the objects and relationships that make up a system. Database system architectures reveal the objects that make up a data-centric software system. Such objects include applications components and their views of data, the database layers (often called the *server architecture*), and the *middleware* (software that connects clients to servers, adding value as needed) that establishes connections between the application and the database.

Each architecture contains such objects and the relationships between them. Architectural differences often center in such relationships.

Studying the history and theory of system architecture pays large rewards to the database designer. In the course of this book, I introduce the architectural features that have influenced my own design practice. By the end of this chapter, you will be able to recognize the basic architectural elements in your own design efforts. You can further hone your design sense by pursuing more detailed studies of system architecture in other sources.

The Three-Schema Architecture

The most influential early effort to create a standard system architecture was the ANSI/SPARC architecture [ANSI 1975; Date 1977]. ANSI/SPARC divided database-centric systems into three models: the internal, conceptual, and external, as Figure 2-1 shows. A *schema* is a description of the model (a metamodel). Each schema has structures and relationships that reflect its role. The goal was to make the three schemas independent of one another. The architecture results in systems resistant to changes to physical or conceptual structures. Instead of having to rebuild your entire system for every change to a storage structure, you would just change the structure without affecting the systems that used it. This concept, *data independence,* was critical to the early years of database management and design, and it is still critical today. It underlies everything that database designers do.

For example, consider what an accounting system would be like without data independence. Every time an application developer wanted to access the general ledger, he or she would need to program the code to access the data on disk, specifying the disk sectors and hardware storage formats, looking for and using indexes, adapting to "optimal" storage structures that are different for each kind of data element, coding the logic and navigational access to subset the data, and coding the sorting routines to order it (again using the indexes and intermediate storage facilities if the data could not fit entirely in memory. Now a database engineer comes along and redoes the whole mess. That leaves the application programmer the Herculean task of reworking the whole accounting system to handle the new structures. Without the layers of encapsulation and independence that a database management system provides, programming for large databases would be impossible.

> *Note: Lack of data independence is at least one reason for the existence of the Year 2000 problem. Programs would store dates in files using two-byte storage representation and would propagate that throughout the code, then use tricky coding techniques based on*

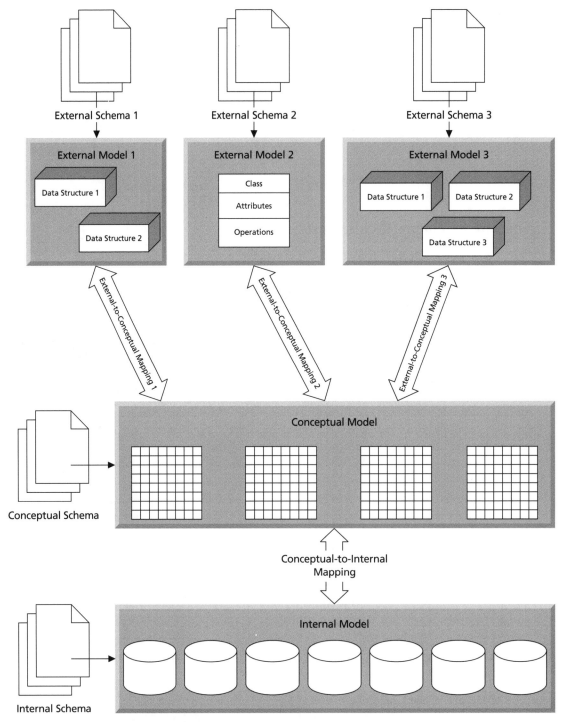

Figure 2-1   *The ANSI/SPARC Architecture*

the storage representation to achieve wonders of optimized pro-
gramming (and completely unmaintainable programs).

The *conceptual model* represents the information in the database. The structures of this schema are the structures, operations, and constraints of the data
model you are using. In a relational database, for example, the conceptual schema
contains the tables and integrity constraints as well as the SQL query language. In
an object-oriented database, it contains the classes that make up the persistent
data, including the data structures and methods of the classes. In an object-
relational database, it contains the relational structures as well as the extended
type or class definitions, including the class or type methods that represent object
behavior. The database management system provides a *query* and *data manipulation language,* such as the SELECT, INSERT, UPDATE, and DELETE statements
of SQL.

The *internal model* has the structure of storage and retrieval. It represents
the "real" structure of the database, including indexes, storage representations,
field orders, character sets, and so on. The internal schema supports the conceptual schema by implementing the high-level conceptual structures in lower-level
storage structures. It supplies additional structures such as indexes to manage access to the data. The mapping between the conceptual and internal models insu-
lates the conceptual model from any changes in storage. New indexes, changed
storage structures, or differing storage orders of fields do not affect the higher-
level models. This is the concept of *physical data independence.* Usually, database
management systems extend the data definition language to enable database administrators to manage the internal model and schema.

The *external model* is really a series of views of the different applications or
users that use the data. Each user maps its data to the data in the conceptual
schema. The view might use only a portion of the total data model. This mapping
shows you how different applications will make use of the data. Programming
languages generally provide the management tools for managing the external
model and its schema. For example, the facilities in C++ for building class structures and allocating memory at runtime give you the basis for your C++ external
models.

This three-level schema greatly influences database design. Dividing the
conceptual from the internal schema separates machine and operating system dependencies from the abstract model of the data. This separation frees you from
worrying about access paths, file structures, or physical optimization when you
are designing your logical data model. Separating the conceptual schema from the
external schemas establishes the many-to-one relationship between them. No application need access all of the data in the database. The conceptual schema, on
the other hand, logically supports all the different applications and their data-
related needs.

For example, say Holmes PLC (Sherlock Holmes's investigative agency, a running example throughout this book) was designing its database back in 1965, probably with the intention of writing a COBOL system from scratch using standard access path technology such as ISAM (Indexed Sequential Access Method, a very old programming interface for indexed file lookup). The first pass would build an application that accessed hierarchically structured files, with each query procedure needing to decide which primary or secondary index to use to retrieve the file data. The next pass, adding another application, would need to decide whether the original files and their access methods were adequate or would need extension, and the original program would need modification to accommodate the changes. At some point, the changes might prove dramatically incompatible, requiring a complete rewrite of all the existing applications. Shall I drag in Year 2000 problems due to conflicting storage designs for dates?

In 1998, Holmes PLC would design a conceptual data model after doing a thorough analysis of the systems it will support. Data architects would build that conceptual model in a database management system using the appropriate data model. Eventually, the database administrator would take over and structure the internal model, adding indexes where appropriate, clustering and partitioning the data, and so on. That optimization would not end with the first system but would continue throughout the long process of adding systems to the business. Depending on the design quality of the conceptual schema, you would need no changes to the existing systems to add a new one. In no case would changes in the internal design require changes.

Data independence comes from the fundamental design concept of *coupling,* the degree of interdependence between modules in a system [Yourdon and Constantine 1979; Fenton and Pfleeger 1997]. By separating the three models and their schemas, the ANSI/SPARC architecture changes the degree of coupling from the highest level of coupling (content coupling) to a much lower level of coupling (data coupling through parameters). Thus, by using this architecture, you achieve a better system design by reducing the overall coupling in your system.

Despite its age and venerability, this way of looking at the world still has major value in today's design methods. As a consultant in the database world, I have seen over and over the tendency to throw away all the advantages of this architecture. An example is a company I worked with that made a highly sophisticated layout tool for manufacturing plants. A performance analysis seemed to indicate that the problem lay in inefficient database queries. The (inexperienced) database programmer decided to store the data in flat files instead to speed up access. The result: a system that tied its fundamental data structures directly into physical file storage. Should the application change slightly, or should the data files grow beyond their current size, the company would have to completely redo their data access subroutines to accommodate new file data structures.

Note: As a sidelight, the problem here was using a relational data-base for a situation that required navigational access. Replacing the relational design with an object-oriented design was a better solu-tion. The engineers in this small company had no exposure to OO technology and barely any to relational database technology. This lack of knowledge made it very difficult for them to understand the trade-offs they were making.

The Multitier Architectures

The 1980s saw the availability of personal computers and ever-smaller server ma-chines and the local-area networks that connected them. These technologies made it possible to distribute computing over several machines rather than doing it all on one big mainframe or minicomputer. Initially, this architecture took the form of *client/server computing,* where a database server supported several client machines. This evolved into the *distributed client/server architecture,* where sev-eral servers taken together made up the distributed database.

In the early 1990s, this architecture evolved even further with the concept of *application partitioning,* a refinement of the basic client/server approach. Along with the database server, you could run part of the application on the client and another part on an application server that several clients could share. One popu-lar form of this architecture is the *transaction processing (TP) monitor* architec-ture, in which a middleware server handles transaction management. The data-base server treats the TP monitor as its client, and the TP monitor in turn serves its clients. Other kinds of middleware emerged to provide various kinds of appli-cation support, and this architecture became known as the three-tier architecture.

In the later 1990s, this architecture again transformed itself through the availability of thin-client Internet browsers, distributed-object middleware, and other technology. This made it possible to move even more processing out of the client onto servers. It now became possible to distribute objects around multiple machines, leading to a multitier, distributed-object architecture.

These multitier system architectures have extensive ramifications for sys-tem and network hardware as well as software [Berson 1992]. Even so, this book focuses primarily on the softer aspects of the architectures. The critical im-pact of system architecture on design comes from the system software architec-ture, which is what the rest of this section discusses.

Database Servers: Client/Server Architectures

The *client/server architecture* [Berson 1992] structures your system into two parts: the software running on the server responds to requests from multiple clients running another part of the software. The primary goal of client/server architecture is to reduce the amount of data that travels across the network. With a standard file server, when you access a file, you copy the entire file over the network to the system that requested access to it. The client/server architecture lets you structure both the request and the response through the server software that lets the server respond with only the data you need. Figure 2-2 illustrates the classic client/server system, with the database management system as server and the database application as client.

In reality, you can break down the software architecture into layers and distribute the layers in different ways. One approach breaks the software into three parts, for example: presentation, business processing, and data management [Berson 1992]. The X-Windows system, for example, is a pure presentation layer client/server system. The X terminal is a client-based software system that runs the presentation software and makes requests to the server that is running the business processing. This lets you run a program on a server and interact with it on a "smart terminal" running X. The X terminal software is what makes the terminal smart.

A more recent example is the World Wide Web browser, which connects to a network and handles presentation of data that it demands from a Web server. The Web server acts as a client of the database server, which may or may not be running on the same hardware box. The user interacts with the Web browser, which submits requests to the Web server in whatever programming or scripting language is set up on the server. The Web server then connects to the database and submits SQL, makes remote procedure calls (RPCs), or does whatever else is required to request a database service, and the database server responds with da-

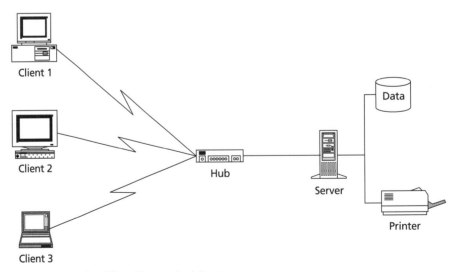

Figure 2-2   *The Client/Server Architecture*

tabase actions and/or data. The Web server then displays the results through the Web browser (Figure 2-3).

The Web architecture illustrates the distribution of the business processing between the client and server. Usually, you want to do this when you have certain elements of the business processing that are database intensive and other parts that are not. By placing the database-intensive parts on the database server, you reduce the network traffic and get the benefits of encapsulating the database-related code in one place. Such benefits might include greater database security, higher-level client interfaces that are easier to maintain, and cohesive subsystem designs on the server side. Although the Web represents one approach to such distribution of processing, it isn't the only way to do it. This approach leads inevitably to the transaction processing monitor architecture previously mentioned, in which the TP monitor software is in the middle between the database and the client. If the TP monitor and the database are running on the same server, you have a client/server architecture. If they are on separate servers, you have a multitier architecture, as Figure 2-4 illustrates. *Application partitioning* is the process of breaking up your application code into modules that run on different clients and servers.

The Distributed Database Architecture

Simultaneously with the development of relational databases comes the development of *distributed databases,* data spread across a geographically dispersed network connected through communication links [Date 1983; Ullman 1988]. Figure

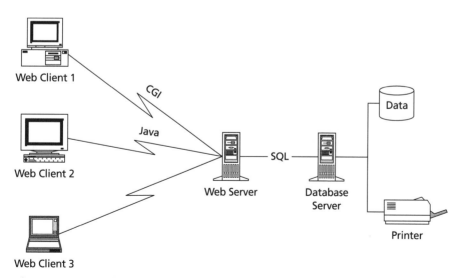

Figure 2-3 *A Web-Based Client/Server System*

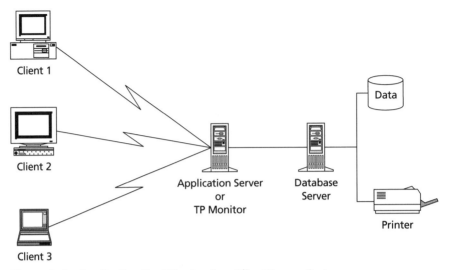

Figure 2-4   *Application Partitioning in a Client/Server System*

2-5 illustrates an example distributed database architecture with two servers, three databases, several clients, and a number of local databases on the clients. The tables with arrows show a *replication* arrangement, with the tables existing on multiple servers that keep them synchronized automatically.

> *Note: Data warehouses often encapsulate a distributed database architecture, especially if you construct them by referring to, copying, and/or aggregating data from multiple databases into the warehouse. Snapshots, for example, let you take data from a table and copy it to another server for use there; the original table changes, but the snapshot doesn't. Although this book does not go into the design issues for data warehousing, the distributed database architecture and its impact on design covers a good deal of the issues surrounding data warehouse design.*

There are three operational elements in a distributed database: transparency, transaction management, and optimization.

Distributed database *transparency* is the degree to which a database operation appears to be running on a single, unified database from the perspective of the user of the database. In a fully transparent system, the application sees only the standard data model and interfaces, with no need to know where things are really happening. It never has to do anything special to access a table, commit a transaction, or connect. For example, if a query accesses data on several servers, the query manager must break the query apart into a query for each server, then combine the results (see the optimization discussion below). The application

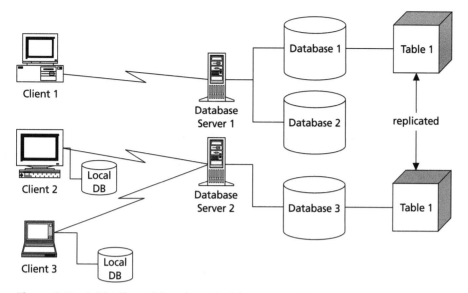

Figure 2-5   *A Distributed Database Architecture*

submits a single SQL statement, but multiple ones actually execute on the servers. Another aspect of transparency is *fragmentation,* the distribution of data in a table over multiple locations (another word for this is *partitioning*). Most distributed systems achieve a reasonable level of transparency down to the database administration level. Then they abandon transparency to make it easier on the poor DBA who needs to manage the underlying complexity of the distribution of data and behavior. One wrinkle in the transparency issue is the heterogeneous distributed database, a database comprising different database management system software running on the different servers.

> *Note: Database fragmentation is unrelated to* file fragmentation, *the condition that occurs in file systems such as DOS or NTFS when the segments that comprise files become randomly distributed around the disk instead of clustered together. Defragmenting your disk drive on a weekly basis is a good idea for improving performance; defragmenting your database is not, just the reverse.*

Distributed database transaction management differs from single-database transaction management because of the possibility that a part of the database will become unavailable during a commit process, leading to an incomplete transaction commit. Distributed databases thus require an extended transaction management process capable of guaranteeing the completion of the commit or a full rollback of the transaction. There are many strategies for doing this [Date 1983;

Elmagarmid 1991; Gray and Reuter 1993; Papadimitriou 1986]. The two most popular strategies are the two-phase commit and distributed optimistic concurrency.

Two-phase commit breaks the regular commit process into two parts [Date 1983; Gray and Reuter 1993; Ullman 1988]. First, the distributed servers communicate with one another until all have expressed readiness to commit their portion of the transaction. Then each commits and informs the rest of success or failure. If all servers commit, then the transaction completes successfully; otherwise, the system rolls back the changes on all servers. There are many practical details involved in administering this kind of system, including things like recovering lost servers and other administrivia.

Optimistic concurrency takes the opposite approach [Ullman 1988; Kung and Robinson 1981]. Instead of trying to ensure that everything is correct as the transaction proceeds, either through locking or timestamp management, optimistic methods let you do anything to anything, then check for conflicts when you commit. Using some rule for conflict resolution, such as timestamp comparison or transaction priorities, the optimistic approach avoids deadlock situations and permits high concurrency, especially in read-only situations. Oracle7 and Oracle8 both have a version of optimistic concurrency called read consistency, which lets readers access a consistent database regardless of changes made since they read the data.

Distributed database optimization is the process of optimizing queries that are executing on separate servers. This requires extended cost-based optimization that understands where data is, where operations can take place, and what the true costs of distribution are [Ullman 1989]. In the case where the query manager breaks a query into parts, for example, to execute on separate servers, it must optimize the queries both for execution on their respective servers and for transmission and receipt over the network. Current technology isn't terrific here, and there is a good way to go in making automatic optimization effective. The result: your design must take optimization requirements into account, especially at the physical level.

The key impact of distributed transaction management on design is that you must take the capabilities of the language you are designing for into account when planning your transaction logic and data location. Transparency affects this a good deal; the less the application needs to know about what is happening on the server, the better. If the application transaction logic is transparent, your application need not concern itself with design issues relating to transaction management. Almost certainly, however, your logical and physical database design will need to take distributed transactions into account.

For example, you may know that network traffic over a certain link is going to be much slower than over other links. You can benchmark applications using a cost-benefit approach to decide whether local access to the data outweighs the remote access needs. A case in point is the table that contains a union of local data from several localities. Each locality benefits from having the table on the local site. Other localities benefit from having remotely generated data on their site. Especially if all links are not equal, you must decide which server is best for all. You can also take more sophisticated approaches to the problem. You can build separate tables, offloading the design problem to the application language that has to recombine them. You can replicate data, offloading the design problem to the database administrator and vendor developers. You can use table partitioning, offloading the design problem to Oracle8, the only database to support this feature, and hence making the solution not portable to other database managers. The impact of optimization on design is thus direct and immediate, and pretty hairy if your database is complex.

Holmes PLC, for example, is using Oracle7 and Oracle8 to manage certain distributed database transactions. Both systems fully implement the distributed two-phase commit protocol in a relatively transparent manner on both the client and the server. There are two impact points: where the physical design must accommodate transparency requirements and the administrative interface. Oracle implements distributed servers through a linking strategy, with the link object in one schema referring to a remote database connection string. The result is that when you refer to a table on a remote server, you must specify the link name to find the table. If you need to make the reference transparent, you can take one of at least three approaches. You can set up a synonym that encapsulates the link name, making it either public or private to a particular user or Oracle role. Alternatively, you can replicate the table, enabling "local" transaction management with hidden costs on the back end because of the reconciliation of the replicas. Or, you can set up stored procedures and triggers that encapsulate the link references, with the costs migrating to procedure maintenance on the various servers.

As you can tell from the example, distributed database architectures have a major impact on design, particularly at the physical level. It is critical to understand that impact if you choose to distribute your databases.

Objects Everywhere: The Multitier Distributed-Object Architecture

As OO technology grew in popularity, the concept of distributing those objects came to the fore. If you could partition applications into pieces running on different servers, why not break apart OO applications into separately running objects on those servers? The Object Management Group defined a reference object model and a slew of standard models for the Common Object Request Broker Architecture (CORBA) [Soley 1992; Siegel 1996]. Competing with this industry standard is the Distributed Common Object Model (DCOM) and various database access tools such as Remote Data Objects (RDO), Data Access Objects (DAO), Object Linking and Embedding Data Base (OLE DB), Active Data Objects

(ADO), and ODBCDirect [Baarns 1997; Lassesen 1995], part of the ActiveX architecture from Microsoft and the Open Group, a similar standard for distributing objects on servers around a network [Chappell 1996; Grimes 1997; Lee 1997]. This model is migrating toward the new Microsoft COM+ or COM 3 model [Vaughan-Nichols 1997]. Whatever the pros and cons of the different reference architectures [Mowbray and Zahavi 1995, pp. 135–149], these models affect database design the same way: they allow you to hide the database access within objects, then place those objects on servers rather than in the client application. That application then gets data from the objects on demand over the network. Figure 2-6 shows a typical distributed-object architecture using CORBA.

> *Warning: This area of software technology is definitely not for the dyslexic, as a casual scan over the last few pages will tell you.*
> *Microsoft in particular has contributed a tremendously confusing array of technologies and their acronyms to the mash in the last couple of years. Want to get into Microsoft data access? Choose between MFC, DAO, RDO, ADO, or good old ODBC, or use all of them at once. I'm forced to give my opinion: I think Microsoft is making it much more difficult than necessary to develop database applications with all this nonsense. Between the confusion caused by the variety of technologies and the way using those technologies locks*

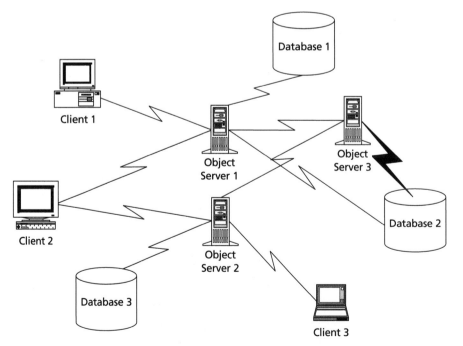

Figure 2-6 *A Simple Distributed-Object Architecture Using CORBA*

you into a single vendor's muddled thinking about the issues of da-
tabase application development, you are caught between the devil
and the deep blue sea.

In a very real sense, as Figure 2-6 illustrates by putting them at the same level, the distributed-object architecture makes the database and its contents a peer of the application objects. The database becomes just another object communicating through the distributed network. This object transparency has a subtle influence on database design. Often there is a tendency to drive system design either by letting the database lead or by letting the application lead. In a distributed-object system, no component leads all the time. When you think about the database as a cooperating component rather than as the fundamental basis for your system or as a persistent data store appendage, you begin to see different ways of using and getting to the data. Instead of using a single DBMS and its servers, you can combine multiple DBMS products, even combining an object-oriented database system with a relational one if that makes sense. Instead of seeing a series of application data models that map to the conceptual model, as in the ANSI/SPARC architecture, you see a series of object models mapping to a series of conceptual models through distributed networks.

> *Note: Some advocates of the OODBMS would have you believe that*
> *the OO technology's main benefit is to make the database disap-*
> *pear. To be frank, that's horse hockey. Under certain circumstances*
> *and for special cases, you may not care whether an object is in mem-*
> *ory or in the database. If you look at code that does not use a data-*
> *base and code that does, you will see massive differences between*
> *the two, whatever technology you're using. The database never dis-*
> *appears. I find it much more useful to regard the database as a peer*
> *object with which my code has to work rather than as an invisible*
> *slave robot toiling away under the covers.*

For example, in an application I worked on, I had a requirement for a tree structure (a series of parents and children, sort of like a genealogical tree). The original designers of the relational database I was using had represented this structure in the database as a table of parent-child pairs. One column of the table was the parent, the other column was one of the children of that parent, so each row represented a link between two tree elements. The client would specify a root or entry point into the tree, and the application then would build the tree based on navigating from that root based on the parent-child links.

If you designed using the application-leading approach, you would figure out a way to store the tree in the database. For example, this might mean special tables for each tree, or even binary large objects to hold the in-memory tree for quick retrieval. If you designed using a database-centric approach, you would simply retrieve the link table into memory and build the tree from it using a graph-building algorithm. Alternatively, you could use special database tools such as the Oracle CONNECT BY clause to retrieve the data in tree form.

Designing from the distributed-object viewpoint, I built a subsystem in the database that queried raw information from the database. This subsystem combined several queries into a comprehensive basis for further analysis. The object on the client then queried this data using an ORDER BY and a WHERE clause to get just the information it required in the format it needed. This approach represents a cooperative, distributed-object approach to designing the system rather than an approach that started with the database or the application as the primary force behind the design.

Another application I worked on had two databases, one a repository of images and the other a standard relational database describing them. The application used a standard three-tier client/server model with two separate database servers, one for the document management system and one for the relational database, and much code on the client and server for moving data around to get it into the right place. Using a distributed-object architecture would have allowed a much more flexible arrangement. The database servers could have presented themselves as object caches accessible from any authenticated client. This architectural style would have allowed the designers to build object servers for moving data between the two databases and their many clients.

The OMG Object Management Architecture (OMA) [Soley 1992; Siegel 1996] serves as a standard example of the kind of software objects you will find in distributed-object architectures, as Figure 2-7 shows. The Open Group Architectural Framework [Open Group 1997] contains other examples in a framework for building such architectures.

The CORBAservices layer provides the infrastructure for the building blocks of the architecture, giving you all the tools you need to create and manage objects. Lifecycle services handle creation, movement, copying, and garbage collection. Naming services handle the management of unique object names around the network (a key service that has been a bottleneck for network services for years under the *nom de guerre* of directory services). Persistence services provide permanent or transient storage for objects, including the objects that CORBA uses to manage application objects.

The Object Request Broker (ORB) layer provides the basic communication facilities for dispatching messages, marshaling data across heterogeneous machine architectures, object activation, exception handling, and security. It also integrates basic network communications through a TCP/IP protocol implementation or a Distributed Computing Environment (DCE) layer.

The CORBAfacilities layer provides business objects both horizontal and vertical. Horizontal facilities provide objects for managing specific kinds of application behaviors, such as the user interface, browsing, printing, email, compound documents, systems management, and so on. Vertical facilities provide solutions

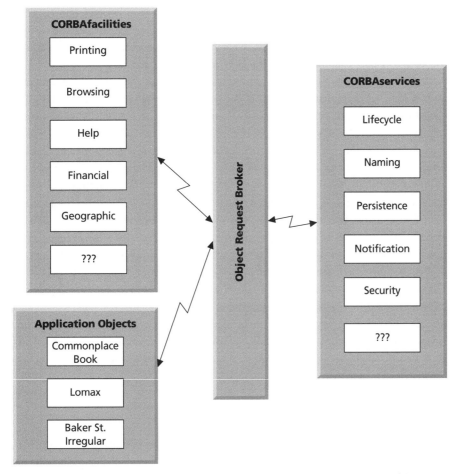

CORBAfacilities

Printing

Browsing

Help

Financial

Geographic

???

Application Objects

Commonplace Book

Lomax

Baker St. Irregular

Object Request Broker

CORBAservices

Lifecycle

Naming

Persistence

Notification

Security

???

Figure 2-7 *The Object Management Group's Object Management Architecture*

for particular kinds of industrial applications (financial, health care, manufacturing, and so on).

The Application Objects layer consists of the collections of objects in individual applications that use the CORBA software bus to communicate with the CORBAfacilities and CORBAservices. This can be as minimal as providing a graphical user interface for a facility or as major as developing a whole range of interacting objects for a specific site.

Where does the database fit in all this? Wherever it wants to, like the proverbial 500-pound gorilla. Databases fit in the persistence CORBAservice; these will usually be object-oriented databases such as POET, ObjectStore, or Versant/ DB. It can also be a horizontal CORBAfacility providing storage for a particular kind of management facility, or a vertical facility offering persistent storage of financial or manufacturing data. It can even be an application object, such as a local database for traveling systems or a database of local data of one sort or another. These objects work through the Object Adapters of the ORB layer, such as the Basic Object Adapter or the Object Oriented Database Adapter [Siegel 1996; Cattell and Barry 1997]. These components activate and deactivate the database and its objects, map object references, and control security through the OMG security facilities. Again, these are all peer objects in the architecture communicating with one another through the ORB.

As an example, consider the image and fact database that Holmes PLC manages, the commonplace book system. This database contains images and text relating to criminals, information sources, and any other object that might be of interest in pursuing consulting detective work around the world. Although Holmes PLC could build this database entirely within an object-relational or object-oriented DBMS (and some of the examples in this book use such implementations as examples), a distributed-object architecture gives Holmes PLC a great deal of flexibility in organizing its data for security and performance on its servers around the world. It allows them to combine the specialized document management system that contains photographs and document images with an object-oriented database of fingerprint and DNA data. It allows the inclusion of a relational database containing information about a complex configuration of objects from people to places to events (trials, prison status, and so on).

System Architecture Summary

System architecture at the highest level provides the context for database design. That context is as varied as the systems that make it up. In this section, I've tried to present the architectures that have the most impact on database design through a direct influence on the nature and location of the database:

- The three-schema architecture contributes the concept of *data independence,* separating the conceptual from the physical and the application views. Data independence is the principle on which modern database design rests.

- The client/server architecture contributes the *partitioning* of the application into client and server portions, some of which reside on the server or even in the database. This can affect both the conceptual and physical schemas, which must take the partitioning into account for best security, availability, and performance.

- The distributed database architecture directly impacts the physical layout of the database through *fragmentation* and *concurrency* requirements.

- The distributed-object architecture affects all levels of database design by raising (or lowering, depending on your perspective) the status of the database to that of a *peer* of the application. Treating databases, and potentially several different databases, as communicating objects requires a different strategy for laying out the data. Design benefits from decreased coupling of the database structures, coming full circle back to the concept of data independence.

Data Architectures

System architecture sets the stage for the designer; data architecture provides the scenery and the lines that the designer delivers on stage. There are three major data architectures that are current contenders for the attentions of database designers: relational, object-relational, and object-oriented data models. The choice between these models colors every aspect of your system architecture:

- The data access language

- The structure and mapping of your application-database interface

- The layout of your conceptual design

- The layout of your internal design

It's really impossible to overstate the effect of your data architecture choice on your system. It is not, however, impossible to isolate the effects. One hypothesis, which has many advocates in the computer science community, asserts that your objective should be to align your system architecture and tools with your data model: the *impedance mismatch* hypothesis. If your data architecture is out of step with your system architecture, you will be much less productive because you will constantly have to layer and interface the two. For example, you might use a distributed-object architecture for your application but a relational database.

The reality is somewhat different. With adequate design and careful system structuring, you can hide almost anything, including the kitchen sink. A current example is the Java Data Base Connectivity (JDBC) standard for accessing databases from the Java language. JDBC is a set of Java classes that provide an object-oriented version of the ODBC standard, originally designed for use through the C language. JDBC presents a solid, OO design face to the Java world. Underneath, it can take several different forms. The original approach was to write an interface layer to ODBC drivers, thus hiding the underlying functional nature of the database interface. For performance reasons, a more direct approach evolved, replacing the ODBC driver with native JDBC drivers. Thus, at the level of the programming interface, all was copacetic. Unfortunately, the basic function of JDBC is to retrieve relational data in relational result sets, not to handle objects. Thus, there is still an impedance mismatch between the fully OO Java application and the relational data it uses.

Personally, I don't find this problem that serious. Writing a JDBC applet isn't that hard, and the extra design needed to develop the methods for handling the relational data doesn't take that much serious design or programming effort. The key to database programming productivity is the ability of the development language to express what you want. I find it more difficult to deal with constantly writing new wrinkles of tree-building code in C++ and Java than to use Oracle's CONNECT BY extension to standard SQL. On the other hand, if your tree has cycles in it (where a child connects back to its parent at some level), CONNECT BY just doesn't work. Some people I've talked to hate the need to "bind" SQL to their programs through repetitive mapping calls to ODBC or other APIs. On the other hand, using JSQL or other embedded SQL precompiler standards for hiding such mapping through a simple reference syntax eliminates this problem without eliminating the benefits of using high-level SQL instead of low-level Java or C++ to query the database. As with most things, fitting your tools to your needs leads to different solutions in different contexts.

The rest of this section introduces the three major paradigms of data architecture. My intent is to summarize the basic structures in each data architecture that form a part of your design tool kit. Later chapters relate specific design issues to specific parts of these data architectures.

Relational Databases

The relational data model comes from the seminal paper by Edgar Codd published in 1972 [Codd 1972]. Codd's main insight was to use the concept of mathematical relations to model data. A relation is a table of rows and columns. Figure 2-8 shows a simple relational layout in which multiple tables relate to one another by mapping data values between the tables, and such mappings are themselves relations. *Referential integrity* is the collection of constraints that ensure that the mappings between tables are correct at the end of a transaction. *Normalization* is the process of establishing an optimal table structure based on the internal data dependencies (details in Chapter 11).

A relation is a table of columns and rows. The *relation* (also called a *table*) is a finite subset of the Cartesian product of a set of *domains,* each of which is a set of values [Ullman 1988]. Each *attribute* of the relation (also called a *column*) corresponds to a domain (the *type* of the column). The relation is thus a set of *tuples* (also called *rows*). You can also see a relation's rows as mapping attribute names to values in the domains of the attributes [Codd 1970].

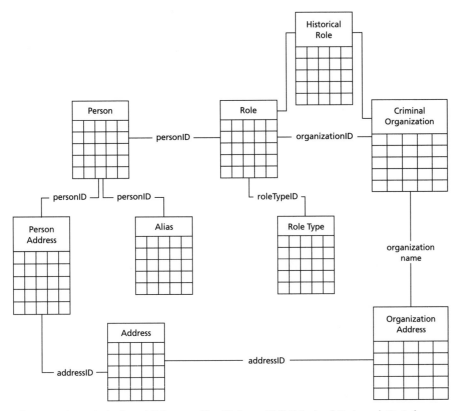

Figure 2-8 *A Relational Schema: The Holmes PLC Criminal Network Database*

For example, the Criminal Organization table in Figure 2-8 has five columns:

- *OrganizationName:* The name of the organization (a character string)
- *LegalStatus:* The current legal status of the organization, a subdomain of strings including "Legally Defined", "On Trial", "Alleged", "Unknown"
- *Stability:* How stable the organization is, a subdomain of strings including "Highly Stable", "Moderately Stable", "Unstable"
- *InvestigativePriority:* The level of investigative focus at Holmes PLC on the organization, a subdomain of strings including "Intense", "Ongoing", "Watch", "On Hold"
- *ProsecutionStatus:* The current status of the organization with respect to criminal prosecution strategies for fighting the organization, a subdomain

of strings including "History", "On the Ropes", "Getting There", "Little Progress", "No Progress"

Most of the characteristics of a criminal organization are in its relationships to other tables, such as the roles that people play in the organization and the various addresses out of which the organization operates. These are separate tables, OrganizationAddress and Role, with the OrganizationName identifying the organization in both tables. By mapping the tables through OrganizationName, you can get information from all the tables together in a single query.

You can constrain each column in many ways, including making it contain unique values for each row in the relation (a *unique, primary key,* or *candidate key* constraint); making it a subset of the total domain (a *domain* constraint), as for the subdomains in the CriminalOrganization table; or constraining the domain as a set of values in rows in another relation (a *foreign key* constraint), such as the constraint on the OrganizationName in the OrganizationAddress table, which must appear in the Organization table. You can also constrain several attributes together, such as a primary key consisting of several attributes (AddressID and OrganizationName, for example) or a conditional constraint between two or more attributes. You can even express relationships between rows as logical constraints, though most RDBMS products and SQL do not have any way to do this. Another term you often hear for all these types of constraints is "business rules," presumably on the strength of the constraints' ability to express the policies and underlying workings of a business.

These simple structures and constraints don't really address the major issues of database construction, maintenance, and use. For that, you need a set of operations on the structures. Because of the mathematical underpinnings of relational theory, logic supplies the operations through relational algebra and relational calculus, mathematical models of the way you access the data in relations [Date 1977; Ullman 1988]. Some vendors have tried to sell such languages; most have failed in one way or another in the marketplace. Instead, a simpler and easier-to-understand language has worked its way into the popular consciousness: SQL.

The SQL language starts with defining the domains for columns and literals [ANSI 1992]:

- Character, varying character, and national varying character (strings)
- Numeric, decimal, integer, smallint
- Float, real, double
- Date, time, timestamp
- Interval (an interval of time, either year-month or day-hour)

You create tables with columns and constraints with the CREATE TABLE statement, change such definitions with ALTER TABLE, and remove tables with DROP TABLE. Table names are unique within a schema (database, user, or any number of other boundary concepts in different systems).

The most extensive part of the SQL language is the query and data manipulation language. The SELECT statement queries data from tables with the following clauses:

- *SELECT:* Lists the output expressions or "projection" of the query
- *FROM:* Specifies the input tables and optionally the join conditions on those tables
- *WHERE:* Specifies the subset of the input based on a form of the first-order predicate calculus and also contains join conditions if they're not in the FROM clause
- *GROUP BY* and *HAVING:* Specify an aggregation of the output rows and a selection condition on the aggregate output row
- *ORDER BY:* Specifies the order of the output rows

You can also combine several such statements into a single query using the set operations UNION, DIFFERENCE, and INTERSECT.

There are three data manipulation operations:

- *INSERT:* Adds rows to a table
- *UPDATE:* Updates columns in rows in a table
- *DELETE:* Removes rows from a table

The ANSI/ISO standard for relational databases focuses on the "programming language" for manipulating the data, SQL [ANSI 1992]. While SQL is a hugely popular language and one that I recommend without reservation, it is not without flaws when you consider the theoretical issues of the relational model. The series of articles and books by Date and Codd provide a thorough critique of the limitations of SQL [Date 1986; Codd 1990]. Any database designer needs to know these issues to make the best of the technology, though it does not necessarily impact database design all that much. When the language presents features that benefit from a design choice, almost invariably it is because SQL either does not provide some feature (a function over strings, say, or the transitive closure operator for querying parts explosions) or actually gets in the way of doing something (no way of dropping columns, no ability to retrieve lists of values in GROUP BY queries, and so on). These limitations can force your hand in designing tables to accommodate your applications' needs and requirements.

The version of SQL that most large RDBMS vendors provide conforms to the Entry level of the SQL-92 standard [ANSI 1992]. Without question, this level of SQL as a dialect is seriously flawed as a practical tool for dealing with databases. Everyone uses it, but everyone would be a lot better off if the big RDBMS vendors would implement the full SQL-92 standard. The full language has much better join syntax, lets you use SELECTS in many different places instead of just the few that the simpler standard allows, and integrates a very comprehensive approach to transaction management, session management, and national character sets.

The critical design impact of SQL is its ability to express queries and manipulate data. Every RDBMS has a different dialect of SQL. For example, Oracle's CONNECT BY clause is unique in the RDBMS world in providing the ability to query a transitive closure over a parent-child link table (the parts explosion query). Sybase has interesting aggregation functions for data warehousing such as CUBE that Oracle does not. Oracle alone supports the ability to use a nested select with an IN operator that compares more than one return value:

```
WHERE (col1, col2) IN (SELECT x, y FROM TABLE1 WHERE z = 3)
```

Not all dialect differences have a big impact on design, but structural ones like this do.

Because SQL unifies the query language with the language for controlling the schema and its use, SQL also directly affects physical database design, again through its abilities to express the structures and constraints on such design. The physical design of a database depends quite a lot on which RDBMS you use. For example, Oracle constructs its world around a set of users, each of which owns a schema of tables, views, and other Oracle objects. Sybase Adaptive Server and Microsoft SQL Server, on the other hand, have the concept of a database, a separate area of storage for tables, and users are quasi-independent of the database schema. SQL Server's transaction processing system locks pages rather than rows, with various exceptions, features, and advantages. Oracle locks rows rather than pages. You design your database differently because, for SQL Server, you can run into concurrency deadlocks much more easily than in Oracle. Oracle has the concept of read consistency, in which a user reading data from a table continues to see the data in unchanged form no matter whether other users have changed it. On updating the data, the original user can get a message indicating that the underlying data has changed and that they must query it again to change it. The other major RDBMSs don't have this concept, though they have other concepts that Oracle does not. Again, this leads to interesting design decisions. As a final example, each RDBMS supports a different set of physical storage access methods ranging from standard B*-tree index schemes to hash indexes to bitmap indexes to indexed join clusters.

There's also the issue of national language character sets and how each system implements them. There is an ANSI standard [ANSI 1992] for representing different character sets that no vendor implements, and each vendor's way of doing national character sets is totally different from the others. Taking advantage of the special features of a given RDBMS can directly affect your design.

Object-Oriented Databases

The object-oriented data model for object-oriented database management does not really exist in a formal sense, although several authors have proposed such models. The structure of this model comes from OO programming, with the concepts of inheritance, encapsulation and abstraction, and polymorphism structuring the data.

The driving force behind object-oriented databases has been the impedance mismatch hypothesis mentioned in the section above on the distributed-object architecture. As OO programming languages became more popular, it seemed to make sense to provide integrated database environments that simultaneously made OO data persistent and provided all the transaction processing, multiple-user access, and data integrity features of modern database managers. Again, the problem the designers of these databases saw was that application programmers who needed to use persistent data had to convert from OO thinking to SQL thinking to use relational databases. Specifically, OO systems and SQL systems use different type systems, requiring designers to translate between the two. Instead, OO databases remove the need to translate by directly supporting the programming models of the popular OO programming languages as data models for the database.

There are two ways of making objects persistent in the mainstream ODBMS community. The market leader, ObjectStore by Object Design Inc., uses a storage model. This approach designates an object as using persistent storage. In C++, this means adding a "persist" storage specifier to accompany the other storage specifiers of volatile, static, and automatic. The downside to this approach is that it requires precompilation of the program, since it changes the actual programming language by adding the persistent specifier. You precompile the program and then run it through a standard C++ compiler. POET adds a "persistent" keyword in front of the "class" keyword, again using a precompiler. The other vendors use an inheritance approach, with persistent classes inheriting from a root persistence class of some kind. The downside of this is to make persistence a feature of the type hierarchy, meaning you can't have a class produce both in-memory objects and persistent objects (which, somehow, you always want to do).

It is not possible to describe the OO data model without running into one or another controversy over features or the lack thereof. This section will describe certain features that are generally common to OO databases, but each system implements a model largely different from all others. The best place to start is the

ODMG object model from the ODMG standard for object databases [Cattell and Barry 1997; ODMG 1998] and its bindings to C++, Smalltalk, and Java. This is the only real ODBMS standard in existence; the ODBMS community has not yet proposed any formal standards through ANSI, IEEE, or ISO.

The Object Model specifies the constructs that are supported by an ODBMS:

- The basic modeling primitives are the *object* and the *literal*. Each object has a unique identifier. A literal has no identifier.

- Objects and literals can be categorized by their *types*. All elements of a given type have a common range of states (i.e., the same set of properties) and common behavior (i.e., the same set of defined operations). An object is sometimes referred to as an *instance* of its type.

- The state of an object is defined by the values it carries for a set of *properties*. These properties can be *attributes* of the object itself or *relationships* between the object and one or more other objects. Typically the values of an object's properties can change over time.

- The behavior of an object is defined by the set of *operations* that can be executed on or by the object. Operations may have a list of input and output parameters, each with a specified type. Each operation may also return a typed result.

- A *database* stores objects, enabling them to be shared by multiple users and applications. A database is based on a *schema* that is defined in ODL and contains instances of the types defined by its schema.

The ODMG Object Model specified what is meant by objects, literals, types, operations, properties, attributes, relationships, and so forth. An application developer uses the construct of the ODMG Object Model to construct the object model for the application. The application's object model specifies particular types, such as Document, Author, Publisher, and Chapter, and the operations and properties of each of these types. The application's object model is the database's (logical) schema [Cattell and Barry 1997, pp. 11–12].

This summary statement touches on all the parts of the object model. As with most things, the devil is in the details. Figure 2-9 shows a simplified UML model of the Criminal Network database, the OO equivalent of the relational database in Figure 2-8.

Note: Chapter 7 introduces the UML notation in detail and contains references to the literature on UML.

Without desiring to either incite controversy or go into gory detail comparing vendor feature sets, a designer needs to understand several basic ODMG concepts that apply across the board to most ODBMS products: the structure of object types, inheritance, object life cycles, the standard collection class hierarchy,

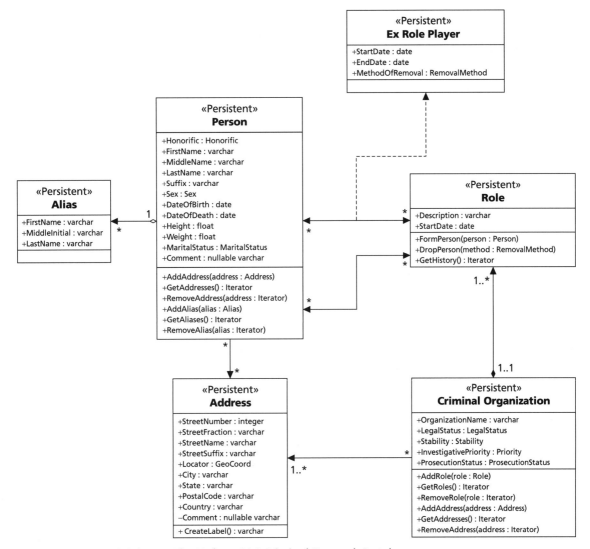

Figure 2-9   *An OO Schema: The Holmes PLC Criminal Network Database*

relationships, and operation structure [Cattell and Barry 1997]. Understanding these concepts will give you a minimal basis for deciding whether your problem is better solved by an OODBMS, an RDBMS, or an ORDBMS.

Objects and Type Structure

Every object in an OO database has a type, and each type has an internal and an external definition. The *external definition,* also called a *specification,* consists of the operations, properties or attributes, and exceptions that users of the object can access. The *internal definition,* also called an *implementation* or *body,* contains the details of the operations and anything else required by the object that is not visible to the user of the object. ODMG 2.0 defines an *interface* as "a specification that defines only the abstract behavior of an object type" [Cattell and Barry 1997, p. 12]. A *class* is "a specification that defines the abstract behavior and abstract state of an object type." A literal specification defines only the abstract state of a literal type. Figure 2-9 shows a series of class specifications with operations and properties. The CriminalOrganization class, for example, has five properties (the same as the columns in the relational table) and several operations.

An *operation* is the abstract behavior of the object. The implementation of the operation is a *method* defined in a specific programming language. For example, the AddRole operation handles adding a person in a role to an organization. The implementation of this operation in C++ might implement the operation through calling an insert() function attached to a set<> or map<> template containing the set of roles. Similarly, the *property* is an abstract state of the object, and its implementation is a *representation* based on the language binding (a C++ enum or class type, for example, for the LegalStatus property). Literal implementations also map to specific language constructs. The key to understanding the ODMG Object Definition Language (ODL) is to understand that it represents the specification, not the implementation, of an object. The language bindings specify how to implement the ODL abstractions in specific OO languages. This separation makes the OO database specification independent of the languages that implement it.

ODMG defines the following literal types:

- Long and unsigned long
- Short and unsigned short
- Float and double
- Boolean
- Octet (an eight-bit quantity)
- Character
- String
- Enum (an enumeration or finite set of distinct values)

Beyond these types, there are four structured types:

- Date, time, timestamp
- Interval

Finally, ODMG lets you define any structure of these types using a struct format much like that of the C language.

Because much of the work in OO databases has to do with collections of objects, ODMG also provides a class hierarchy of collection classes for use with methods and relationships (see the following section, "Relationships and Collections," for details).

Inheritance

Inheritance has many names: subtype-supertype relationship, is-a relationship, or generalization-specialization relationship are the most common. The idea is to express the relationship between types as a specialization of the type. Each subtype inherits the operations and properties of its supertypes and adds more operations and properties to its own definition. A cup of coffee is a kind of beverage.

For example, the commonplace book system contains a subsystem relating to identification documents for people. Each person can have any number of identification documents (including those for aliases and so on). There are many different kinds of identity documents, and the OO schema therefore needs to represent this data with an inheritance hierarchy. One design appears in Figure 2-10.

The abstract class IdentificationDocument represents any document and has an internal object identifier and the relationship to the Person class. An *abstract class* is a class that has no objects, or *instances,* because it represents a generalization of the real object classes.

In this particular approach, there are four subclasses of Identification Document:

- *ExpiringID:* An ID document that has an expiration date

- *LawEnforcementID:* An ID document that identifies a law enforcement officer

- *SocialSecurityCard:* A U.S. social security card

- *BirthCertificate:* A birth certificate issued by some jurisdiction

All but the social security card have their own subclasses; Figure 2-10 shows only those for ExpiringID for illustrative purposes. ExpiringID inherits the relationship to Person from IdentificationDocument along with any operations you might choose to add to the class. It adds the expiration date, the issue date, and the issuing jurisdiction, as all expiring cards have a jurisdiction that enforces the expiration of the card. The Driver's License subclass adds the license number to expiration date, issue date, and issuing jurisdiction; the Passport

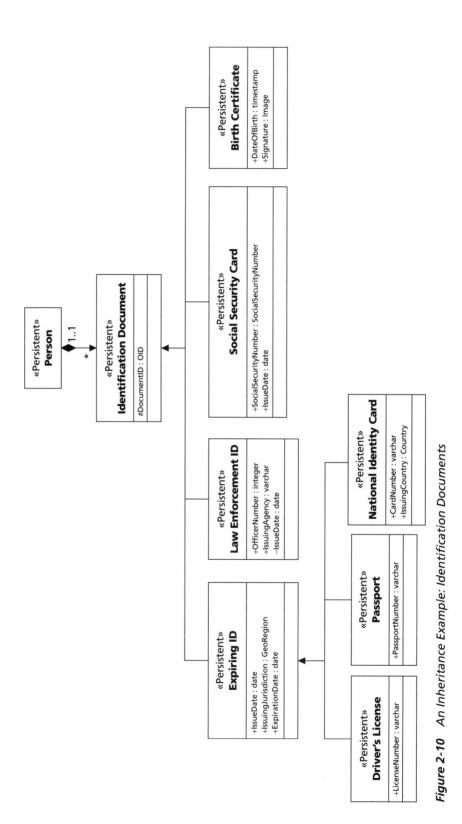

Figure 2-10 An Inheritance Example: Identification Documents

adds the passport number; and the NationalIdentityCard adds card number and issuing country, which presumably contains the issuing jurisdiction. Each subclass thus inherits the primary characteristics of all identification documents, plus the characteristics of the expiring document subclass. A passport, for example, belongs to a person through the relationship it inherits through the Identification Document superclass.

> *Note: The example here focuses primarily on inheriting state, but inheritance in OO design often focuses primarily on inheriting behavior. Often, OO design deals primarily with interfaces, not with classes, so you don't even see the state variables. Since this book is proposing to use OO methods for designing databases, you will see a much stronger focus on class and abstract state than you might in a classical OO design.*

Object Life Cycles

The easiest way to see the life cycle of an object is to examine the interface of the ObjectFactory and Object classes in ODMG [Cattell and Barry 1997, p. 17]:

```
interface ObjectFactory {
  Object      new();
};
Interface Object {
  enum       Lock_Type{read, write, upgrade}
  exception LockNotGranted{}
  void       lock(in Lock_Type mode) raises (LockNotGranted);
  boolean    try_lock(in Lock_Type mode);
  boolean    same_as(in Object anObject);
  Object     copy();
  void       delete();
};
```

The new() operator creates an object. Each object has a unique identifier, or object id (OID). As the object goes through its life, you can lock it or try to lock it, you can compare it to other objects for identity based on the OID, or you can copy the object to create a new object with the same property values. At the end of its life, you delete the object with the delete() operation. An object may be either *transient* (managed by the programming language runtime system) or *persistent* (managed by the ODBMS). ODMG specifies that the object *lifetime* (transient or persistent) is independent of its type.

Relationships and Collections

A relationship maps objects to other objects. The ODMG standard specifies binary relationships between two types, and these may have the standard multiplicities one-to-one, one-to-many, or many-to-many.

> Relationships in this release of the Object Model are not named and are not "first class." A relationship is not itself an object and does not have an object identifier. A relationship is defined implicitly by declaration of *traversal paths* that enable applications to use the logical connections between the objects participating in the relationship. Traversal paths are declared in pairs, one for each direction of traversal of the binary relationship. [Cattell and Barry 1997, p. 36]

For example, a CriminalOrganization has a one-to-many relationship to objects of the Role class: a role pertains to a single criminal organization, which in turn has at least one and possibly many roles. In ODL, this becomes the following traversal path in CriminalOrganization:

```
relationship set<Role> has_roles  inverse Role::pertains_to;
```

In practice, the ODBMS manages a relationship as a set of links through internal OIDs, much as network databases did in the days of yore. The ODBMS takes care of referential integrity by updating the links when the status of objects changes. The goal is to eliminate the possibility of attempting to refer to an object that doesn't exist through a link.

If you have a situation where you want to refer to a single object in one direction only, you can declare an attribute or property of the type to which you want to refer instead of defining an explicit relationship with an inverse. This situation does not correspond to a full relationship to the ODMG standard and does not guarantee referential integrity, leading to the presence of *dangling references* (the database equivalent of invalid pointers).

You operate on relationships through standard relationship operations. This translates into operations to form or drop a relationship, adding a single object, or to add or remove additional objects from the relationship. The to-many side of a relationship corresponds to one of several standard collection classes:

- *Set<>:* An unordered collection of objects or literals with no duplicates allowed
- *Bag<>:* An unordered collection of objects or literals that may contain duplicates
- *List<>:* An ordered collection of objects or literals
- *Array<>:* A dynamically sized, ordered collection of objects or literals accessible by position

- *Dictionary<>:* An unordered sequence of key-value pairs *(associations)* with no duplicate keys

You use these collection objects through standard interfaces (insert, re-move, is_empty, and so on). When you want to move through the collection, you get an Iterator object with the create_iterator or create_bidirectional_iterator operations. These iterators support a standard set of operations for traversal (next_position, previous_position, get_element, at_end, at_beginning). For ex-ample, to do something with the people associated with a criminal organization, you would first retrieve an iterator to the organization's roles. In a loop, you would then retrieve the people through the role's current relationship to Person.

It is impossible to overstate the importance of collections and iterators in an OO database. Although there is a query language (OQL) as well, most OO code retrieves data through relationships by navigating with iterators rather than by querying sets of data as in a relational database. Even the query language retrieves collections of objects that you must then iterate through. Also, most OODBMS products started out with no query language, and there is still not all that much interest in querying (as opposed to navigating) in the OODBMS application com-munity.

Operations

The ODMG standard adopts the OMG CORBA standard for operations and sup-ports overloading of operations. You *overload* an operation when you create an operation in a class with the same name and signature (combination of parameter types) as an operation in another class. Some OO languages permit overloading to occur between any classes, as in Smalltalk. Others restrict overloading to the subclass-superclass relationship, with an operation in the subclass overloading only an operation with the same name and signature in a superclass.

The ODMG standard also supports exceptions and exception handling fol-lowing the C++, or *termination,* model of exception handling. There is a hierar-chy of Exception objects that you subclass to create your own exceptions. The rules for exception handling are complex:

1. The programmer declares an exception handler within scope **s** capable of handling exceptions of type **t**.

2. An operation within a contained scope **sn** may "raise" an exception of type **t**.

3. The exception is "caught" by the most immediately containing scope that has an exception handler. The call stack is automatically unwound by the run-time system out to the level of the handler. Memory is freed for all ob-jects allocated in intervening stack frames. Any transactions begun within

a nested scope, that is, unwound by the run-time system in the process of searching up the stack for an exception handler, are aborted.

4. When control reaches the handler, the handler may either decide that it can handle the exception or pass it on (reraise it) to a containing handler [Cattel and Barry 1997, p. 40].

Object-Relational Databases

The object-relational data model is in even worse shape than the OO data model. Being a hybrid, the data model takes the relational model and extends it with certain object-oriented concepts. Which ones depend on the particular vendor or sage (I won't say oracle) you choose. There is an ISO standard, SQL3, that is staggering toward adoption, but it has not yet had a large impact on vendors' systems [ISO 1997; Melton 1998].

> Note: C. J. Date, one of the most famous proponents of the relational model, has penned a manifesto with his collaborator Hugh Darwen on the ideas relating to the integration of object and relational technologies [Date and Darwen 1998]. The version of the OR data model I present here is very different. Anyone seriously considering using an OR data model, or more practically an ORDBMS, should read Date's book. It is by turns infuriating, illuminating, and aggravating. Infuriating, because Date and Darwen bring a caustic and arrogant sense of British humour to the book, which trashes virtually every aspect of the OR world. Illuminating, because they work through some serious problems with OR "theory," if you can call it that, from a relational instead of OO perspective. Aggravating, because there is very little chance of the ORDBMS vendors learning anything from the book, to their and our loss. I do not present the detailed manifesto here because I don't believe the system they demand delivers the benefits of object-oriented integration with relational technology and because I seriously doubt that system will ever become a working ORDBMS.

Depending on the vendor you choose, the database system more or less resembles an object-oriented system. It also presents a relational face to the world, theoretically giving you the best of both worlds. Figure 2-11 shows this hybrid nature as the combination of the OO and relational structures from Figures 2-8 and 2-9. The tables have corresponding object types, and the relationships are sets or collections of objects. The issues that these data models introduce are so new that vendors have only begun to resolve them, and most of the current solutions are ad hoc in nature. Time will show how well the object-relational model matures.

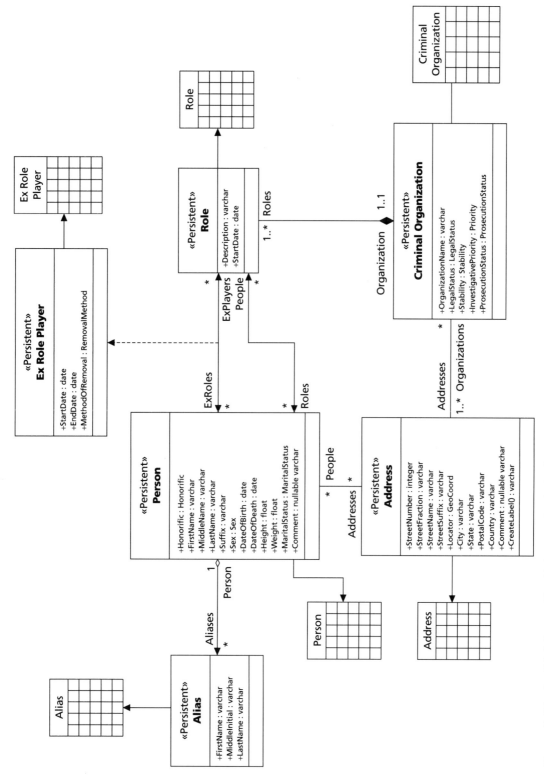

Figure 2-11 An OR Schema: The Holmes PLC Criminal Network Database

In the meantime, you can work with the framework that Michael Stone-braker introduced in his 1999 book on ORDBMS technology. That book suggests the following features to define a true ORDBMS [Stonebraker 1999, p. 268]:

1. Base type extension
   a. Dynamic linking of user-defined functions
   b. Client or server activation of user-defined functions
   c. Integration of user-defined functions with middleware application systems
   d. Secure user-defined functions
   e. Callback in user-defined functions
   f. User-defined access methods
   g. Arbitrary-length data types
   h. Open storage manager
2. Complex objects
   a. Type constructors
      - set of
      - record of
      - reference
   b. User-defined functions
      - dynamic linking
      - client or server activation
      - securer user-defined functions
      - callback
   c. Arbitrary-length complex data types
   d. SQL support
3. Inheritance
   a. Data and function inheritance
   b. Overloading
   c. Inheritance of types, not tables
   d. Multiple inheritance
4. Rule system
   a. Events and actions are retrieves as well as updates
   b. Integration of rules with inheritance and type extension
   c. Rich execution semantics for rules
   d. No infinite loops

Note: While this definition provides a good basis for academic wrangling over truth and beauty, it probably is neither a necessary nor a sufficient definition of the data model from the perspective of the practicing data architect. Certainly it doesn't cover all the issues that interest me, and it smacks of the same logic that led to the Ten-Year War over the true character of the "object." It is counterproductive, I believe, to treat a list of features as a definition. Until there is a formal, mathematical model that extends the relational model with whatever constructs are appropriate, I choose to leave truth to the academic communities' debates. It's also important to note that

*these features reflect Stonebraker's interest in Illustra, the product
he designed based on his work in the ORDBMS arena, since acquired
by Informix and shipped as the Informix Dynamic Server with Universal Data Option.*

In the following sections, I will cover the basics of these features. Where useful, I will illustrate the abstraction with the implementation in one or more commercial ORDBMS products, including Oracle8 with its Objects Option, DB2 Universal Database [Chamberlin 1998], and Informix with its optional Dynamic Server (also known as Illustra) [Stonebraker and Brown 1999].

Types and Inheritance

The relational data architecture contains types through reference to the domains of columns. The ANSI standard limits types to very primitive ones: NUMERIC, CHARACTER, TIMESTAMP, RAW, GRAPHIC, DATE, TIME, and INTERVAL. There are also subtypes (INTEGER, VARYING CHARACTER, LONG RAW), which are restrictions on the more general types. These are the *base types* of the data model.

An OR data model adds *extended* or *user-defined* types to the base types of the relational model. There are three variations on extended types:

- Subtypes or distinct data types

- Record data types

- Encapsulated data types

Subtypes   A *subtype* is a base type with a specific restriction. Standard SQL supports a combination of size and logical restrictions. For example, you can use the NUMERIC type but limit the numbers with a precision of 11 and a scale of 2 to represent monetary amounts up to \$999,999,999.99. You could also include a CHECK constraint that limited the value to something between 0 and 999,999,999.99, making it a nonnegative monetary amount. However, you can put these restrictions only on a column definition. You can't create them separately. An OR model lets you create and name a separate type with the restrictions.

DB2 UDB, for example, has this statement:

```
CREATE DISTINCT TYPE <name> AS <type declaration> WITH COMPARISONS
```

This syntax lets you name the type declaration. The system then treats the new type as a completely separate (distinct) type from its underlying base type, which can greatly aid you in finding errors in your SQL code. Distinct types are part of the SQL3 standard. The WITH COMPARISONS clause, in the best tradition of

IBM, does nothing. It is there to remind you that the type supports the relational operators such as + and <, and all base types but BLOBs require it. Informix has a similar CREATE DISTINCT TYPE statement but doesn't have the WITH COMPARISONS. Both systems let you cast values to a type to tell the system that you mean the value to be of the specified type. DB2 has a CAST function to do this, while Informix uses a :: on the literal: 82::fahrenheit, for example, casts the number 82 to the type "fahrenheit." Both systems let you create conversion functions that casting operators use to convert values from type to type as appropriate. Oracle8, on the other hand, does not have any concept of subtype.

Record Data Types   A *record data type* (or a *structured type* in the ISO SQL3 standard) is a table definition, perhaps accompanied by methods or functions. Once you define the type, you can then create objects of the type, or you can define tables of such objects. OR systems do not typically have any access control over the members of the record, so programs can access the data attributes of the object directly. I therefore distinguish these types from encapsulated data types, which conceal the data behind a firewall of methods or functions.

> Note: SQL3 defines the type so that each attribute generates ob-
> server and mutator functions (functions that get and set the attrib-
> ute values). The standard thus rigorously supports full encapsula-
> tion, yet exposes the underlying attributes directly, something
> similar to having one's cake and eating it.

Oracle8 contains record data types as the primary way of declaring the structure of objects in the system. The CREATE TYPE AS OBJECT statement lets you define the attributes and methods of the type. DB2 has no concept of record type. Informix Dynamic Server offers the row type for defining the attributes (CREATE ROW TYPE with a syntax similar to CREATE TABLE), but no methods. You can, however, create user-defined routines that take objects of any type and act as methods. To a certain extent, this means that Oracle8 object types resemble the encapsulated types in the next section, except for your being able to access all the data attributes of the object directly.

Encapsulated Data Types and BLOBs   The real fun in OR systems begins when you add encapsulated data types—types that hide their implementation completely. Informix provides what it calls *DataBlades* (perhaps on the metaphor of razor blades snapping into razors); Oracle8 has Network Computing Architecture (NCA) *data cartridges*. These technologies let you extend the base type system with new types and the behaviors you associate with them. The Informix spatial data blade, for example, provides a comprehensive way of dealing with spatial and geographic information. It lets you store data and query it in natural ways rather than forcing you to create relational structures. The Oracle8 Spatial Data Cartridge performs similar functions, though with interesting design limitations (see Chapter 12 for some details). Not only do these extension modules let you represent data and behavior, they also provide indexing and other access-method-related tools that integrate with the DBMS optimizer [Stonebraker 1999, pp. 117–149].

A critical piece of the puzzle for encapsulated data types is the *constructor,* a function that acts as a factory to build an object. Informix, for example, provides the row() function and cast operator to construct an instance of a row type in an INSERT statement. For example, when you use a row type "triplet" to declare a three-integer column in a table, you use "row(1, 2, 3)::triplet" as the value in the VALUES clause to cast the integers into a row type. In Oracle8, you create types with constructor methods having the same name as the type and a set of parameters. You then use that method as the value: triplet(1, 2, 3), for example. Oracle8 also supports methods to enable comparison through standard indexing.

OR systems also provide extensive support for LOBs, or large objects. These are encapsulated types in the sense that their internal structure is completely inaccessible to SQL. You typically retrieve the LOB in a program, then convert its contents into an object of some kind. Both the conversion and the behavior associated with the new object are in your client program, though, not in the database. Oracle8 provides the BLOB, CLOB, NCLOB, and bfile types. A BLOB is a binary string with any structure you want. The CLOB and NCLOB are character objects for storing very large text objects. The CLOB contains single-byte characters, while the NCLOB contains multibyte characters. The bfile is a reference to a BLOB in an external file; bfile functions let you manipulate the file in the usual ways but through SQL instead of program statements. Informix Dynamic Server also provides BLOBs and CLOBs. DB2 V2 provides BLOBs, CLOBs, and DBCLOBs (binary, single-byte, and multibyte characters, respectively). V2 also provides file references to let you read and write LOBs from and to files.

Inheritance Inheritance in OR systems comes with a couple of twists compared to the inheritance in OODBMSs. The first twist is a negative one: Oracle8 and DB2 V2 do not support any kind of inheritance. Oracle8 may acquire some form of inheritance in future releases, but the first release has none. Informix Dynamic Server provides inheritance and introduces the second twist: inheritance of types and of tables. Stonebraker's definition calls for inheritance of types, not tables; by this he seems to mean that inheritance based only on types isn't good enough, since his book details the table inheritance mechanism as well. Type inheritance is just like OO inheritance applied to row types. You inherit both the data structure and the use of any user-defined functions that take the row type as an argument. You can overload functions for inheriting types, and Dynamic Server will execute the appropriate function on the appropriate data.

The twist comes when you reflect on the structure of data in the system. In an OODBMS, the extension of a type is the set of all objects of the type. You usually have ways to iterate through all of these objects. In an ORDBMS, however, data is in tables. You use types in two ways in these systems. You can either declare a table of a type, giving the table the type structure, or you declare a column in the table of the type, giving the column the type structure. You can therefore declare multiple tables of a single type, partitioning the type extension. In current systems, there is no way other than a UNION to operate over the type extension as a whole.

Inheritance of the usual sort works with types and type extensions. To accommodate the needs of tables, Informix extends the concept to table inheritance based on type inheritance. When you create a table of a subtype, you can create it under a table of the supertype. This two-step inheritance lets you build separate data hierarchies using the same type hierarchies. It also permits the ORDBMS to query over the subtypes.

Figure 2-10 in the OODBMS section above shows the inheritance hierarchy of identification documents. Using Informix Dynamic Server, you would declare row types for IdentificationDocument, Expiring Document, Passport, and so on, to represent the type hierarchy. You could then declare a table for each of these types that corresponds to a concrete object. In this case, IdentificationDocument, Expiring Document, and LawEnforcementID are abstract classes and don't require tables, while the rest are concrete and do. You could partition any of these classes by creating multiple tables to hold the data (US Passport, UK Passport, and so on).

Because of its clear distinction between abstract and concrete structures, this hierarchy has no need to declare table inheritance. Consider a hierarchy of Roles as a counterexample. Figure 2-9 shows the Role as a class representing a connection between a Person and a CriminalOrganization. You could create a class hierarchy representing the different kinds of roles (Boss, Lieutenant, Soldier, Counselor, Associate, for example), and you could leave Role as a kind of generic association. You would create a Role table as well as a table for each of its subtypes. In this case, you would create the tables using the UNDER clause to establish the type hierarchy. When you queried the Role table, you would actually scan not just that table but also all of its subtype tables. If you used a function in the query, SQL would apply the correct overloaded function to the actual row based on its real type (dynamic binding and polymorphism). You can use the ONLY qualifier in the FROM clause to restrict the query to a single table instead of ranging over all the subtype tables.

ORDBMS products are inconsistent in their use of inheritance. The one that does offer the feature does so with some twists on the OODBMS concept of inheritance. These twists have a definite effect on database design through effects on your conceptual and physical schemas. But the impact of the OR data architecture does not end with types. They offer multiple structuring opportunities through complex objects and collections as well.

Complex Objects and Collections

The OR data architectures all offer complex objects of various sorts:

- *Nested tables:* Tables with columns that are defined with multiple components as tables themselves

- *Typed columns:* Tables with columns of a user-defined type

- *References:* Tables with columns that refer to objects in other tables

- *Collections:* Tables with columns that are collections of objects, such as sets or variable-length arrays

  Note: Those exposed to some of the issues in mathematical modeling of data structures will recognize the difficulties in the above categorization. For example, you can model nested tables using types, or you can see them as a special kind of collection (a set of records, for example). This again points up the difficulty of characterizing a model that has no formal basis. From the perspective of practical design, the above categories reflect the different choices you must make between product features in the target DBMS.

Oracle8's new table structure features rely heavily on nested structures. You first create a table type, which defines a type as a table of objects of a user-defined type:

```
CREATE TYPE <table type> AS TABLE OF <user-defined type>
```

A nested table is a column of a table declared to be of a table type. For example, you could store a table of aliases within the Person table if you used the following definitions:

```
CREATE TYPE ALIAS_TYPE (...);
CREATE TYPE ALIAS AS TABLE OF ALIAS_TYPE;
CREATE TABLE Person (
  PersonID NUMBER PRIMARY KEY,
  Name VARCHAR2(100) NOT NULL,
  Aliases ALIAS)
```

The Informix Dynamic Server, on the other hand, relies exclusively on types to represent complex objects. You create a user-defined type, then declare a table using the type for the type of a column in the table. Informix has no ability to store tables in columns, but it does support sets of user-defined types, which comes down to the same thing.

Both Oracle8 and Informix Dynamic Server provide references to types, with certain practical differences. A *reference,* in this context, is a persistent pointer to an object stored outside the table. References use an encapsulated OID to refer to the object it identifies. References often take the place of foreign key relationships in OR architectures. You can combine them with types to reduce the complexity of queries dramatically. Both Oracle8 and Informix provide a navigational syntax for using references in SQL expressions known as the dot notation. For example, in the relational model of Figure 2-8, there is a foreign key relationship between CriminalOrganization and Address through the OrganizationAddress relationship table. To query the postal codes of an organization, you might use this standard SQL:

```
SELECT a.PostalCode
  FROM CriminalOrganization o, OrganizationAddress oa, Address a
 WHERE o.OrganizationID = oa.OrganizationID AND
       oa.AddressID = a.AddressID
```

To get the same information from an ORDBMS, you might have represented the address relationship as a set of references to addresses, which are a separate type. To query these, you would use this SQL in Informix:

```
SELECT deref(*).PostalCode
  FROM (SELECT Addresses
          FROM CriminalOrganization)
```

The SELECT in the FROM clause returns a set of object references of type Address, and you dereference this set and navigate to the PostalCode attribute of the type in the main SELECT clause expression.

Oracle8 works from a position much closer to the relational model, as it does not support this kind of set retrieval. Instead, you can retrieve the address references and dereference them in the context of an object view and its type. An object view is a view you define with the CREATE VIEW statement to be a view of objects of a certain type. This lets you encapsulate a query of indefinite complexity that builds the objects. In this case, for example, you might build a view of criminal organization address objects that includes the name of the organization and a VARRAY of addresses for each organization. You would then typically select an object into a PL/SQL data structure and use the standard dot notation to access the postal code element of the individual members of the VARRAY.

The Oracle8 VARRAY is a varying length array of objects of a single type, including references to objects. The varying array has enjoyed on-again, off-again popularity in various products and approaches to data structure representation. It provides a basic ability to structure data in a sequentially ordered list. Informix Dynamic Server provides the more exact SET, MULTISET, and LIST collections. A SET is a collection of unique elements with no order. A MULTISET is a collection of elements with no order and duplicate values allowed. A LIST is a collection of elements with sequential ordering and duplicate values allowed. You can access the LIST elements using an integer index. The LIST and the VARRAY are similar in character, though different in implementation.

DB2 V2 comes out on the short end for this category of features. It offers neither the ability to create complex types nor any kind of collection. This ORDBMS relies entirely on lobs and externally defined functions that operate on them.

Rules

A *rule* is the combination of event detection (ON EVENT x) and handling (DO action). When the database server detects an event (usually an INSERT, UPDATE, or DELETE but also possibly a SELECT), it fires an action. The combination of event-action pairs is the rule [Stonebraker 1999, pp. 101–111]. Most database managers call rules *triggers*.

While rules are interesting, I don't believe they really form part of the essential, differentiating basis for an ORDBMS. Most RDBMSs and some OODBMSs also have triggers, and the extensions that Stonebraker enumerates do not relate to the OO features of the DBMS. It would be nice if the SQL3 standard finally deals with triggers and/or rules in a solid way so that you can develop portable triggers. You can't do this today. The result is that many shops avoid triggers because they would prevent moving to a different DBMS, should that become necessary for economic or technical reasons. That means you must implement business rules in application server or client code rather than in the database where they belong.

Decisions

The object-relational model makes a big impact on application design. The relational features of the model let you migrate your legacy relational designs to the new data model, insofar as that model supports the full relational data model. To make full use of the data model, however, leads you down at least two additional paths.

First, you can choose to use multiple-valued data types in your relational tables through nested tables or typed attributes. For certain purposes, such as rapid application development tools that can take advantage of these features, this may be very useful. For the general case, however, I believe you should avoid these features unless you have some compelling rationale for using them. The internal implementations of these features are still primitive, and things like query optimization, indexes, levels of nesting, and query logic are still problematic. More importantly, using these features leads to an inordinate level of design complexity. The nearest thing I've found to it is the use of nested classes in C++. The only real reason to nest classes in C++ is to encapsulate a helper class within the class it helps, protecting it from the vicious outside world. Similarly, declaring a nested table or a collection object works to hide the complexity of the data within the confines of the table column, and you can't reuse it outside that table. In place of these features, you should create separate tables for each kind of object and use references to link a table to those objects.

Second, you can use the object-oriented features (inheritance, methods, and object references) to construct a schema that maps well to an object-oriented conceptual design. The interaction with the relational features of the data model provide a bridge to relational operations (such as the ability to use SQL effectively with the database). The OO features give you the cohesion and encapsulation you need in good OO designs.

Summary

This introductory chapter has laid out the context within which you design databases using OO methods. Part of the context is system architecture, which contributes heavily to the physical design of your database. Another part of the context is data architecture, which contributes heavily to the conceptual design and to the choices you make in designing applications that use the database.

The rest of this chapter introduced you to the three major kinds of database management systems: RDBMSs, ORDBMSs, and OODBMSs. These sections gave you an overview of how these systems provide you with their data storage services and introduced some of the basic design issues that apply in each system.

Given this context, the rest of the book goes into detail on the problems and solutions you will encounter during the typical orderly design process. Remember, though, that order comes from art—the art of design.

Gathering Requirements 3

Ours is a world where people don't know what they want and are willing to go through hell to get it.

Don Marquis

Requirements hell is that particular circle of the Inferno where Sisyphus is pushing the rock up a hill, only to see it roll down again. Often misinterpreted, this myth has roots in reality. Sisyphus has actually reached the top of the hill many times; it's just that he keeps asking whether he's done, with the unfortunate result of being made to start over.

Perhaps the answer to getting requirements right is not to ask. On the other hand, I suspect the answer is that you just have to keep going, rolling that requirements rock uphill. This chapter lays out the terrain so that at least you won't slip and roll back down.

The needs of the user are, or at least should be, the starting point for designing a database. Ambiguity and its resolution in clearly stated and validated requirements are the platform on which you proceed to design. Prioritizing the requirements lets you develop a meaningful project plan, deferring lower-priority items to later projects. Finally, understanding the scope of your requirements lets you understand what kind of database architecture you need. This chapter covers the basics of gathering data requirements as exemplified by the Holmes PLC commonplace book system.

Ambiguity and Persistence

Gathering requirements is a part of every software project, and the techniques apply whether your system is database-centric or uses no database at all. This section summarizes some general advice regarding requirements and specializes it for database-related ones.

Ambiguity

Ambiguity can make life interesting. Unless you enjoy the back-and-forth of angry users and programmers, however, your goal in gathering requirements is to reduce ambiguity to the point where you can deliver a useful database design that does what people want.

As an example, consider the commonplace book. This was a collection of reference materials that Sherlock Holmes constructed to supplement his prodigious memory for facts. Some of the relevant Holmes quotations illustrate the basic requirements.

This passage summarizes the nature of the commonplace book:

> "Kindly look her up in my index, Doctor," murmured Holmes without opening his eyes. For many years he had adopted a system of docketing all paragraphs concerning men and things, so that it was difficult to name a subject or a person on which he could not at once furnish information. In this case I found her biography sandwiched in between that of a Hebrew rabbi and that of a staff-commander who had written a monograph upon the deep-sea fishes.
>
> "Let me see," said Holmes. "Hum! Born in New Jersey in the year 1858. Contralto—hum! La Scala, hum! Prima donna Imperial Opera of Warsaw—yes! Retired from operatic stage—ha! Living in London—quite so! Your Majesty, as I understand, became entangled with this young person, wrote her some compromising letters, and is now desirous of getting those letters back." [SCAN]

Not every attempt to find information is successful:

> My friend had listened with amused surprise to this long speech, which was poured forth with extraordinary vigour and earnestness, every point being driven home by the slapping of a brawny hand upon the speaker's knee. When our visitor was silent Holmes stretched out his hand and took down letter "S" of his commonplace book. For once he dug in vain into that mine of varied information.
>
> "There is Arthur H. Staunton, the rising young forger," said he, "and there was Henry Staunton, whom I helped to hang, but Godfrey Staunton is a new name to me."
>
> It was our visitor's turn to look surprised. [MISS]

The following passage illustrates the biographical entries of people and their relationship to criminal organizations.

> "Just give me down my index of biographies from the shelf."
>
> He turned over the pages lazily, leaning back in his chair and blowing great clouds from his cigar.
>
> "My collection of M's is a fine one," said he. "Moriarty himself is enough to make any letter illustrious, and here is Morgan the poisoner, and Merridew of abominable memory, and Mathews, who knocked out my left canine in the waiting-room at Charing Cross, and finally, here is our friend of tonight."

He handed over the book, and I read:

Moran, Sebastian, Colonel. Unemployed. Formerly 1st Bangalore Pioneers. Born London, 1840. Son of Sir Augustus Moran, C.B., once British Minister to Persia. Educated Eton and Oxford. Served in Jowaki Campaign, Afghan Campaign, Charasiab (dispatches), Sherpur, and Cabul. Author of *Heavy Game of the Western Himalayas* (1881), *Three Months in the Jungle* (1884). Address: Conduit Street. Clubs: The Anglo-Indian, the Tankerville, the Bagatelle Card Club.
On the margin was written, in Holmes's precise hand:
The second most dangerous man in London. {EMPT}

Here is an example of the practical use of the commonplace book in criminal investigating:

We both sat in silence for some little time after listening to this extraordinary narrative. Then Sherlock Holmes pulled down from the shelf one of the ponderous commonplace books in which he placed his cuttings.
"Here is an advertisement which will interest you," said he. "It appeared in all the papers about a year ago. Listen to this:
"Lost on the 9th inst., Mr. Jeremiah Hayling, aged twenty-six, a hydraulic engineer. Left his lodging at ten o'clock at night, and has not been heard of since. Was dressed in—"
etc. etc. Ha! That represents the last time that the colonel needed to have his machine overhauled, I fancy. [ENGR]

And here is another example, showing the way Holmes added marginal notes to the original item:

Our visitor had no sooner waddled out of the room—no other verb can describe Mrs. Merrilow's method of progression—than Sherlock Holmes threw himself with fierce energy upon the pile of commonplace books in the corner. For a few minutes there was a constant swish of the leaves, and then with a grunt of satisfaction he came upon what he sought. So excited was he that he did not rise, but sat upon the floor like some strange Buddha, with crossed legs, the huge books all round him, and one open upon his knees.
"The case worried me at the time, Watson. Here are my marginal notes to prove it. I confess that I could make nothing of it. And yet I was convinced that the coroner was wrong. Have you no recollection of the Abbas Parva tragedy?"
"None, Holmes."
"And yet you were with me then. But certainly my own impression was very superficial. For there was nothing to go by, and none of the parties had engaged my services. Perhaps you would care to read the papers?" [VEIL]

Holmes also uses the commonplace book to track cases that parallel ones in which a client engages his interest:

"Quite an interesting study, that maiden," he observed. "I found her more interesting than her little problem, which, by the way, is a rather trite one. You will find parallel cases, if you consult my index, in Andover in '77, and there was something of the sort at The Hague last year. Old as is the idea, however, there were one or two details which were new to me. But the maiden herself was most instructive." [IDEN]

This use verges on another kind of reference, the casebook:

"The whole course of events," said Holmes, "from the point of view of the man who called himself Stapleton, was simple and direct, although to us, who had no means in the beginning of knowing the motives of his actions and could only learn part of the facts, it all appeared exceedingly complex. I have had the advantage of two conversations with Mrs. Stapleton, and the case has now been so entirely cleared up that I am not aware that there is anything which has remained a secret to us. You will find a few notes upon the matter under the heading B in my indexed list of cases. {HOUN]

Certain limitations of the commonplace book medium clearly limited the ways in which Holmes ordered his cases:

"Matilda Briggs was not the name of a young woman, Watson," said Holmes in a reminiscent voice. "It was a ship which is associated with the giant rat of Sumatra, a story for which the world is not yet prepared. But what do we know about vampires? Does it come within our purview either? Anything is better than stagnation, but really we seem to have been switched on to a Grimms' fairy tale. Make a long arm, Watson, and see what V has to say."

I leaned back and took down the great index volume to which he referred. Holmes balanced it on his knee, and his eyes moved slowly and lovingly over the record of old cases, mixed with the accumulated information of a lifetime.

"Voyage of the *Gloria Scott*," he read. "That was a bad business. I have some recollection that you made a record of it, Watson, though I was unable to congratulate you upon the result. Victor Lynch, the forger. Venomous lizard or gila. Remarkable case, that! Vittoria, the circus belle. Vanderbilt and the Yeggman. Vipers. Vigor, the Hammersmith wonder. Hullo! Hullo! Good old index. You can't beat it. Listen to this, Watson. Vampirism in Hungary. And again, Vampires in Transylvania." He turned over the pages with eagerness, but after a short intent perusal he threw down the great book with a snarl of disappointment.

"Rubbish, Watson, rubbish! What have we to do with walking corpses who can only be held in their grave by stakes driven through their hearts? It's pure lunacy." [SUSS]

These quotations show how Holmes constructed his commonplace books:

He took down the great book in which, day by day, he filed the agony columns of the various London journals. "Dear me!" said he, turning over the pages, "what a chorus of groans, cries, and bleatings! What a rag-bag of singular happenings! But surely the most valuable hunting-ground that ever was given to a student of the unusual! This person is alone and cannot be approached by letter without a breach of that absolute secrecy which is desired. How is any news or any message to reach him from without? Obviously by advertisement through a newspaper. There seems no other way, and fortunately we need concern ourselves with the one paper only. [REDC]

One winter's night, as we sat together by the fire, I ventured to suggest to him that, as he had finished pasting extracts into his commonplace book, he might employ the next two hours in making our room a little more habitable. [MUSG]

The first day Holmes had spent in cross-indexing his huge book of references. [BRUC]

As evening drew in, the storm grew louder and louder, and the wind cried and sobbed like a child in the chimney. Sherlock Holmes sat moodily at one side of the fireplace cross-indexing his records of crime, . . . [FIVE]

These passages from the Holmes canon illustrate both the painstaking nature of Holmes's approach to detection and the nature of ambiguity in requirements gathering. Holmes, despite his best efforts, was unable to conceive of his commonplace book system in unambiguous terms. "Voyage of the Gloria Scott," for example, as an entry in volume "V" seems a bit mysterious.

Ambiguity is a state in which you find multiple, conflicting interpretations of a text or situation. You create ambiguity when you state the requirements for your system or database that someone might interpret in different ways. Gause and Weinberg cite three specific kinds of ambiguity that are important for requirements gathering [Gause and Weinberg 1989]:

- *Missing requirements:* Needs that are a key part of resolving the differences in interpretation

- *Ambiguous words:* Words in the requirement that are capable of multiple interpretations

- *Introduced elements:* Words you put in the mouth of the stakeholder

In designing the commonplace book system, we have perhaps a bit less access to Holmes than we would ordinarily like, given his busy schedule and general terseness. This situation is certain to lead to missing requirements and introduced elements. With some persistence, we can work out the details.

For example, in the quotations above, the system seems to require several types of fact:

- *Biographical facts:* Facts relating to the history of individual people

- *Case history:* Facts relating to the history of criminal cases from Holmes's work and cases of interest from around the world

- *Encyclopedia articles:* Facts relating to things of interest to the consulting detective (vampires, for example, or gilas)

- *Classified advertisements:* The agony columns where people advertise for lost family members or place communications to others
- *Periodical articles:* Text from newspapers and magazines that contributes interesting facts relating to people, places, and events of interest to the consulting detective

With a little thought, you can see that there might be many more sources of information that are critical to the investigator. Did Holmes exclude these for a reason, or did they simply not come up in the conversation? What about Web articles? How about government data? What about information about corporations, limited partnerships, and other business entities? Television infomercials (relating to consumer fraud, for example, possibly on a large scale)?

Also, we have to infer from the quotations that the information in the commonplace book is not random or universal. But it seems difficult to make the direct claim that the book contains only those bits of fact that relate to things of interest to the detective. This is ambiguous both because the terms are ambiguous (what is of interest?) and because we are putting words in Holmes's mouth. How can we resolve these questions?

Observing and Asking the Right Questions

In a word: exploration. You need to explore the requirements to clarify, as much as possible, what problem you need to solve [Gause and Weinberg 1989]. The first question is a simple one: Can a solution for the problem exist? That is, if you've stated the problem correctly, is there in fact a way to solve it?

What is the essential problem that the commonplace book system solves? In the work of a consulting private detective, it is critical to reason about a situation from a basis in factual data, both about the situation and about the context of that situation. In the quotations, Holmes uses his written commonplace book to get the facts he needs to interpret events and situations. The problem statement thus might be the following:

> *Holmes PLC needs a way to make facts relevant to their consulting detective practice available to the consulting private detective.*

This statement gives you the flavor of the problem, but it hasn't enough detail to state a solution. In this case, however, we're starting with a *norm:* an existing solution. With this kind of starting point, you want to refine your problem definition using the existing system as a guide. In the process, you identify the limitations of that system and perhaps the underlying problems that system tries to address.

The next step in the exploration is to ask context-free questions, usually beginning with the familiar pronouns *who, what, why, when, where,* and *how.* Process questions ask about the nature of the design process, product questions ask about the nature of the design product, and metaquestions ask questions about the questions. For example, here are some issues you might raise in the first set of questions about the commonplace book:

- The client for the commonplace book is the consulting private detective at Holmes PLC. This system is proprietary and is part of the intellectual property of Holmes PLC.

- The value of this system to the client is at least 20 million pounds sterling over a five-year period in increased revenues. These revenues come from better identification of revenue opportunities and better results of investigations, leading to increased marketability of detective services.

- There is increasing pressure for an automated solution to this problem from the clients, who want faster access to better information than the current system provides. There have been too many Godfrey Stauntons of late.

- The content of the system ranges from critical information about criminals and criminal events to "nice-to-have" information about vampires and vipers. Critical information includes biographical data about criminals and relevant people and organizations, case histories from Holmes PLC and police files, and agony column entries (though this fine old paper-based institution for advertising for assistance is now being superseded by Web/Internet chat rooms).

- Not all information must be available immediately. Recent information is more important, and you can add historical information as time permits. Biographical information needs to be present in the first release for all criminals known to the agency. Information in the current paper-based system is more important than other information.

- The clients would like to have the existing paper system accessible through computer searching within a year. The old system must continue to exist until the new system is up and running with equivalent information.

- Information is more important than time, in this case. It would be better to have more complete information than to get the system running in a year.

- The information addresses the detectives' need for factual information about criminals and others involved in cases. These facts provide the basis for deductive and inductive detective work; without them, you cannot reason effectively. The computer system solves the problem of accessing a huge quantity of information quickly. It also solves the problem of cross-indexing the information for access by concept. A potential for conflict exists here because the cognitive maps of different clients differ greatly: Holmes might have an interest in "Voyages," while Watson might want to look for "Gloria Scott."

- Data quality is vital. The wrong information is not just worthless, it actually impedes deductive and inductive thought. That means that data validation tools are an essential component of the system, as are processes for accomplishing validation. It also means that the database must be secure from damage, either through accident or malicious intent.

- Security during system access not only is important for data validity, it also ensures that the client maintains confidentiality and secrecy during ongoing investigations. Subjects of investigations should not be able to determine whether the system has information about them or whether clients are accessing such information.

- The most important problem with this system is a combination of invasion of privacy and intellectual property issues. Much of the material from which Holmes PLC gathers information is public. As time goes on, Holmes PLC will increasingly use information gathered from individual informants, police agencies, and other private organizations. This could cause problems with privacy laws and regulations, particularly wiretapping and electronic eavesdropping laws in varying jurisdictions around the world. Also, material gathered from public sources may be subject to copyright or other intellectual property restrictions.

Given all this, you might wonder where the ambiguity is. Each and every statement above has ambiguity; the question is whether there is enough ambiguity to raise the risk of doing the wrong thing to the intolerable level. For example, one requirement says that completeness is vital, even at the expense of getting the system done in a year. You could not proceed with the requirement in this form. Take it apart. What does "complete" mean? It could mean many things depending on the set of data in question. For example, for criminal biographies, complete might mean all police records relating to a person, or it could mean police records, newspaper accounts, informer reports, and any number of other sources of information. And just when is informer reporting "complete"? These are the kinds of questions you must resolve by going back to the clients, posing situations, and probing into the meaning more deeply. You would presumably come out of this process with an understanding of how to assess the adequacy of information about a subject, potentially with some kind of metric indicating how adequate the information is, or a reliability metric for informers. This kind of metadata metric conveys real information to the client about how much they can rely on the data in the database. It is a capital mistake to theorize ahead of your data, and knowing what your data really is becomes vital to judging the relevance of your theories.

Persisting

Persisting here means two things: keep rolling that rock, and figure out what the requirements mean for your persistent data.

You can spend your entire life gathering requirements rather than developing systems. Although endless acquisition of knowledge is useful, unless someone pays you for just that, at some point you need to start developing your software. Knowing when to persist in gathering and interpreting requirements and when to move on comes from experience. You can use sophisticated metrics to judge the adequacy of your requirements, or you can use your intuition. Both require a good deal of experience, either to gather benchmark data or to develop your feelings to the point of being able to judge that you've done enough. It's important to probe to the level of ambiguity resolution that suits the needs of the project.

Persistence also extends to the data itself. Since this is a book on database design, it focuses on the requirements for such design. The last section listed various requirements for the system as a whole. Running through all those requirements are hidden assumptions about persistent data. Examining a few of the requirements shows you what this means.

- *The client for the commonplace book is the consulting private detective at Holmes PLC. This system is proprietary and is part of the intellectual property of Holmes PLC.*

  Nothing much related to databases here.

- *The value of this system to the client is at least 20 million pounds sterling over a five-year period in increased revenues. These revenues come from better identification of revenue opportunities and better results of investigations, leading to increased marketability of detective services.*

  Nor here.

- *There is increasing pressure for an automated solution to this problem from the clients, who want faster access to better information than the current system provides. There have been too many Godfrey Stauntons of late.*

  Here the first assumption appears about the underlying technology. "Faster access to better information" implies the storage of that information and the existence of access paths to it. The only qualifier is "faster," which could mean anything. In this case, "faster" refers to the current paper-based system. Pushing down on the requirement would probably elicit some details such as the need for access from mobile locations, the need for immediate response over a wide-area network, and the distribution of the data to Holmes PLC locations around the world. "Faster" then becomes relative to the current system, in which detectives need to call into a central office to get information, which researchers look up in paper-based file storage. The term "better" probably refers to the later requirement about "complete" data, meaning that not only must we move the database into electronic form but we must improve its content.

- *The content of the system ranges from critical information about criminals and criminal events to "nice-to-have" information about vampires and vipers. Critical information includes biographical data about criminals and relevant people and organizations, case histories from Holmes PLC and police files, and agony column entries.*

Here is some specific data that must persist: biographical and police information about criminals. There is also information about relevant other people, information about organizations (criminal, corporate, nonprofit, and so on), case history data, and media publications that reflect potential criminal or "interesting" activity.

- *Not all information must be available immediately. Recent information is more important, and you can add historical information as time permits. Biographical information needs to be present in the first release for all criminals known to the agency. Information in the current paper-based system is more important than other information.*

This requirement is similiar to the "faster access" one the came previously.

- *The clients would like to have the existing paper system accessible through computer searching within a year. The old system must continue to exist until the new system is up and running with equivalent information.*

This requirement helps us prioritize the data requirements. See the next section for details.

- *Information is more important than time, in this case. It would be better to have more complete information than to get the system running in a year.*

These are broad requirements relating to data content. The last section discussed the huge degree of ambiguity in this requirement, so it will need quite a bit of probing to refine it into something useful. It is, however, a critical requirement for the persistent data. "Complete" in this sense certainly applies to the persistent data, not to the software that accesses it. You should realize, however, that this requirement is unusual; time is often as or more important than completeness of information. Sometimes it's better to have incomplete data now than complete data on Tuesday, after the alleged felon has been acquitted by a jury for lack of evidence. This database focuses on a longer-term perspective, which is vital to understanding how to structure the application and database.

- *The information addresses the detectives' need for factual information about criminals and others involved in cases. These facts provide the basis for deductive and inductive detective work; without them, you cannot reason effectively. The computer system solves the problem of accessing a huge quantity of information quickly. It also solves the problem of cross-indexing the information for access by concept. A potential for conflict exists here because the cognitive maps of different clients differ greatly: Holmes might have an interest in "Voyages," while Watson might want to look for "Gloria Scott."*

Here we have two elements that relate to persistent data: access methods and second-order data. The "huge quantity" implies that there will be terabytes of data, which requires special database management software, extensive hardware analysis, and specific requirements for access paths such as indexing, clustering, and partitioning. These will all be part of the physical database design. As well, "cross-indexing" requires data about the data—data that describes the data in ways that permit rapid access to the data you want to see. There are several different ways to organize second-order data. You can rely on text searching, which is not particularly good at finding relevant information. You can develop a keyword system, which is quite labor intensive but pays dividends in access speed: this is what Holmes did with his paper-based "indexes." You can use a simple enumerative scheme such as the Dewey decimal system that libraries use, or you can develop more elaborate systems using *facets,* dimensions of the problem domain, in various combinations. This is the classic style of data warehousing, for example. Probing a bit may elicit requirements in this case for extensible indexing, letting the client add facets or classifications to the scheme as needed rather than relying on a static representation.

- *Data quality is vital. The wrong information is not just worthless, it actually impedes deductive and inductive thought. That means that data validation tools are an essential component of the system, as are processes for accomplishing validation. It also means that the database must be secure from damage, either through accident or malicious intent.*

This one definitely impacts persistent data. It means a number of things. First, you must have some way to tell whether conflicting information is part of the reality your database represents or is simply wrong. People disagree, for example, in their recollection of events and things. This is not a data quality problem but an information issue. You need not concern yourself with anything but data quality. Second, you must establish a process for data entry and validation. Third, you must err on the side of caution in establishing enforcement of referential integrity constraints and other business rules. Fourth, you must defer to the database in such enforcement. Fifth, you must impose security on the persistent data. You must protect the data going in and coming out.

- *Security during system access not only is important for data validity, it also ensures that the client maintains confidentiality and secrecy during ongoing investigations. Subjects of investigations should not be able to determine whether the system has information about them or whether clients are accessing such information.*

While you might think this requirement affects the software rather than the persistent data, it can affect the data also. For example, if you want the greater security of a mandatory access security scheme, you need to associate security labels with the data at all levels of the system, including the database and operating system. This quickly narrows down your technology choices, as there aren't many operating systems and database managers that support this level of security. It also has implications for authentication and access to the persistent data, which overlaps with the previous requirement relating to data integrity. Also, espionage is now easier than ever with Internet access to data. Holmes PLC depends upon the confidentiality of its trade secrets and other types of intellectual property in the database. Security at the database level protects those secrets from access through other mechanisms than applications.

- *The most important problem with this system is a combination of invasion of privacy and intellectual property issues. Much of the material from which Holmes PLC gathers information is public. As time goes on, Holmes PLC will increasingly use information gathered from individual informants, police agencies, and other private organizations. This could cause problems with privacy laws and regulations, particularly wiretapping and electronic eavesdropping laws in varying jurisdictions around the world. Also, material gathered from public sources may be subject to copyright or other intellectual property restrictions.*

The major implication of this requirement is a need to store licenses and permissions relating to proprietary and restricted data. This is another kind of second-order data. This also relates back to the security requirement, as keeping intellectual property secure is often required, as is privacy of data applying to individuals.

Getting Your Priorities Straight

Collecting the requirements is not the end of your work. Not every requirement is as important as every other requirement. The next task is to prioritize the requirements by understanding them, by relating them to one another, and by categorizing them. This is an iterative process that often requires deeper analysis through use cases, the subject of the next chapter. Until you get a reasonable level of detail, you may have a hard time figuring out what the real priorities are and which things depend on which other things. As you get into design, you will often find that there are technology dependencies that you must take into account as well, forcing you to revisit your priorities once again. Once you have your basic requirements, though, you can make a start on creating a framework for system and database development.

Understanding Requirements

Just because you have a list of what people expect from your system does not mean that you understand the requirements. The logic of failure dictates that every system resists the efforts of human beings to change it. The first thing you must do is to step back from your hunting and gathering efforts and think about them. And think, not just about the requirements you've gathered, but also about the ones you haven't, and about their side effects. Get people involved in this effort who both understand the domain and who have extensive experience with solving problems in that domain. Get training in problem solving. Consider the following recommendations from cognitive psychology [Dörner 1996]:

- State goals clearly
- Understand where you must compromise between conflicting goals
- Establish priorities, then change them when needed
- Model the system, including side effects and long-term changes
- Understand how much data you need, and get it
- Don't be excessively abstract
- Don't reduce everything to a nutshell, a single cause or fact
- Listen to others when they tell you you're going down the wrong path
- Apply methods when useful, and avoid them when they get in the way
- Study your history and apply the lessons you learn to the new system
- Think in terms of systems, not in terms of simple requirements

The more you do this, and the more you learn from your mistakes, the better you will be at gathering requirements.

Categorizing Requirements

At the most fundamental level, you can categorize requirements into operational objectives, object properties, rules, and preferences.

Operational Objectives

Operational objectives express the purpose behind the system and the approach you intend to take to achieve that purpose. Goals, functions, behaviors, operations, all are synonymous with operational objectives. Objectives are the most important kind of requirement because they express the underlying meaning behind the system, the *why* of what you are doing [Muller 1998].

For example, consider the following requirement from the last section:

- *The content of the system ranges from critical information about criminals and criminal events to "nice-to-have" information about vampires and vipers. Critical information includes biographical data about criminals and relevant people and organizations, case histories from Holmes PLC and police files, and agony column entries.*

This requirement expresses several overlapping operational objectives of the commonplace book system related to information needs:

- To give detectives the information they need to conduct their work through an appropriate computer interface to a database

- To provide information about known criminals through biographical and case history data

- To provide information about people of interest to detectives in their work through biographical data and personal advertising in various media

- To provide information about criminal cases of interest through case history data from Holmes PLC and police investigations and through news items from various media

- To provide information about facts of use in criminal investigations through encyclopedia entries (vampires and vipers)

- To enable quick and easy integration of up-to-date information through flexible interface technology that links the system to other similar systems owned by the police and media sources for much of the information required by clients

These requirements express a purpose (to do something) and a way of achieving that purpose (through data or behavior). Some of these objectives relate to the user of the system, such as the above objectives. Other objectives may be hidden from the user, existing only to enable some other objective or to make the system more flexible or easier to use. In this case, the dog that didn't bark in the nighttime (the clue that told Holmes that the abduction of Silver Blaze was an inside job [SILV]) is the interfacing requirement. The system needs to have a flexible data interface that lets Holmes easily integrate new information into the database. The detective doesn't really care how the information gets into the system, just that it is available when needed.

Object Properties

As you develop the data requirements for the system, you begin to see the objects (entities, tables, classes, and so on) that will exist in the system. As you think about them, you start to see their properties. *Object properties* are the second category of requirement, and probably the most important to the database designer. Properties can be table columns, object attributes, or class data members.

For example, a key object in the information requirement in the last section is the case history. You can immediately think of certain basic properties of this object:

- An identifier for the case

- A set of jurisdictions with interest in the case

- A set of people associated with the case in various roles (criminal, accessory, investigator, criminalist, medical examiner, witness, victim, judge, juror, and so on)

- A set of evidentiary facts (look up the Nicole Simpson murder case to see the minutiae that can result)

- The value of the property involved in the case

- The agency expenditure for the case

These are classic data elements. Not all object properties relate directly to database elements, of course: reliability, usability, nontoxicity are all object properties that apply to the software system in the large. Mostly, good object properties are very specific: the system must be available 24 hours a day, or the information should reflect all known information related to death or injury, or the system response must be two seconds or less for any given piece of information. Much ambiguity lies concealed in object properties: puzzle it out.

Rules

Rules are conditional requirements on object properties. For the value of a property to be acceptable, it must satisfy the condition.

Most referential integrity constraints come under this category of requirement. For example, if a case history refers to a particular criminal under a specific alias, both criminal and alias must exist in the database.

Timing rules also come under this category. For example, you may have an operational objective that the system must respond within two seconds of a request for information. That translates into a rule that all information in the database must have access characteristics that will permit retrieval in two seconds or less.

A third category of rule is a quality rule. You can specify tolerances for error that become part of your requirements. For example, if you store DNA evidence, the error in identifying the individual person must be less than .0001, meaning that the results are statistically significant with a probability value of 0.9999. These kinds of rules establish tolerances or boundaries beyond which the data cannot go.

Think a bit before you create a rule. Rules have a tendency to become laws, particularly in a software project with a deadline. Be reasonably sure that your rule is necessary before imposing it on your project. You may have to live with it for a long time.

Preferences

A *preference* is a condition on an object property that expresses a preferred state. For example, a detective would prefer to know the criminal behind every crime. Realistically, you must have unsolved case histories in the system—case histories that have no criminals. Requiring a case history to relate to a criminal is not possible. However, you can express a preference that case histories have a criminal with a requirement that the information source make every effort to specify this information. Alternatively, you can qualify "suspects" or something similar with some sort of probability value to permit detectives to proceed. You can also use initial values or default values—values that the database assigns if you don't specify anything—to represent preferences.

Usually, preferences take the form of "as much as possible" or "optimal" or "on balance" or something similar. You need to understand the difference between rules and preferences. A rule says "must" or "will" or "shall." It's a matter of integrity versus a matter of desire (as are so many other aspects of life).

Relating Requirements

Requirements are not isolated pearls of wisdom that exist independently of one another. The next step in understanding requirements is to treat them as a system, relating them to one another. The synergistic combination of requirements often can change the nature of your approach to design.

With data requirements, you usually express relationships directly through data models that contain the objects and their relationships. The later design chapters show you how to do this in detail. Briefly, more general requirements have more general relationships.

For example, storing a case history related to a criminal requires relating a criminal to some kind of event. The criminal is in a way a property of the event. The existence of the criminal as a separate object makes him or her an object in the system relating to other objects such as crimes.

More generally, the commonplace book system relates case histories by analogy. That is, some cases are "like" other cases. Detectives would like (love, actually) to retrieve all cases that are like the one they are investigating. This is a hard problem and unlikely to make it into the serious objectives for the common-place book. Still, there are relationships between cases that require additional rules in the database. For example, a consistent classification language for crimes could express a good deal of the similarity between crimes, including motive, means, and opportunity. It is actually quite difficult to express this in a database format [Muller 1982], but you could give it a shot.

It is important to understand how requirements cluster. The connections you can establish between requirements will usually tell you how your system architecture can organize its subsystems. If a particular set of requirements relate to one another strongly but are relatively unconnected to other requirements, you have a subsystem candidate. On the other hand, if you intuitively feel that several requirements belong together but you haven't found any relationship between them, think harder. You've missed something.

In the commonplace book system, for example, the case history is a central requirement. You can link a case history to criminals, crime and other events, people, organizations, and investigations. Vampires, on the other hand, link to very little. The former objects are the heart of the subsystem relating to the main purpose of the commonplace book: to record information about past events and people to help in resolving current investigations. Case histories pull together all the different strands into a single whole. The vampire encyclopedia entry, however, is almost a random bit of information that happened to be of interest in a single case. That item, and items like it, probably belongs in a separate encyclopedia subsystem outside the scope of the case history subsystem.

There is also a close internal relationship between people, criminals, and organizations. These requirements probably belong in a subsystem as well, showing that systems can contain other systems, or can overlap with them. The criminal organization, for example, maps certain kinds of people, such as Colonel Sebastian Moran, to organizations and to case histories and events. The criminal organization of which Moran was a part was a key target of Holmes's investigative efforts. This suggests it deserves a separate data subsystem to track the complex web of relationships between people, organizations, and events. This system overlaps with the biographical system and with the case history system as well as with the event system. You can see the stirring of the architectural dragon, even at the early requirement stage.

Relationships such as these are the domain of the analyst. Often, part of a system such as this will include data mining, statistical analysis, and other such tools to aid the analyst in identifying and quantifying relationships.

The increasing impact of your understanding of the requirements on the scope and direction of your project leads naturally into the next topic: prioritizing what you've understood.

Prioritizing Requirements

Requirements come in many guises. Some are vital to the project; others are fluff. Unfortunately, you have to go through a lot of fluff to train your mind to distinguish between fluff and the real thing. One aspect of this is the relativity of priorities. They depend on the nature of the people involved with the project. This configuration of beliefs and attitudes can change radically from project to project. In many ways, you must look at priorities as completely fresh in each project. Each of the different types of requirement has a different set of priorities.

You prioritize operational objectives by their contribution to the basic mission of the system. If system success requires successful achievement of the objective, the objective is critical. If you can skip the objective with only minor problems, it's marginal. If the objective is unrelated to the mission, it is a bad requirement.

You prioritize object properties into similar categories: must have, want, and ignore. A "must have" property is one without which the system will not achieve its mission. A "want" is something that is nice to have. An "ignore" is something that might be useful but either probably isn't or isn't worth the cost of building it.

You prioritize rules and preferences by their nature. Rules apply to must-have situations. If you've expressed a rule, you have to build it. Preferences, on the other hand, come in shades of gray, not in black and white. Defining "possible" and "optimal" is one of the hardest things to do in requirements gathering, though necessary.

Deciding the Style of Database

At this point in the project life cycle, you should be getting an image in your mind of the technology you expect to use. You've already begun to see subsystems, you've begun to identify data model elements, and your technical intuition is probably stirring. You may be wrong in your expectations, but it's a good idea to at least draw a line in the sand at this point. If nothing else, you'll see who thinks you're wrong and why. Feedback is the essence of good design.

There are several basic styles of database that apply to radically different situations. An *OLTP database* (online transaction processing) is one that supports many small transactions, usually on a very large database. For example, creating an entry for a new identification document or entering a new criminal into a criminal organization is a small transaction repeated many times in parallel. A *data warehouse* is a database that supports ad hoc queries on a very large database. You could see the historical features of the commonplace book as a data warehouse. A *data mart* is a data warehouse on a small scale, perhaps at a departmental level in an enterprise. A local biographical or geographical database fits this bill, for example. Then there are specialty databases such as multimedia databases, CAD databases, geographical information systems (GIS), and statistical databases. GIS systems, for example, could provide a means for representing location data for crimes, addresses, and other geographical information in the commonplace book (see Chapter 12 for an example of this use). Then there are the databases for the rest of us.

You will find these categories fit only the most generic or the most specific of problems. Holmes PLC, for example, certainly is not an OLTP system. You could see it as a data warehouse, but the style of analysis that data warehouses and data marts represent is not the kind of use that Holmes PLC expects to have. The data model is generally more complex than a simple star topology expressing dimensions. Perhaps the best way to think about the Holmes PLC database is as a multimedia search database, but with emphasis on classification by facet rather than on text-based searching.

You should also be seeing the relationships that will lead you to choose a given type of data model (relational, object-relational, or object-oriented). If your system will involve navigational access through complex OO software written in C++ or Java, you should be looking at OODBMS products. If your system is an OLTP application based on simple forms and ad hoc queries, look at relational systems. If you have complex storage needs such as multimedia or geographical information and you need ad hoc query access to that information, consider the ORDBMS products as your first choice.

As you become more familiar with these data models and the technologies that implement them, you will be able to use more sophisticated decision rules in choosing your DBMS product. This book gives you a beginning.

Summary

Gerald Weinberg quotes Bertrand Russell on the relationship between what is meant versus what is done:

> I agree entirely that, in this case, a discussion as to what is meant is important and highly necessary as a preliminary to a consideration of the substantial

question, but if nothing can be said on the substantial question it seems a waste of time to discuss what it means. These philosophers remind me of the shopkeeper of whom I once asked the shortest way to Winchester. He called to a man in the back premises:

"Gentleman wants to know the shortest way to Winchester."

"Winchester?" an unseen voice replied.

"Aye."

"Way to Winchester?"

"Aye."

"Shortest way?"

"Aye."

"Dunno."

He wanted to get the nature of the question clear, but took no interest in answering it. This is exactly what modern philosophy does for the earnest seeker after truth. [Russell 1956, pp. 169–170]

Requirements must lead to solutions, not just to more requirements. Having gathered the requirements, the next step is to analyze them a bit more rigorously with use case analysis.

Modeling Requirements with Use Cases 4

The court assembles. Hamlet sits by Ophelia and makes bawdy jests that trouble her, and also makes remarks to disturb the King and Queen. With pantomime and spoken action the Players enact a murder like that of Hamlet's father, and the wooing of the Queen. The King rushes out in agitation and the court disperses in confusion. Hamlet says the ghost has proved trustworthy.

A scenario describing Act 3, scene 2, of Shakespeare's *Hamlet* [Fuller 1966]

A scenario, in literature, is a summary of a scene or story that describes the plot in terms a reader can easily understand. The UML *use case* performs a similar function for the software system. Like scenarios for plays, use cases can at best give you a pale reflection of the real workings of the system. For all that, they are more than useful; they are essential. Done properly, the use cases for a system describe at a high level what the system should do. A use case has at least four major effects on database design:

- A use case represents an atomic transaction through the system [Rational Software 1997b]. Knowing the system transactions lets you design the logical and physical database and the architecture to accommodate the transaction processing requirements of the system.

- A use case shows how the system uses data elements, both internally through inserting, updating, and deleting, and externally through querying. Knowing the set of data elements lets you organize them into user schemas and relate them to the overall conceptual schema of the system. The use case is the basis for the business rules that constrain your database design.

- A use case provides the infrastructure for measurement of the database product. The function points you estimate for the use case let you measure the value your database contributes to your project.

- A use case provides the basis for validation of your database product. As you move through incremental design and construction of the database, you validate what you've done by relating it back to the use cases that drive it. As your scope changes, you change the use cases to reflect new requirements and trace new work directly to those requirements.

The use case comes from Jacobson's original work, which is still the primary source for the intimate details [Jacobson et al. 1992]. The UML uses the term *scenario* for a use case instance, a particular path through a use case [Rational Software 1997a].

All the World's a Stage

The *UML Notation Guide* defines the *actor* [Rational Software 1997a, p. 77]:

> An actor is a role of object or objects outside of a system that interacts directly with it as part of a coherent work unit (a use case). An Actor element characterizes the role played by an outside object; one physical object may play several roles and therefore be modeled by several actors.

The UML uses a stick figure icon to represent the actor in use case diagrams, as in Figure 4-1.

Actors represent the context of the use case. By developing your actor model carefully, you can better understand who or what is going to use which parts of your system. As you map use cases to your database design, you will fill in blanks as you realize that certain actors need access to certain data elements in specific ways.

An actor may be a user, but an actor may also be another software subsystem or even a piece of hardware [Rational Software 1997b]. Use cases do not limit you to representing the overall system. You can represent the use of any interface, internal or external, with use cases. For example, consider a subsystem that represents image processing of crime scene photographs. This subsystem provides a series of services to other subsystems of the overall commonplace book system. Developing a use case diagram for this subsystem provides you with measurable, testable requirements for the crime scene subsystem as a part of the overall system. The end user may not be the actor for this use case, however. Instead, the other subsystems of the commonplace book become its actors.

To develop your actor model for a system, you must first carefully define the boundaries of the system. The requirements gathering process in Chapter 3 results in a broad description of the system. You can start with these requirements to work out your first pass at an actor model.

For example, for the commonplace book system, various requirements refer to certain roles in the system:

- Consulting private detective (the main client of the system)

- Marketing and sales person (identifies revenue opportunities and gathers testimonial data)

- Police and media suppliers (supply information to the system)
- Data entry clerk (enters new data)
- Data quality engineer (ensures high quality of data in database)
- Database administrator (maintains database)
- Security administrator (maintains security system)
- Legal representatives (resolve privacy and intellectual property issues)

These actors all have some reason to use the system, and the system must supply transactions (use cases) for those actors.

It may be that certain actors relate to other actors in generalization relationships. For example, a security administrator may be a kind of database administrator, or a database administrator may also use the system as a consulting private detective. A detective can also be a data entry clerk if you decide to integrate data entry of case information with the query interface, letting detectives enter case information as they get it. Figure 4-1 shows an actor model with some actor hierarchies. In this case, the model breaks down the consulting private detective into several types based on the type of case with which they deal. The different kinds of actors will use different parts of the commonplace book. You could alternatively break down detectives by security classification if that will have a major impact on system structure.

Modeling actors in a hierarchy lets you simplify your use case descriptions. In this context, inheritance means that a subactor inherits the role played by its super-actor parent. Anything a consulting private detective can do, an administrator can do. If you didn't model these overlaps in roles, you would need to connect administrators to the same use cases as the detectives. Now, all you need to do is to model the detective use cases, then show where administrators do something in addition to what a detective can do. This works both ways, of course. A detective uses a certain set of use cases in the system, sharing these with the administrator. But the administrator uses certain use cases not available to the detective.

Actors also perform passive roles in the system. You can define various external elements that the system controls or uses as actors if it has an impact on requirements. An important use for this approach is to define "the database" as an actor. You can integrate your knowledge about the database structure in a first cut at system architecture. For example, it may be that the commonplace book system requires four databases. The first is a U.S. database containing facts relevant to detective practice in the United States. The second is a U.K. database containing facts relevant to international operations around the world. The third is an image database containing photos, fingerprints, DNA profiles, and other images. The fourth is a text database containing media text and graphics. These latter two systems also provide different interfaces (image searching and text searching

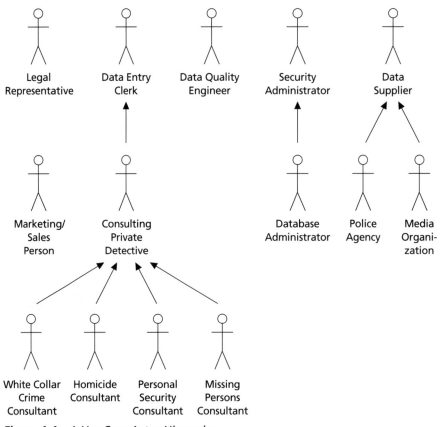

Figure 4-1 *A Use Case Actor Hierarchy*

engines, for example) that distinguish them from the standard SQL fact databases. You can use these actors to show how the different use cases use the database systems.

The database actors also provide a way for you to specify the use of data elements from the database in the use cases. In the details of the use case, you can enumerate the tables and columns or objects that you will use and relate them to the specific database schema in which they appear. See the section "Data Elements and Business Rules Summary" for details.

Defining the hierarchy of actors gives you the staff to use in populating your stage: the use case model.

Actors on Stage

With the actor model in place, you can now develop the main part of the use case model. While this is an iterative process, defining the actors first usually helps you to define your use cases more clearly. You will usually find yourself refining your actor model during use case development, though. You may also find opportunities for connecting actors to use cases in unanticipated ways, rendering certain actors irrelevant to the system.

Use Case Diagrams

The use case diagram is a context diagram that shows the top-level relationships between actors and use cases. You can also include relationships between use cases (uses and extends relationships) in these diagrams. Figure 4-2 illustrates a very high level use case diagram for the commonplace book system. The rounded rectangle is the system boundary for the commonplace book system. The actors appear on the outside of the system boundary, while the use cases are inside it. The use cases are labeled ovals with no internal structure whatever. The idea is to model the transactions of the system at the highest level.

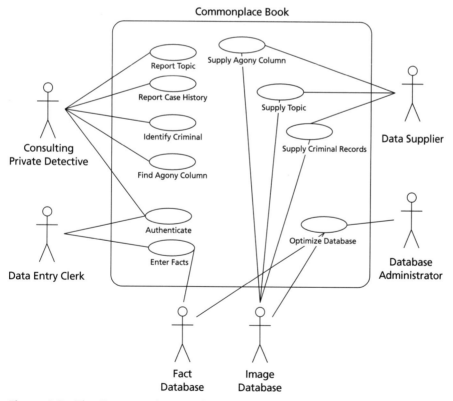

Figure 4-2   *The Commonplace Book Use Case Diagram*

Starting with each actor, think about the transactions that actor initiates. Create a use case in the system for each of these and connect it to the actor with an *association* (a line from the actor to the use case). The association is a communication relationship showing that the actor communicates with the use case in some way (active or passive). You usually start with the top-level actors in your actor hierarchy and work downwards, adding specialized use cases for the subactors.

Now, think about the transactions you've created and decide whether they are truly atomic. This is a critical part of defining both the system and its databases. *Atomicity* is a property of a transaction that relates to its coherence as a set of operations. A transaction has a series of operations that the use case describes. Making that series atomic means that you must complete the entire series or remove the effects entirely from the system. You cannot complete only part of the series. This concept of atomicity is fundamental to database transactions. It is also fundamental to system transactions and forms the basis for your use case.

Finally, think about the other actors. Do any of them also communicate with a use case that you've defined? If so, connect them. Remember that you only need to associate actors that don't inherit from the other actors in the actor model. That is, if an actor is a subactor for the one for which you've defined the use cases, that actor automatically shares the communication you've already drawn for the first actor to the use cases.

Now that you've finished thinking about all this, take the use cases and present them to real people who play the roles of the actors you've created. Observe their work, interview them, talk with them casually about the use cases. Close the feedback loop by integrating the real world with your model of it.

A Brief Example

For example, start with the consulting private detective. A first cut at transactions might yield something like this:

- *Authenticate:* Connect to the system as an authenticated user
- *Report Case History:* Report a case history with text and multimedia details
- *Report Event:* Report on a set of events based on factual and text search criteria
- *Report Criminal:* Report a criminal biography with text and multimedia details, including police file data and case histories involving the criminal
- *Identify with Alias:* Find a criminal's identity based on alias

- *Identify with Evidence:* Find a criminal's identity based on evidence analysis such as fingerprint, DNA, and so on

- *Report Topic:* Report an encyclopedia topic

- *Find Agony Column:* Find an agony column entry (a newspaper or Web advertisement of a personal nature) based on text search criteria

- *Find Mob:* Find information about criminal organizations based on factual search criteria

- *Explore:* Explore relationships between people, organizations, and facts in the database

Figure 4-3 shows this first cut with associations. It also shows some associations to other actors, such as the databases and the police and media suppliers of data. These actors in turn supply other use cases, such as the addition of police files, fingerprint records, photos, media text, and all the other bits of fact the commonplace book needs to satisfy the needs of the detectives. A complete system use case for the commonplace book might involve 150–200 use cases over five or six levels, perhaps more.

At the point where you have the basic use cases fleshed out, take it on the road. Present an overview with high-level descriptions of the important transactions to the detectives around the world. You will doubtless find additional use cases that people want you to consider putting into the system. You will also find that you have misunderstood some of the requirements, resulting in changes to your use cases.

Transactions and Use Cases

As you continue your system analysis, you break down each use case into several use cases, creating a nested series of use cases that combine to form the overall system. For example, Report Case History breaks down into several use cases, one for each basic element of the case history. These include Report Criminal Information (another high-level use case), Report Case Police History, Report Case Media History, Report Case Evidence, and Report Case Cross References (to information about criminal organizations, for example).

These use cases illustrate certain aspects of transaction analysis. Most of the high-level use cases are general query transactions. Each is a transaction because each retrieves a specific set of information with a clear beginning and end. The Add Police Case History use case is an example of a transaction that changes the database. The police organization that enters the case history does so in a single, atomic transaction. If the transaction fails, either for hardware reasons or because

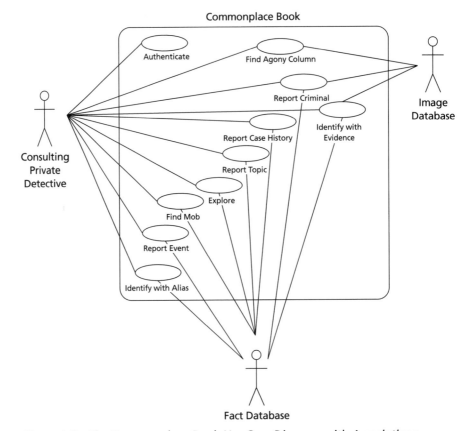

Figure 4-3   *The Commonplace Book Use Case Diagram with Associations*

of violation of business rules (no authorizing signature, for example), no information from the case history appears in the database. The system rolls back the transaction.

The breaking down of use cases into internal use cases brings up the issue of transaction management. There are really two kinds of use cases from the transaction perspective, atomic use cases and subatomic ones. You can easily distinguish these: atomic use cases have communication associations with actors, while subatomic use cases extend other use cases or are used by other use cases (for details on «extends» and «uses» relationships, see the section on "Use Case Relationships"). Some OODBMS products support a nested transaction model that lets you nest atomic transactions within transactions. Most RDBMS products give you the concept of a *checkpoint,* a point in the sequential set of actions in a transaction to which you can roll back. If you are using either model, you can build transactions (or partial transactions to a checkpoint) that represent the subatomic transactions. You can commit or roll back any level of the transaction.

Warning: Using nested transactions and checkpoints is definitely advanced database management. Don't try this at home, and don't expect it to be easy or bug free.

You can avoid some of these transaction issues by putting all the use cases at the top level. This kind of model gets hard to understand very quickly, however. Divide-and-conquer design is an extremely useful way to limit complexity and promote understanding. You do have to trade off such usefulness against the possible illogic you introduce into the system transaction model. How might a real user accomplish the use case through the user interface of the system? If you can make a case for a single menu choice or button driving the use case, then it is probably right to treat it as a high-level use case. But also think about how hard a system with 200 menu items is to use. You may want to remove chunks of the system into other systems, modules that you can access on demand. This yields a more complex system configuration that is much easier to use.

You may also want to consider some of the implications for transaction processing in defining your transactions. The cardinal rule in designing transactions is to make them as short as possible. If you are updating a row, lock the row just before updating it, not when you read it. Use update locks rather than exclusive locks to allow readers to read even while you're contemplating the update. If you are inserting or deleting a row, don't acquire an exclusive lock on the table at the beginning of the transaction; let the DBMS handle the locking transparently. If your DBMS doesn't handle locking in a reasonable way, consider getting a new DBMS; yours is out of date. Surprisingly, I've encountered problems with locking (particularly *deadlocking*, where multiple users have conflicting locks that mutually lock each other out, causing transactions to fail or wait indefinitely) in leading RDBMS and OODBMS products. You should investigate and prototype your technology choice early in your project to avoid surprises on the back end. Particularly if you have transactions with a lot of data (100,000 rows or more in a query is a lot), don't assume that tests with simple and limited data are telling you what will really happen when you go live. While these technology issues seem to be implementation issues, not requirements issues, you will find that your use case transactions are the source of many problems if they don't take transaction processing basics into account.

Use Case Relationships

There are two relationships between use cases in the UML: «extends» and «uses». Both are stereotyped extensions to the UML that permit a special relationship to exist between two use cases. The «extends» relationship says that the extending use case conditionally occurs within the extended use case. One implication is that the extension is not a complete transaction but rather is a conditional part of a transaction. The «uses» relationship unconditionally uses a use case that two or more use cases share, thus permitting a fan-in style of modularization in use case development. You can create shared use case transactions that larger transactions share, reducing the complexity and redundancy of the overall system.

The *UML Semantics* guide defines the two stereotypes [Rational Software 1997b, p. 95]:

> Commonalities between use cases are expressed with *uses* relationships (i.e., generalizations with the stereotype «uses»). The relationship means that the sequence of behavior described in a used use case is included in the sequence of another use case. The latter use case may introduce new pieces of behavior anywhere in the sequence as long as it does not change the ordering of the original sequence. Moreover, if a use case has several uses relationships, its sequence will be the result of interleaving the used sequences together with new pieces of behavior. How these parts are combined to form the new sequence is defined in the using use case.
>
> An *extends relationship,* i.e., a generalization with the stereotype «extends», defines that a use case may be extended with some additional behavior defined in another use case. The extends relationship includes both a *condition* for the extension and a reference to an *extension point* in the related use case, i.e., a position in the use case where additions may be made. Once an instance of a use case reaches an extension point to which an *extends* relationship is referring, the condition of the relationship is evaluated. If the condition is fulfilled, the sequence obeyed by the use case instance is extended to include the sequence of the extending use case. Different parts of the extending use case sequence may be inserted at different extension points in the original sequence. If there is still only one condition (i.e., if the condition of the extends relationship is fulfilled at the first extension point), then the entire extending behavior is inserted in the original sequence.

The «uses» relationship lets you consolidate a part of a use case into a separate use case that you can share between multiple transactions. This permits you to identify shared behavior corresponding to shared code in the design. It also lets you simplify to some extent the use case model by eliminating chunks of use case description from multiple use cases. The most common «uses» relationship is the sharing of a simple chunk of behavior such as display of a graphic or calculation of an algorithmic value.

In the commonplace book model, there is a «uses» relationship between the Identify with Alias use case and the Identify with Evidence use case (Figure 4-4). Both use cases use the Identify Criminal use case, which presents information to the actor identifying a person with a criminal record, including the criminal's name and aliases, fingerprints, DNA profile (if available), and picture(s). In the first case, the transaction queries the criminal's identity using an alias. In the sec-

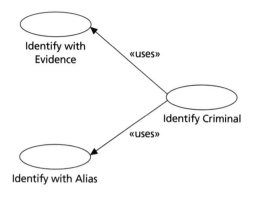

Figure 4-4   *The «uses» Relationship*

Figure 4-5   *The «extends» Relationship*

ond case, the use case identifies the criminal using some kind of evidentiary profile such as a fingerprint or DNA profile.

The «extends» relationship lets you simplify a use case by excluding conditional elements that are distractions from the main point of the transaction: "exceptions." The most common example of this is error handling. Under a certain condition, a use case "exits" with an error. For example, in the commonplace book system, you can try to find a criminal through his or her alias and fail. Instead of including this in the use case description, you extend the use case by adding an extension with the error condition and the resulting behavior. For example, you could display an alert with the text "Could not identify suspect." Figure 4-5 illustrates this relationship between the Identify Criminal with Alias and the Could Not Identify Suspect use case. You can extend different use cases with the same extension, of course. This lets you build up a library of extensions for your error-handling procedures. This usually translates into an exception-handling library in your system design.

The next most common example of an extension is the use of menu and keypress use cases throughout a system. Within any use case, you can access shared actions by choosing a menu item or pressing a key. You can thus represent

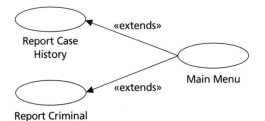

Figure 4-6   *The Main Menu Use Case and Its «extends» Relationship*

the menu and keypress selections as use cases related to your main use cases through the conditional choosing of a menu item or keypress. Figure 4-6 illustrates the use case diagram with the Main Menu use case. That use case represents the available main menu for the Report Case History and Report Criminal and windows of the commonplace book application. This diagram assumes that these two use cases are main transactions of the system. Usually, these use cases correspond to "documents" or windows in a multiple-document interface.

The use of «extends» and «uses» relationships have two major effects on your use case model. First, it simplifies the model by removing conditional distractions and shared behavior. Second, it lets you measure the value of your system more accurately by representing the same behavior once instead of many times.

The use case model structures your requirements into a straightforward representation of the system you need to build. The next step is to build the detailed use case that tells your architect and builder what he or she needs to do.

Setting the Scene

The point of a *use case description* is to convey to an audience the meaning and behavior of the system that the use case represents. That can be as simple as a paragraph of text or as complex as a complete state model of the system. You need to use your judgment about the level of detail and formality in the use case. Most books that describe use cases [Jacobson et al. 1992; Harmon and Watson 1998] tend to rely on a simple description of a process: a use case story. I usually go one step further and include an activity diagram, mainly because my audience usually includes a tester. The test model for a use case usually is some kind of control or data flow model [Muller 1996]. The activity diagram serves as that model given its representation of the branching control flow of the use case.

The audience for a use case consists of at least four roles.

First, *you* are your own audience. Knowing and exploring requirements gives you the big picture. Analyzing them systematically as you write down use cases crystallizes your thoughts and forces you to make connections that you would not otherwise make.

Second, your *team* is your audience. Depending on the size of the system, you can develop use cases with a team effort. The other team members need to know what different parts of the system do, both to aid in understanding their requirements and to make it easier to reuse commonalties in the set of use cases. The use case is a good place to communicate the background and context that team members need to design and code your system.

Third, your *client* is your audience. A use case is an excellent way to get the client to buy into the system you intend to build. They've given you their expectations, and you've explored their informal requirements. With the set of use cases for the system, you can go back to them and take them through scenarios in a low-fidelity prototyping process. This lets them understand what you think they think, and it also lets them express any concerns and to buy into your understanding of the system.

Fourth, your *organization* is your audience, primarily in the role of reviewer. Chapter 5 goes into some detail on testing your use cases. A big part of that process is reviewing the use cases with fresh eyes. The easier you make it for a reviewer to understand your use cases, the more likely you will uncover problems and oversights.

The form of the use case can vary widely depending on your orientation toward these audiences. Generally, you want to have a summary of the use case, a narrative and/or diagrammatic description of the details, and a clear statement of business rules and data elements to which the use case refers.

Summaries

The *use case summary* is a short paragraph that describes what the use case does. The paragraph should convey the essence of the use case, not the details. The purpose of the summary is to give the reviewer a quick understanding of the use case. This can be very useful:

- It focuses the reviewer's attention on the essence of the use case by removing details that might confuse basic understanding. It does the same for you when you write the use case, often clarifying a fuzzy understanding of the basic purpose of the case.

- It permits rapid understanding of a use case related to the one the reviewer is inspecting in detail.

- It provides a text that you can use in situations that require a comment about the use case, such as a short report on the use cases or a comment in code that traces back to the use case.

The Report Case History use case, for example, has this summary paragraph:

> The Report Case History use case builds a report of one or more criminal cases for a Consulting Private Detective using the Fact and Image Databases. For each case, the report contains a summary of the case, a list of people and organizations associated with the case, any objects (photographs, documents, sound or video recordings) relevant to the case, and a list of evidence (including analyses of the evidence) related to the case.

The summary should mention the actors that communicate with the use case. In the Report Case History example, the summary mentions that the report is for a Consulting Private Detective and that it uses the Fact and Image Databases.

For use cases that express commonalties or exceptions through «extends» and «uses» relationships, you should summarize the purpose and mention the shared nature of the case or the condition or conditions likely to raise the case. There are two goals you need to satisfy. First, the summary should tell the reviewer that the use case is not a complete transaction in itself. Second, prospective reusers of the use case (either in this project or in a later project) should be able to understand what the use case delivers for reuse. Here are two examples using the previous examples of the «extends» and «uses» relationships:

> The Identify Criminal use case provides shared behavior for more specific use cases such as Identify with Alias or Identify with Evidence. The use case starts with a list of identifiers for criminals created by the related use case. It then displays the name of the criminal, a picture, a list of aliases, a list of identification documents, and a brief summary of the criminal history of the individual.
>
> The Could Not Identify Suspect use case extends other use cases with an exception meaning that the related use case could not identify a criminal. The use case occurs when the related use case queries the identity of a criminal or criminals from a database and comes up with nothing.

You can optionally include a use case diagram with the use case, the actors that use it, and any use cases related to the case through «extends» or «uses» relationships. This can supplement the summary text with a picture. Some reviewers understand the use case relationships better if they see a graph; others prefer straight text. This difference leads into the way you present the details of the use case as well, through narratives and/or activity diagrams.

Note: You can also include background information in your summaries, though you should keep it short and sweet. Define basic terms,

identify basic players, explain the fundamental concepts that a ca-
sual reader of the use case would need to understand the why *of*
the use case. Did I say keep it short and sweet?

Narratives

The *use case narrative* is a series of text descriptions of the detailed steps in the use case. This usually takes the form of a numbered list of steps that alternate between the actor(s) and the system. The "system," in this case, is the software that implements the use case.

There really aren't many rules for constructing these narratives. The primary objective is to be as clear as possible. As you write, think about the audience for the use case, and shape the text to their level of understanding of the events. If you find it difficult to describe what goes on in the use case in language comprehensible to your audience, you might want to back off and redo the use cases in your system to reflect better what needs to happen. Keep it simple.

Also, you should stay away from describing specific user interface or system details, keeping the narrative as abstract as possible. This technique (*essential* use case analysis) pushes the user interface decisions into the design stage, leaving the requirements to deal only with the generic behavior of the application. This delayed commitment to an interface can save you a good deal of stress and bother when you start designing your user interface. On the other hand, sometimes you really do have user interface requirements because of early architectural decisions or even because of explicit client expectations. For example, if a high-up manager at Holmes PLC hands you a copy of a case history report and tells you they want it to look exactly like that with such-and-such changes, you should put the specific interface requirements into your use case. You should always probe a bit under these circumstances to make sure the client really wants that format. Propose some alternatives and listen carefully to the response. For example, I once was required to develop a report in a specific format. The format allowed the client to print the report onto a half-page form already printed by the company. After questioning, it turned out that we could dispense with the printed forms if the report writer could produce printouts of comparable quality, which it could. On the other hand, the basic format needed to stay the same; the people using the form had used it for years and didn't want to have to learn a whole new layout.

In the end, if the client really wants a specific screen control or report format, you should make that a formal part of the requirements.

If the use case makes explicit reference to the database, you can express the step using the database access language. For an SQL database, that means an SQL statement. For an OO database, it might mean C++ code or OQL statements.

You should keep your SQL or OQL as generic as possible, using only ANSI/ODMG standard language for the same reason that you avoid specific user interface controls or formats. Each statement should form a complete step in the narrative and in the activity diagram of the use case.

The use of SQL or OQL at this stage of development implies that you have a schema. As you iterate through creation of use cases, you will determine the classes of persistent objects the use cases require. Chapter 7 discusses the UML *static structure diagrams* (diagrams of classes, objects, and associations) that represent these objects. You should develop these diagrams in parallel, or at least iteratively, while you develop your use cases. This approach gives you a basic schema, with object or table names and attribute or column names that you can use in your SQL and OQL use case steps.

Using SQL or OQL in your use cases also gives you a clear picture of how your system will access the database. You can use such use cases during a design phase to understand more clearly how the system uses the database in terms of transaction processing and performance.

Your narrative should refer to «uses» relationships directly in the steps that use the shared behavior. However, you should not refer to «extends» relationships at all in your narrative. The whole point of the «extends» relationship is to remove the extension from the main use case to simplify it. Putting it back into the narrative would therefore be counterproductive. Usually, you add a section at the end entitled "Extensions" that contains a list of the extensions. In each element of this list, you detail the conditions under which the extension extends the use case and refer to the extension by name. You should identify the point in the narrative where the extension condition appears, but that's all. The reader can then look up the extension use case to see its details if needed.

This narrative describes the Identify Criminal with Alias use case, in this case using the RDBMS/ORDBMS SQL approach:

1. The Identify Criminal with Alias use case begins with the Consulting Private Detective asking the System to identify a criminal by entering an alias, a character string.
2. The System looks up the criminal, returning the identity of the criminal (PersonID, Name), using this SQL statement:

```
SELECT PersonID, Name
   FROM Person p, Alias a
WHERE p.PersonID 5 a.PersonID AND
      Alias 5 :Alias
```

3. The System uses the Identify Criminal use case to display information relating to the criminal's identity. This ends the transaction.

The first step in this narrative tells you where the use case begins. For use cases relating to actors, this usually means identifying the actor and what the actor communicates to the system. Communications are either control ("asking the system to identify a criminal") or data ("by entering an alias, a character string"). You can regard the data as parameters to the use case. This step starts the transaction.

The second step in this narrative tells you what the system does in response to the user's request. In this case, it uses an SQL statement to describe the input (:Alias, a "host variable"), the processing (a join of the Person and Alias tables on PersonID and a selection based on an equality comparison to the alias string), and the output (a projection of PersonID and Name).

The third step identifies a «uses» relationship. This kind of narrative step identifies the other use case by name. It can also identify any special issues regarding the relationship. For example, you can intermingle the steps in the other use case with steps in this one. I generally have found this is counterintuitive, so I avoid this kind of relationship. This step also explicitly ends the transaction. You should try to end a transaction explicitly in only one place, the last step of the use case. Many use case designers will find that overconstraining because they want to leave the use case based on some conditional determination earlier in the sequence. It does clarify the logic of the use case a good deal to structure the logic with a single ending point.

> *Note: You do not mention «extends» relationships in this part of the narrative. The whole point of this kind of relationship is to get the other use case and the conditional logic involved out of the use case proper.*

In the second step, you could have used extended ORDBMS SQL or OQL to specify the query. For example, using an ODBMS, you could have a Boolean method on the Person object that returns true if the person has an alias that matches the input alias string. The method could use some kind of complex pattern-matching algorithm. Your OQL might look like this:

```
SELECT p.PersonID, p.Name
  FROM Person p
 WHERE p.matchesAlias(:Alias)
```

It's a good idea to keep the steps to a single SQL statement. This keeps the purpose of the step clear and the narrative easy to understand. The exception is when you have nested SQL statements in some kind of iteration, where you are doing the SQL inside the loop for each row from the outer SQL.

You might also think about identification and realize that it is both a fuzzy process and one that can result in ambiguity. In database terms, with this specification, you can't guarantee that you will return only a single row or object from this query. The step should read, "The System looks up the set of criminals that match the input alias, returning the identity of the criminals (PersonID, Name), using this OQL statement."

For the Identify Criminal use case, you have two choices for the first step. If the use case can stand on its own (usually a good idea), then you begin the use case just as for the previous one:

1. The Identify Criminal use case begins with the Consulting Private Detective asking the System to identify a criminal by entering a person identifier (a unique integer for the person).

If the use case always extends another, and thus never interacts with an external actor, you need to state that in the first step.

1. The Identify Criminal use case begins *with another use case using it,* passing it a unique person identifier (a unique integer for the person). This requests the System to display aliases, criminal history, and identification information for the criminal.

You should also state this in the use case summary.

The last part of the narrative is a section on extensions. In this section, you identify all the «extends» relationships for the use case and the conditions under which they occur. For example, it is possible that the alias you pass to Identify Criminal with Alias results in no criminal identifications. You can add an extension use case, No Criminal Identified, that displays an error message. In the extensions section, you add this paragraph:

1. The No Criminal Identified use case extends the Identify Criminal with Alias use case when the query in step 2 fails to return any rows or objects.

If your use case has conditional logic, often you can best express it through substeps. For example, the Identify Criminal use case step 5 conditionally displays information about the role of the person in a criminal organization:

5. Display the role of the person in criminal organizations. Query the set of roles that the criminal plays with this SQL statement:
```
SELECT p.Name, o.OrganizationID, o.OrganizationName, rt.ShortType
   FROM Person p, Role r, RoleType rt, CriminalOrganization o
WHERE p.PersonID 5 r.PersonID AND
      r.RoleTypeID 5 rt.RoleTypeID AND
      r.OrganizationID 5 o.OrganizationID AND
      p.PersonID 5 :PersonID
```
   a. If there are no roles for this person, display the text "<Name> has no known association with any criminal organization."
   b. If there are roles, for each role display the role's short type and the organization's name in this text: "<p.Name> plays the <ShortType> role in the <OrganizationName> criminal organization."

You can refer to these steps as "step 5a" and "step 5b" in other parts of your narrative and in an activity diagram. You show loops in the same way, as multiple steps within a larger step.

The use case is usually part of a larger system of models that include the class model and the interaction diagram. Depending on the level of detail you want at the requirements level, you can abstract the "things" in your use case narrative into a class model. You can connect the use case to it through interaction diagrams [Jacobson et al. 1992]. Chapter 7 goes into detail on using static structure models for database design. The section "Data Elements and Business Rules Summary" in this chapter suggests some ways to connect database elements with these other diagrams as well. As with other parts of the OO development process, you revise all these models incrementally and iteratively. As you design your class model, you will learn things about your use cases: what elements are missing, what things you could reorganize to take advantage of synergy between classes, and so on. You then can return to your use cases to make them better requirements models. You'll find a similar benefit in formalizing the narrative through UML activity diagrams.

UML Activity Diagrams

Every computer programmer knows the *activity diagram* as a "flow chart," though there are some differences in notation and semantics. You use the activity diagram to represent the control logic of the use case in a graphical format. This model also formalizes to some extent the control flow of the use case. You can use this control flow to structure system testing of the use case. Chapter 5 contains a detailed description of how this works.

> *Note: Activity diagrams are good at representing procedural flow of control. They do not handle situations with external or asynchronous events. If a use case must respond to external input other than through the initial state of the use case, or if it must respond to external, asynchronous events, you should use a UML statechart (a hierarchical state transition diagram). You generally use statecharts to model the behavior of objects and activity charts to model the behavior of individual methods or processes such as use cases. Both are excellent ways to create test models as they directly represent the flow of control.*

Elements of the Activity Diagram

The UML activity diagram reflects two of the basic control structures: sequence and condition. The sequence is the directed connection between the elements; a

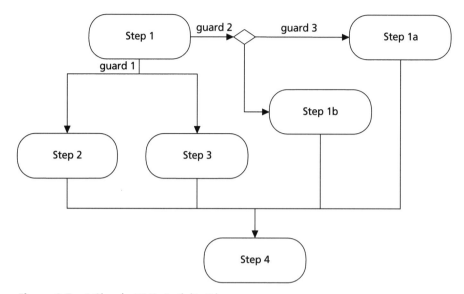

Figure 4-7 *A Simple UML Activity Diagram*

condition is the equivalent of an IF statement. Figure 4-7 is a simple activity diagram. You can also represent iteration through a sequence that connects to an ancestral sequence element (an element already executed).

The activity chart is a special case of the statechart [Rational Software 1997a]. *Action states,* the rounded rectangles in Figure 4-7, are states that represent an action with no internal transitions, at least one transition at the completion of the action, and potentially multiple transitions with guards or conditions. Transitions are the directed arrows in Figure 4-7. The action state corresponds to the process in a flow chart, and the transition corresponds to the flow of control arrow. You can show the guard conditions as labels on the transitions, or you can place a diamond on the transition and split it to show a decision, as in Figure 4-7. The decision format is closer to the flow chart and is better for understanding the conditional flow of control. The guard conditions must be Boolean (true or false) and cannot have associated events.

> Note: Because the SQL language, and databases in general, support null values in a three-valued logic, it makes sense to allow a three-valued logic for these guards in use cases based on SQL processing. If you don't understand the concept of three-valued logic, consult a standard book on SQL [Groff and Weinberg 1994] or one of Chris Date's articles on the subject [Date 1986, pp. 313–334]. Since most programming languages do not support a three-valued logic, this won't help much in translating your use cases into programming

language code. It does help you to understand the result of an SQL query, however, and can flag potential problems with returning null values. On the other hand, if you are using OQL or another form of OODBMS logic based on C++ or Smalltalk, you probably should stick to the two-valued logic, as these languages don't support null values.

In Figure 4-7, the use case starts in step 1. Step 1 has two possible transitions, one for the condition "guard 1" and one for the condition "guard 2." The transition based on guard 2 results in a further decision (a multiple-part predicate, for example) that requires doing step 1a if guard 3 is true and step 1b otherwise. Steps 2 and 3 happen in parallel, which the branching line from step 1 shows. You must complete steps 2 and 3 (and possibly 1a or 1b) before you can start step 4, the final step in the use case.

Figure 4-8 shows the logic of the example from the prior section on "Narratives." This activity diagram isn't very complex, but it does immediately convey the basic structure of the use case. Each action state corresponds to a step in the use case. In this use case, the transitions are sequential and there are no conditional guards or decisions. You can put the SQL or OQL into the action state, as Figure 4-8 illustrates, unless it is too extensive. The SQL directly and clearly expresses the content of the step. It also aids in understanding the test requirements of the use case.

The Activity Diagram as Test Model

A *test model* is a system model that represents the elements of the system of interest to testers. Usually, this means control. The two main forms of test model are the control flow diagram and the state transition diagram. The control flow diagram represents a system through its flow of control; the state transition diagram represents the states of the system and the possible transitions between states. Both help focus testers on system elements likely to fail, which is the whole point of testing. A system at rest does not fail, it just sits there. The system making a

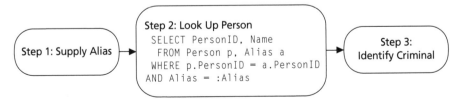

Figure 4-8 *The Activity Diagram for the Identify Criminal with Alias Use Case*

decision about where to transfer control or which transition to make is a system with the potential to fail.

Chapter 5 goes into detail on system testing and use cases. That chapter puts use cases into a context of system quality, showing how you can take advantage of the natural form of the use case to structure system testing.

Data Elements and Business Rules Summary

The final section of the use case lets you express the details of your database requirements. Your narrative and activity diagram have referred to data elements and constraints, perhaps in an informal way. This section gives you a place to collect your requirements to show the overall impact of the use case on the database. You can also use this section in counting function points to estimate complexity factors [Garmus and Herron 1996].

Expanding a bit beyond the database, you can also summarize the set of objects and operations that the use case uses. As the section "Narratives" mentioned, these elements find their expression in design-related diagrams such as the class diagram and interaction diagrams. Whether or not you decide to link your use cases explicitly to these diagrams, it is useful to summarize their use in the use case itself.

Any data element to which your SQL or OQL statements refer should appear here, organized within their table, type, or class. The Identify Criminal with Alias use case, for example, refers to these data elements with Table 4-1.

Business rules are constraints on the data or operations. Use cases mention both simple and complex constraints because the use of the data is the context in which such constraints usually apply. Often, however, your design will move these constraints into the database as triggers or constraints in the database schema. Regardless, the use case specifies the rules to ensure that the point of view of the user of the system comes through to the design. Since multiple use cases impose different rules on the data, the database design may reflect the input of several use cases, not just one. Sometimes the business rules even conflict between different use cases, making it necessary to design negotiation layers to handle the conflict. The source of these business rules is the use case narrative. Again, to make it easy for the user and designer to understand the rules, placing them in a summary is very useful.

For example, a simple rule is that a Person must own an Alias. That is, there is a foreign key constraint that requires the Alias to have an associated PersonID to identify the person. PersonID is therefore part of the primary key of the Alias table as well as being a foreign key to the Person table. What about an alias that you know about but that you can't yet link to a person? For example, Sherlock Holmes once dealt with a very secret informer [VALL]:

Table 4-1 *Identify Criminal with Alias Use Case Data Elements Table*

Table	Column	Comments
Person	PersonID	Unique integer that identifies the person
	Name	The composed name of the person (concatenation of first and last names)
Alias	PersonID	A foreign key to Person.PersonID
	Alias	An alias name of a person; the actor passes this alias in to use to look up the person

"Porlock, Watson, is a nom-de-plume, a mere identification mark; but behind it lies a shifty and evasive personality. In a former letter he frankly informed me that the name was not his own, and defied me ever to trace him among the teeming millions of this great city."

. . ."Did you never trouble to see who called for [these letters]?"

"No."

The inspector looked surprised and a little shocked. "Why not?"

"Because I always keep faith. I had promised when he first wrote that I would not try to trace him."

"You think there is someone behind him?"

"I know there is."

"This professor that I have heard you mention?"

Given the circumstances, perhaps the business rule about linking each alias to a person is getting in the way. This is a fairly common design problem. You could dispense with the business rule and have aliases that don't correspond to people. Unfortunately, that would mean that querying people through aliases would simply miss Porlock, since there would be no associated person row. An alternative is to create a "fake" row in the Person table for an as-yet-unknown person. Taking the OO approach, you could create a subclass of Person called UnknownPerson that would serve this purpose admirably. The object could behave just like a regular person, but the name would be "Unknown" or something like that. When the consulting detective figures out who the person is, the UnknownPerson mutates into a person and carries its aliases with it.

Another problem: What if "Fred Porlock" is a *nom de plume* for several people, not just one? Expressing a strong link between a person and an alias would make this impossible. You would need to enter the alias several times, once for each person you know uses it. A better design solution is to create a many-to-many relationship between Alias and Person with a constraint that there must be at least one row in the relationship for each Alias row. This is an additional business rule that should appear in your use case business rule summary.

Here is the business rule summary:

> A person may have several aliases. Several people may use an alias. An alias must refer to at least one person, even if you don't know that person right now.

If you wish, you can express business rules in SQL, OQL, or an equivalent logical language. Unless the logic is critical, it's usually best to leave it in a simply stated natural language format that your audience can easily understand. Leave it to the class model to express the constraints formally.

Summary

Before even starting to develop your use cases, you develop a model of who uses them: actors. Actors provide the context for the system, the "who" that motivates what you're doing. Actors can be either stakeholders or external systems such as databases that you access.

Use cases themselves represent the transactions (logical units of work) that the actors perform. You can break the system down using the «extends» and «uses» relationships to create subatomic use cases that you can share between transactions. Each use case contains a summary, a narrative description, an optional activity diagram, a table of data elements that the use case uses, and a set of business rules that constrain the use case.

The use case is a critically important part of any database development project. A software system, however, like a play, does not consist of scenarios alone. The actors, the props, the stage, the playbook, the audience all play their part in the experience. The next chapter briefly discusses the role of use cases and requirements in testing, preparing you for the rest of the book, which focuses on design.

Testing the System 5

It is commonly said, and more particularly by Lord Shaftesbury, that ridicule is
the best test of truth.

Wit and Wisdom of Lord Chesterfield, Epigrams

The quality of a thing reflects the value of the work that goes into it. A well-
done steak is, well, a mistake—unless that's what the customer wants. The
trick to getting a high-quality database application system is not to load large
amounts of data in the wild hope that, by brutalizing the system, you will find out
what's wrong with it. Instead, you must compare the end result of your effort to
the needs and wants of your customers. In this short chapter, I hope to cover
some of the techniques I've learned over the years for testing databases against requirements.

There are two parts to such testing: the database and the requirements. If
you are going to hold the database design and development accountable for meeting a set of requirements, you must be reasonably sure that the set is correct and
complete. That means that you must verify your requirements in the same way
that you verify your design and code. As with all testing, this is not a one-time,
do-or-die testing effort that you must complete before moving on to design. You
do it over and over as your design and implementation progress, always questioning, always testing the limits of your requirements. You start with presenting the
use cases to your clients and getting their feedback on completeness and accuracy
of the use cases as statements of their requirements. As your design and implementation proceed, you find parts of the use cases that need revision, missing use
cases, and different ways of thinking about the problem (as opposed to the solution). These changes lead you back to validation through more client interviews
and observations, always subject to the need of your project to complete its tasks
on schedule within a reasonable budget. Life is a trade-off.

On the other side of the equation, the validation process compares the
end result of a project increment against its requirements. System validation testing of the database against its requirements is the critical test your project must

pass to deliver a working database application. The section "Systems and Truth" in this chapter shows you how to tie your end result back to requirements through testing.

Requirements and Truth

The main risk in project requirements is that they do not accurately reflect the real needs of project stakeholders. *Verifying* requirements means reducing this risk below your tolerance for failure. In practice, this means getting agreement from the stakeholders that the use cases accurately reflect what they want from the system. A *requirements review* is a meeting for the purpose of verifying the system requirements, thus reducing the risk of failure.

Your use cases have two audiences: the users of the system and the designers of the system. The users are the source for the requirements, while the designers are the "consumers" of the requirements. Both must participate in a requirements review through capable representatives. You should also include subject matter experts who can objectively comment on the correctness and completeness of the use cases. You may also have other stakeholders (upper management, government regulators, labor unions, and so on) that need to participate at various times.

> *Warning: Conducting requirement reviews with only people from your project participating is a waste of time. You must involve stakeholders that will actually use the system in such reviews, or you will not truly validate your use cases. I was involved in a largish 1000-function-point project that proceeded with only internal reviews of the use cases by the programming team. They found all the cases where objects were never deleted and all the instances where the use cases were inconsistent with each other. They did not find any features missing. Talking to customers revealed the need for at least five major use cases that no one on the programming team even understood, much less perceived as missing. Internal reviews are good at checking consistency, but not at validating the connection between your use cases and the real world, which is the real point of such reviews.*

The goal of the review is to discover problems with the requirements. A requirements review must deal with all of these types of problems [Freedman and Weinberg 1990, pp. 294–295]:

- *Completeness:* Are all the requirements there that must be there? Are any database elements or business rules missing?

- *Correctness:* Are there any errors in the requirements? Are all the data element definitions correct?

- *Clarity:* Does any ambiguity remain in the requirements?

- *Consistency:* Are there any conflicts between requirements? Have you stated all trade-off assumptions clearly? Are there any data elements that will conflict with each other? Are there business rules that contradict one another?

- *Relevancy:* Do all the requirements really apply to the problem and solution? Are all data elements really necessary? Do some data or business rules apply only to things outside the scope of the current project?

- *Testability:* Will it be possible to determine whether the end product meets each requirement? Given a working database schema, will it be possible to validate the design and construction of the database against the requirements? Will the database be so large that testing it will be intractable with current testing tools?

- *Traceability:* Will it be possible to trace all features back to the source requirement? Do you have tools and procedures in place to link database deliverables to requirements?

- *Feasibility:* Is each requirement possible given the time, resources, and tools available? In particular, are there requirements for the schedule and budget that conflict with the feature requirements? Can the database technology you've chosen handle the performance and storage requirements?

- *Necessity:* Do the requirements include just the detail needed, leaving out unnecessary specification of design details? Are there data elements in the requirements that aren't necessary for meeting the requirements? Do you have elements or rules in your use cases that exist for "compatibility" or that are there "just in case we'll need them in the future"? Take them out. They'll just confuse your testing.

- *Manageability:* Is the set of use cases capable of controlled change? Can you modify a requirement without any impact on the others? Do you have a change control process for the database schema and/or data in the database?

Systematically examining your use cases in these categories can yield a surprising number of problems. The extent to which you resolve the problems depends on both the contribution of the problem to the overall risk of failure and your tolerance for such risk. For example, you may find it possible to leave a requirement ambiguous by deciding to fix it later, after you have design experience with the system. Or, you might find that the requirement's value is small enough that you can tolerate the system not meeting it (a "nice-to-have" priority on the requirement).

Systems and Truth

Testability doesn't seem very important, just one of many things on the checklist for your use cases. However, this factor is actually one of the most critical because your use cases form the basis for your system testing. Most of the other factors you must review relate as well to testability. For example, an incorrect requirement means a requirement you can't test, as does an ambiguous requirement.

A system test is a test of the system as a whole, as opposed to tests of the pieces that make it up [Muller 1996; Muller, Nygard, and Crnkovic 1997; Siegel and Muller 1996]. Object or unit tests test individual code units (classes and methods), and integration tests test subsystems that don't stand on their own as working systems. These tests should comprise the bulk of your verification efforts and can uncover most serious bugs long before they get to system test. When you deliver a working version of your system, your testing becomes a different thing.

There are several different kinds of system test [Muller, Nygard, and Crnkovic 1997]:

- *Validation/acceptance test:* A test that validates the system against its requirements; an acceptance test is when the customer plans and executes the tests, as opposed to the developer of the system

- *Performance test:* A test that verifies specific performance requirements and that serves as a performance benchmark for future iterations of the system

- *Configuration test:* A test that verifies the proper operation of the system under different hardware and software environments

- *Installation test:* A configuration test that verifies installation procedures under an array of different environments

- *Field test:* A configuration test that tests the system in the field using real customer data

- *Recovery test:* A test that verifies the proper recovery of system data after a disabling failure

- *Security test:* A test that verifies the ability of the system to prevent undesirable intrusion or access to data by unauthorized users of the system

- *Stress test:* A test that verifies the ability of the system to handle saturation-level use (many users, many transactions, large volumes of data, and so on); the objective is to observe how the system fails, gracefully or disastrously

A *test model* is a system model that abstracts the characteristics of the system under test that are of interest to the tester [Siegel and Muller 1996; Muller 1998]. For example, the source code of a C++ member function is not a test model for the function; its purpose is to represent the operation of the function in terms a programmer can understand and that a compiler can translate into machine code. A test model is a control flow or state transition model that describes the flow of control through the member function, which is what interests a tester. The actual program statements don't interest the tester, only the points at which decisions can go wrong or loops can go on endlessly.

The use cases are the test model for your validation/acceptance system test. They can include performance and security requirements or other capability requirements, but usually the use cases do not formally model these characteristics of the system. If they do, then you must validate the system against these requirements just as with any other requirements. Otherwise, the use cases are irrelevant to the other kinds of system test. Use cases represent the objects of interest to a validation/acceptance tester: the steps that an actor goes through to use the system.

What this means in practice is that you use the narratives or the activity charts in your use cases to build your test cases. A test case is a single instance of the test model. For a use case, that means a test case is a scenario, a specific instance of the use case. If you use activity charts to model your use case, you can achieve branch coverage of the use case by having a single test case for each possible path through the flow chart. You can generate additional test cases by developing equivalence classes of data inputs to the use case.

The database affects system testing in several ways. First, the database often serves as a test bed for your system. A *test bed* is a configuration of data that the system uses in a test case or *test suite* (a collection of test cases related to one another in some way). The test bed you develop must enable you to exercise the right level of testing of your test models. In other words, your test data must permit thorough exercise of your use cases.

> Note: There are several test data generation tools on the market. Let me be blunt. They don't work for me. Especially with the style of design this book presents, these tools are simply not capable of producing data that looks reasonable taking into account all the associations, inheritance generalizations, and other semantic aspects of the data. For example, if you have a table with a foreign key to a table with a foreign key to a superclass table, which in turn has a foreign key to an association class table with foreign keys to three other tables, each of which have aggregate composition associations to children tables, it's hopeless for these tools. They don't understand the connection at the semantic level, only at the structural level. Random data generation just doesn't make it for these test beds. I have failed to generate effective test beds in every single case where I've tried to use these tools on a database of any complexity.

Second, the database often contains behavior as well as data, especially for OODBMS- and ORDBMS-based products, but increasingly even in RDBMS-based products. Stored procedures, triggers, methods, and operators all perform specific elements of the system use cases on the database server rather than on the application server(s) or clients. Database testing then begins to look much like any kind of system testing, not just data testing.

Third, the database may contain data you integrate from different sources. The data itself becomes part of the system under test. For example, Holmes PLC integrates multimedia documents and objects, police files, fingerprint records, and DNA sample profiles into the database. These data objects are as much a part of the system as the code that displays it. If your data is dirty, your system will fail to achieve its purpose. Data testing is thus an essential part of constructing the database-centric application system. It comprises both testing the data against the business rules (hint: don't disable integrity constraints on data loading, then forget to turn them back on) and testing data accuracy and content for correctness. Random sampling is often the best way to verify content.

In any event, getting your use cases right is critical for adequate system testing. Since system testing comes after delivery of the system, you must also keep your use cases up-to-date. If you let them diverge from your current understanding of the requirements as you iterate through design and construction, you will find it very difficult to develop effective validation test cases during system test. You must also feed back changes to the use cases into your test bed so that it accurately reflects the requirements of the system.

Summary

Your main risk at this point is that your requirements do not reflect the real needs of your stakeholders. To address this risk, you must verify requirements with a review of the use cases. Such reviews should involve both team members and external stakeholders.

You must also make sure that requirements are testable. Preparing for the system validation test that validates the finished system against its requirements means developing both test models and test beds that you can use in such tests. As always, this is an iterative process that requires revisiting the test models and test beds as your requirements change throughout the project.

Now that you are comfortable with the *whys* of the system, it is time to turn to the *how:* database design.

Building Entity-Relationship Models 6

The excellency of every art is its intensity, capable of making all disagreeables
evaporate, from their being in close relationship with beauty and truth.

John Keats, to T. and T. Keats, January 13, 1818

Over the last 20 years, the intense art of data modeling has grown and
changed with the needs of designers, though not perhaps in beauty and
truth. In today's database design world, the dominant method of modeling information is the entity-relationship (ER) diagram. While I am proposing to do away
with this method, or at least to expand its capabilities greatly, you cannot design
databases without a familiarity with the techniques of ER diagramming. If for no
other reason, you'll need to explain yourself to those who have exposure only
to ER techniques. The source of many of the techniques that the UML offers origi-
nate in ER modeling. Understand ER models, and you are more than halfway to
understanding object models. In particular, this chapter introduces some of the
really basic modeling concepts that you use in data modeling of whatever variety.

This chapter briefly surveys ER diagramming and data modeling without
going into full detail on design methods. The following chapters go into great detail on modeling techniques using UML. Usually, the comparison to ER models is
easy to make; the later chapters explicitly mention any great departures from
things that ER models do. This chapter introduces you to the basic data modeling
concepts through ER diagrams, and the following chapters then show you how to
use UML to accomplish the same things in a broader, OO context.

First, some history. Peter Chen invented the ER diagram in the early days
of relational databases to model the design of those databases from a more abstract perspective [Chen 1976]. At the time, relational databases contended with
network and other types of databases, particularly in academic research. Chen
wanted a way to represent the semantics of the data model that would unify these
database models, so he invented ER models to do exactly that.

Ten years later, ER modeling was becoming broadly used, but many competing forms emerged as the various communities that needed database design

tools began to address those needs. A major leap forward came when Teorey and his coauthors proposed the extended ER model in 1986 [Teorey, Yang, and Fry 1986]. Because this paper coincided with the rise of the CASE tool as the next silver bullet, it became a standard through these tools. The extended ER model included generalization (inheritance) as a major extension to Chen's original model. The extensions came from the same work on semantic networks that informed the rise of the original OO design and programming methods.

Several other models became current in different regions of the world. Europeans focused on Natural-language Information Analysis Method (NIAM) and data modeling techniques based on it, while Americans continued to develop variations on ER diagrams. In the 1990s, the information systems industry began to adopt widely two such variations: IDEF1X [Bruce 1992] and Information Engineering dialects, often known as "crow's-foot diagramming" [Everest 1986].

> *Note: These references may seem a bit long in the tooth for the fast-moving software industry. While I'd like to be able to refer you to more recent innovative training materials on these techniques, there aren't any.*

About the same time, the first stirrings of the OO world began to suggest ways to use OO methods in database design. The developers of the Object Modeling Language (OML) published a paper that described how you might use OML to design databases [Blaha, Premerlani, and Rumbaugh 1988] and followed it up recently with a comprehensive book [Blaha and Premerlani 1998]. OML object modeling itself derives from ER modeling [Rumbaugh et al. 1992, p. 271], as does the Shlaer-Mellor approach [Shlaer and Mellor 1988]. Since much of the work in OO modeling had its roots in data modeling, the fit with database design was fairly good. People began to experiment tentatively with these techniques, but because of the slow adoption rate of OO, the techniques did not become popular. As OO adoption speeds up, that is changing quickly, as evidenced by the techniques in this book.

So what exactly is entity-relationship diagramming, and what can it do for you?

Entities and Attributes

An *entity* is a data object. You can get quite baroque about terminology if you go into this formally. Briefly, you have to distinguish between a particular thing, a set of things with similar properties, the definition of that set, and the set of such definitions. When you see the word "entity" in a database design book, it generally refers to the definition of the set of things. It could potentially refer to a particular thing or even to the set of particular things. Other names for particular things include entity instance, entity occurrence, object, tuple, or row (for the relationally inclined). Other names for sets of things are entity set, result set, object collection, extension, relation, or table. Other names for the definitions are entity type, intension, object type, class, relation (just to be confusing), or relvar (short for *relational variable*, Date's formal term for this concept). Other names for the set of definitions are schema, database (very inexact usage), data model, or even database design.

In practice, you use the term "entity" to refer to the rectangle in an entity-relationship diagram [Teorey 1999]. Formally, this is a model of the intensional definition of a set of objects. The *extension* of the entity is the set of objects in the database that the entity models. Figure 6-1 shows a Chen ER entity, a rectangle with a name. The circles connected to the rectangle are the *attributes* (properties, columns) of the entity.

The entity Person consists of objects that all have the properties PersonID, Name, Sex, DateOfBirth, Height, Weight, MaritalStatus, and Comment. Name is a complex attribute that consists of a series of attributes (Honorific, FirstName, MiddleName, LastName, and Suffix). All of these attributes have values for each instance of the entity (each person). The underlined attribute PersonID is the identifier or primary key for the person, a value that uniquely identifies each object.

Figure 6-2 shows the IDEF1X version of the Person entity. The entity is a box with its name over the top of the box. Inside the box appear the same attributes. The box has two sections. The top section contains all the attributes of the primary key (the identifying attributes). The lower box contains all other attributes. This format consumes quite a bit less space than the attribute circle

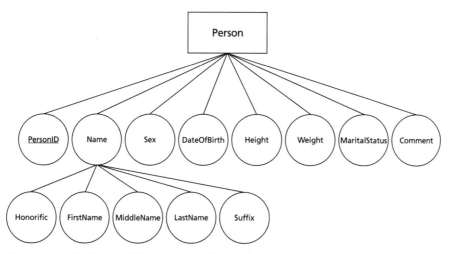

Figure 6-1 *A Chen Entity and Its Attributes*

Figure 6-2   *An IDEF1X Entity and Its Attributes*

approach. It is also quite close to the UML class in format, as Chapter 7 will demonstrate.

> *Note: In the IDEF1X approach, there is no way to show complex attributes. IDEF1X shows attributes in first normal form, meaning that there are no internal components in an IDEF1X attribute. You must model the complex name as a separate entity, then relate it to the Person through a relationship. As you will see in Chapter 7, UML has a similar requirement, but it comes from a different source: encapsulation of the internal structure of objects. See Chapter 11 for more information on normal forms.*

Relationships

The other half of the ER diagram is the relationship. A *relationship* is a model of the association between objects of one or more different entity types. You can do the same kind of formal language expansion for relationships that appeared in the above section "Entities and Attributes" for entities. Relationships show how each entity connects to other entities. They correspond to mappings between attributes of the different entities. These mappings can be objects in their own right, having properties and primary keys (more on that later in the section "ER Business Rules"). Figure 6-3 shows two entities, Person and CriminalOrganization, mapped to one another with a relationship "plays a role in."

The ER relationship is omnidirectional; that is, each entity relates to all the other entities in the relationship and can "see" those entities. Each side of the relationship (the line connecting the diamond to the rectangle) is a *role,* the function of the entity in the relationship. You can name each role for clarity, though you need not. Conventionally, you use verbs for relationship and role names and nouns for entity names. You then construct sentences with the appropriate subject and object.

Figure 6-4 shows the relationship between the Person entity and the Identification entity. From the person's perspective, a person is identified by a set

Figure 6-3   *A Relationship between Two Entities*

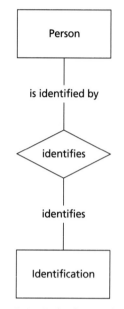

Figure 6-4   *Roles in a Relationship*

of identification papers. From the identification perspective, an identification identifies a person. The person-side role name is therefore "is identified by," while the identification-side role name is "identifies." This active-passive mode naming is very common, though certain kinds of relationships evade such easy naming. You can choose to name the relationship with one or the other role name or a separate name that makes sense in the context. In the case of Figure 6-4, the relationship is "identifies," which makes sense in the context.

> *Note: A common trap is to fall into the* uniqueness fallacy *when naming roles. For years, all names in a database had to be unique. There was no concept of* scope, *or* name space. *All database systems now let you scope most names to an appropriate level in the schema, so there is really no reason to make all attribute names unique. Role names (which may correspond to attribute names in the relational table or class) need not be unique either. The point of the role name is clarity: what the relationship means in the context of the entity. "Has" is often good enough, or you might want to*

*include a noun object ("has an address," for example, in the relation-
ship between Person and Address). In OO design, encapsulation up-
grades this feature to a principle; names within a class should reflect
the perspective of the class, not the unique names of all the other
classes in the system. As you will see in Chapter 7, another way to
think of role names is as class property names, which are of necessity scoped to the class and therefore unique only within the class.*

IDEF1X dispenses with the diamonds and represents the relationships with
just a labeled line. The crow's-foot notation similarly represents relationships.
Figure 6-5 shows the "identifies" relationship in those notations.

Figure 6-6 illustrates a special relationship. The recursive relationship relates entity objects to others of the same type. In this example, you want to model
the relationship between criminal organizations. A criminal organization can be a
part of another criminal organization, or indeed several such organizations. Figure 6-6 shows this relationship in Chen, IDEF1X, and crow's-foot notations.

A relationship can have properties of its own in addition to the entities that
it relates. For example, you might want to have an attribute on the "plays a role
in" relationship in Figure 6-3 that names the role (Boss, Underboss, Lieutenant,
and so on). This feature of ER diagramming expands the semantics of the relationship to considering the relationship as an object in its own right with its own
properties. The classic example of this is marriage. A marriage is a relationship

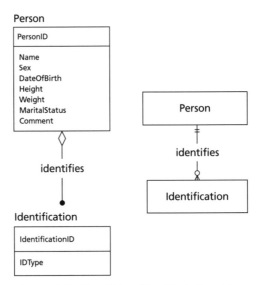

Figure 6-5   *The "identifies" Relationship
in IDEF1X and Crow's-Foot Notations*

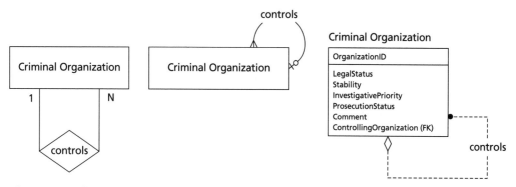

Figure 6-6   *The Recursive Relationship in Various Notations*

between two people that has legal properties as an object. You can model these objects as entities, but they are really relationships with all the associated semantics of relationships.

A relationship has several properties of interest to the database designer:

- The number of objects that *can* participate in a role
- The number of objects that *must* participate in a role
- The number of entities that participate in the relationship
- Whether the relationship is strong (independent) or weak (dependent)

These properties are the major way an ER diagram defines business rules, the subject of the "ER Business Rules" section that follows. Every dialect has a different way to express these constraints. First, however, there are some extensions to ER modeling that introduce a different kind of relationship: a semantic one.

Semantic Relationships: Subtyping and Aggregation

During the 1970s, there were several strands of software research that cross-pollinated each other with ideas about the semantic relationships between data structures. The term "semantic" means of or relating to the meaning of an object, as opposed to its structure (syntax) or its use (pragmatics). Chen's ER notation introduced part of this background data theory by integrating relationships and their constraints as abstractions that made a valuable modeling contribution. Later ER notations went even further, introducing the concept of subtyping [Teorey, Yang, and Fry 1986] and aggregation [Bruce 1992].

Tip: You can usually do a perfectly good database design using ER diagramming techniques without worrying much about subtyping and aggregation. Once you start moving in the direction of OO design with UML, however, you will find these issues much more important.

Subtyping is also known by several other names: generalization, inheritance, is-a, is-a-kind-of, or subclassing. Each comes from using the basic concept of generalization in different contexts. The *generalization* relationship specifies that a supertype generalizes the properties of several subtypes. In other words, the supertype contains the properties that the subtypes share, and all subtypes inherit the properties of the supertype. Often the supertype is purely an abstract type, meaning that there are no instances of the supertype, just of the subtypes.

Note: Chapter 7 goes into much more detail on inheritance, which is a fundamental property of class modeling. It also discusses multiple inheritance (having multiple supertypes), which you never find in ER models, or at least I haven't observed it in the ER salt marshes I've visited.

Figure 6-7 illustrates a subtype relationship expressed in IDEF1X notation. An identification is an abstract type of object that identifies a person, and there are many different kinds of identification. The subtype hierarchy in Figure 6-7 shows an additional abstract subtype, identifications that have expiration dates (passports, driver's licenses, and so on), as opposed to those that do not (birth certificates).

You can add *mutual exclusivity* as a constraint on this relationship as well [Teorey, Yang, and Fry 1986; Teorey 1999]. If the subtypes of an entity are mutually exclusive, it means that an object or instance of the entity must be precisely one of the subtypes. The identification hierarchy represents this kind of subtyping. You can't have an identification document that is simultaneously a passport and a driver's license, for example. If subclasses are not mutually exclusive, then the subtypes overlap in meaning. You could imagine a document that would be simultaneously a passport, driver's license, and birth certificate, I suppose. A better example would be an organization that is both a criminal organization and a legal company, a very common situation in the real world. The underlying reality of this way of looking at subtypes is as overlapping sets of objects. Mostly, you want to avoid this, as it makes the objects (rows in the database) interdependent and hence harder to maintain through changes. On the other hand, if the underlying reality really does overlap, your modeling should reflect that.

Finally, you can constrain the generalization relationship with a *completeness* constraint [Teorey, Yang, and Fry 1986; Teorey 1999]. If the subtypes of an entity are complete, it means that an object of that kind must be one of the

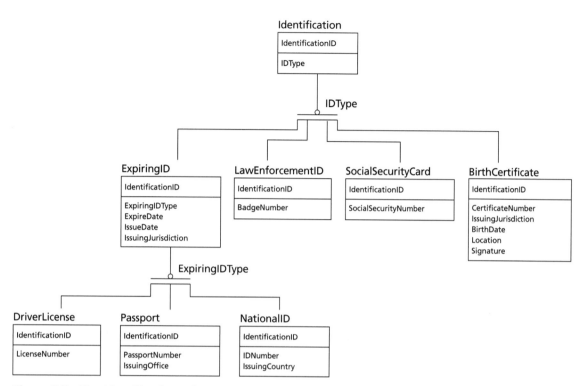

Figure 6-7 *The Identification Subtype Hierarchy Using IDEF1X Notation*

subtypes, and that there are no additional (unknown) subtypes. This constraint lets you express the situation where your subtypes are a logical division of the supertype that exhaustively covers the possibilities. Descriptive objects such as identity documents are almost never complete. Usually, this constraint applies to divisions that you make to handle conceptual or abstract categorizations of the data, such as grouping organizations into the categories of criminal, legitimate, and "other." Having the "other" category makes this set of subtypes complete.

Aggregation links two entities in a relationship that is tighter than the usual relationship. The aggregation relationship is often called a "part-of" relationship, because it expresses the constraint that one entity is made up of several other entities. There is a semantic difference between being a part of something and something "having" something else [Booch 1994, pp. 64–65, 102, 128–129; Rumbaugh et al. 1992, pp. 57–61; Teorey 1999, p. 26].

The most common situation in which you find aggregation useful is the parts explosion, or more generally the idea of physical containment. A *parts explosion* is a structural situation where one object is made up of a set of other objects, all of the same type. The parts explosion thus represents a tree or graph of parts. Querying such a tree yields the *transitive closure* of the graph, the collection of all the parts that make up the tree.

> *Note: The parts explosion or transitive closure is a hard problem for relational databases. Some SQL dialects, such as Oracle SQL, have operators that do this kind of query (CONNECT BY), but most don't. As a result, SQL programmers generally spend a lot of time programming the retrieval of these structures. Identifying an aggregate thus tells you interesting things about the amount of work involved in your application, at least if you're using a standard relational database.*

Holmes PLC is as much interested in parts as in wholes:

He passed close beside us, stole over to the window, and very softly and noiselessly raised it for half a foot. As he sank to the level of this opening, the light of the street, no longer dimmed by the dusty glass, fell full upon his face. The man seemed to be beside himself with excitement. His two eyes shone like stars, and his features were working convulsively. He was an elderly man, with a thin, projecting nose, a high, bald forehead, and a huge grizzled moustache. An opera hat was pushed to the back of his head, and an evening dress shirt-front gleamed out through his open overcoat. His face was gaunt and swarthy, scored with deep, savage lines. In his hand he carried what appeared to be a stick, but as he laid it down upon the floor it gave a metallic clang. Then from the pocket of his overcoat he drew a bulky object, and he busied himself in some task which ended with a loud, sharp click, as if a spring or bolt had fallen into its place. Still kneeling upon the floor, he bent forward and threw all his weight and strength upon some lever, with the result that there came a long, whirling, grinding noise, ending once more in a powerful click. He straightened himself then, and I saw that what he held in his hand was a sort of a gun, with a curiously misshapen butt. He opened it at the breech, put something in, and snapped the breech-block. Then, crouching down, he rested the end of the barrel upon the ledge of the open window, and I saw his long moustache droop over the stock and his eye gleam as it peered along the sights. I heard a little sigh of satisfaction as he cuddled the butt into his shoulder, and saw that amazing target, the black man on the yellow ground, standing clear at the end of his foresight. For an instant he was rigid and motionless. Then his finger tightened on the trigger. There was a strange, loud whiz and a long, silvery tinkle of broken glass. At that instant, Holmes sprang like a tiger on to the marksman's back, and hurled him flat upon his face.

. . . Holmes had picked up the powerful air-gun from the floor, and was examining its mechanism.

"An admirable and unique weapon," said he, "noiseless and of tremendous power: I knew Von Herder, the blind German mechanic, who constructed it to the order of the late Professor Moriarty. For years I have been aware of its existence, though I have never before had the opportunity of handling it. I commend it very specially to your attention, Lestrade, and also the bullets which fit it." [EMPT]

Figure 6-8 illustrates the basic parts explosion in IDEF1X notation. Each gun component is a part of another, with the top-level ones (the air-gun in the above quotation, for example) having a null relationship (no parent). This structure represents a forest of mechanical trees, a one-to-many relationship between mechanisms and parts. There is a case for making the relationship many-to-many, representing a forest of graphs or networks instead of hierarchical trees. The aggregation adornment is the diamond shape at one end of the relationship line. The relationship is strong, or "nonidentifying," so the entity gets a foreign key attribute that is not part of the primary key ("is part of") and a dashed line (see the later section "Strong and Weak Relationships" for more information about nonidentifying relationships).

While aggregation can be interesting and useful, it seldom has many consequences for the underlying database design. The main consequence is to couple the design more tightly. When you design a system, you break the system into subsystems, uncoupling the elements as much as possible. This permits the reuse of the elements in different situations. When you identify an aggregate, you are usually saying that you can't separate the aggregate from the entity it aggregates. That generally means you can't break the two apart into separate subsystems. Often, genericity (templates or generics) provides a way to gain reuse while still allowing for the tight coupling of the entities (as instantiated templates or generics). As ER diagramming has no concept of genericity, however, the concept isn't of much value in ER aggregation situations.

Also, in OO design, aggregation is a kind of abstraction, just like inheritance. In this case, you are abstracting and encapsulating the aggregated objects under the aggregate. Usually, your aggregate will have operations that manipulate the encapsulated objects that make it up, hiding the structural details. For example, to search a tree, you create an operation that returns an iterator, which in turn lets you walk the tree in some well-defined order. In design terms, if you don't want this level of encapsulation, you shouldn't designate the relationship as an aggregate.

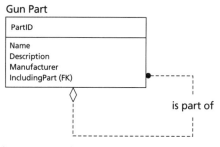

Figure 6-8 *The Air Gun Parts Explosion*

> *Note: You can see almost any component relationship as aggregation if you stretch the semantics enough. You can call the attributes of an entity an aggregation, for example: the entity is made up of the attributes. While this may be possible, it isn't useful for design. You should limit your use of aggregation to situations such as parts explosions or physical containment, where the result means something special for your design and code. This is especially true when it means something for your database structures, as in the case of the criminal organization tree.*

ER Business Rules

Business rules are any logical conditions that must be true at the end of a transaction. Broadly defined, a business rule is any policy that you want to impose on your data handling, no matter how complex. From the database design perspective, these business rules fall into two categories: integrity constraints and database policies. There are other business rules that you enforce at the application level, such as process flow requirements and other policies that affect transient data. Those rules do not concern the database designer unless they have some impact on transactions. In an object system, there is usually an object model or domain layer that represents the system's objects, and that layer of the application manages the business rules.

> *Note: The GUIDE International Business Rules Project Final Report does an excellent job of defining formally the concept of business rules [GUIDE 1997]. You should consult that document to get a full discussion of all the issues with business rules.*

An *integrity constraint* is a logical relationship between entities that imposes some restriction on those entities. The concept directly corresponds to the relationship in the last section. A *database policy* is a constraint independent of particular entities that the database must enforce, such as security or physical layout constraints. In the context of ER diagramming, you find three basic constraints: multiplicity, the relationship itself ("foreign key constraint"), and primary key. You also can constrain how foreign keys and primary keys interact; ER diagramming does this using strong and weak relationships. You can also specify domain constraints on the kind of data that an attribute represents.

Multiplicity

Multiplicity is the number of objects that can participate in a role of a relationship. That is, multiplicity constrains the range of the number of objects that relate to other objects through a particular role. In Chen's original approach [Chen 1976], you put variable letters or constant integers on the roles to indicate their multi-plicity. The "plays a role in" Chen relationship, for example, in Figure 6-9, shows an "M" on one side and an "N" on the other. This is a many-to-many relationship: a person may play a role in many (M) criminal organizations, and a criminal orga-nization may have several people (N) playing a role in the organization. You could replace these with a number to indicate a specific number of items; the usual constant is 1, meaning the role is a one rather than a many role.

The crow's-foot notation uses its eponymous line adornments to show to-many roles. Figure 6-9 shows the crow's feet on both sides of the relationship, meaning that it's a many-to-many relationship. There are variations on the sym-bols that let you show that a role may have no value for a given object (multiplic-ity 0) or must have exactly one (multiplicity 1).

IDEF1X shows multiplicity with specific adornments on the relationship roles, at least in its incarnation in the ERwin modeling tool [Logic Works 1996], now a product of Platinum Technology. A "P" indicates a to-one-or-more con-straint, a "Z" indicates a to-zero-or-one constraint, and an integer indicates an exact-number constraint. However, although there is a notation for many-to-many relationships, IDEF1X models usually create an associative entity for the re-lationship, then put one-to-many or one-to-one relationships from the entities to the associative entity. Figure 6-10 illustrates both formats for the "plays a role in" relationship. In the first, the black dots at both ends of the relationship indicate its many-to-many character. In the second, the relationship becomes an associative entity with two relationships, one to Person and one to CriminalOrganization.

The relationship between Person and Identification is a one-to-many rela-tionship named "is identified by," shown in Figure 6-11. A person is identified by some number of identification documents, while an identification document identifies a single person. In this case, the Person role has multiplicity 1, and the Identification role has multiplicity" many," making it a one-to-many relationship.

You can also have one-to-one relationships, many of which are really sub-type relationships, others of which represent objectified candidate keys. Figure

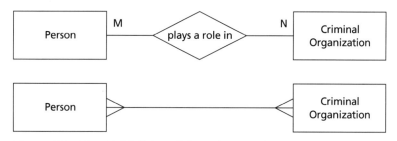

Figure 6-9 *The Multiplicity of the "plays a role in" Relationship in Two Notations*

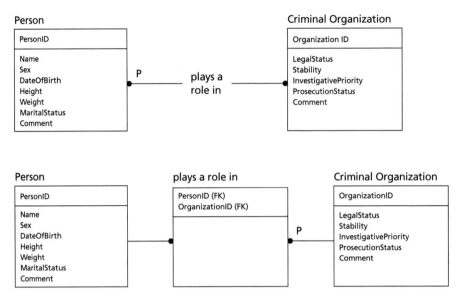

Figure 6-10   *The Multiplicity of the "plays a role in" Relationship in IDEF1X*

6-8 shows the subtype relationship in IDEF1X notation. A birth certificate is a subtype of an identification document, as is a passport or a driver's license or an identity card. All of these entities are separate and linked by a relationship. In Chen's notation, which does not provide generalization or subtyping notation, this is a simple, one-to-one relationship. One passport corresponds to one identification document. IDEF1X and crow's-foot notations show the generalization relationship directly without indicating the one-to-one nature of it, but the methodology implies that from the way generalization and subtyping works.

Other one-to-one relationships relate two objects that are both unique in their own collections. That is, one entity has a unique attribute that refers to another entity's unique key (a set of attributes that uniquely identifies an object, see the following section on "Keys and Relationships" for details). You can identify both entities if you know the value of the attribute. This situation is relatively rare. An example: every person has a unique set of fingerprints and a unique DNA profile. The relationship between the Person entity and the FingerprintRecord entity is thus one-to-one, as is the DNAProfile relationship to Person. These relationships usually show up as simple connections with 1 for both role multiplicities.

> *Note: If you are using ER modeling and encounter a one-to-one relationship, analyze it carefully to see whether the data model should actually express this as a subtype. If not, consider*

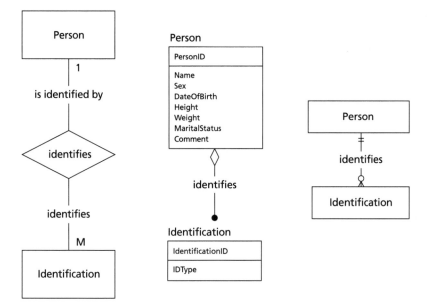

Figure 6-11 *The Multiplicity of the "is identified by" Relationship in Various Notations*

whether one entity can be usefully collapsed into an attribute or attributes of the other entity. You could, for example, have a FingerprintProfile as an attribute of the Person rather than as a one-to-one relationship if the profile was just a single value (a picture, say). On the other hand, you may want to break up a single table into two or more tables related to each other one-to-one as a physical design technique to minimize retrieval time, separating data that you use all the time and data you use relatively infrequently. This is not really a logical design issue, however.

Multiplicity has many names. The term "multiplicity" is the best one I've found; it comes from the UML and originated in OMT [Rumbaugh et al. 1992]. Various design methods name this with other terms:

- Cardinality [Teorey 1999; Logic Works 1996]
- Cardinality Ratio [Fleming and von Halle 1989]
- Connectivity [Teorey, Yang, and Fry 1986]
- Designation [Date 1986, pp. 437–438]
- Frequency Occurrence [Halpin 1995]
- Functionality [Ullman 1988]

> *Note: In the ER world, you usually use the term "cardinality," which comes by analogy from set theory in mathematics, where it refers to the size of a set. Given that this is really a constraint on the range of such sizes, not the size itself, I prefer to use the term "multiplicity," which has no unfortunate conflicts in meaning. It's also the term that the UML (and its precursor, OMT) uses to describe this design specification.*

Relationships and their multiplicities connect the different entities in the schema design. The constraints they create imply certain things about the structure of the entities: primary and foreign keys.

Keys and Relationships

A *key* is a set of attributes that identifies an object. The *primary key* of an entity is one key that uniquely identifies the entity that owns the attributes. An *alternate* or *candidate key* is a unique identifier other than the primary key. An entity can have any number of keys, though having more than a single alternate is quite unusual. A *foreign key* is a key that identifies an object in another entity; it acts as a data pointer to the other kind of entity, relating the two entities. A *composite key* is a key where the set has more than one attribute in it; I don't think there is a special name for the key with a one-element set, which is far more common.

> *Note: As with everything to do with computer science, somebody somewhere has probably given this a name. More likely, there are multiple names for the concept. I just haven't run into them. As with cardinality and multiplicity, the name isn't as important as the concept.*

In Chen diagrams, you show the primary key either by an asterisk on the attribute name or names or by underlining them, as in Figure 6-12. There is no way of showing alternate keys. The IDEF1X notation puts the primary key attributes in the upper division of the entity and marks alternate keys with an "AK<n>" in parentheses after the attribute name, with <n> being an integer identifying the key if it has several attributes. The crow's-foot notation, which does not show attributes, has therefore no way of showing primary keys. CASE tools extend the notation with notations similar to Chen or IDEF1X. Those tools depend on this information to generate the correct relational tables, including key constraints.

The foreign key does not exist formally in the ER diagram, as it is really the relational way of representing the many side of a one-to-many relationship. When they generate a relational schema from the ER diagram, most ER case tools take such relationships and include attributes from the primary key of the one side in

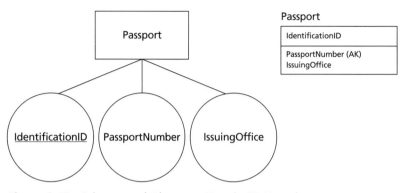

Figure 6-12   *Primary and Alternate Keys in ER Notations*

the table on the many side. A foreign key is thus a set of attributes that represents a relationship to another group of entities. IDEF1X represents this explicitly using "(FK<n>)" to mark the foreign key attributes, again with <n> identifying the key over multiple attributes.

Many-to-many relationships create foreign keys in a completely separate object, one that represents the relationship itself. The "plays a role in" relationship of Figure 6-10, for example, is a many-to-many relationship between a person and a criminal organization. That is, one person may play a role in several criminal organizations, and one criminal organization has at least two and possibly more persons playing a role in it. In this case, you can see that placing the primary key attributes in either of the two entities isn't going to work. You have to put their primary keys in the relationship, which then explicitly represents the connections between people and organizations. The relationship's primary key is then the combination of the two foreign keys. Using the IDEF1X notation, the two keys appear together in the upper part of the entity box, both marked with the (FK) adornment to indicate they are foreign keys.

> *Note: These kinds of associative entities are also examples of weak or identifying relationships; see the following section on "Strong and Weak Relationships" for details.*

You can have relationships that relate more than two entities to one another. A binary relationship is a two-way relationship with two roles. A ternary relationship is a three-way relationship with three roles. You can keep going, but there are very few relationships with four or more roles. As an example of a ternary relationship, consider the "plays a role in" relationship again. Figure 6-13 shows in Chen notation an expanded relationship that includes the RoleType entity. One use for this might be to create a description of the role that several

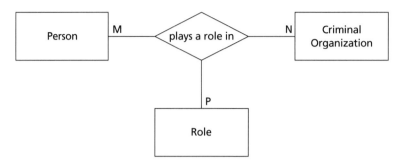

Figure 6-13   *A Ternary Relationship in Chen Notation*

people play in different organizations. Another use might be to permit modeling of the role structure of organizations with a graph structure (Underboss reports to Boss, Lieutenant reports to Underboss, and so on).

The relationship contains three keys, one for Person, one for Criminal Organization, and one for Role. It represents a specific role played by a specific person in a specific criminal organization. This particular ternary relationship expresses a many-to-many-to-many multiplicity. That is, each of the relationship roles is a to-many role. Often, there are functional dependencies that limit ternary roles to a to-one role. For example, you might want to say that a person can play a role in only one criminal organization, not several. Then the criminal organization role (the link from the relationship to criminal organization) would be a to-one link, and the relationship would be many-to-many-to-one. This constraint is a functional dependency from the person and role to the criminal organization. Chapter 11 discusses functional dependencies and their impact on relational database design and normal forms in more detail. In that context, putting the relations into fifth normal form requires breaking the relationship into three tables, showing the relationships between person and criminal organization, person and role, and role and criminal organization. Combining these tables using a relational join lets you express any fact about the relationship without introducing spurious facts or losing any information. The ER model shows you the relationship directly and lets you express the real semantics of the situation in a very direct way.

The foreign key, as a surrogate for relationship, is at the center of the storm in the data modeling world. More than anything else, the foreign key and the relationship provide the differentiator between most design notations and methods as well as the DBMS physical models that implement the relationships. The foreign key is essentially a relational concept. Chen, in creating the relationship, tried to abstract the notion away from the relational data model to accommodate the needs of other models. Later ER models such as IDEF1X downplay this aspect of the relationship by forcing you to create what is essentially a relational model. In-

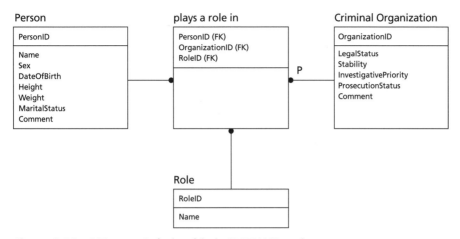

Figure 6-14   *A Ternary Relationship in IDEF1X Notation*

stead of many-to-many relationships or ternary relationships, for example, you create an *associative entity* [Logic Works 1996] with one-to-many relationships to the entities that make it up. Figure 6-14 shows the expanded "plays a role in" ternary relationship in the equivalent IDEF1X notation.

The "plays a role in" relationship is now an entity with the appropriate relationship links to the three components. The primary key of the associative entity consists of the three primary keys of the three related entities. These keys are now foreign keys that are part of the primary key, making the associative entity a weak or dependent entity. This kind of entity, and its reliance on foreign keys, has a special representation in ER diagrams.

Strong and Weak Relationships

Chen introduced the idea of *weak relationship* to describe the relatively common situation where the foreign key is part of the primary key [Chen 1976]. That is, a *weak entity* is an entity whose primary key includes the primary key of a related entity. IDEF1X, for example, automatically shows the elements of the primary key from the many side as part of the primary key in the upper section of the entity box if you link the entities with an *identifying* relationship. The relationship itself (Figure 6-14) is a solid line rather than the *nonidentifying (strong)* relationship's dashed line. Chen's notation just shows the relationship as a double-line diamond and the corresponding weak entity as a double-line rectangle.

In Chen diagrams, weak entities are rare because there are few existence constraints between real entities. Chen's original example was to have a Dependent entity related to an Employee entity with a weak relationship. The

Dependent's primary key combined the employee's EmployeeID and the name of the dependent. Making this a weak relationship asserted that the dependent person was of no interest other than as a dependent of the employee. If you think a bit about this, however, and think about the real-world situations that might confront the hapless human resource clerk (multiple addresses for divorced dependents of ex-employees with ongoing COBRA coverage and on and on), you realize that the real world does not often present opportunities to use weak relationships with real entities.

Almost all associative entities, however, are weak entities because their existence depends essentially on the existence of the entities they associate. They are relationships, not freestanding entities. So the weak or identifying relationship is much more important in ER diagramming techniques that use associative entities, such as IDEF1X.

Weak entities depend on the existence of their related entities. If you delete the related entity, you must cascade that deletion to the weak entities that contain the primary key you've deleted.

> Note: The implications of the weak entity are much more interesting in the object world. The equivalent situation in object design is when an object creates and owns another object rather than just having a reference to the object. If you delete the main object, it must delete all the dependent objects that it owns. If the objects are independent, one object simply refers to the other object. When you delete the referring object, the relationship disappears, but the other object still exists.

Domains

A *domain* is a set of values to which an attribute maps an object. That is, each value for an attribute in an entity set must come from the domain of the attribute. This is a very simple form of integrity constraint. It puts restrictions on the values in a very direct way.

> Note: The value domain is completely unrelated to the Microsoft Windows NT domain, a network naming concept.

ER diagrams do not directly represent domains, but all CASE tools that I've used let you put the domain information into the repository for each attribute. Since a critical feature of a CASE tool is the generation of the data definition language or the schema itself, you have to have a way of specifying the required domain constraints. Often you can specify a separate set of domain requirements for each target DBMS, as they all have different features relating to domains.

Summary

Entities, relationships, and the ER diagrams they populate are the meat and pota-toes of the database design world. Entities are rectangles connected to other enti-ties by relationship lines, with many variations in different modeling techniques ranging from Chen notation to NIAM to data modeling to IDEF1X.

Most ER diagramming notations support these concepts:

- *Entity:* A set of objects

- *Attribute:* A property of an entity

- *Relationships (both strong and weak):* A link between two or more entities, corresponding to foreign keys in relational databases

- *Role:* One side of a relationship

- *Multiplicity:* The number of objects that participate in a role (one-to-one, one-to-many, many-to-many)

- *Primary and candidate keys:* Attributes that uniquely identify objects

- *Domains:* A set of values to which an attribute maps an object

You've now seen all the different elements of standard data modeling using ER diagrams. The next chapter turns this on its head and introduces you to the concepts of modeling objects.

Building Class Models in UML 7

There are more things in heaven and earth, Horatio, than are dreamt of in your philosophy.

Shakespeare, Hamlet I:v

The ER modeling techniques in Chapter 6 are a good start at the methods you need for effective data modeling. This chapter expands on these basic techniques by extending them into the world of object orientation. Instead of modeling entities, now you are going to learn how to model objects. Hamlet was right: there are more things in heaven and earth than you can conceive—but at least you can model more effectively what you can conceive.

The Unified Modeling Language (UML) is a notation that combines elements from the three major strands of OO design: Rumbaugh's OMT modeling [Rumbaugh et al. 1992], Booch's OO Analysis and Design [Booch 1994], and Jacobson's Objectory [Jacobson et al. 1992]. The UML shows every sign of becoming a standard. OMG has adopted the UML as the standard notation for object methods. The UML is ubiquitous in trade show presentations. Several professional books now cover the UML in greater or lesser detail in presenting their analysis and design methods [Douglass 1998; Eriksson and Penker 1997; Fowler, Jacobson, and Kendall 1997; Harmon and Watson 1998; Larman 1997; Muller, Nygard, and Crnkovic 1997; Quatrani 1997; Texel and Williams 1997].

Note: There are thus many ways to learn UML. Rather than tutoring you in UML, this chapter focuses on teaching you the elements of UML you need to model data. By no means does this exhaust the language. As an OO designer, you should become familiar with all the different parts of the UML. The most direct way to do this is to download the UML specification documents from the Rational or OMG Web sites [Rational Software 1997a, 1997b, 1997c]. Reading these documents and using one of the many tutorials the above paragraph references will introduce you to all the OO features of the UML. All of the following material draws on the three UML documents for details; please consult those documents for more information on any individual elements of the class diagrams. You can acquire additional understanding through the readings in the preceding paragraph and their examples. Fowler is a good introduction [Fowler, Jacobson, and Kendall 1997], Larman and Harmon are good intermediate texts [Larman 1997; Harmon and Watson 1998], and Eriksson is a particularly good advanced text [Eriksson and Penker 1997].

Chapter 4 covered one type of UML diagram, the use case. This chapter covers the class diagram, which models object classes. Object-oriented analysis and design using class diagrams can get quite complex; this chapter's objective is to cover just those elements of class diagrams that you use to model information. The first section covers object structure: packages, classes, and attributes. The second section covers the structure of object behavior: operations and methods. The third section covers relationships and their representation of referential business rules. The final section expands the coverage of business rules to object identity and uniqueness, domain constraints, and more general constraints.

Packages, Classes, and Attributes

The UML class and its structure corresponds closely to the entity type and its structure in ER diagramming. In the UML:

> A *class* is a description of a set of objects that share the same attributes, operations, methods, relationships, and semantics. A class may use a set of interfaces to specify collections of operations it provides to its environment. [Rational Software 1997b, p. 20]

There are quite a few words with specific meanings in this definition, all of which are relevant to the database designer:

- *Attribute:* "A named slot within a classifier [an interface, type, class, subsystem, database, or component] that describes a range of values that instances of the classifier may hold" [Rational Software 1997b, p. 149]. This is very similar to the relational definition of an attribute as a named mapping to a domain [Codd 1972].

- *Operation:* "A service that can be requested from an object to effect behavior. An operation has a signature [name and parameters, possibly including the returned parameter], which may restrict the actual parameters that are possible." [Rational Software 1997b, p. 155]

- *Method:* "The implementation of an operation. It specifies the algorithm or procedure that effects the results of an operation." [Rational Software 1997b, p. 154]

- *Relationship:* "A semantic connection among model elements. Examples of relationships include associations and generalizations." [Rational Software 1997b, p. 156]

- *Association:* "The semantic relationship between two or more classifiers that involves connections among their instances." [Rational Software 1997b, p. 149]

- *Generalization:* "A taxonomic relationship between a more general element and a more specific element. The more specific element is fully consistent with the more general element and contains additional information. An instance of the more specific element may be used where the more general element is allowed." [Rational Software 1997b, p. 152]

- *Interface:* "A declaration of a collection of operations that may be used for defining a service offered by an instance." [Rational Software 1997b, p. 153]

The *classifier* is a fundamental concept in the UML that may confuse even many OO design experts. This is an abstract UML class that includes the various UML notational subclasses you can use to classify objects in some way by their structure and behavior. Classes, types, interfaces, subsystems, components, and databases are all kinds of classifiers. Often the UML diagramming notations apply to classifiers in general, not just to classes.

These terms combine to form the semantics of the class as it appears in the UML class diagram. That is, to be meaningful, you must build your class diagram with notation that corresponds to these concepts as the UML defines them. This section discusses classes and attributes, while the following sections discuss operations, relationships, and other business rules.

A *class diagram* is a structural or static diagram with which you model the structure of a system of classes. In many ways, class diagrams strongly resemble ER diagrams. If you compare the definition of the class given above to the definition of the entity type for ER diagrams, you'll see they are substantially the same. Differences emerge mainly in the modeling of operations and relationships. All this is hardly surprising, since the OO notations on which UML was founded all developed from ER notations.

> *Note: The UML class diagram is really broader than just classes, as it can model interfaces, relationships, and even individual class instances or objects. An alternative and sometimes preferable name for the class diagram is thus the "static structural diagram," which*

*many of the books on the UML use instead of the more common
"class diagram." Since the focus here is on classes and their relationships, I have chosen to use the term "class diagram."*

But before getting into the details of class diagramming, you first need to understand how to structure your system as a whole, and that means packages.

Packages

Most UML-capable design tools let you organize your classes independently of the UML diagram structure, as the UML specification suggests. That is, you can model all your classes in a single diagram, or you can break them up into chunks across several diagrams. Some tools let you do both, letting you define your classes in a repository or single diagram from which you create other diagrams that refer back to the repository for class and relationship structure. You can thus show different views of your system without duplicating your actual modeling efforts.

In many ways, the organization of your diagrams depends on the tools you use to draw them. Using a simple drawing tool, you can organize the classes however you like, but it's a lot of work. Using a comprehensive tool such as Rational Rose or one of its competitors, you can let the tool do most of the work. However, you pays your money and you takes your choice: you must often structure your diagrams the way the tool requires.

Part of the art of OO project management is to structure your project and organization along the lines of your product architecture [Hohmann 1997; Muller 1998]. One aspect of the project is the data model, and modeling your information is just as subject to architectural structuring as every other part of the project. This may seem kind of vague and difficult, but it isn't really if you understand how object systems work in architectural terms.

An OO software *system* is a working software object that stands alone, such as a software product or a framework library. These systems in turn comprise various smaller systems that do not stand alone but which come together to make up the system as a whole. I call these subsystems *clusters* [Muller 1998]; others call them everything from packages to subsystems to layers to partitions to modules.

A UML *package* is a grouping of model elements. A UML *subsystem* is a kind of package that represents the specification and realization of a set of behaviors [Rational Software 1997b, pp. 130–137], which is close to my concept of cluster. A subsystem is also a kind of classifier, so you can refer to it anywhere that you can use a class or interface. The *specification* consists of a set of use cases and their relationships, operations, and interfaces. The *realization* is a set of classes and other subsystems that provide the specified behavior. You relate the specification and the realization through a set of *collaborations,* mappings between the use cases and the classes or interfaces, in a collaboration diagram, which this book doesn't cover. These subsystems are the building blocks or components that make up your software system. They, not classes or files, should be the basis for configuration management in your system, if your source control tools are smart enough to understand subsystems [Muller 1998]. Usually a subsystem groups several classes together, though you can have single-class subsystems or even subsystems that are merely facades for other subsystems, with no classes at all, just interfaces. In terms of system architecture, subsystems often correspond to static (LIBs) or dynamic link libraries (DLLs), which present the external interfaces of the subsystem for reuse by other libraries.

Packages are really just name spaces, named groupings of elements that have unique names within the group. Subsystems are much more substantial and form the basis for your system design. You can use packages as such to create lightweight groups within your subsystems without needing to develop separate use cases and collaborations. How to decide what needs a subsystem and what is OK to leave as just a package is up to you.

The UML *model* is a package that contains a complete representation of your system from a given modeling perspective. You can have different models of the system using different perspectives or levels. For example, you can have an analysis model consisting entirely of use cases and a design model consisting of subsystems or classes.

Besides models and subsystems, there are several kinds of packages identified only by adding stereotypes to the package name. A *stereotype* is a phrase in guillemets, « », that you place on a symbol to represent an "official" extension to the semantics of the UML.

- *«System»:* The package that contains all the models of the system

- *«Facade»:* A package that consists solely of references to other packages, presenting the features of those packages in a view

- *«Framework»:* A package that presents an extensible template for use in a specific domain, consisting mainly of patterns

- *«Top-level package»:* A package that contains all the other packages in a model, representing all the nonenvironmental parts of the model

- *«Stub»:* A package with a public interface and nothing more, representing design work that is not yet complete or that is deferred for some reason

Note: The way you structure your packages and subsystems is a part of the general process of OO system architectural design [Rumbaugh et al. 1992, pp. 198–226; Booch 1994, pp. 221–222; Booch 1996, pp. 108–115]. There is much more to system architecture than just the aspects relevant to database design, so please

> consult these references for more details. The UML semantics
> specification is also a very useful reference for system architecture
> concepts [Rational Software 1997b].

This concept of system architecture as related and nested packages helps you to structure the system for optimal reusability. The point of packaging model elements is to let you uncouple large parts of the system from one another. This in turn lets you encapsulate large parts of the system into the packages, which become your reusable components. In other words, the package is the focus for creating reusable components, not the class. Packages typically have a package interface or set of interfaces that model the services that the package provides. Other packages access the packaged elements through those interfaces but know nothing about the internal structure of the package.

It's best to be clear: you should think about your system architecture as a set of packages and their interfaces, not as a collection of interrelated database entities. This focus on packaging is the critical difference between the ER approach to designing databases and the OO methods I am presenting in this book. The consequences of this type of thinking go all the way through to the database—or, I should say, databases. You should consider the subsystems different schemas and hence different databases, even if you actually build them all together in a single physical schema. The databases themselves become packages at some level, representing shared data, when you're detailing the actual implementation structure of your system. Breaking up your system into multiple databases gives you the option of modularizing your system for reuse. You can create a Person package that lets you model people and their related objects (addresses, for example). You can use that package in several systems, reusing the database schema nested within it along with everything else. You might even be able to reuse the database implementation, which is after all the point of the three-level ANSI/SPARC architecture.

You will find two central organizing principles behind most of your packages. The first is purely structural: How do the classes within the package relate to classes outside the package? Minimizing such interrelationships gives you a clear metric for judging whether to include a class in one package or another. From the database perspective, you have another consideration: transactions. Minimizing the number of packages that are part of a transaction is usually a good idea. Keeping transactions within a single package is ideal.

A good way to approach the packaging of your classes is through your use cases. To start developing your classes, as the next section describes, you go through your use cases looking for objects and their attributes. As you do this, also look at the transaction structure. You'll often find that you can simplify your package structure by understanding how the use case scenarios affect objects in the database. Start building subsystems by grouping the use cases that affect similar objects together. You will also often find that you can think of interesting ways to modify the use cases to simplify your transactions. As you build your packages, think about how the use cases map to the transactions involving the classes in the package. If you can find a way to restate the requirements to minimize the number of packages, you will usually have a better system in the end. Since your use cases correspond to transactions, this method guarantees that transactions center within packages rather than being spread all over the system.

All this is part of the iterative nature of OO design. You will find yourself moving from the microdesign level back to the architectural level or even back to requirements, then moving forward again with a better system. Your subsystems grow from a set of use cases to a complete subsystem package with classes, interfaces, and collaborations as well as the use cases. Your use cases may get more detail as you understand more about what is really going on within them. As long as you have it under control, such iteration is the essence of good design.

Enough abstraction. How do packages work in practice? When you first begin designing an architecture, you should usually have gone through building a set of use cases. You've gotten some basic ideas about the classes you'll need, and a reasonably clear idea of the sorts of transactions in the system. You should be able at this point to brainstorm a few basic packages that will form a basis for building your system architecture model. You have a few class hierarchies in mind, and you've almost certainly identified a few major subject areas of the system.

For example, the commonplace book system has several major areas of interest. Recall the use cases from Chapter 4:

- *Authenticate:* Connect to the system as an authenticated user

- *Report Case History:* Report a case history with text and multimedia details

- *Report Event:* Report on a set of events based on factual and text search criteria

- *Report Criminal:* Report a criminal biography with text and multimedia details, including police file data and case histories involving the criminal

- *Identify with Alias:* Find a criminal's identity based on alias

- *Identify with Evidence:* Find a criminal's identity based on evidence analysis such as fingerprint, DNA, and so on

- *Report Topic:* Report an encyclopedia topic

- *Find Agony Column:* Find an agony column entry based on text search criteria

- *Find Mob:* Find information about criminal organizations based on factual search criteria

• *Explore:* Explore relationships between people, organizations, and facts in the database

The System Architecture model contains a top-level subsystem called Commonplace Book that contains all the other subsystems. You can see several major areas of interest here. Authentication implies that something needs to keep track of users of the system and their security attributes. You might call this subsystem the Security package or the User package. Other subsystems all check with Security before allowing access. Case histories and events have their own subsystems. There are a series of use cases relating to criminals, who are people, and use cases that refer to other kinds of people as well, so you have a Person subsystem. You could create a Criminal subsystem layered on top of Person, or generalizing Person, that holds things such as aliases and roles in criminal organizations. You need a CriminalOrganization subsystem, certainly, to accommodate the needs of the Report Case History, Report Criminal, and Find Mob use cases. The first two use cases are part of the Event and Criminal subsystems, while Find Mob becomes part of the CriminalOrganization subsystem. You also need Encyclopedia and Media Report packages to hold information about these elements of the use cases. Finally, Explore requires a separate subsystem called Ad Hoc Query that offers a set of operations permitting users to explore the relationships in the other subsystems.

Thinking a bit more about the needs of case history reports and criminal record reports, you might create some additional packages for the multimedia objects such as fingerprint records, photos, DNA profiles, and other data elements of the commonplace book. These are perhaps a bit too detailed for the first pass. You might benefit from doing some class design before creating packages for these things, or at least making sure you iterate a few times before putting it all in the freezer.

You can also take a first crack at relating the packages, resulting in the package diagram in Figure 7-1.

The package diagram shows the overall structure of your system. Each package is a named file folder icon with the package name and the appropriate stereotype. You show dependencies between the packages with dashed, directed arrows. In Figure 7-1, for example, both the Ad Hoc Query subsystem and the Role package depend on the CriminalOrganization subsystem. The Role package depends on both the Criminal and the CriminalOrganization subsystems, and the Case History subsystem depends on the Role. The Commonplace Book subsystem depends on all the other subsystems except for Person; it also uses the Role package. Security does this as well, but I've hidden the arrows for clarity. Keeping the diagram from resembling a plate of pasta is always a problem; using straight lines helps, and hiding minor lines helps even more. The solid arrow with a white ar-

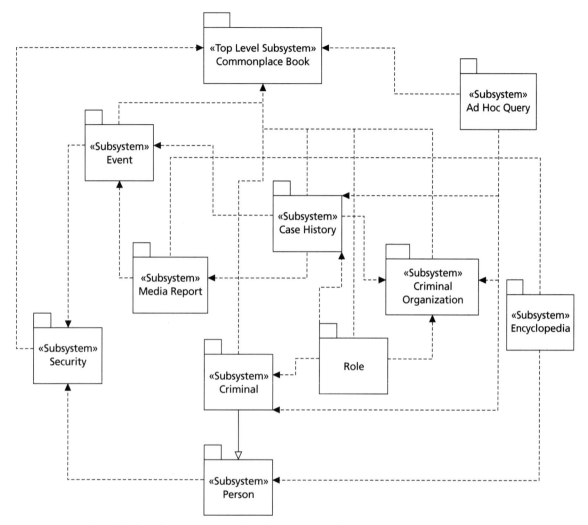

Figure 7-1   *The Initial Package Diagram for the Commonplace Book*

rowhead from Criminal to Person is a generalization, meaning the Criminal sub-system inherits from the Person subsystem (a criminal is a kind of person).

You could actually label all these as «Stub» until you're ready to push down the design, but in this example the intent is to complete the subsystem designs in the current design process step. If you tasked several people with designing the different pieces in separate design steps, you could stub the subsystems until the first complete design is ready.

As you progress in defining the details of the system, your packages acquire internal details such as use cases, classes, interfaces, and collaborations. By the end of your design effort, you should have a reasonably solid set of packages that are mostly independent of one another and that interact through well-defined, re-usable interfaces. Each package should break down into a set of class diagrams that you can use to document and direct the construction of the actual code for the system, including the database creation and manipulation code.

Again, while architectural design is different from database design, you will find your subsystems and packages do have direct effects on the underlying database architecture in the end. You do the database design within the structure you set as you design the classes with their attributes.

In many ways, this iterative architecture is similar to the way Holmes built his case against Moriarty:

> But the Professor was fenced round with safeguards so cunningly devised that, do what I would, it seemed impossible to get evidence which would convict in a court of law. You know my powers, my dear Watson, and yet at the end of three months I was forced to confess that I had at last met an antagonist who was my in-tellectual equal. My horror at his crimes was lost in my admiration at his skill. But at last he made a trip—only a little, little trip—but it was more than he could af-ford, when I was so close upon him. I had my chance, and, starting from that point, I have woven my net round him until now it is all ready to close. In three days—that is to say, on Monday next—matters will be ripe, and the Professor, with all the principal members of his gang, will be in the hands of the police.
>
> . . . Now, if I could have done this without the knowledge of Professor Moriarty, all would have been well. But he was too wily for that. He saw every step which I took to draw my toils round him. Again and again he strove to break away, but I as often headed him off. I tell you, my friend, that if a detailed account of that silent contest could be written, it would take its place as the most brilliant bit of thrust-and-parry work in the history of detection. Never have I risen to such a height, and never have I been so hard pressed by an opponent. He cut deep, and yet I just un-dercut him. This morning the last steps were taken, and three days only were wanted to complete the business. [FINA]

As always, that last 10% of the project was the hardest to complete.

Classes and Attributes

Returning to the class, now you need to define the structure that you will trans-form into your database schema design. Of course, there's more to it than that. Your database design is really a part of the larger design process that includes de-signing all the objects in your system, including both the in-memory ones and the persistent ones. You need to do some special things to the persistent ones. This section goes over certain aspects of this database-related customization but defers other things to the following sections, "Relationships" and "Object Constraints and Business Rules."

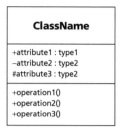

Figure 7-2   A Simple Class Symbol

The class diagram can contain a number of different things, ranging from classes to interfaces to packages and all the relationships between these things. The package diagram from the last section is really a very high level class diagram that only contains packages. Each of the subsystems usually has its own class diagram that describes the classes and interfaces that realize the subsystem. This section focuses on the classes and their attributes, leaving the operations and relationships to later sections.

The symbol for a class is a rectangle with up to three compartments, as Figure 7-2 shows. The top compartment contains the class name and properties, if any. The middle compartment contains a list of attributes and their properties. The lower compartment contains a list of operations and their properties. You can hide or display as much detail as you need. You usually hide most of the details when you import the class into another diagram, showing it only as a reference. You can also do it to display the class diagram as a high-level view of the class model for clarity, as the lists can get quite involved for large subsystems.

The class name is unique within the package. Again, a package represents a *name space,* a scope for the names of the package elements. You can have classes with the same name in different packages. To refer to an object in another package, you prefix the name to the package name in the format "package::class." The :: symbol is a scope resolution operator that attaches the name space name to the class. You can nest name spaces, so you can have multiple prefixes for the class name: package1::package1.1::package1.1.3::class, for example, means that package1.1.3 defines the class within the package1.1 package, which in turn nests within the package1 package.

The upper compartment contains more than just the class name. Classes that you intend to be persistent have a stereotype indicating that: «persistent». The persistent stereotype tells you that the system does not destroy the state of an instance when it destroys the instance. The «persistent» class converts later to the underlying implementation (relational table, object-relational type, or object-oriented persistent class, for example). Chapters 11 to 13 go into more detail on using component diagrams to represent these model elements in the implementation model of the system.

An *abstract class* is a class that has no instances. It exists primarily to represent a common abstraction that several subclasses share. The UML suggests that the class symbol show abstraction by italicizing the class name. You can also display the property below the class name in curly braces: {abstract}. Making a persistent class abstract has no relationship to data in the relational or object-relational database, unlike its effect on transient objects and OO databases. Because of the way you translate the OO data model into the schema, the relational databases do have data for the abstract class. This data represents the part of the concrete objects that comes from the abstract class, not an instance of the abstract class itself.

Figure 7-3 shows the Person class as a simple example of an abstract persistent class with various attributes and operations.

The second compartment in Figure 7-3 also illustrates the list of attributes, while the third compartment shows the operations on the class. The attributes, like the class name in the upper compartment, have various qualifiers that you can suppress at will: stereotype, visibility, data type, and constraints and properties. This is the syntax of an attribute expression:

```
stereotype visibility name : type-expression =
        initial-value { property-string }
```

In the case of Figure 7-3, you see visibility, name, and type-expression. There are three symbols for visibility, all taking their meaning from the C++ access qualifier concepts:

+ *Public* visibility, meaning that any other class may directly examine or
change the attribute's value

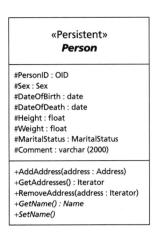

Figure 7-3   *The Person Persistent Class*

Protected visibility, meaning that only methods of the class or of a public or protected subclass can directly examine or change the attribute's value

- *Private* visibility, meaning that only methods of the class (but not of inheriting classes) can directly examine or change the attribute's value

The standard UML notation does not define any stereotypes for attributes. The later section on "Object Constraints and Business Rules" suggests some extensions for attribute tagged values.

The initial-value is the value that the system automatically gives to the attribute when you create an instance of the class. This translates directly into the DEFAULT value in an SQL CREATE TABLE statement, for example.

The abstract persistent Person class in Figure 7-3 has several protected attributes and several public operations. During the next round of design, you would add more public operations to get and set the various attributes as required. You might, for example, add a constructor that supplied most of the data on object instantiation, plus a series of get operations to give access to the values, plus a few set operations to set things like DateOfDeath that might change during the person object's life cycle.

You can adopt some simplifying conventions for get and set attributes. If you make an attribute public, your implementation standards can translate this into a protected data structure accompanied by a get and a set operation. You can add the {readonly} tagged value to the attribute to specify creation of just the get operation. This is the scheme that the CORBA IDL uses for class generation, for example.

> *Tip: Good OO design practice makes all attributes either protected or private, allowing direct access only within the class hierarchy or class, respectively. With persistent types, this is less clear, as relational and object-relational implementations may not be able to represent the visibility. Often these DBMSs only provide public attributes and hence no encapsulation. Still, you are designing the class both for the database and for the domain model of the system, so it's usually a good idea to encapsulate your attributes. Choosing between protected and private is a matter of deciding whether you want subclasses to be able to use the attributes. I've generally found protected visibility a better choice in reusable persistent classes, particularly for relational or object-relational target implementations. On the other hand, making attributes private uncouples the class from the subclasses, reducing the overall data coupling in your system.*

The data type expression is language dependent. When specifying persistent classes, I generally use SQL-92 or ODMG-2 ODL data types (see the later section on "Domain Constraints" for details). This lets you produce standard SQL or ODL while also providing enough information to produce other programming language declarations. Both SQL-92 and ODL have language bindings that translate SQL/ODL data types into programming language data types. Unfortunately, the SQL-92 standard has no bindings for OO programming languages, but you can add a standard binding to your development standards for this. You could also specify C++, Java, or other such data types, then provide the translation to SQL types. ODL has standard bindings for these languages.

> *Note: Data type expressions are a part of the more general concept of domain constraints. See the section on "Domain Constraints" in the later section on "Object Constraints and Business Rules" for more details on data type expressions and other domain constraints. You can use the UML type classifier to define your data types for use in other diagrams, as that section does.*

One question that always comes up is when to declare an attribute and when to declare an association. The UML equates attributes with associations: the attribute data type is the name of a class or type, thus showing an association to that class or type [Rational Software 1997a, p. 29]. For the general case of OO design, I recommend specifying attributes only for the primitive language data types (INTEGER, VARRAY(FLOAT), or char[1000], for example). To represent objects that are instances of classes, you should always use associations. Let your CASE tool or conversion algorithm do the work of creating the appropriate attributes in your tables, object types, or class declarations. For the special case of persistent class design, you should specify attributes that convert into the standard primitive data types of your target DBMS. In Figure 7-3, all the types are standard SQL except for Sex and MaritalStatus. These are simple enumerated types taking on a range of specific code values ('M' and 'F' for Sex, 'Single' and 'Married' for MaritalStatus, for example). Most DBMS products have some way of representing these types directly, though some don't. If you are unsure about the type, make it a class and an association rather than an attribute.

Certain attributes (and operations) in OO systems apply to the class as a whole rather than to each instance. For example, if you create a Criminal object, it has all the attributes from Person in Figure 7-3 as distinct values for that object. You can make an attribute a class-scope attribute by showing it underlined in the attribute list. A class-scope attribute has a single value for all objects of the class; that is, all objects share the same value, and all see any change to that value. Relational tables don't have class-scope attributes, but OR and OO types often do. In C++, the class-scope attribute becomes a variable with storage class static. A common use for this in domain factory classes is to represent a static SQL statement with which the factory queries a collection of objects. It has fewer applications in the persistent classes themselves.

Persistent class attributes have some needs that go beyond the standard UML properties. In particular, you need to be able to specify nullability, keys, uniqueness, and domain constraints. The later section "Object Constraints and Business Rules" discusses the special UML properties that correspond to these constraints, such as {OID}, {alternate OID}, and {nullable}.

The lower compartment of the class box contains the operations. You can specify operations with return data types as in Figure 7-3. The following section, "Operations," goes into detail on operations and their syntax in class diagrams as well as their use in data modeling.

With class and attribute information, your class notation lets you define a nearly complete data model. Extending classes with behavior through operations, methods, and interfaces gives you even more power to specify your database design. The class diagram, however, becomes much more interesting when you relate classes to one another with generalization and association relationships. The next two sections deal with these two topics.

Operations

Normally, you wouldn't think you'd need to specify operations if you are just building a data model. Don't believe it. With stored procedures and functions in relational databases and with methods in object-relational and object-oriented databases, you can almost guarantee the presence of operations on the database server.

Unless you resolve to avoid any coding of behavior in the database server, you should specify operations on your classes. You can decide later whether the methods that implement the operations translate to stored procedures or other such constructs. See Chapters 11 to 13 for more advice on converting operations to server-based methods for specific kinds of conceptual data models.

Operations, Methods, and Interfaces

An *operation* is a service that you can request of a class instance, or object. The operation requests the abstract interface of the service. A *method* is the concrete implementation of the interface, the executable code that you call when you request the service. An *interface* is a classifier that represents an abstract collection of operations. A class may have one or more interfaces, and interfaces can group operations of several different classes.

An operation has a name and a list of parameters, which are variables you can pass to the operation to affect its behavior or that the operation can pass back to return information. Operations appear in the third compartment of the class

box, optionally with their parameter list and various other characteristics. This is
the syntax for operations:

```
stereotype visibility name ( parameter-list ) : return-type-expression
{ property-string }
```

The three stereotypes in the UML for operations are «create», «destroy»,
and «signal». The first two stereotypes represent constructors and destructors,
operations that create and destroy instances of the class. You use these in the normal way to define the various methods for building objects and destroying them.
For data modeling, they have a different purpose, particularly when combined
with visibility. Visibility takes on the same values as for attributes (public, protected, or private). If you declare a constructor protected instead of public, it
means that other objects can't construct the object without some special qualities
giving them access. In the database, this means your applications can't add rows
to the object's table, or the equivalent in OR and OO systems. You can also use it
to model a situation where the database comes with one or several rows that applications can't add to under any circumstances.

The «signal» stereotype has a special use for data modeling; see the later
section on "Triggers" for details.

The parameter-list is a list of variables and data types in a language-specific
syntax, as is the return-type-expression. The combination of the name, parameter
list types, and return type constitutes the *signature* of the operation, which must
be unique within the scope of the class. If a second operation appears with the
same signature, the UML considers it a method—the implementation of the operation that the first appearance of the signature defined. You specify the parameter
list with this syntax:

```
kind name : type-expression = default-value
```

The kind is one of several possibilities describing the access of the operation
to the parameter value:

- *in:* The operation can read the value but cannot change it (pass by value).
- *out:* The operation can change the value but cannot read it or use it.
- *inout:* The operation can both read the value and change it (pass by
  reference).

The default-value is a value that the parameter takes on if you don't pass the
parameter when you call the operation.

You can mark an operation with the {query} property. Specifying an operation as {query} means that it has no side effects—that it does not change system state. If you transform the operation into persistent programming language
(stored procedure or function) program units, often this designation is useful in
the implementation of the unit. For example, Oracle lets you extend SQL expres-

sions with stored functions that have no side effects, but not with functions that may have side effects. In Figure 7-3, the GetAddresses operation is a query operation. You generally use the "Get" verb prefix to indicate queries that return attributes or related objects of the class. The "Set" prefix indicates a nonquery operation that updates the attributes or related objects.

> *Note: You can use a constraint (a formal Boolean expression that evaluates to true or false at the end of each transaction and that has no side effects) as the specification for a {query} operation. Any method that implements the operation must satisfy the constraint. For details on constraints, see the later section on "Complex Constraints."*

You can also give an operation the property {abstract}. Just as with class names in the top compartment of the class box, you can show this by italicizing the operation name. An abstract operation is one that has no corresponding method (implementation). C++ calls this a pure member function, for example. You use abstract operations in abstract classes to show interfaces for which subclasses provide an overriding implementation. Polymorphism and dynamic binding resolve the call to the appropriate subclass method at runtime.

In the Person class in Figure 7-3, the GetName class is an abstract query operation. Person, being an abstract class, needs to provide an interface that constructs a name object for the person. Subclasses of person will provide GetName methods that actually implement this service, but the Person operation is abstract and has no implementation. When you instantiate a Person object, you are really instantiating a Criminal or some other kind of person. Say you then request the GetName operation on what you perceive as an object of class Person, which is really a Criminal or some other subclass. The runtime system resolves this through dynamic binding to the method that implements GetName for the particular subclass. You might, for example, get the criminal's best-known alias embedded in the name: Salvatore "Lucky" Luciano, for example.

An interface is a collection of operations. Interfaces have a special role in UML diagrams. They are a kind of classifier, meaning that you can specify an interface anywhere you can specify a class. This abstraction permits you to define packages with interfaces that abstract the internal structure of the package as a set of operations. It also lets you use the same interface in different classes and packages. The Java language has its "implements" keyword, for example, which lets you include an interface in a class without requiring you to inherit it from its superclasses. As Java does not support multiple inheritance, this facility lets you mix in behavioral abstractions that many classes can share without complicating the inheritance model.

To specify an interface, you build a class box using the «interface» stereotype. Figure 7-4 shows the Person interface as opposed to the Person class. Notice

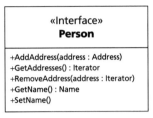

Figure 7-4   *The Person Interface*

there are no attributes, just a collection of operations. Also notice there are no italics; everything in an interface is abstract, so there is no need to distinguish the abstract elements.

You connect an interface to a package or class with a labeled line ending in a circle. The label is the name of the interface. This shorthand lets you add interfaces in a very compact way. It also lets you connect the classes or packages that use the interface by drawing a dashed connection from the using classifier to the interface. This means that the using classifier uses some or all of the interface. Figure 7-5 is a package diagram that shows the Person subsystem with its two interfaces, the Person interface and the Address interface. The Role subsystem uses the Person interface but not the Address interface.

There are really two kinds of interfaces: interfaces for packages and interfaces for classes. Class interfaces are small collections of operations that many classes use. The UML uses the example of the Comparable interface, which has a hash() operator and an isEqual() operator. You include this in any class that needs comparison operations instead of specifying the operations over and over again. Package interfaces, on the other hand, provide an abstraction for the package that lets you formalize the package interface for use and reuse by other packages. This permits you to rigorously construct subsystems that are highly reusable through careful interface development.

Where an operation turns into actual object behavior depends on how and where you implement the operation. You can implement the operation as application behavior, or you can do it as server behavior. These implementations have very different characteristics.

Application Behavior

Operations translate into application behavior by putting methods into classes that are part of the domain model for your application. *Application behavior* is thus behavior you associate with persistent objects that runs as part of the application.

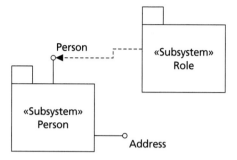

Figure 7-5 *Using the Person Interface*

Until recently, most persistent object behavior was application behavior, as DBMS products had no way to execute object behavior on the database server. You would write all your source code and compile it as part of the application, then retrieve the data and conduct the operations on it. Now you usually have the choice of performing services in either the application or the database. In the application, you can opt for a standard domain model consisting of the persistent classes and various helpers and aggregates (classes that aggregate instances of the persistent classes), or you can be more complex.

Such complex behavior takes its format from the way you build your object subsystems. For example, you can build classes using the multithreading support of modern compilers and operating systems, and you can make your operations multithreaded or multitasking. You can designate some operations as signals that respond to events and interrupts instead of being called by other objects. Multithreading lets you operate on objects in parallel in your application. It also means you need to build concurrency management into your objects, which makes them a bit more complicated than otherwise. This concurrency management is completely separate from the transaction management relating to database concurrency; it exists only to manage the transient objects.

When you create your conceptual schema, you ignore the application operations. It thus makes sense to extend the UML property persistence to operations: {persistence=transient} means that the operation is application behavior, while {persistence=persistent} means that the operation is server behavior. These are extended properties, not standard UML properties.

Database Server Behavior

Server behavior is behavior you associate with persistent objects that executes through the database server. Where it actually executes and how is completely up to the database server and its optimization. For example, say you have a DBMS with parallel processing capabilities, and you are running on a hardware setup with multiple CPUs available. The DBMS could run the operations in parallel without your application knowing the difference.

There are three basic kinds of server behavior that most DBMS products offer in one way or another: methods, stored procedures, and triggers. This means another UML extension—the {format} property, which takes one of three values: method, stored procedure, or trigger, with method being the default (consistent with standard UML). For example, you could specify that GetName in Figure 7-3 was a server operation implemented as a stored procedure by attaching the property {format=stored_procedure} to the operation in your class diagram.

> Note: This UML extension is very high level, as there are many options you can specify about implementation in most DBMS products. You should extend the UML properties as required by your needs. Just make sure you standardize the extensions as part of your development design standards so that everyone adding to the design is using the same extensions.

Methods

A method is the concrete implementation of the operation. In the database world, only object-relational and object-oriented databases have methods.

OODBMS products tend to view methods as application methods. Typically, you create the OO schema by coding classes with attributes and methods. The attribute structure goes into the database, while the methods remain as transient. When you query objects from the database, you instantiate transient objects by converting the stored data into transient data, then you call the transient operations on the transient data in the application. No behavior actually executes on the database server.

ORDBMS products let you define the methods as server extensions. Some ORDBMS products such as Oracle8 let you code the methods in the database programming language. In the case of Oracle8, that means PL/SQL (and according to Oracle Corporation marketing plans, Java). Others, such as DB2 UDB, let you integrate externally compiled methods written in "real" programming languages such as C or C++. Still others, such as Informix Dynamic Server, let you create extension modules that define methods for the classes as part of the module (NCS cartridges for Oracle8 and DataBlades for Informix).

RDBMS products don't have methods because tables don't have behavior and aren't types. If you use an RDBMS, you must define your methods as transient and execute them in the application, not on the server. However, you can fake it with stored procedures, as the following section, "Stored Procedures," describes.

There is no support from the ODBC or JDBC standards for method invocation.

If you are designing your class operations to be persistent methods, this restricts your options to just a few of the available DBMS products, mostly the ORDBMS products. A better strategy is to design your operations leaving the implementation open. This lets you design operations that can translate into different implementations should you need to support other databases.

Stored Procedures

A stored procedure is an operation that the system does not explicitly attach to a class. Compare this to a global function in C++, for example. Anything that can see the stored procedure can execute it by passing in the required arguments, with no need for having an object instance to qualify the call.

Stored procedures emerged from the attempts of Sybase, Oracle, Informix, and other RDBMS vendors to provide server behavior in their relational database products. Sybase defined a language, Transact-SQL, that it integrated with its server; Oracle did the same with PL/SQL. Oracle also made PL/SQL available as an application programming tool through its Developer/2000 product, letting you build libraries of PL/SQL that the application executes rather than the server.

The ANSI SQL-92 standard provides no support for stored procedures. ODBC and JDBC support invoking stored procedures through a special escape syntax [Jepson 1996; Signore, Creamer, and Stegman 1995]:

```
{? = CALL <procedure name>(<parameter list>)}
```

The question mark represents the value that the procedure returns, if any, and you can retrieve one or more result sets that the procedure creates using SQLFetch and its siblings. You can thus code the implementation of your operation as a stored procedure, then call it using the special syntax in the transient method you create in your object domain model.

This technique can be quite useful when your target DBMS is relational. Using the standard security mechanisms, you can essentially make your relational database invisible to applications except for a well-defined set of stored procedures. For example, you can create a CriminalOrganization table and not GRANT it to any users. No user but the table's owner can see it. You can then define insert, update, and delete stored procedures that perform those common operations on the criminal organization, granting execution privileges (no, not that kind of execution) on the procedures to the appropriate users. The applications then can call the stored procedures but can't perform the underlying operations on the table, effectively encapsulating the table data just as a class does its protected and private attributes.

Your UML design for this situation is a fairly standard design with protected attributes and well-defined interface methods for creation, removal, updating of attributes (Set operations), and queries (Get operations and more extensive «query» operations). Just specify the property {format=stored_procedure} and your design is complete.

Triggers

A trigger is an event handler. That is, it is executable code that executes when a certain event happens in the database server. The ANSI SQL-92 standard says nothing about triggers or the events that signal them. Most DBMS products do have triggers at this point in one form or another, but there is no standard format for them.

The most common set of triggers are before and after event triggers for the three standard relational data manipulation events: insert, update, and delete. That is, an event occurs at the following points in database processing:

- Before Insert
- After Insert
- Before Update
- After Update
- Before Delete
- After Delete

These row-oriented triggers perform extended business rule checking and other implementation functions. For example, one use is to implement referential integrity constraints (foreign key constraints) across databases through triggers. When you insert a row in a table in one database, for example, the Before Insert trigger checks to make sure the foreign key you've specified exists in a foreign key reference to a table in another database. You need this in multiple-database environments because the SQL integrity constraint mechanism requires all the tables to be in the same database, which isn't very helpful.

ORDBMS and OODBMS systems could presumably develop more complex trigger mechanisms. You can generalize triggers into rules, for example [Stonebraker and Brown 1999]. Not many mainstream systems yet give you much in the way of such things, though, as they can have a big impact on performance and reliability of the database engine.

Using UML, you can declare triggers by the use of the standard «signal» stereotype on the method. You might want to add a property with the name of the event that signals the operation. You could even go so far as to define standard interfaces with the appropriate event operations defined, then refer to the interface in your class diagram to show the presence of triggers. This can be complex, however, since you don't want each and every class to catch each and every event and fire an operation. You just want the events that need the server to do something when they happen. Unfortunately, if you include an interface, you must implement all the operations in the interface. I've found the best way to model triggers is to create individual trigger interfaces with one operation for a single event. You can at least standardize the signature and semantics that way.

> *Note: You can also specify many triggers through constraints such as pre- and postcondition constraints on operations or classes. Constraints must have no side effects, so you can't use them for triggers that update, insert, or delete from the database, just validation constraints that cause the transaction to fail if certain integrity conditions aren't met.*

Now you've seen how UML lets you model classes, attributes, and operations in the class box. The next step is modeling the connections between class boxes.

Relationships

A class *relationship* is a connection between classes that relates one class to other classes (or back to itself). For data modeling, the UML has two kinds of relationship: generalization and association.

Inheritance and Generalization

A *generalization* relationship is a "taxonomic relationship between a more general element and a more specific element. The more specific element is fully consistent with the more general element and contains additional information. An instance of the more specific element may be used where the more general element is allowed" [Rational Software 1997b, p. 152]. Generalization relationships between classes define the inheritance hierarchy, the graph showing which classes inherit the elements of what other classes.

Chapter 6 described an example of an inheritance hierarchy surrounding the concept of identification in the section "Semantic Relationships: Subtyping and Aggregation." A brief recap: an Identification is an abstract concept that breaks down into ExpiringId, LawEnforcementID, SocialSecurityCard, and BirthCertificate. ExpiringID breaks down into several classes as well: DriverLicense, Passport, and NationalID. Recasting this example in terms of the

UML generalization relationship language: DriverLicense, Passport, and NationalID are more specific than ExpiringID, which is more specific than the abstract Identification class. Each of these three elements is fully consistent with ExpiringID and contains more information (license number, issuing office, and issuing country, for example). You can use a passport anywhere you can use an expiring identification (or the even more general identification). Figure 7-6 shows the UML class diagram for the Identification class hierarchy.

The arrows with white arrowheads are generalization relationships. The arrow points to the more general class, variously known as the *superclass* or the *base class*. The arrow comes from the more specialized class, variously known as the *subclass* or the *derived class*. A *leaf class* is a class with nothing more specialized (no incoming generalization relationship). A *root class* is a class with nothing more general (no outgoing generalization relationship).

Superclasses with several subclasses, such as Identification or ExpiringID, may have a named discriminator in the UML. The discriminator becomes an attribute of the superclass that identifies the subclass, although you don't specify the attribute in the list of attributes, just as the label for the generalization. For example, the ExpiringID has an attribute, ExpiringIDType, which has three possible values: DriverLicense, Passport, or NationalID. Since the ExpiringID class is abstract, the attribute cannot be null; the object instance must always be one of the three subclasses.

Inheritance and generalization are the most difficult and complex concepts in OO design. The following discussion gives you an overview of the concepts and issues without going into the great detail you would need to become an expert in using generalization in OO design. Instead, it touches on the basic concepts from the data modeling perspective. Please consult other books on OO design for a more complete discussion [Booch 1994; Jacobson et al. 1992; Rumbaugh et al. 1992].

Generalization

The human mind has tried to make sense of the world with generalization at least since Aristotle and Plato, and probably before. Perhaps the pyramids, or cuneiform and hieroglyphic writing, represent even older abstraction and generalization. The human mind makes great use of its ability to abstract the common structure and behavior of a set of different things into a more general class of things.

For example, in Figure 7-6, the various kinds of identification that share an expiring date combine into an abstract class, ExpiringID, which then contains the expiring date. That abstraction, together with nonexpiring identification classes, generalizes into the abstract concept of identification. That's *generalization* to the abstract. When you instantiate a passport or a driver's license, that subclass object

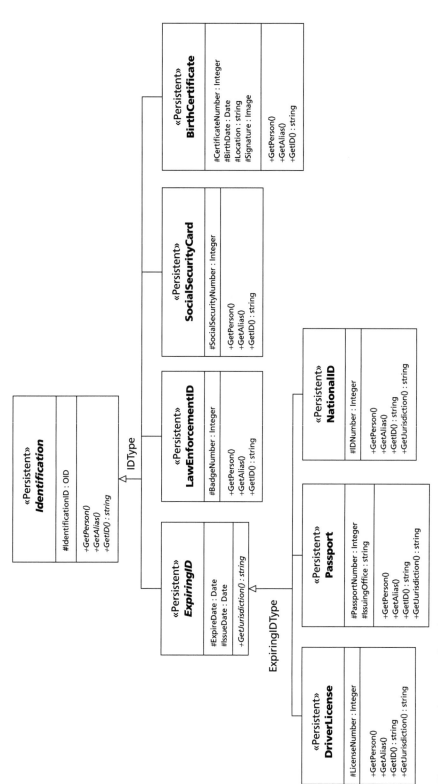

Figure 7-6 *The UML Identification Class Diagram*

inherits the expiring date attribute from its superclass, ExpiringID. That's *inheritance* from the abstraction.

Going in the other direction—*specialization*—the subclass extends or restricts the superclass. Extending the superclass means adding attributes, operations, or associations to those present in the superclass and inherited by the subclass. Restricting the superclass means overriding the behavior of the superclass with polymorphic or virtual operations.

Polymorphism

Polymorphism is the ability of the language to use the same name for different operations. Using C++ terminology, there are two basic kinds of polymorphism. *Overloading* is the ability to provide operations with the same name but different signatures (parameter types differ, although the name may be the same). *Overriding* is the ability to define, in a subclass, an operation which restricts or changes the behavior but has the same signature.

Overloading provides several different opportunities for the creative designer to simplify (or complicate) programming. For example, you can use overloading to provide a "single" operation that you can apply to many different kinds of objects. In reality, of course, you must create many different overloaded operations; the programmer who uses them doesn't need to worry about that, however. Another example is to overload the name to provide slightly different behaviors depending on different types of input.

Overriding is a key feature in most OO programming languages. Those languages all support *late* or *dynamic binding,* the ability of the runtime system to determine which method to execute depending on the type of an object. Figure 7-6 has an extended example of overriding. The abstract class Identification has three operations: GetPerson, GetAlias, and GetID. These are themselves abstract operations (an interface) with no method implementations. The ExpiringID subclass, also an abstract class, does not define any implementations, but all the other concrete classes override the three operations to provide specific implementations. Consider a person who has several identification documents. From the person's perspective, this is a set of Identification objects, not objects of the individual types (Passport, BirthCertificate, and so on). When you instantiate a Passport, for example, and request the ID using GetID from the object (as an Identification object), the runtime system resolves the call to Identification::GetID() as a call to Passport::GetID() by late binding. The method that implements the operation looks up the passport number attribute and converts it to a string, then returns it. This behavior restricts the abstract behavior of the superclasses.

Warning: Overloading and overriding give you the ability to change the behavior of a subclass dramatically. As with all homonyms, if the

meaning is sufficiently different, you will get nothing but confusion.
Overloaded and overridden operations should have substantially
similar semantics in their different classes.

What is the relevance of overloading and overriding to data modeling? If you're using an OODBMS or ORDBMS as your target implementation, they both support (more or less) the concepts of polymorphism. Even some relational databases (Oracle7 and Oracle8) support overloading: using the Ada model, PL/SQL packages let you have multiple program units with the same name and different signatures.

You can go quite far with persistent versions of operations. Since you are using your class model as a proxy for both your transient and your persistent models, keeping clear on overloading and overriding operations is essential to keeping things straight between your in-memory objects and your persistent database objects.

Abstract and Concrete Classes and Inheritance

Another recap: remember that an abstract class is one that has no instances, while a concrete class is one that can have instances. An interface is an abstract class that has no attributes and that contains only abstract operations. The more general case of the abstract class may have both.

Abstract classes are meaningless without generalization relationships. What good, for example, would the Identification class be as an abstract class without its subclasses? Since you can't instantiate an object of the class, the only reason for its existence is to set up the common properties of its concrete subclasses for inheritance when you instantiate their objects.

Abstract classes represent the opportunity to express intermediate concepts in your semantic hierarchy, such as ExpiringID. You create abstract classes when you see common properties that make sense as a cohesive cluster of behavior. Sometimes this corresponds to an easily understood object, and sometimes it doesn't. If it doesn't, check and double-check your design to make sure you're not introducing too much abstraction. Simpler is better, and the shallower you keep your inheritance hierarchy the better.

Note: An interface is an abstract class, but not all abstract classes are
interfaces. While you can't have methods implementing operations
in an interface, you can in an abstract class that is not an interface.
This lets you share common behavior in concrete subclasses.

What is the place of abstract classes in a data model? The abstract class gives you a place to put attributes and operations that you would otherwise spread around many classes. You are reducing redundancy by centralizing the implementation of these objects. When the design translates into the database schema, the lower redundancy will usually result in a more flexible schema. You may see more complexity in relational schemas because of the extra tables, but you will see fewer normalization problems and easier table management and maintenance.

Multiple Inheritance

Classes can have more than one more general parent superclass. If this is part of your design, you are using multiple inheritance. The world is full of such things, in reality, because the human mind imposes classification on the world, not vice versa. Humans are, if nothing else, inconsistent and complex, and we can find endless ways to classify things. Our thinking tends to overlap—good for thought, lousy for software system design.

A common reason for using multiple inheritance is the presence of more than one dimension to the data. If you model dimensions using inheritance trees, you wind up with multiple subtrees from a common superclass. As you break things down, you begin to see objects that combine the dimensions in meaningful ways, so you use multiple inheritance to bring the trees together.

One aspect of the commonplace book is the tracking of stolen property.

"The goose, Mr. Holmes! The goose, sir!" he gasped.

"Eh! What of it, then? Has it returned to life, and flapped off through the kitchen window?" Holmes twisted himself round upon the sofa to get a fairer view of the man's excited face.

"See here, sir! See what my wife found in its crop!" He held out his hand, and displayed upon the centre of the palm a brilliantly scintillating blue stone, rather smaller than a bean in size, but of such purity and radiance that it twinkled like an electric point in the dark hollow of his hand.

Sherlock Holmes sat up with a whistle. "By Jove, Peterson," said he, "this is treasure trove indeed! I suppose you know what you have got?"

"A diamond, sir? A precious stone. It cuts into glass as though it were putty."

"It's more than a precious stone. It's *the* precious stone."

"Not the Countess of Morcar's blue carbuncle!" I ejaculated.

"Precisely so. I ought to know its size and shape, seeing that I have read the advertisement about it in *The Times* every day lately. It is absolutely unique, and its value can only be conjectured, but the reward offered of £1000 is certainly not within a twentieth part of the market price."

. . . When the commissionaire had gone, Holmes took up the stone and held it against the light. "It's a bonny thing," said he. "Just see how it glints and sparkles. Of course it is a nucleus and focus of crime. Every good stone is. They are the devil's pet baits. In the larger and older jewels every facet may stand for a bloody deed. This stone is not yet twenty years old. It was found in the banks of the Amoy River in southern China, and is remarkable in having every characteristic of the carbuncle, save that it is blue in shade, instead of ruby red. In spite of its youth, it has already a sinister history. There have been two murders, a vitriol-throwing, a suicide, and several robberies brought about for the sake of this forty-grain weight of crystallized charcoal. Who would think that so pretty a toy would be a purveyor to the gallows and the prison? I'll lock it up in my strong box now and drop a line to the Countess to say that we have it." [BLUE]

In tracking these objects, there are two dimensions to consider: the kind of property involved and the insurance status of the property. Figure 7-7 shows an inheritance structure starting with the property. One branch of the hierarchy divides property into types by their nature: collectibles, jewelry, cash, security, personal, or "other" (to make the classification complete). The other branch of the hierarchy divides property into uninsured, privately insured, or publicly insured depending on the source of the theft insurance. These are all abstract classes.

The tricky part of this hierarchy comes when you need to create an actual object: you must combine the two subtrees into joint subclasses, such as Uninsured Jewelry or Publicly Insured Securities. In this case, you might practically have to define a subclass for the Cartesian product (all possible combinations of the abstract classes).

> Note: I am not advocating this style of design. If anything, you should avoid this kind of design like the plague. There are ways around it, depending on your needs. The primary justification for this sort of design is to override operations in, and add structure to, the various dimensions. If you don't have much need to extend or restrict operations and structure, you shouldn't even consider the dimensional hierarchy approach; just use enumerated data types for the dimensions. In OR and OO products, you have many different options for representing dimensions. You should try to limit your inheritance to just what you need rather than going overboard with semantic distinctions that are pragmatically the same.

This form of multiple inheritance exhibits the infamous diamond shape, where the superclasses eventually merge in a single parent. This structure results in some hard problems in programming language design. If you call an operation, and that operation exists in both immediate superclasses and in the shared parent, which actual method executes? C++ forces you to specify the exact operation through a scope operator identifying the class owner, which increases your coupling. Worse, because of its structural logic, C++ gives you two copies of the shared parent, StolenProperty. You have to declare the intermediate classes virtual base classes in C++ to tell the compiler to share the parent. This has the result of forcing you to modify several classes if you want to add a class using multiple inheritance, again increasing coupling.

Think about the structure translated into persistent structures. You have a StolenProperty table, a table for each of the property types, and a table for each of

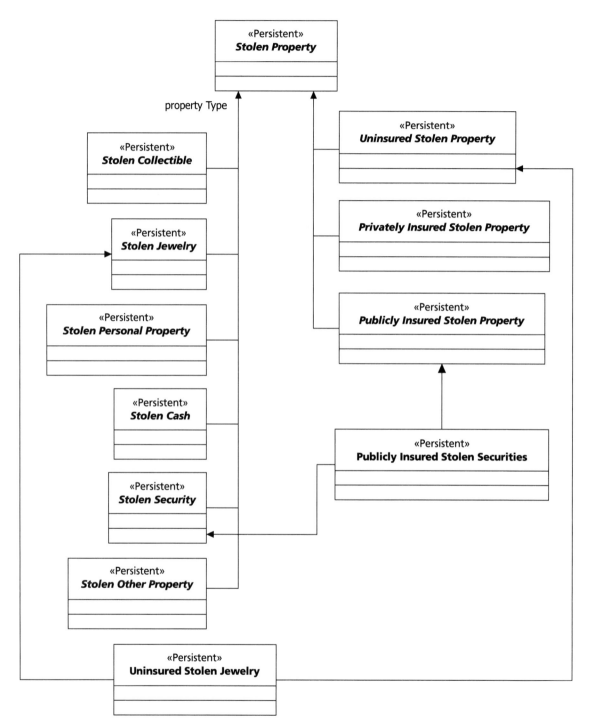

Figure 7-7   *Dimensional Multiple Inheritance of Stolen Property*

the insurance types. It seems natural to add an InsuredStolenJewelry table if you need to represent attributes or operations that such an account has that its two parents do not. The object ID for stolen property flows through these tables representing the generalization relationships. A row in InsuredStolenJewelry has a one-to-one relationship with rows in InsuredStolenProperty and StolenJewelry. This represents the fact that an InsuredStolenJewelry object is also an InsuredStolenProperty and a StolenJewelry object.

If you then reverse-engineer this back into a UML diagram, your natural choice would be to use associations, not generalization, making the joint table a relationship rather than an entity. That is, instead of inheriting operations and structure, you refer to InsuredStolenJewelry as an association between StolenJewelry and InsuredStolenProperty, not as a subclass of both of them. This is one workaround for this kind of multiple inheritance—factoring the dimensions into separate classes and using associations to relate them [Blaha and Premerlani 1998, p. 60].

Dimensional multiple inheritance is not the only kind there is. A different reason for using it is to combine two unrelated classes (that is, classes with no common parent). In most cases, this reflects the mix-in approach: you are mixing in behavior or structure that the subclass needs. For example, you may want at some point to treat fingerprints as identification, but the Fingerprint class is a kind of image. Figure 7-8 shows what this looks like as multiple inheritance.

What this design does is to integrate the operations and structure from the Identification class into the Fingerprint class by subclassing both using multiple inheritance. The resulting FingerprintIdentification class acts as both a fingerprint record (with image) and as a kind of nonexpiring identification.

Note: Again, there are better ways to do this. Mix-in inheritance is better done through the use of interfaces. You create the interface you need for any kind of identification, then include it in the Fingerprint class or a subclass. See the next section, on "Subtypes: Type versus Class versus Interface," for a look at this example.

Multiple inheritance lets you say that a thing is a kind of several other things. To the extent that this reflects the true meaning of the thing, that's fine. Unfortunately, what you're doing when you subclass two or more classes is exponentially increasing the coupling of the system through inheritance. Inheritance coupling isn't all bad. For any given class, your shared attributes, operations, and associations inherited from a superclass make perfect sense from the perspective of the object. But as you increase the number of superclasses, you increase the interdependence of more and more parts of the system.

When you then make a change to a part of the system, that change affects all its subclasses in some way. At the very least, you need to retest them. In a data model with persistent classes, that change is by definition persistent: you're

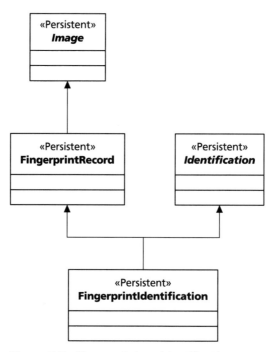

Figure 7-8   *Fingerprints as Identification*
Using Mix-in Multiple Inheritance

changing the database schema. Migrating schemas under these circumstances is, if anything, more difficult than maintaining spaghetti code with meatball objects floating in it. The more interconnections you have, the more difficult maintenance and extension becomes. So, it's in your best interest to use multiple inheritance—and single inheritance, for that matter—with great restraint.

The double-edged sword of multiple inheritance exists for one reason: to model objects that you want to use as a subtype of two or more different types. This is not as simple as it might appear.

Subtypes: Type versus Class versus Interface

Even the UML definition of generalization embeds the concept of subtype: "An instance of the more specific element may be used where the more general element is allowed." In a strongly typed system, the behavior of an object depends on its type, and you can't call operations or access attributes in contexts that require objects of a different type. *Subtyping* lets you extend the concept of "the same type" to a hierarchy of related objects rather than just to the objects of a single class.

Computer scientists carefully distinguish the notions of type and subtype from the concept of inheritance. Programming language designers are less careful for the most part, though some OO languages do make the distinction. Languages such as Smalltalk have no typing at all, just inheritance. In Smalltalk, for example, you can send a message to any object that provides the method with the signature your message specifies.

The rationale for strong typing is that this kind of flexibility leads inevitably to defects, for at least three reasons. You can accidentally set up your system at runtime to call a method on an object that doesn't exist, yielding an exception (falling off the top of the inheritance hierarchy). You can call a method that does something entirely unrelated to what you intended. You can pass objects that differ enough in format to yield operating system or runtime system errors such as divide-by-zero or access violations.

C++ combines subtyping and inheritance into a single structure, the inheritance hierarchy. A subclass is a subtype in C++. You can use a C++ subclass object anywhere you can use one of its parents. This in turn provides the rationale for multiple inheritance. Since strong typing prevents you from using an object that doesn't inherit from the designated superclass, you must use multiple inheritance to inherit that superclass. Otherwise, you have to turn off strong typing by using void pointers or something similar.

The interface provides an alternative to multiple inheritance through introduction of a completely different subtype relationship. In systems that support interfaces as types, you can use an object that supports an interface anywhere you can use the interface. Instead of declaring variables with the class type, you use interface types. This then permits you to refer to the interface operations on any object that provides those methods. It's still strong typing, but you get much of the flexibility of a weakly typed system such as Smalltalk without the complexity and strong coupling of multiple inheritance. The Java programming language supports this kind of typing. The downside to interfaces is that you can't really use them to inherit code, just the interface specification. You must implement all the operations in the interface with appropriate methods when you apply it to a class.

Interfaces support a special UML relationship: the "realizes" relationship. This is a kind of generalization relationship that represents not inheritance, but type *realization*. That is, when you associate an interface with a class, you are saying that the class realizes or implements the interface. The class can thus act as a subtype of the interface. You can instantiate objects of the class, then assign them to variables typed with the interface and use them through that interface. This is similar to what you do with superclasses, but you have access only to the interface, not to all the operations on the subclass.

Interface realization permits you to use overriding and late binding outside the class hierarchy, freeing you from the artificial constraints imposed by inheritance in a tree structure. For example, instead of instantiating the different Identification subclasses and putting them into a container typed with the Identification class, you can type the container as the Identification interface. This gives you the best of both worlds. You still have strong typing and type safety, but you can access an object through multiple mixed-in interfaces. Multiple inheritance gives you this ability as well but with a much greater degree of system coupling between classes, never a good idea.

Figure 7-9 shows the Identification hierarchy redone using interfaces. The diagram is simpler, and you have the additional flexibility of being able to use the Identification interface in other classes beyond the Identification hierarchy. Consider again the fingerprint identification example from the earlier section on "Multiple Inheritance." Just adding the Identification interface to Fingerprint, then building the appropriate methods to realize the three interface operations, lets you extend FingerprintRecord and use it wherever you use an Identification interface.

Figure 7-9 also shows the two forms of the realization relationship. The dashed arrow with the white arrowhead is a formal realizes relationship, showing the connection of Identification to BirthCertificate. The other classes, to save space, show the realizes relationship as a small, labeled circle connected to the class. The label is the interface name.

Figure 7-9 is less complex, but you can easily see why interfaces are not the preferred way of doing every kind of subtyping. Although inheriting the GetExpireDate abstract operation is logically the same as inheriting the ExpireDate attribute, practically the latter makes more sense. This is especially true in a data model destined for implementation in a DBMS logical schema. As a rule, if you have meaningful attributes as common properties, you should use a generalization; if you have only operations, you should use interfaces. Identification meets this test (ignoring the object identifier), while ExpiringID does not. The FingerprintRecord class is the best example of good interface realization. If you can use the phrase "is used as," as in "a fingerprint record is used as identification," you are looking at interface realization. If you use the phrase "is a," as in "a passport is an expiring ID," that's generalization.

Finally, Figure 7-9 also shows a feature of interfaces: interface inheritance. The ExpiringID interface inherits the Identification interface, and you can use an object with an ExpiringID interface anywhere you use an Identification interface.

There is a third kind of type-related concept in programming languages: genericity. Languages that support templates (C++) or generics (Ada, Eiffel) give you the ability to create multiple versions of an implementation of a class or function, each one parameterized with a series of types and/or objects. When you instantiate an object typed with the generic class, you supply appropriate types and objects as parameter arguments. All the operations and attributes take on the appropriate types, and you can use the object in a strongly typed system. Classic

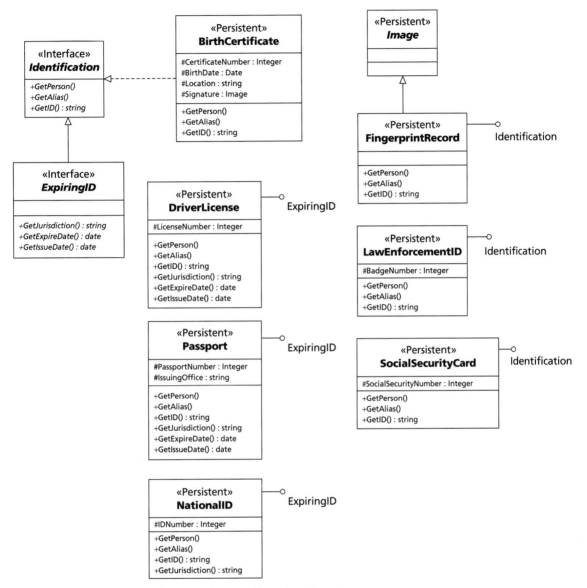

Figure 7-9 *The Identification Interface and Interface Realization*

uses for generics are basic data structures such as stacks and trees and generic algorithms such as sorts. You parameterize the kind of objects the aggregate structures contain, for example.

Data modeling can make good use of typing. Most database programming languages are strongly typed, though some of them are curious in that regard. For example, SQL does not regard a table definition as a type. When you create a named table, you are creating an aggregate object (Date's "relvar" or relational variable), not a type you can use to specify the type of an attribute somewhere. Cursors provide a generic way to access these objects. You can look at most current relational DBMS CASE tools for the specific consequence for data modeling. When you define the schema, you create an entity. When you forward-engineer that schema, that entity becomes a table in the database. If you want to define multiple tables with the same structure, you have to copy the existing entity or create a new one that looks identical. These things don't behave as types. The later section on "Domain Constraints" discusses some of these attribute type issues in more detail.

ORDBMS products extend the typing system with user-defined types (UDTs in the jargon of the vendors and the SQL3 standard). You define the type, then instantiate tables from it. You can access all the objects of a given type with specific variations on the SELECT statement, or you can access just those in a single table instance [Stonebraker and Brown 1999]. This opens up a world of interesting storage options by freeing up the storage of the rows/objects from their type definition. In the RDBMS, you need to define the physical model for the entire set of objects of the entity. In the ORDBMS, you can store multiple tables of the same type in totally different locations. ORACLE8's table partitioning scheme lets you automate the process without introducing instance logical location issues. The table is one table stored in multiple locations defined by the data, not multiple tables of the same type, though you can do that too.

Most OODBMS products adopted the C++ model (Gemstone being the early exception with its Smalltalk format). For better or worse, this has meant the integration of typing and inheritance in OODBMS schemas. One difference with the OODBMS products is that you create objects of the type and store them in logical (not physical) containers.

Not one of these products, as far as I am aware, supports interfaces or generics directly. Interfaces are useful in the data model as a way of expressing the realization relationship, but the translation to the logical and physical models requires quite a bit of work. Generics or templates simply don't exist in the database world.

While generalization in all its variety is a powerful data modeling tool, it pales in the light of the other major type of relationship: the association.

Associations, Containment, and Visibility

An *association* relationship is the "semantic relationship between two or more classifiers that involves connections among their instances" [Rational Software

1997b, p. 149]. In other words, associations show how an object of a class relates to other objects. The network of associations defines the *containment hierarchy,* a graph showing which kinds of objects contain what other kinds of objects. It also defines the *visibility hierarchy,* a graph showing which kinds of objects can see and use what other kinds of objects.

Containment is important because object ownership is a critical business rule. Ownership affects where you create objects, what happens when you delete objects, and how you store objects in all the different kinds of DBMSs. The key choice you make when you create an association is to decide whether the association represents a reference to an independent object or an ownership link.

Visibility is important because encapsulation is important. In an OO design, you want to limit the visibility of an object as much as possible. Limiting visibility through encapsulation is the best way to reduce coupling in your system, which leads to much more maintainable and robust software. In the database, visibility (and encapsulation) has always been a problem. With the newer ORDBMS and OODBMS products, you can increasingly control visibility; with most RDBMS products, your ability to control visibility is at best moderate.

Before getting into details, here is some notation. Figure 7-10 shows the basic association notation from the UML. There are two kinds of association: binary and other. The relationship between Person and Address, for example, is a *binary association,* an association between two classes. The association "influences" between CriminalOrganization and itself is a *recursive binary association.* The association "plays" between CriminalOrganization, Role, and Person is a *ternary association* (three classes related to one another rather than two). The binary association is a line connecting two classes, while the ternary and higher association is a series of lines connecting the various classes through a central diamond representing the association. You can have as many participants in an association as you need, though (as Chapter 6 mentioned for ER diagrams) there are very few realistic associations beyond ternary. The exception is in data warehouse star schemas, which invert the usual design into a massive association between a series of dimensional objects, with the central fact object being a multidimensional association.

Association names are generally verb phrases, just like ER relationship names. You will usually have quite a few associations that you can't name more specifically than "has." Just leave these names off and assume that a nameless association means that one class "has" instances of another class.

As with ER diagrams, each side of the association is a *role,* the part played by the class in the relationship. Each role has an optional name, a multiplicity, and an optional navigability. You can optionally make the relationship an aggregation, showing ownership, and you can include a qualifier to show multiple relationships.

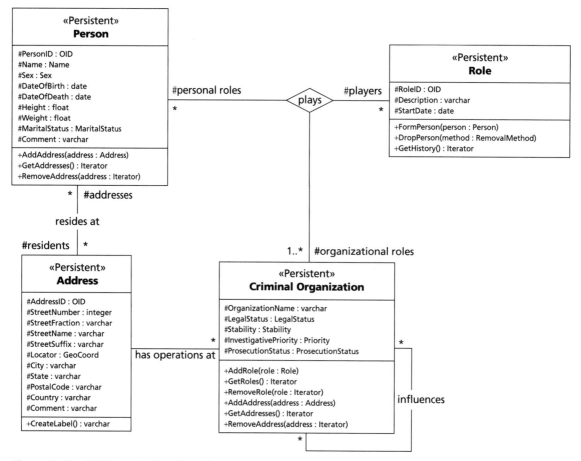

Figure 7-10   *UML Association Notation*

Roles and Role Names

A role is one end of the association. A binary association thus has two roles, a ternary one three roles, and so on. You can name a role to clarify the nature of the
association, though you don't have to do so. In Figure 7-10, for example, you see
role names on the binary association between Person and Address and on the ternary association between Role, CriminalOrganization, and Person.

Unlike roles in ER diagrams, which generally are verb phrases, most roles in
UML are noun phrases corresponding to the subjects and objects of the fact that
the association represents. For example, from the perspective of a Person, a person resides at a set of addresses. From the perspective of the address, a set of residents resides at the address. The verb phrase is the name of the association, while
the subject and object noun phrases are the roles.

Role names translate directly into variable names in the class implementation. If you're having trouble thinking what to call the role, think about the name you will give to the attribute or method that implements the role in the class. For example, in the Person class, you have a series of methods for manipulating addresses. GetAddresses obtains an iterator to the collection of addresses for a person. AddAddress adds an address to the set of addresses, while RemoveAddress gets rid of one identified by an iterator. Thus, "addresses" represents the name you call the set of addresses. It will usually become the name of the internal variable that represents the set (a C++ STL set<> instance, for example, or an ODL relationship set<>).

> *Note: Figure 7-10 does not show similar methods on Address. Why? The requirements do not call for accessing people through their addresses, though that's a perfectly reasonable thing to do. The class itself may need to iterate over the set of residents, but users of the class do not. Thus you have a role name but no corresponding operations. The lesson here is that operations and roles are distinct: operations package roles, they don't implement them. This distinction is fundamental to the encapsulation of the associations within the class and limiting visibility to just what you need.*

You can also specify a visibility for the role (public, protected, or private, with the same symbols as for attributes and operations). This lets you complete the specification of the association variable in your implementation for OO systems that support access control in some way.

You should understand, however, that not all relationships are equally meaningful. For example, the Person role in the ternary relationship in Figure 7-10 is quite hard to name. I chose "players" for this role name. The objects involved are the people and organizations in which they play the role, a very abstract concept. From the perspective of the role, there is very little meaning. It does support queries such as "Give me the names and addresses of all the bosses in criminal organizations in London." The person and the organization are critical, while the role simply qualifies the relationship.

Role names are very useful in data modeling because they translate into the names the logical schema gives to columns, collections, or other logical artifacts that represent the associations when you construct the schema. Choosing a meaningful role name results in meaningful schemas.

Multiplicities and Ordering

The *multiplicity* is a property of the role that represents a business rule or constraint on the number of objects that participate in the association from the perspective of the role. Recall from Chapter 6 that ER diagramming sees multiplicity as one-to-one, one-to-many, or many-to-many qualifiers on the association. The "one" and the "many" are the role multiplicities. UML takes this a bit further than ER models.

Each role multiplicity consists of a specification of integer values, usually a range of such values. Here are some alternatives:

- *0..*:* Zero or more objects
- *0..1:* No more than one optional object
- *1..*:* At least one object
- *1:* Exactly one object
- **:* Zero or more objects
- *2..6:* At least two but no more than six objects
- *1, 3, 5-7:* At least one object but possibly three, five, six, or seven objects

The asterisk "*" represents an unlimited upper bound. The range is inclusive; that is, the range includes the values separated by the ".." range indicator. The multiplicities "*" and "1" are the most common, with "1..*" for not-optional to-many and "0..1" for optional to-one following closely behind.

You can also specify that objects associated with a multiplicity greater than one (to-many) are in some order using the {ordered} property on the role. This qualification means you have to use some kind of ordered representation in the logical schema. In the relational schema, this translates into an ordering attribute in the appropriate table. In the OR and OO schemas, it translates into the use of an ordered collection relationship, such as a vector, a list, a stack, or a queue, for example. If it were unordered, it might be a set or a bag.

Multiplicity is critical in the data model because it translates directly into the structure of the foreign key business constraints in the logical schema (see Chapter 6 for details in the ER diagram context). If you specify a 0..* role, this translates into a to-many null foreign key attribute in a relational database, for example, or to a relationship set<> with optional membership in ODL. Getting the multiplicities right in the data model lets you create the right schemas; getting them wrong definitely means a wrong schema.

Navigability and Symmetric Visibility

The navigability property of the role lets you specify the visibility relationships between the classes. Navigability is the ability to navigate to the class to which the role attaches from the other classes in the association. The association thus becomes a directed association. By default, the roles in a UML class diagram are undirected, meaning you have full navigational access to each class participating in the association. Adding an arrowhead to the association turns this off, specifying navigation in only that direction.

This introduces *asymmetric* visibility, the ability of one class in a relationship to see the others without having the others being able to reciprocate. Judicious use of navigability can reduce the coupling in the data model to just that necessary to satisfy the requirements. It does, however, impose constraints on your ability to reuse the model, as you are explicitly saying that you can't see certain things even if it makes sense in a new situation. Used sparingly, navigability can improve your design; used to excess, you can wind up with something very hard to reuse.

In data modeling, navigability gives you the ability to have one-way relationships. Translating this into the conceptual schema, navigability can be very useful for OR and OO schemas that support unidirectional relationships, as most do. That is, you create a relationship that exists in one class, but the other class can't see the related objects in the first class. In the ODL, this corresponds to a relationship that has no inverse traversal path, for example.

Aggregation, Composition, and Ownership

Aggregation is a part-whole relationship between two classes. The UML lets you specify two kinds of aggregation: weak or shared aggregation and strong or composite aggregation. *Shared aggregation* lets you model a part-whole relationship in which one object owns another object, but yet other objects can own that object as well. *Composition* lets you model the part-whole relationship where one object exclusively owns the other object.

> Note: Composition aggregation corresponds directly to the ER modeling concept of the weak relationship, just to be thoroughly confusing about the terminology.

The UML represents aggregation as a diamond shape at the end of the association line that terminates in the owner class. A shared aggregation is a hollow diamond, while the composite aggregation role is a black-filled diamond. Figure 7-11 shows two aggregation relationships. The first one describes the shared aggregation relationship between a photographic image and a person. The second shows the composite aggregation role between people and identification.

The shared aggregation describes the situation in which a thing aggregates some other thing. In this case, a photo aggregates a set of people. But also, any given person may appear in more than one photo. The "*" multiplicities make this explicit. Given the semantics, there is no ownership: the photo does not own the person, and the person doesn't disappear (at least, from the database) when you delete the photo.

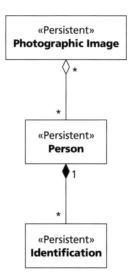

Figure 7-11   UML Aggregations

The composite aggregation, on the other hand, is quite explicit about ownership. You identify a person by one or more identification documents, and the person owns those documents. If the person disappears, the documents disappear. You thus identify the identification documents by their relationship to the person.

Only one role in an association can have an aggregation marker. By definition, only one object can "own" the other one. An *n*-ary association with more than two associated classes cannot have any aggregation [Rational Software 1997b, p. 27]. A composite aggregation, by definition, must have a multiplicity of 1, 1..1, or 0..1 on the role corresponding to the aggregate owner.

Composite aggregation is critical to data modeling because it represents the weak relationship. Translated into the conceptual schema of a relational or object-relational database, a composite aggregate association becomes a foreign key that is part of the primary key of the dependent object (in this case, the identification document). Even in object-oriented databases, there is an implication of cascading deletes: should you delete the aggregation, all the aggregated parts disappear as well. This in turn translates into a cascaded delete specification or trigger on the table in the conceptual schema.

Qualified Association

The *qualified association* is an association with a *qualifier:* "an attribute or list of attributes whose values serve to partition the set of objects associated with an ob-

Figure 7-12   *The UML Qualified Association*

ject across an association. The qualifiers are attributes of the association" [Rational Software 1997a, p. 58]. Figure 7-12 shows a qualifier on the association between Person and Identification. The qualifier translates into an associative array or map, a collection indexed by some attribute. In this case, the IDType attribute identifies the various kinds of identification, and the multiplicities on the association indicate that the person may have any number of identifiers. Putting the qualifier on this association means that you can have only one identifier of each type—in this case a reasonable business rule.

The qualifier is relatively rare in data modeling, but you can use it to advantage when you have this particular kind of constraint. In a relational data model, the concept translates to a table containing the qualifier attribute and the rest of the object attributes, with the qualifier a part of the primary key of the table. The IDType attribute would appear in the Identification table, where it also serves as a discriminator for the different subclasses of Identification. In the case of an OO data model, you can use a map, dictionary, or similar data structure for associative access to represent the collection. The Person would have an attribute defined as a map<IDType,Identification> type, where the first template parameter is the enumerated type containing all the different types of ID and the second is the Identification type.

Association Classes

Associations are generally quite simple—or as simple as roles, multiplicities, aggregation, and qualifiers allow them to be. Some associations, however, contain information not just about the related classes, but about the association itself. To add attributes to an association, you create an *association class,* a class that acts as an association but has its own attributes and operations.

The UML represents the association class as a class box attached to the association with a dashed line. The class has the name of the association. Figure 7-13 shows an association class that represents special properties of the ternary relationship between Person, Role, and CriminalOrganization. This class has several attributes: tenure (the length of time in the role), start date, end date, and termination method (for those individuals no longer playing a role—promotion, demotion, removal by various ugly methods, such as might have happened to Porlock in Moriarty's organization).

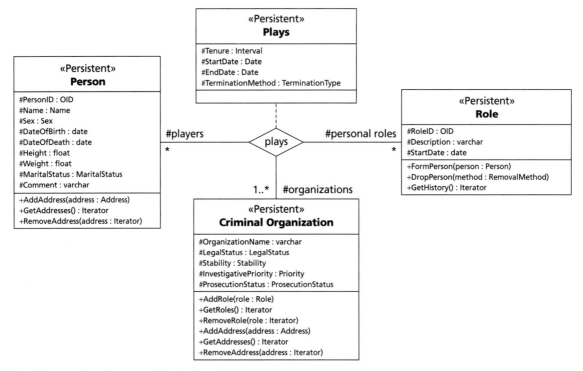

Figure 7-13   *The UML Association Class*

By carefully defining association classes, you can model relationships as first-class objects in your conceptual schema design. Association classes translate directly into conceptual schema classes (tables in a relational database).

Generalization and associations provide many of the constraints that a data model requires to produce a complete conceptual schema. There are still a few constraints you will need to add to your model, including keys, domains, and more complex constraints.

Object Constraints and Business Rules

Associations let you constrain the relationships between classes and objects with referential integrity, and these constraints form the bulk of your conceptual data model. The remaining constraints—primary keys, domains, and complex constraints—complete the data model. If you haven't already done so, please read the section "ER Business Rules" in Chapter 6. This section expands on the discussion there, putting the different constraints in the context of UML class diagrams.

Object Identity and Uniqueness Constraints

Any database data model must contain a way to identify each unique object in the database. Holmes's identification of the individual weapon used at Thor Bridge shows the value of individuality.

> "No doubt she blamed this innocent lady for all those harsh dealings and un-kind words with which her husband tried to repel her too demonstrative affection. Her first resolution was to end her own life. Her second was to do it in such a way as to involve her victim in a fate which was worse far than any sudden death could be.
>
> "We can follow the various steps quite clearly, and they show a remarkable sub-tlety of mind. A note was extracted very cleverly from Miss Dunbar which would make it appear that she had chosen the scene of the crime. In her anxiety that it should be discovered she somewhat overdid it, by holding it in her hand to the last. This alone should have excited my suspicions earlier than it did.
>
> "Then she took one of her husband's revolvers—there was, as you saw, an arse-nal in the house—and kept it for her own use. A similar one she concealed that morning in Miss Dunbar's wardrobe after discharging one barrel, which she could easily do in the woods without attracting attention. She then went down to the bridge where she had contrived this exceedingly ingenious method for getting rid of her weapon. When Miss Dunbar appeared she used her last breath in pouring out her hatred, and then, when she was out of hearing, carried out her terrible pur-pose. Every link is now in its place and the chain is complete. The papers may ask why the mere was not dragged in the first instance, but it is easy to be wise after the event, and in any case the expanse of a reed-filled lake is no easy matter to drag unless you have a clear perception of what you are looking for and where."
> [THOR]

Most database systems provide unique, proprietary, and hidden identifiers for rows and objects (ROWIDs in Oracle, for example). OO database managers provide uniqueness through the *object identifier,* or *OID.* Identifying an object through this kind of surrogate is *implicit,* or *existence-based,* identification [Blaha and Premerlani 1998, pp. 193–194]. The alternative is *explicit,* or *value-based,* identification. With explicit identification, you can identify the object with the values of one or more attributes of the object. Object identity corresponds to the ER modeling concept of primary key. I use the term "OID" to refer to any kind of key that uniquely identifies an object.

To recap the key definitions, this time in terms of objects: a *candidate key* is a set of implicit or explicit attributes that uniquely identify an object of a class. The set of attributes must be complete in that you should not be able to remove any attribute and still preserve the uniqueness of the objects. Also, no candidate key can be null, as this would logically invalidate the equality comparison you need to apply to ensure uniqueness. A *primary key* is a candidate key that you choose to become the identifier of the class, the OID. An *alternate key* is a candidate key that is not the primary key. The alternate key thus represents an implicit or explicit *uniqueness constraint*.

> *Note: In the UML, objects have identity but data values do not. Data values are values of primitive types, types such as int or VARCHAR that have no assumption of underlying object identity. Objects are instances of classes. See the section "Domain Constraints" for a complete discussion of data values and object values.*

The UML does not provide any standard means of expressing object identity because it assumes that object identity is a basic, implicit, and automatic property of an object. To include the concept in UML data modeling, therefore, you must extend the UML with some additional properties for attributes. You define explicit keys in a UML class diagram with two extended tagged values, {OID} and {alternate OID}. Again, these are *not* standard UML notation; they are custom UML extensions for data modeling.

These two properties identify those attributes that serve to identify a unique instance of the class. By attaching the {OID} tagged value to an attribute, you specify that attribute as part of the primary key, or object identifier. By attaching the {alternate OID=n} tagged value to an attribute, you specify it as part of alternate key n, where n is an integer.

The {OID} and {alternate OID} properties constrain the objects of the class regardless of storage. They correspond to the SQL PRIMARY KEY constraint and the UNIQUE constraint, respectively. If, for example, you create an object-relational type and instantiate two tables from that type, the {OID} property on the attributes constrains all of the objects in both tables to have unique values with respect to each other.

> *Note: You only specify the {OID} property on the primary key attributes of the regular classes you build, not association classes. The OID of an association class is always implicit and consists of the combined oid attributes of the classes that participate in the relationship.*

Figure 7-14 shows the oids for the Person and Identification classes. The Person class is a complete object in itself and has strong object identity. If you need to make identity explicit, you usually add an attribute with a suitable type to serve as the object identifier, in this case the PersonID: OID {OID} attribute.

In relational and object-relational systems, this corresponds to an identifier you generate, such as a sequence in Oracle or an IDENTITY in SQL Server. Be careful, though: if you create the OID on a table basis, its scope is the table, not

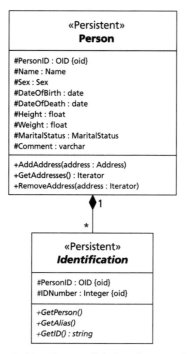

Figure 7-14   *The Explicit {OID} Tagged Value*

the class. That is, if you define multiple tables from a class, the OID will not uniquely identify the objects across the two tables, just within each table. In most OODBMS systems, objects have built-in oids that you can access and use for establishing identity. Usually referential integrity happens automatically because of the way you relate objects to one another, and the systems use the oids in representing the relationships. Codd described this problem and its requirements for "complete" RDBMS products. He specified that relational systems must behave in a similar way, treating a primary key as potentially shared between several tables [Codd 1990, pp. 25–26, 36–37]. Specifically, the attributes share a common, composite domain from which all the participating tables draw their values. Defining this in terms of domains lets you preserve strong typing under joins and set operations as well as in comparison expressions [Codd 1990, p. 49].

   When you build a generalization hierarchy, you specify the {OID} property at the top of the hierarchy. The subclasses of the root class inherit the explicit object identifier from that class. You can always add {alternate OID} specifications lower in the generalization hierarchy. Multiple inheritance, of course, throws something of a monkey wrench into this scheme, just as it does for object structure. If a class inherits {OID} attributes from more than one parent, you must override the property in the inheriting class to specify one or the other attribute set as the {OID} of the multiply inheriting subclass. You can also specify a completely new {OID} property if that makes sense.

> *Tip: Making sense of multiple inheritance is hard. This is just another reason to avoid multiple inheritance in data modeling. One way or another, this is going to complicate your life. Try to avoid it. If you can't avoid it, make the OID implicit and let the system handle identity through object existence rather than through inheritance. If you won't do that, all I can say is that I feel your pain.*

Similarly, a class related to another through composite aggregation (a weak relationship in ER terms) gets the OID from the aggregating class. This does not constitute the complete OID for the aggregated class, though; you need to specify any additional attributes required to identify the individual element within the aggregate. For example, in Figure 7-14, the Identification class OID is the combination of the Person OID from the aggregating person and the identification number. This usage is a bit unusual in UML.

In OO design and programming, and hence in the UML, every object has implicit identity. In transient systems, identity often is the address in memory of the object. In persistent OODBMS systems, each object has an OID that often contains physical or logical storage information. In relational and ORDBMS products, there is usually a similar way to identify each row. None of these identifiers is explicitly part of the conceptual schema or class design, it just happens automatically. This is most of the reason why there is no standard way to refer to oids in UML diagrams; other constructs such as relationships, classes, and objects imply the whole concept.

Which approach is better, explicit or implicit identity? From the purist OO perspective, you should leave out the explicit OID attributes entirely. Figure 7-15 shows what Figure 7-14 would look like using this approach. Given this diagram, when you generate a relational database schema, you would add a column that uniquely identified each row in the Person table corresponding to a Person object. The aggregation relationship between the two classes implies that there is a foreign key in Identification pointing to a single person. The aggregation implies that the foreign key is also part of the primary key. Instead of generating a unique OID column for Identification, therefore, you generate two columns. First is the Person OID that refers back to the person table as a foreign key. You follow it with a unique number for each row with the same Person oid. You could specify the attribute to use as the second OID element by using a different tagged value, {aggregate OID}. This tags the attribute as the element to add to the aggregating object's OID to create the new object's oid. If you wanted to replace the implicit OID with an explicit set of attributes, you would just specify the {OID} tagged value on those attributes. There would be no implicit OID in the underlying conceptual schema.

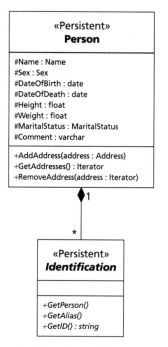

Figure 7-15   *The Implicit OID Approach*

The second approach makes all this explicit at the design level, much as in Figure 7-14. The explicit approach has the benefit of keeping all the attributes clear and open in your design. This makes the connection between your data model and your conceptual schema in the target data model more direct. Since the objects are persistent, you will usually have to have methods on your classes that manipulate the oids on their way from persistent memory to transient memory. OODBMS products handle this automatically, but RDBMS and ORDBMS products usually don't. Making the OID explicit gives you the ability to design OID handling into your persistent classes. The implicit approach, on the other hand, hides the details and lets you do the work when you convert the data model to the conceptual schema in your target database. As long as you have standard OID handling built into your persistent class hierarchy in some way, this works fine. In relational databases, this requires a good deal of additional work.

You can have an explicit OID spanning two or more attributes of a class, which corresponds to the ER composite key from Chapter 6. When you join sets of objects (tables or whatever) on the primary key, and that key has more than one attribute, the syntax for the join condition can get very messy, especially for outer joins. You need one comparison expression for each attribute in the join. You can simplify coding a good deal by replacing multiple-attribute explicit oids (composite keys) with single-attribute explicit oids that you generate. This usage is somewhere between an explicit and an implicit oid. It's implicit because it depends on existence. It's explicit because it has to be an actual attribute of the class, since you're creating it for explicit use.

Yet another issue arises as your data model grows in size. For largish databases, you may find that consistency in your choice of identity approach yields productivity benefits. Consistency, in this case, means the implicit approach. With a large number of tables, programmers may get easily confused by a plethora of different OID attributes scattered around the database. With implicit OIDs, and with a standard OID naming convention for persistent attributes in the conceptual schema, programmers will usually be able to code without confusion about which attributes are identifying ones.

Domain Constraints

The section on "Domains" in Chapter 6 defined the *domain* of an attribute as a set of values to which the attribute maps. There are an infinite number of potential sets of possible values. This section classifies domains to provide a structure for talking about the things without falling into a morass of detail. Some philosophy is useful, though.

> Note: For an excellent discussion of domains in the context of the extended relational model, consult Codd's book on RM/V2 [Codd 1990, pp. 43–59] or Date and Darwen's Manifesto [Date and Darwen 1998], which discusses the relationships between domains and other aspects of the object-relational system. Blaha goes into some detail on OO domain concepts with a slightly different perspective than the following classification [Blaha and Premerlani 1998, pp. 45–46].

There are really only two types of domains: extensional and intensional. These terms come from mathematical logic and denotational semantics. Don't confuse the attribute domain with the completely separate use of "domain" to refer to the specific business area to which a software system relates (or to the NT network domain, either). Defining a "domain model" in OO design refers to setting up the classes for a business area, not to defining the basic data types of your system. Also, don't confuse the definition of the type with the definition of the set of values or objects typed. That is, don't confuse the definition of integer with a set of integer values. The definition of the type tells you about all possible values of the type, while the definition of a set of values tells you about the actual values in a particular context such as a database or table.

The *intension* of a set is a logical predicate (a combination of relations and operators on those relations such as AND, OR, NOT, FOR ALL, and FOR ANY) that defines the contents of the set. For example, you can define the set of all criminal organizations as "the set of all organizations organized for the purpose of engaging in criminal activities." This definition is close to that of the Racketeer-Influenced and Corrupt Organizations (RICO) Act that defines the U.S. federal government's approach to organized crime. If you define a set by its intension, you are stating a condition that you can apply to an object to discover whether it is a member of the set.

The *extension* of a set is the collection of objects that belong to the set, the set's *elements*. If you define a set by intension, the objects that satisfy the intensional definition constitute the extension of the set. Again referring to criminal organizations, the actual criminal organizations are the elements of the set of criminal organizations. Using the intensional definition, only those organizations that satisfy the condition are part of the extension of the set. If you define a set extensionally, you are defining it by listing out the members. For example, you define the set of Arabic digits as {0, 1, 2, 3, 4, 5, 6, 7, 8, 9}.

You can define some domains easily with an intensional definition, such as criminal organizations. The "easy" part is the definition, not the application. For example, the U.S. government tried the Hell's Angels in California federal court as a criminal organization under the RICO statute. But the court decided that they were just a motorcycle club with some people in it who sold illegal drugs—not a criminal organization. Certain domains, such as the set of integers, the set of colors, or the set of JPEG images, can only have an intensional definition. There is literally no way to list the elements, as there is an infinite number of them. Practically, of course, the computer's internal numeric representation scheme limits the number of integers. Color is really all possible combinations of three 32-bit integers. The number of images must be finite in reality as there are only a finite number of atoms in the universe to serve as bits. Still, reality should not constrain designers too much. After all, who could possibly use more than 64K of memory?

You can define other domains best through an extensional definition, such as a short list of possible values. For example, the possible states of the legal status of a criminal organization include "legally defined," "on trial," "alleged," and "unknown." This is a *nominal scale,* a set of values with no intrinsic ordering or comparison operator defined other than equality [Fenton and Pfleeger 1997]. You can use it to define an enumerated type in most modern programming languages.

> *Note: It's interesting that the C++ and ODL enum type does not completely conform to the definition. The type is defined to be an integer, and therefore has an internal order. Many C and C++ programmers take advantage of this by assigning the integers and using conversions to get the actual integer values when they need them, usually for comparisons or sorting. This kind of programming violates the mathematical assumptions of the nominal scale, unfortunately, and can have misleading results, particularly in statistical applications. You should try to avoid it in database programming in*

*particular because of the data constraints implicit in the domain.
This only applies to C++-based OO database systems for the most
part, fortunately.*

The domain can be *simple* (the set of integers, or the set of valid dates, or
the set of JPEG images), it can be *structured* (a struct or other record type), it can
be *multivalued* (an array or collection of objects of some domain), it can be
extensional (an enumerated list of possible values), or it can be *intensional* (a logical predicate that defines a set of possible values as its extension).

*Note: There is no room in this book to go into the deeper theoreti-
cal details of domains. If you want to understand the mathematics
behind domains, consult one of the standard works on measurement theory [Fenton and Pfleeger 1997; Roberts 1979]. In particular,
pay attention to the organization of data with respect to compara-
bility and other operations. If you mix or convert data between incompatible types, it is impossible to determine the meaning of the
results of operations on such data.*

The simple domains correspond to the standard single-valued data types. In
SQL, that means exact or approximate numbers, character strings in various
forms, dates, times, timestamps, and intervals [ANSI 1992]. Using CHECK constraints, you can impose restrictions on the simple domains to create new domains. You can't define them separately and specifically as domains; you have to
write out the CHECK constraint on each attribute. In certain ORDBMS products
such as DB2, you can define subtypes that apply such constraints [Chamberlin
1998].

In OQL, there are more choices: floating point, integer, character, string,
Boolean, octet, date, time, timestamp, and interval [Cattell and Barry 1997].
There is also an "any" type to give you the ability to refer to any object. ORDBMS
products let you add simple types through extensions to the type system.

The structured domains include various forms of the record, a collection of
attributes coming from different domains. The multivalued domains include arrays and other ways of representing a collection of objects coming from the same
domain.

An extensional domain defines the domain through a simple list of values.
This is also known as an enumerated type. In SQL, you do this through a CHECK
constraint, usually using an IN expression with a list of elements: CHECK
LegalStatus IN ('Legally Defined', 'On Trial', 'Alleged', 'Unknown'). In SQL, these
are integrity constraints on individual attributes, not separate domains. That
means, for example, that you must put the CHECK constraint separately on all
the attributes that must conform to the list of values. In ODL, there is an explicit

enum type that lets you define the domain, then apply it to several properties [Cattell and Barry 1997].

The UML does not specify any particular domain model—just the reverse. The UML specification implicitly makes the data type "implementation defined," letting you specify the domain model to use based on your target programming language. The UML defines the semantics of the data type this way:

> A *data type* is a type whose values have no identity, i.e., they are pure values. Data types include primitive built-in types (such as integer and string) as well as definable enumeration types (such as the predefined enumeration type boolean whose literals are false and true). [Rational Software 1997b, p. 22]

There are three subclasses of the DataType classifier in the UML metamodel: Primitive, Structure, and Enumeration. These are stereotypes you can use to qualify the classifier (class box) that you set up to represent the type and its operations.

For data modeling, you should carefully define a set of data types for your data models as a separate package of classifiers. Figure 7-16 illustrates a data type package based on the ODL (and OMG) type model.

Figures 7-17 through 7-19 show the details of the individual packages (AtomicLiteral, CollectionLiteral, and StructuredLiteral). The OMG object model

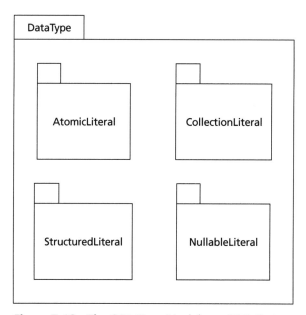

Figure 7-16 *The ODL Type Model as a UML Data Type Package*

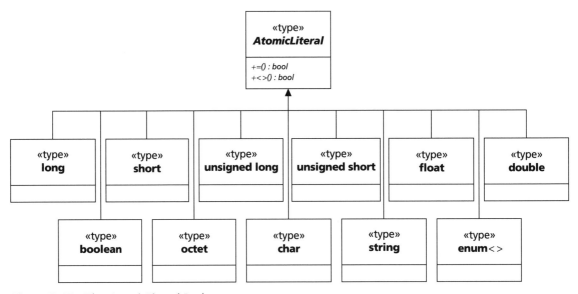

Figure 7-17   *The AtomicLiteral Package*

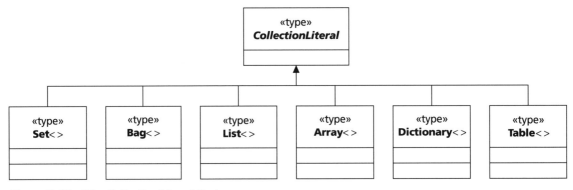

Figure 7-18   *The CollectionLiteral Package*

does not define standard operations on these types, though the SQL data type model does (operators +, -, *, and /, for example, on numeric types). You could add operations, as Figure 7-17 illustrates for the Atomic Literal type. Once you've defined this type model package, you can then refer to the types and the operations you've defined on them in your designs without confusion. You can also define standard relationships between the type model data types and the target data model or DBMS data types. This then permits you to generate the correct DBMS data types for different target DBMS products. You can also define subtypes as subclasses with constraints such as range constraints.

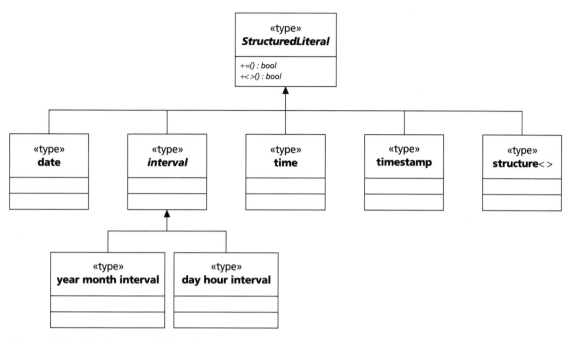

Figure 7-19   *The StructuredLiteral Package*

The enum<> type is parameterized by a set of literals in the ODL object model. It thus produces instances of the generic enumerated type. You can then use these instances to define attributes or parameters. This approach is an example of using genericity instead of inheritance to construct varieties of an object with different qualities (in this case the enumeration constants). If you have the ability to define subtypes, you can name the specific instance with its own name and use that name. For example, to define LegalStatus, you can use this direct declaration:

```
attribute enum<LegallyDefined, OnTrial, Alleged, Unknown> LegalStatus;
```

Alternatively, you can define a subtype and use a declaration with the subtype name:

```
type enum<LegallyDefined, OnTrial, Alleged, Unknown> LegalStatusType;
LegalStatusType LegalStatus;
```

The second usage is better because you can reuse the type for several different attributes while still defining the type as an instance of a generic enum type. Unfortunately, not all target languages support enums, genericity, or subtyping, so you may have to do things in another way.

Because of the three-valued logic of SQL (true, false, and null), the ODL defines a mirrored type hierarchy for null literals (nullable_float, nullable_set, and so on, not illustrated here) [Cattell and Barry 1997, p. 34]. You can use these types to define attributes that can be null. Remember, though, that null is not a value, it is the absence of a value. SQL (and OQL) uses IS null for comparisons to null rather than the "= null" syntax, which would imply that null is a value.

Tip: If you choose to use another approach, you can express nullability as an extended UML property of the attribute: {nullable}.

Complex Constraints

To this point, the UML has expressed the simple business rules such as integrity constraints and domain constraints with standard notation. There are many business rules that go beyond these simple constraint expression mechanisms in the UML. The UML therefore provides a formal language for expressing these constraints: the UML Object Constraint Language (OCL) [Rational Software 1997c]. There is no room to go into the details of the OCL here; consult the language specification if you want to use it.

Note: You can express constraints in whatever language is appropriate as long as it meets the requirements. A constraint is a Boolean expression that evaluates to true or false (not null) at the end of each transaction in whatever context you place it. The expression cannot have side effects on the state of that context object. You can use an SQL or OQL expression, for example, instead of OCL, or you can use Java, Smalltalk, or first-order predicate calculus if that makes sense to you. In some systems such as Oracle8, you do have to avoid language that results in side effects on object state, which you can't use in constraints.

Where can you use OCL expressions in UML diagrams?

- *Classes and types:* Constraints on all instances of the class or type (class invariants)

- *Operations:* Pre- and postconditions and other constraints on operation behavior

- *Transitions/flows:* Guard conditions in state transition and activity diagrams

As an extension, you can also use the class invariant expressions on the individual attributes of a class diagram to express rules on each attribute. As with SQL CHECK constraints, there is really no limit on what you can express with

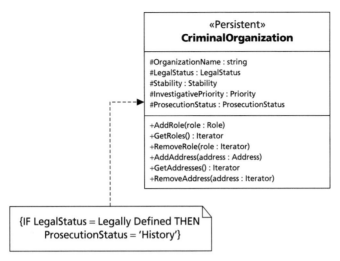

Figure 7-20   *A UML Constraint on CriminalOrganization*

such constraints, but it is often convenient to place the rule with the attribute to which it applies.

The UML notation for constraints is a note attached to the constrained object. Figure 7-20 shows a simple class invariant constraint on the Criminal-Organization class. The constraint, expressed in SQL, tells you that a criminal organization cannot simultaneously have a LegalStatus of "LegallyDefined" and a Prosecution Status of anything but "History". In English, if you have successfully had a court define an organization as a criminal organization, your prosecution status must be "History", meaning you've won your case.

Summary

This exceptionally long chapter is very hard to summarize, since it is itself a summary of a much larger corpus, the UML specification. The chapter focuses on those parts of the UML notational system that are of direct use in data modeling and database design.

Most of the UML classifiers play some kind of role in database design: packages, subsystems, types, interfaces, databases, and classes are all elements of such a design. As well, the association, generalization, and realization relationships of UML play a direct role in data modeling by relating classifiers to one another.

You use packages and subsystems to build the high-level architecture of your database application. These classifiers represent a name space that organizes your classes and other subsystems into cleanly separable units. You specify those units with transactional use cases, and you realize the use cases with the various classifiers that collaborate with each other. In this way, you build up the data model that realizes the transactions your requirements specify.

Classes may be abstract (no instances) or concrete. Each class has a set of attributes and operations, with attributes and their data types representing the state of the class (the data) and operations being the behavior. Methods are the implementation of the operations. Both attributes and operations have public, protected, or private visibility, a feature that gives you the ability to encapsulate your data and operations within the class, reducing overall coupling in your subsystems.

The generalization relationship lets you relate classifiers into an inheritance hierarchy, with either single or multiple inheritance. You should avoid multiple inheritance in your design whenever possible. You can use interfaces to avoid mix-in multiple inheritance while still maintaining a strongly typed design.

The association relationship lets you relate classifiers into a visibility hierarchy. Each side of an association is a role that a classifier plays. Each role has a multiplicity (1, *, 0..*, 2..6, and so on) that tells you how many objects may link to other objects through the association. A composite aggregation strengthens the association to ownership instead of just visibility: the parent owns the child object. Associations can themselves become objects through association classes, which have their own attributes and operations.

Finally, you can use UML to specify constraints on your classifiers and relationships. Object identity may be implicit (the UML standard) or explicit (the extended {OID} and {alternate OID}) tags. You can place domain constraints on attributes through types (either value types such as string or object types you define with the type classifier). You can use extended tags to specify data model constraints, such as {nullable}. You can specify arbitrarily complex constraints through constraint comments, boxes you attach to the constrained notation. You can use any kind of constraint language ranging from the UML's OCL to SQL expressions.

Now you've seen most of the UML relevant to data modeling. The next chapter brings everything together in the process of data model design.

Patterns of Data Modeling 8

Imagination continually frustrates tradition; that is its function.

John Pfeiffer

Design in the object-oriented world has taken an odd turn in recent years. The usual course of design in the software world is revolution upon revolution. Every new generation of designer ignores what came before and builds a new way of doing what needs doing. The evolution of programming languages over the last 30 years reflects this revolutionary way of thinking, to the consternation of experienced language designers.

In the OO world, designers have begun to accept that there are aspects of design that should not change, or should change very little. Much of the rationale for this thinking comes from the fact that OO designers emphasize reusability. Once OO thinking moved beyond programming, designers realized that some of the lessons of architectural design thinking and philosophy could apply just as well to software design. These software architects adapted the work of Christopher Alexander, the great architectural philosopher, to software design through the concept of the *pattern:*

> Design patterns capture solutions that have developed and evolved over time. Hence they aren't the designs people tend to generate initially. They reflect untold redesign and recoding as developers have struggled for greater reuse and flexibility in their software. Design patterns capture these solutions in a succinct and easily applied form. [Gamma et al. 1995, p. xi]

The essence of a pattern is tradition. The tradition is the core of the solution. The funny thing about traditions is that they constantly confront imagination, and vice versa. Design patterns, like most traditions, help establish a context for your solution to a design problem. Your imagination then takes over to move beyond the tradition to solve the problem. Occasionally, your imagination comes up with the beginnings of a new pattern—"out of the box" thinking, as many people now call it. If you spend all your time out of the box, however, you won't get very far with your work.

This chapter shows you how to use patterns in your data modeling. It provides examples of some common abstract and concrete solutions to data modeling problems and suggests ways you can move beyond patterns to achieve working solutions to specific problems.

The art of building a database-centric system doesn't lie with the notation you use but rather with your use of the notation. As you go through the examples of analysis and design patterns, think about the modeling techniques from Chapter 7 and how they apply to the patterns. The thinking itself, and its expression through UML, is the essence of designing databases. This data modeling, reusing patterns and integrating views of the data, prepares the way for the more concrete tasks of implementing the conceptual and physical schemas.

Modeling with Reusable Design Patterns

A *design pattern* is a reusable system that describes a design problem and its solution. You can vary the structure of your pattern descriptions. However, the basic nature of a pattern consists of a name, a problem description, a solution description, and a discussion of issues, trade-offs, and consequences of the pattern [Gamma et al. 1995].

The name of the pattern is literally the key to the pattern. When you talk about patterns, or any tradition for that matter, you refer to it by a catch phrase that everyone in the culture recognizes. Each person may have personal variants of the pattern, but each understands its basic nature when you refer to it by name. You can put the name into a comment in the code or design diagram, and reviewers will immediately understand what they are seeing. The name is an abstraction that contains all the pain that went into developing the tradition.

The problem is the set of circumstances that lead to the need for a solution. Often the most helpful part of a design pattern, the problem tells you when to apply the pattern. If your problem doesn't match the problem description well, the design solution probably isn't appropriate. Small variations are not important in this comparison, only the essential problem elements, so when you read the problem description, focus on the essential elements, not the details.

As with most abstract discussions, the problem description often seems ambiguous and indefinite until you fully understand it. The pattern almost always benefits from a concrete problem description, a real-world issue that maps to the abstract problem. Be careful not to get caught up in the particular example, however, as there may be significant differences between it and the problem you are trying to solve. Don't force one real world onto another that isn't the same.

The solution is the design that solves the problem. In the present case, this is a UML data model that represents the abstract design in general terms. You then convert this model by naming the various elements with your classes and relationships as they apply to your specific problem.

The discussion of the pattern contains all the things you can think of that a designer might want to consider when applying the pattern. It includes one or two extended examples of the application of the pattern to real problems. Providing working code is usually a good idea if you can do it. You should certainly mention any limitations on the implementation in different languages, portability issues, or situations that might lead to problems in one way or another.

The following sections present some patterns as examples of what you might do as a pattern designer. The level of detail is not as thorough as it might be because of space limitations.

> *Tip: You should definitely consult more complete pattern books for ideas and details, especially if you are a software architect about to embark on pattern design of your own. The Gang of Four's book [Gamma et al. 1995] is required reading. Also, one pattern I don't specify here is the Star pattern, which lets you create a multidimensional representation of a complex data warehouse. This book doesn't discuss data warehousing modeling. See the Preface for a discussion of the star schema and its fact-dimension tables. These correspond to a simple UML pattern with a central n-ary relationship (the fact association and its class) and the participating objects (the dimension classes).*

The design patterns that you adopt from other sources and the ones you develop yourself are part of your portfolio of reusable systems. You should catalog and index them so that designers in your business can find and use them, just as with any reusable system.

There are two kinds of pattern of direct interest to data modelers: abstract patterns and analysis patterns. The following sections give you some examples of both of these types.

Abstract Patterns

An *abstract pattern,* in the context of data modeling, is a pattern of classes and relationships that describe a generic solution to a generic problem. The names are often very general ("composite," for example, or "mediator") and don't map directly to the objects you are considering in your design problem.

The following subsections each present a single pattern from the Gang of Four or from my own work, transformed into a database pattern. These are the patterns for which I've been able to see direct uses in a database application.

Other patterns relate more to the application design, and especially to abstractions or behavior in the application code rather than in the database server. There is much overlap in coding techniques in modern DBMS software with application software (triggers, server extensions and plug-ins, stored procedures, persistent class methods, and so on). You may well find other patterns to be of direct interest in your designs.

The Singleton Pattern

The Singleton pattern ensures that a class has only one instance in the database.

The Problem

Often in data modeling you find you have an abstraction for which there can be only one object instance. There are several common examples of this in relational databases: a row that represents a default value for a table, a row that represents a pointer to one row in another table, and a row that represents the control state of the system. For example, you may have an organization table that represents the hierarchy of organizations and a singleton table that contains the primary key of your organization, the main one concerning you. Or you can have an object that represents a time interval after which objects in the database cannot change.

You use the Singleton when you must have one object and when you may want to extend that object through subclassing. Subclassing the Singleton class doesn't create a different instance, it creates an extended version of the instance that replaces the original one's behavior with polymorphic behavior in the subclass.

The Solution

Figure 8-1 represents the Singleton data model.

The Singleton class in Figure 8-1 has a single instance. The relationship UniqueInstance is a one-to-one relationship where both objects in the relationship are identical, and UniqueInstance is a class attribute, so there can be only one instance of the class. You can make all the attributes class attributes, since there is only one instance, though that isn't necessary.

You use the Instance operation to get a reference to the single instance. In a relational database, this corresponds to a static query that retrieves the row from the database. In an ORDBMS, it might also execute a constructor function to create the instance if it doesn't already exist. In an OO database, it retrieves the instance object (or creates it if necessary) using a static object identifier or other means of reference to the instance from the class.

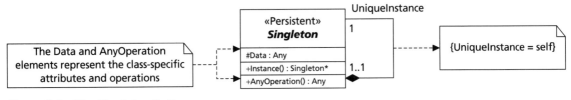

Figure 8-1 *The Singleton Pattern*

Discussion

The Singleton pattern at the application level is usually the means of setting up a single object and getting access to it. The main event loop in the system is usually a Singleton, for example. If you make things like that persistent in an OODBMS, they are usually Singletons. In relational databases, the Singleton plays a distinctly less central role, being confined to utility tables that other tables join to or use to set values.

Enforcing the Singleton constraint requires making any constructors private or protected so that only the Instance operation can create the instance if it isn't already there. The UniqueInstance attribute/relationship also enforces the Singleton constraint. A relational database has no constructors or access protection. You thus implement the constraint with a trigger or through procedural encapsulation, hiding the table behind security privileges and allowing access only through an Instance stored procedure.

Using the Instance operation to create the instance avoids having to create the single instance if you don't need it. In most database applications, this isn't an issue, since you define and store the instance for use in multiple applications through retrieval. It's conceivable, though, that you might find a use that required the instance creation only under certain circumstances. Holmes PLC could implement an intruder shutdown system, for example, by creating a Singleton instance, the presence of which would disable access to any sensitive data from a particular user or for all users. The DBA would then investigate the situation and resolve it by removing the instance. This kind of extremity would require lots of auditing and other data about the security violation, of course.

The Composite Pattern

The Composite pattern represents a tree structure made up of different kinds of related objects, all of which share the same interface. You use the Composite pattern to represent part-whole hierarchies in your database.

The Composite pattern is a very common one in application modeling. Database designers new to OO modeling and patterns may find it difficult at first because of its apparent complexity, but the flexibility you gain is well worth the extra complexity you add.

The Problem

One of the classic modeling problems in relational database theory is the parts explosion problem. Despite its exciting name, this does not refer to active components of military databases and is rarely dangerous except to the unfortunate SQL programmer that must deal with it. A parts explosion is a tree structure of data that models a series of product parts, some of which contain other parts. The part, in this case, is not the instance or object itself but rather the *type* of part. For example, the structure of a commonplace book encyclopedia entry contains various objects. For lots of different reasons, you want to consider these different objects to all be of a common class: the part. Each type of part has a part number that identifies it.

Figure 8-2 illustrates a simple parts explosion using document components as the parts. The encyclopedia article contains other articles as well as text, images, and sounds.

The task is to generate a complete list of all the parts that a given part requires. Since some parts contain other parts, the structure is a tree, as Figure 8-2 shows, and this task requires that you walk the tree to find all the parts. The mathematical term for this operation is *transitive closure,* the set of all the parts in the database that you can reach from the root part.

There are a couple of additional issues with this structure that motivate the Composite pattern. First, the parts are not uniform; they are not all members of the same class. Second, the parts all must share a common interface because you want to access them uniformly. In the example in Figure 8-2, you want to retrieve all the components of the encyclopedia article and display them without needing to know the specific kind of thing, a classic use of interface polymorphism. In the classic OO model, this last requirement means that all the different classes must inherit from a common abstract superclass.

The Solution

Figure 8-3 shows the Composite pattern. The Component is the abstract superclass, and there are two types of subclass, a Leaf class that has no children and a Composite class that does have children, all of which are Component objects. The children association produces the tree structure by allowing Composite objects to contain other Composite objects or Leaf objects as they require.

The Component class is the abstract interface for all the objects in the tree. It contains both abstract operations and operations that provide default behavior.

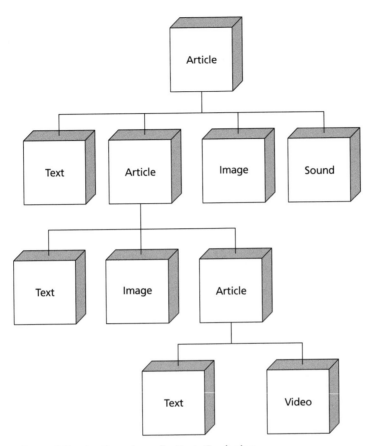

Figure 8-2 *An Encyclopedia Parts Explosion*

It also may contain attributes that all component objects share. The Component thus provides all the operations that you can do on any component object, including iterating over the children of the object. The Leaf class operations and methods provide the ultimate behavior of the system through implementations of the basic component operations.

The Composite class actually stores the children, as indicated by the composite aggregation diamond on the children association to the class. It also provides operations and methods that override the abstract operations of Component to manage the children, such as Add(), Remove(), and GetChildren().

In the case of the parts explosion of Figure 8-2, the Article class is the Composite, and the Text, Video, Image, and Sound classes are all Leaf subclasses (along with Article) of the Component class. Figure 8-4 shows the EncyclopediaComponent class hierarchy that contains all these classes.

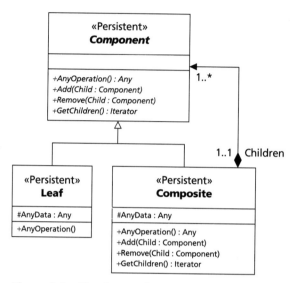

Figure 8-3   *The Composite Pattern*

Discussion

Most designers seeing the Composite pattern for the first time have the irresistible impulse to ask, What about operations on the leaves that don't make any sense on other leaves or on the composite? The answer: don't do it. The objective of the Composite pattern is to treat all the objects in the tree as identical Component objects, not as the Leaf. If the Leaf classes have semantics that demand special operations, define separate classes and encapsulate them within the leaf classes. You can then maintain the objects in a separate table and refer to them through the tree as needed while preserving the data and operations of the individual class. The MPEG File and WAV File classes are examples of this approach in Figure 8-4. The EncyclopediaComponent just displays the component; the two file classes have the various file operations that let you manipulate them within the Display operation. If you want to manipulate the files specifically as MPEG or WAV files outside the tree, retrieve them separately and do so.

Implementing the Composite can be a challenge in a database. Relational databases, for example, complicate the implementation because they don't have sets to hold the children. The pattern specifies storing the children in the Composite, as the Leaf classes do not inherit the relationship. In a relational database, you store the parent OID in the child. For example, if you transform Figure 8-4

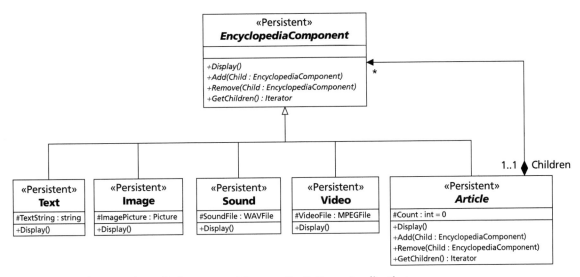

Figure 8-4   *The EncyclopediaComponent Composite Pattern Application*

into an Oracle schema, you would create an EncyclopediaComponent table. You then add an attribute to store the identifier for the encyclopedia component that is the parent. The root component gets a null parent value.

In this case, you almost certainly want to create a separate table to represent the relationship, even though that seems more complicated than necessary. Create a separate ComponentChildren table that maps the Encyclopedia-Component identifier for a child to a parent. You can then join all three tables (EncyclopediaComponent, ComponentChildren, and EncyclopediaComponent) to get the children of a given component (or its parents, for that matter). This fifth-normal-form approach also permits expanding the pattern to enable a component to have multiple parents (component sharing), which is not possible with the other design. That changes the composite aggregation (the black diamond on Composite) to shared aggregation (a white diamond). See the section on "The Flyweight Pattern" for a design alternative.

With the ORDBMS and OODBMS products, you can store REFs or sets directly, so this pattern is not so much of a problem.

You can add an {ordered} tag to the Children role to specify that the children have a specific ordering. This would allow you to process the encyclopedia article in the same order each time, if that had some use in laying out the screen, for example.

The composite aggregation implies the management of deletion by the composite. That is, when you remove a composite, you also delete all of its children. That may mean some special trigger code or referential integrity constraint definitions in a relational database.

The Flyweight Pattern

The Flyweight pattern could be considered an example of the crow's feet coming home to roost. This pattern "uses sharing to support large numbers of fine-grained objects efficiently" [Gamma et al. 1995, p. 195].

The Problem

Translating this goal to the database context reduces it to eliminating redundancy by separating intrinsic and extrinsic data—in other words, normalization. *Extrinsic data* is data that varies with the context rather than with the object; *intrinsic data* varies with the object. In database terms, an OID (a primary key) identifies an object. Intrinsic data is data that, in the context of a set of objects, varies with the oid. In relational database terms, this translates to a functional dependency on the entire primary key, or fourth normal form (more on this in Chapter 11). Reducing the redundancy means creating objects with only intrinsic data and putting the extrinsic data in a separate place. The difference between the situation that leads to the Flyweight pattern and the concept of normalization is sharing.

If the application uses a large number of objects, the duplication of intrinsic data among all the objects can be extreme, depending on the size of each object's intrinsic data. All this duplication can lead to a bloated database and a bloated application. By sharing the data, you can reduce the overall storage requirements a great deal—always an advantage in database (and application) design.

Consider a situation in the commonplace book encyclopedia system, for example. Many of the images in the database are composite images made up of different components. Many of these components are the same, just positioned and colored differently in each image. If you store the images as parent-child composites, with each component accompanied by its location and color, you store all the components of each composite image separately. That means there is quite a lot of redundancy in the database. By sharing the components, you can greatly reduce the overall storage requirements. You can separate the images and store only the coloring and location information with the composite along with a pointer to the shared image.

This situation is common with computerization of real-world things. The first blush look at any situation yields millions of things; only on carefully analyzing the objects do you begin to see the similarities. In the extreme, you need theoretical science and its ability to break through irregularity with systematic innovation that reduces the chaos to a series of laws.

The Solution

The Flyweight pattern breaks apart the objects into intrinsic and extrinsic properties to enable the system to represent as few objects as possible by sharing. Figure 8-5 illustrates the abstract Flyweight pattern.

The Flyweight class is an abstract class that represents the needs of the subclasses for extrinsic information. The various bits of extrinsic information are all elements of the various interface operations. The FlyweightFactory class is the class that manages the collection of Flyweight objects, sharing them among various client objects. It has builder methods that either construct the shared object for the first time or just return it if it already exists. It may also have builder methods for Flyweight subclasses that just create the unshared objects every time you call the method. The FlyweightFactory also owns the transient aggregate data structure that holds the objects and the query code that reads them from the database. The ConcreteFlyweight class represents the actual intrinsic state of the Flyweight object shared between various classes.

Figure 8-6 shows the image example as a Flyweight pattern. This example simplifies the interface. The ImageFactory produces either a shared image or an unshared composite image, depending on what its client wants. It stores the collection of shared images, querying them from the database as needed (or all at once if that makes sense). The interface in FlyweightImage imports context and location information as needed. The image bitmap (or whatever the Image data type is) is the intrinsic state in the shared concrete Flyweight class SharedImage. The other concrete class, CompositeImage, stores the set of children as a Composite pattern—no sharing.

In the database, a central table or object cluster stores the shared images. Another table or class, which Figure 8-6 does not show, stores the location and coloring information for the images, mapping these to the shared image through a

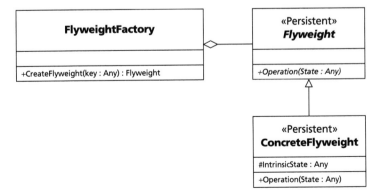

Figure 8-5 *The Flyweight Pattern*

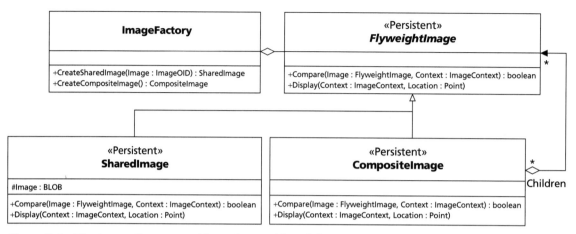

Figure 8-6   *The Image ComponentHierarchy as a Flyweight Pattern*

foreign key or association of some kind. When the application needs a shared image, the client asks the Factory for it, supplying an Image OID identifier as the key. The factory manages the querying of previously created images or the creation of new ones.

> Note: To keep things simple, the example in Figure 8-6 does not include the operations to implement the Composite pattern, such as First and Next or GetIterator.

Discussion

Persistent Flyweights differ from your usual persistent objects mainly in the relationships they have with other objects. In a relational database, the number of links to the Flyweight should be high enough to justify keeping it normalized instead of denormalizing to reduce the overhead of joins in the application.

Much of the Flyweight pattern is about how to represent the objects in memory, not how to store them in the database. In an OODBMS, for example, you have the option of making the Factory a persistent class and storing the links to shared Flyweights as persistent links in a set association. You then just retrieve the Factory and use the interface to retrieve the Flyweights into memory. With a relational database, this isn't really useful, since the Factory object has no state to store in a relational mapping. You can just as easily create the Factory and query the OIDs of the shared objects into an internal mapping structure, then query the objects as the clients request them through the Factory interface.

A critical fact of life with the Flyweight pattern is that all the subclasses must use the same types of extrinsic information. If you have any complexity in this regard (subclasses using different kinds of information) you need to extend the Flyweight with an aggregating pattern. That pattern lets you represent multiple kinds of interfaces in a single class hierarchy. In a Flyweight, data is either intrinsic or extrinsic, with all extrinsic data being passed through the Flyweight interface.

Sharing, as Chapter 7 points out, is a different kind of aggregation. When you share objects, you can no longer rely on the parent creating the object and managing it. Like any joint venture, the shared Flyweight needs a separate management to survive. That means a Factory, or some other manager object, that controls the set of Flyweights and implements the sharing capability of the set. For the most part, the Factory is a transient object in charge of creating and destroying Flyweight objects from persistent data. You can potentially make the Factory persistent if it contains data about the Flyweight, such as a special way to refer to the object (an indexing scheme for image elements based on strings, for example).

The original pattern [Gamma et al. 1995] states that the effectiveness of the pattern increases as the amount of object state that you can make extrinsic increases. Actually, the effectiveness increases as the amount of object state that you can make *intrinsic* increases. The more you can share, the better off you are.

If the extrinsic state is complex and requires additional normalization structuring, you may find that you are approaching the number of objects you had in your original problem. This is the classic case for *denormalization*, the recombining of elements of a normalized database to reduce join complexity and increase performance. Denormalization reduces the total number of objects (rows in a relational database) and the number of operations you must perform to navigate between objects. Consult Chapter 11 for a complete discussion of normal forms, normalization, and denormalization. If you find yourself creating a huge number of classes as you implement your Flyweight, you're almost certainly a candidate for flypapering the thing and denormalizing your database.

A relational database implements a Flyweight as a straightforward series of tables. The superclass Flyweight (FlyweightImage in Figure 8-6) shows the abstract, extrinsic interface for the various image components. Since it has no state, the table contains only the primary key for the subclass tables. You could alternatively define the Flyweight class as a UML interface instead of inheriting from it as a superclass and eliminate it entirely from the relational database. This produces the classic normalization scenario. In both cases, the references are a classic referential integrity foreign key relationship.

In an ORDBMS, the Flyweight pattern uses types and references rather than table nesting. Table nesting is a classic example of a composite aggregation, where the parent table owns the nested table. Instead, you break out the Flyweight class from the extrinsic classes and refer to it from them. You must maintain referential integrity in your application or in triggers, though, as references don't have automatic referential integrity mechanisms (see Chapter 12 for details).

In an OODBMS, you create the Flyweight superclass and its subclasses and retrieve the extent of the Flyweight through that class or the individual extents through the subclasses. You can also make the Factory persistent and thus make the set of Flyweight objects a persistent association using an OODBMS. You thus access the Flyweights through the Factory, just as you would in a purely transient organization. You use bidirectional relationships with automatic referential integrity maintenance for all these associations (see Chapter 13 for details).

The Metamodel Pattern

The Metamodel pattern models the structure of an object as a series of objects. This lets you build very general models of very complex, arbitrary data relationships.

> *Note: Metamodel is not a Gang-of-Four pattern but rather an original pattern from work I've done in the past. Other authors have similar structures [Hay 1996, pp. 61–65].*

The Problem

At times, reality can give you a reality check. This happens most when the complexity of the structure of objects is so great that your model explodes with subclasses and alternatives. It can also happen when your model starts out simple, then meets the real world when the customer uses it. The customer comes back with demand after demand, each of which adds more classes and attributes to your database.

There are two issues with this situation. The more complexity you have in your data model, the harder it is to maintain over time. It becomes harder to understand and harder to change. Second, the changes often affect a very small part of the population of users. You essentially wind up having to customize the system for each user and then transmit the customizations to all users.

The Solution

The Metamodel pattern builds structures using building blocks from the structural paradigm. Figure 8-7 illustrates the Metamodel pattern. The Client class represents a class of objects to which you want to add an attribute. The Attribute class represents a data attribute you add to the Client class. The Value association class models the many-to-many relationship between attribute and target client. You have one ConcreteValue subclass for each type of data you want to model.

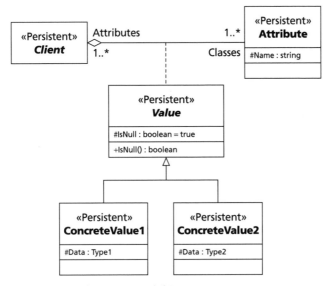

Figure 8-7 *The Metamodel Pattern*

The Metamodel pattern solves the feature creep problem by letting you "modify" the structure of the database without actually modifying the structure of the database. Instead, you add data to the metamodel structures, and your application presents that data as though it were actually part of the Client. Your program can present a fixed set of attributes, or you can provide an interface for the user to add attributes through the application.

Discussion

If you know the specific kind of database your system will use, you can modify the pattern to represent the conceptual model structures rather than using classes and attributes. For example, in a relational metamodel, you can model columns rather than attributes.

The biggest problem with the Metamodel pattern is the restriction on data retrieval. Attributes and values are not really database structures, and you can't use SQL or OQL to query them directly. You cannot, for example, use the attribute in a WHERE clause with a value literal to retrieve a subset of rows from a table. One way around this limitation is to provide a way for the system to create real structures in the database on the fly, which most databases can do. That means putting a bit more information into the Attribute and Value classes. The extra information lets you create SQL or ODL statements that build the correct structures and fill them in with data taken from the Value objects. Your application can then generate the appropriate SQL or OQL queries on the new objects.

> *Note: In the last few years, CASE and other software development tools have begun to use repositories, databases of metadata about software. These databases are a clear example of the Metamodel pattern.*

Analysis Patterns

An *analysis pattern* [Fowler 1997] is a model of concrete, domain-specific objects generalized for reuse in different situations. These are patterns that emerge from years of designing databases. You keep seeing the same tables or objects over and over until you just know what to do when you see the situation in a new context. The generalization is not to the level of the design patterns in the "Abstract Patterns" section, though. The analysis models have specific semantic ties to particular domains.

There are a huge number of domains for data models, as fine-grained as a system for representing utility patents and as coarse-grained as a model of people and organizations. There are some basic domain-specific models that have an intermediate granularity, such as the ones this section presents, and these models can be very reusable across domains with finer granularity.

> *Note: This section draws on the pioneering work of various people [Blaha and Premerlani 1998, pp. 81–88; Fowler 1997; Hay 1996; Silverston, Inmon, and Graziano 1997]. The models I present are modifications of that work, redrawn and redesigned using the UML modeling techniques of Chapter 7 and using the succinct style of the abstract pattern. The analysis patterns this section presents are just a few of those available. Also, because of space limitations, this section can't go into the kind of detail that the original authors did; please consult those works for more details on the domain-specific patterns. Where I have seen improvements, I mention them in the discussion rather than "improving" the original pattern. I'll leave that to a future book on database patterns.*

The Party Pattern

The Party pattern models, not celebrations, but people and organizations and their basic relationship: employment.

The Problem

Most business domains at one point or another involve people and organizations—people because people make up organizations, and organizations because businesses without organizations generally don't need databases. An organization is, however, more than just a simple aggregation of people. In certain ways, it is a kind of legal person in its own right, especially as the corporation or limited company. Both have names and addresses, and several people and organizations can share an address.

Employment is a relationship between a person and an organization. Unless your organization lives in a time warp, however, people and organizations have different employment relationships over time. People employed in a single organization over time can assume different positions with different job titles.

Finally, people and organizations relate to one another in reporting hierarchies. People report to other people, and organizations report to other organizations. The exact form of such relationships is often more general than a simple hierarchy, as people report through complex matrix arrangements and organizations associate to one another in networks.

The Solution

A *party* is a generalization of a person or an organization. Figure 8-8 shows the Party pattern that models people and organizations, their addresses (sites), their employment relationships, and their reporting relationships.

The Party relates to other parties in a many-to-many reporting relationship between a set of Superiors and a set of Reports. This is a completely general relationship between parties that handles any kind of reporting relationship. The special employment relationship is separate, however, as an association between people and organizations. The Party has "placements" at one or more sites, each of which has a purpose (Residence, Office, Manufacturing, and so on) and a text address (presumably with embedded line returns for mailing labels). Each site places any number of parties (people or organizations).

The Person has whatever data is of interest to the particular domain, as does the Organization. The two mutually relate as Employees and Employers, with the Employment class being an association class holding the time period over which employment extends. That class in turn associates with the Position Assignment class, which assigns a series of positions to a particular employment period. Each position relates to a given organization (composite aggregation), which is responsible for defining the position.

Discussion

A major problem with this pattern is the way it handles contact information. There are no telephone numbers, and the Site structure for addresses leaves something to be desired. If you wanted to query all people located in San

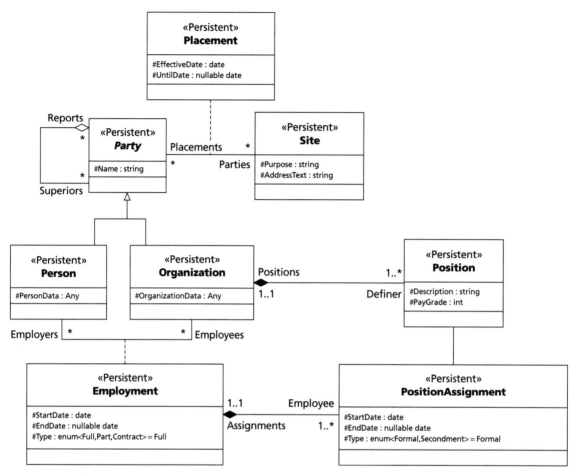

Figure 8-8 *The Party Pattern*

Francisco, for example, Site isn't going to help. The telephone problem might be just attributes in Person or Organization or even Party; unfortunately, there is more structure to contact than that. Each party can have multiple contact points, including several phones (home, office 1, office 2, cell, car), several email addresses, faxes, and different mailing addresses as well as their physical site location. Generally these come in some kind of priority—call this number first, then email, and so on. The Party pattern doesn't handle any of this.

The pattern also points up a common problem with analysis patterns—word choice. I would not choose the word "Party," for example, or "Placement." In different contexts and domains, the structure might be valid, but the semantics of the words might not be as appropriate. As an example, Figure 8-9 shows the commonplace book CriminalOrganization domain with some modifications to

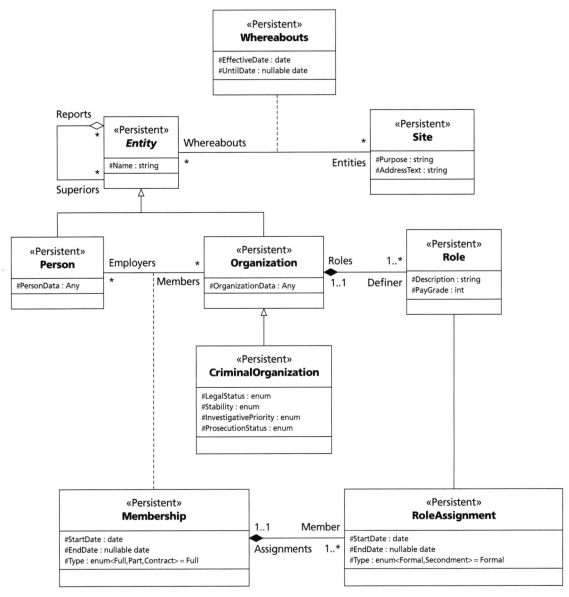

Figure 8-9   The CriminalOrganization as a Party

the class names that help the pattern make more sense in that context. The the-saurus can be your best friend as a data modeler.

Figure 8-9 also points up a further generalization. Instead of modeling Posi-tion, it models Role. This is a more general construct than Position, though it has much the same structure. You can model things that don't correspond to job positions using Role without stretching the semantics of the class title. You might generalize and simplify the structure further by modeling the relationship as a three-way relationship between Organization, Person, and Role rather than having the intermediate Employment class. Employment could be one role a person takes in an organization, while his specific position is yet another role. This greatly simplifies the complexity of an association to an association class in the original pattern.

The Geographic Location Pattern

The Geographic Location pattern models networks of geographical areas.

The Problem

Many businesses, organizations, and government entities need to model geographic locations. They need to track all kinds of different geographical areas, often for different reasons. Geopolitical locations provide data about countries, cities, states, counties, and other legally defined areas. They need to track surveyed areas such as townships and sections, usually established by a county assessor for tax purposes or ownership recording. They need to track specific types of areas, such as bodies of water, oil or other mineral deposits, or natural habitat areas. They need to track administrative regions. All of this goes far beyond site management, which requires only an address. Most applications need to understand at a relatively deep level how all these locations relate to one another.

Geographical information systems (GIS) provide an application interface and database structure for these kinds of applications. If you are designing your own, what kind of database structure do you need?

The Solution

The Geographic Location pattern provides a basic breakdown of kinds of locations and a way to relate locations to one another. Figure 8-10 illustrates the pattern. This particular version of the pattern reflects some of the requirements of a land management government agency at the third level, but the second-level categories are quite general.

The many-to-many relationship between locations reflects the fact that any given location may overlap with any other location, spatially and politically. For example, a government agency dealing with Native American affairs would require geopolitical areas for tribal land areas. These areas would overlap states, counties, and other geopolitical units as well as national forests and other management areas.

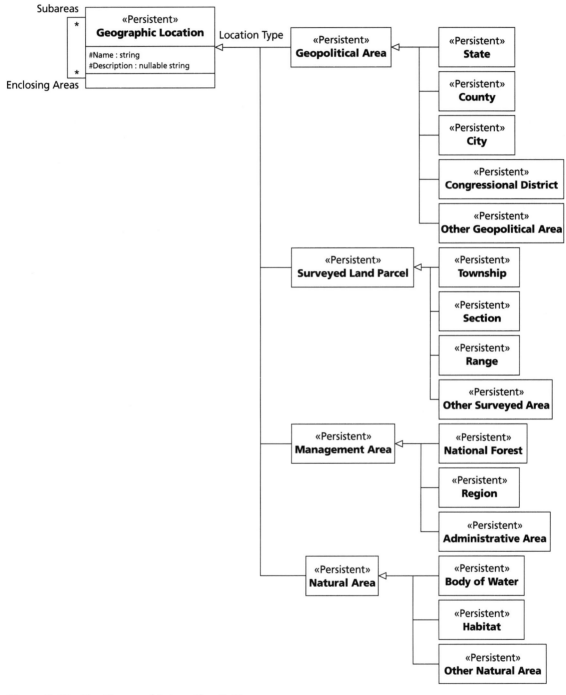

Figure 8-10   *The Geographic Location Pattern*

Discussion

While you can effectively represent addresses using Geographic Location, it's probably overkill. You could represent the site as a surveyed area, the city, the state, the zip code, and the country all as geographic locations related to one another. However, this pattern better represents demographic information or complex area management data, such as for a government agency or a resource exploration company.

The other problem with this pattern is its relatively arbitrary nature. Without too much thought, you can reclassify geographical areas in several different ways, raising the specter of multiple inheritance and infinite complications. This might be an instance where less is more: perhaps you should model location as a concept and let the data model the detailed classifications. In other words, use the Classification pattern to model classification and use the Location pattern to model location, then combine them to produce classifications of locations.

The Process Pattern

The Process pattern models continuous manufacturing processes. A good deal of manufacturing conforms to the discrete models of process that you usually find in work flow systems, with input objects moving along a path through transforming machines into new output states. Continuous manufacturing requires a different sort of model because it involves flows of materials such as oil or chemicals, not discrete items such as parts.

The Problem

Business models that model assets and part explosions are fine for modeling auto production or other manufacturing processes that produce bigger parts from smaller parts. Confronted with liquid flows as in a chemical production plant or sewage facility, these models fail. They are adequate to model the production facilities, machines, and pipes, but not to model the processes that result in products. For these processes, the concept of flow of material, and in particular the rate of flow, is the most important thing to model. As well, to ensure quality through process planning and measurement, you must distinguish between actual flows and potential flows. You want to measure what's supposed to happen as well as what actually does happen.

The Solution

Figure 8-11 is a rather complex representation of the Process pattern. It models a number of different aspects of the problem:

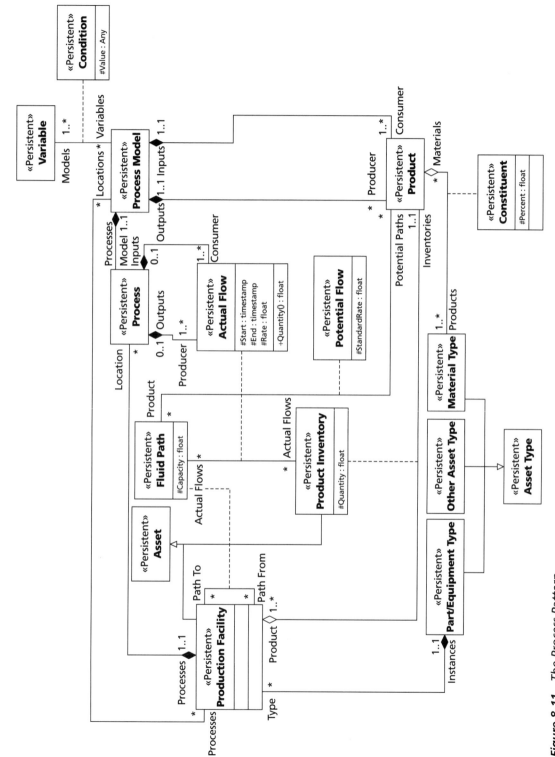

Figure 8-11   The Process Pattern

- The process models (conditions and potential inputs and outputs for processes)
- Process material requirements (products, flows, and constituents)
- Facility structures (facilities, product inventories, fluid paths)
- Process operations (potential and actual product flows through process instances)

> *Note: The original pattern [Hay 1996, pp. 187–196] is very different from Figure 8-11. As I translated the original pattern, I discovered many problems moving from the CASE*Method diagramming style into an OO style. In particular, the modeling of relationships as entities made it very difficult to translate Hays's pattern effectively. I have therefore taken the liberty of revising the pattern into a design that is more compatible with OO concepts.*

This pattern is an example of an explicit, detailed pattern for a particular middle-level domain. The details of the pattern are clearly beyond what an abstract pattern would represent. Yet it still is quite general, and it can apply to any number of industries, not just firms in a specific industry. You can see how the levels of detail of patterns can vary between your particular problem, your company's problems, your industry's problems, your type of industry's problems, and generic problems.

The process is also an example of the transitive qualities of associations in a software system. Figure 8-11 has several association classes that represent realized relationships between classes:

- *ProductInventory:* The relationship between Product and ProductionFacility; a facility contains an inventory of a product, which is a mixture of different materials
- *Constituent:* The relationship between MaterialType and Product, the composition of the Product mixture
- *FluidPath:* The relationship between two Production Facilities; literally, a pipe connecting two facilities that permits product to flow between processes
- *Condition:* The relationship between a ProcessModel and a set of Variables; the variables control the conditions under which the processes modeled can proceed
- *Actual Flow:* The relationship between ProductInventory and FluidPath; the actual flow of material mixtures (products) through the pipes (fluid paths)

Actual Flow is an example of a relationship on a relationship. The actual flow of materials from inventory to process follows the relationships between production facilities. Although seemingly complex in abstract form, you can easily see how all this works in the real world. You have mixtures of product in tanks. The product flows from the tanks through production facilities that apply processes controlled by models to transform the input products into output products. These outputs in turn flow into yet other tanks, and potentially become the input to yet other processes.

Discussion

When you start seeing this kind of reliance on associations, you should think about OODBMS products and schemas instead of RDBMS or even ORDBMS schemas. Your application is almost certain to concern itself primarily with navigation along the paths and flows, not with class-extent queries over entity types. The navigational qualities of OODBMS sets are much more likely to provide the facilities you need in your application. In these systems, you typically want to follow the pipes or flows, not retrieve tabular data about them.

The constraints in a pattern of this complexity are hard to get right. Looking at Figure 8-11, how would you automatically apply the process model to actual processes, for example? The model tells you what inputs a process expects and what outputs it produces, and it tells you the conditions of the variables under which it produces the product. Relating this to the production facilities means knowing where the inventories with the right mixtures are, what products can flow through which fluid paths at what capacities, and so on. The pattern contains the basic information, but there are many details still missing, such as scheduling of flows, tracking of samples and process measurements, and inventory management features. The Process pattern is a start at measuring the process relationships, but it doesn't provide everything you need for a continuous manufacturing domain by any stretch of the imagination.

The Document Pattern

The Document pattern lets you model documents, including structured documents and their users.

The Problem

The librarian's problem is the infinite, as one of the most famous librarians has pointed out, dreaming (perhaps) of an infinite number of hexagonal rooms, poorly lit, with books containing all possible combinations of the alphabet [Borges 1962]. The problem is to find the document that contains the information that you want among the huge volume of such things. As different media take hold in the publishing world, the librarian's job just gets more challenging.

The Solution

The Document pattern lets you describe the universe of documents that you choose to collect in your library. Figure 8-12 shows the Document pattern.

The first aspect of this pattern is the modeling of document types. Instead of using generalization for this, the pattern models the document types as a separate class using the Metamodel pattern. Because there are potentially an infinite number of kinds of documents with very little to distinguish them in structure or behavior, this provides a way to classify documents without complicating your design model. In this case, each document has a single type for classification purposes.

Next, you must represent copies and versions of documents. A document is the abstract concept of the document; a copy is a real instance of this abstraction. For example, Mark Twain's *Huckleberry Finn* is a document; the dog-eared copy on the third shelf from the left in Room 23 is a copy of the document. The key elements of the copy are a way to identify it and a location.

A version of a document is an abstraction, but at a finer grain than the document itself. There are two kinds of versions: the amendment and the edition. An

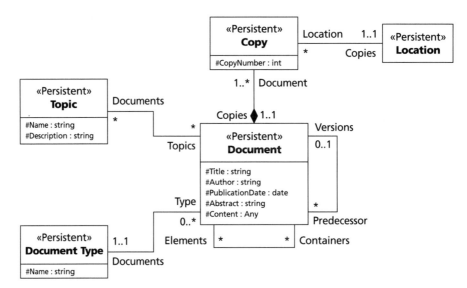

Figure 8-12   *The Document Pattern*

amendment adds a second document that extends the first one and becomes (usually legally) a part of it. An edition replaces the document with a revised version. Continuing the Mark Twain example, someone can publish the original edition with an amending preface that contains biographical and historical material that sets the context. Another example is a contract document and later amendments to that contract that change the terms of the contract after the signing of the contract. As an example of the edition, a publisher has just come out with a revision of Huckleberry Finn based on an extensive analysis of original manuscripts and author's notes that extensively revises and adds to the material in the original edition of the book. The pattern assumes that you can have multiple versions but only one predecessor. That is, you can produce multiple branches of versions, but each branch leads back to a single document.

The Document pattern lets you associate topics with documents however you like. You can find a particular topic in any number of documents, and a particular document may address any number of topics. The structure assumes that a document can address no topics. This lets you create a document without indexing it immediately; it also lets you store documents that you cannot access through the topic index.

Discussion

Obvious applications of the document pattern apply to areas such as knowledge management or World Wide Web content searching and other indexing functionality. Going beyond such indexing and searching, the next step in document management is managing work flow. You can add in the Party pattern and connect it through roles to show how documents move from role to role in a work flow process. One such role could replace the Author attribute with a relationship to a Party. Others could link a Person as the current owner of the document, the signer of the document, or any other related role. You would also record the history of the process as a series of role ownership records.

You might also choose to extend the Document class hierarchy with inheritance while still continuing to use the DocumentType objects. This would give you two ways to classify documents, one relating to structure and behavior and the other as a purely abstract categorization. Both may be useful at different times for different reasons. For example, you may have structured information available for a document that you want to use to search or otherwise process the data. Rather than adding extensive metamodeling, it might prove more efficient to create subclasses in the database for different kinds of documents. For example, the IdentificationDocument hierarchy might contain detailed data that you could use for query purposes, or you might have fingerprint documents with special category elements useful in quickly searching for records.

Summary

A design pattern is a reusable system that describes a design problem and its solution. The generic pattern contains a number of elements:

- A name
- A problem description
- A solution description
- A discussion of issues, trade-offs, and consequences of the pattern

An abstract pattern is a pattern of classes and relationships that describe a generic solution to a generic problem. This chapter gave several examples of abstract data model patterns:

- *Singleton:* Ensures that a class has only one instance in the database
- *Composite:* Represents a tree structure made up of different kinds of related objects, all of which share the same interface; a part-whole hierarchy or parts explosion in your database
- *Flyweight:* Uses sharing to reduce redundancy in the system (normalization)
- *Metamodel:* Represents data about data to enable flexible and extensible data modeling

An analysis pattern is a model of concrete, domain-specific objects generalized for reuse in different situations. This chapter gave several examples of analysis patterns:

- *Party:* Jointly represents people and organizations (entities)
- *Geographic Location:* Represents an extensive variety of physical places
- *Process:* Represents a flow-oriented manufacturing process
- *Document:* Represents an extensive variety of documents and searching features

Abstract patterns and analysis patterns give you a leg up on your data modeling. The next chapter shows you how to get a clue as to how big the horse is that you're mounting.

O mighty Caesar! Dost thou lie so low? Are all thy conquests, glories, triumphs, spoils, Shrunk to this little measure?

Shakespeare, *Julius Caesar* III.i.148

I considered titling this chapter "Measures *of* Success." I thought about it a little and instead opted to use the word "for." Measuring is not passive. It is an active, indeed aggressive approach to forcing success to emerge out of a situation. At its essence, measuring is feedback. It is the process of obtaining information to use to guide your work to a successful conclusion.

Many of the measurement efforts in which I've participated have been passive measurement. Passive measurement collects data because that's what professionals do, or because a consultant recommended it, or because somebody's read a book. This is making measurement into a magical talisman, an amulet you can wear to ward off evil spirits. Although amulets may have their place, software development isn't it.

To measure aggressively, you must first know why you are measuring. What kind of feedback are you trying to get? Are you trying to decide whether your approach is too complex? Are you hoping to improve the quality of your product through measuring defect rates? Are you hoping to improve productivity? Are you trying to understand the effectiveness of the systems you've put in place to get results? If you can't articulate a specific reason for measuring, you shouldn't be measuring because you won't use the results.

Goals, Metrics, and Scales

A *metric* is a method of measuring some empirical aspect of the real world. In this case, the metric is a tool that measures the achievement of the goal you've articulated. The metric lets you measure how well the system you've designed matches the goals you've set for it.

Designing a valid metric for a particular goal is hard. You need to worry about three things:

- You have to be able to measure your goals.
- You have to use the right kind of scale for the type of goal.
- You have to use a metric that lets you make meaningful statements about the state of the object.

Some goals are not measurable, however cunning the metric. Vague goals or goals with little structure prevent you from measuring the results. If you can't get good empirical data with the metric, and if you can't relate that data directly to the objective, you do not have a valid metric. If you can't build a metric or state a measurable goal, you should rethink your objective.

A *scale* is a mapping from an empirical system to a numerical system. The *representation problem* occurs whenever the relationships between empirical elements are the same as the relationships between numerical elements [Roberts 1979, pp. 54–55]. The *uniqueness problem* is how unique this homomorphism (mapping between elements) is. That is, what kinds of transformations can you apply to the data without destroying the representation? Measurement theory specifies a standard set of scale types it identifies by the kind of transformation. Table 9-1 shows the standard scales and their characteristics.

For example, your goal might be a simple true-or-false goal, such as "to represent criminal organizations." You would use a nominal metric (1 or 0 for true or false). If your goal relates to an ordering, such as "to order criminal organizations by prosecutor priority," use an ordinal metric (1, 2, and 3 for high, medium, and low priority). A goal with no zero value, such as "to make data available to prosecutors within two days of acquisition," should use an interval metric such as the data acquisition date. A quantifiable goal, such as "to achieve manageable schema complexity," needs a ratio metric (a measurable schema complexity metric such as number of relationships divided by number of classes). Finally, an absolute goal of some kind, such as "to count number of burglaries in West Sussex," requires an absolute metric (number of burglaries).

It doesn't do any good to measure achievement of a goal that has no meaningful characteristics. For example, controversy continues about the measurement of intelligence, and in particular its application to determining the intellectual success of individuals. None of the words in the previous sentence are in themselves *meaningful,* much less measurable. Does IQ measure "intelligence," and if so, how? Effectively measurable goals should stick to relatively commonplace things in the real world, such as effort, time, and money. It also doesn't do any good to try to apply metrics that use a certain kind of scale to goals that re-

Table 9-1 *Types of Measurement Scales from Measurement Theory*

Scale	Characteristics	Example
Nominal	Any one-to-one transformation is possible. There is no ordering of numbers and no ability to add, subtract, or relate any two numbers other than a basic equality comparison. Uses numbers as labels or names.	Boolean values (true/false), categorizations (good, bad, don't care), alternative codes such as WBS numbers or object identifiers
Ordinal	Any order-preserving transformation is possible. Only order is important, not the relative distance between numbers or the value of the numbers in themselves.	Rankings (good, better, best), grades, mineral hardness
Interval	Linear transformations of the type $\phi(x) = ax + b$ for $a > 0$. An ordered scale with an arbitrary origin b and a unit of measurement a, allowing you to compare intervals between scale values.	Temperature (Celsius or Fahrenheit), time
Ratio	Linear transformation of the type $\phi(x) = ax$ for $a > 0$. Scale values are unique with respect to an arbitrary unit of measurement a, allowing you to compare the numbers themselves. The scale fixes the origin (zero), however.	Length, mass, absolute temperature, and similar physical quantities; time intervals; effort; most kinds of value where there is a concept of no (zero) value
Absolute	No transformations possible.	Count of objects

quire a different scale. For example, consider a goal "to deliver the object within 10% of the estimated effort." You decide to measure this goal with a metric that rates effort for an object as "too little, just right, too much." You're going to have trouble making the objective have any real meaning.

Table 9-2 sets out several characteristics that you can use to evaluate your metric [Osgood, Suci, and Tannenbaum 1957, p. 11; Henderson-Sellers 1996, pp. 33–38]. The more of these criteria that your metric satisfies, the better is the metric.

Finally, measure the measurement. Keep track of the impact of your measuring activities, and improve them just as you would any other system.

The key areas in which you need to measure include the size of your model, its complexity, how well it hangs together (cohesion), and how well you've divided things up (coupling). The ultimate value of your model is in its reuse

Table 9-2 *Evaluation Criteria for Metrics*

Criterion	Definition
Objectivity	Does the metric yield reproducible data? Can different data collectors measure the same object with the same results?
Reliability	Does the metric yield the same results under the same conditions, within acceptable margins of error?
Validity	Can you validate the data that the metric yields with other similar data that measures a similar kind of goal? Is there another metric that you can use to provide assurance that you are getting valid data?
Sensitivity	Does the metric yield data capable of distinguishing differences at the level of your goal?
Comparability	Can you apply the metric to all objects having the same or a similar goal?
Utility	Can you collect meaningful data at a reasonable rate and with reasonable effort?

potential, both for the model itself and for the system you build from it. The following sections summarize some of the metrics you can use to measure these aspects of your data model.

Size Measures

A critical measure by any standard is the metric for the size of your system. The most common measure, lines of code, is nearly useless for measuring database-centric systems, since code is not really your concern. For these kinds of systems, your measurement goals are to understand how big the database will be for storage resource estimation and how big the data model will be for effort estimation.

Database Size

Sizing a database is a tricky thing, even when you have an actual database to measure. At the data modeling stage, your resources are even more limited. This is especially true if your choice of underlying DBMS technology is still uncertain, or if you have multiple DBMS targets for your system. At the data modeling stage, your best bet is to get an order-of-magnitude metric based on the number of classes and the average estimated number of persistent objects per class. You can get this latter number by looking at existing systems or the logical definition of the system to determine how many objects the system might create in some typical time interval.

Schema Size

Sizing a schema for estimation purposes is easy, right? You just count the classes, and voila! Perhaps, but if you are going to be using the size metric for estimating effort, you'll find that not all classes are created equal, at least for that purpose.

The best all-around metric for schema size that I've found is the function point. A function point is an ordinal-scale metric (with some interval-ratio tendencies) that measures the functionality of a software system. There is no room for an extensive description of function points here, so you should consult a tutorial for more details [Dreger 1989; Garmus and Herron 1996; IFPUG 1994; Jones 1991].

Once you have your use cases, you can count function points for your system as a whole. The total number of adjusted function points gives you a clear measure of the size of the software system, including the database-centric aspects. In counting function points, you divide the functionality of your system into five separate countable types of functions:

- *External inputs (EIs)*: Transactions that result in input across the application boundary
- *External outputs (EOs)*: Transactions that result in output across the application boundary
- *External queries (EQs)*: Transactions that send inputs to the application and get back outputs without changing anything in the database
- *Internal logical files (ILFs)*: Data the application manages
- *External interface files (EIFs)*: Data the application uses but doesn't manage

For schema sizing, these last two counts are the most important. ILFs are for the most part the persistent classes in your data model. To qualify as an ILF, your persistent class must be within the application boundary; that is, your application must create persistent objects of the class as part of its essential function. ELFs, on the other hand, are classes that you refer to but don't maintain. That is, your application does not create or update persistent objects, it just uses them after retrieval from the database.

To count ILFs and ELFs, you need your data model and your use cases. First, divide the classes in your model according to whether the application manages them or just queries them. For example, in the commonplace book system, the bulk of the classes represent data that the application queries for the Holmes PLC operatives without letting them change anything. These are ELFs, such as Person and CriminalOrganization. There are some classes that represent operatives' input into the system, such as Case Note, in which operatives record their reports on current cases. These are ILFs. Most systems have many small tables that an administrator maintains, such as lists of cities and states, data type codes, and security information. These are usually ELFs in most applications. The tables critical to a given application are usually ILFs, but not always, as in the common-place book. Such systems are usually query-only systems for the most part.

> *Tip: If your data model consistently marks the operations of classes with the {query} tag, you should consider adding a {query} tag to the class to indicate that it is an ELF rather than an ILF in your application. This makes counting function points even easier.*

The second part of function point counting is determining the complexity of the count for a given item. To do this for the two file counts, you need to determine the record element types (RETs) and data element types (DETs) for the file. With respect to function points, complexity is a weighting factor by which you multiply the raw counts to get an "unadjusted" function point count (I'll get to "adjusting" those counts later).

DETs are "unique user recognizable, nonrecursive fields/attributes, including foreign key attributes, maintained on the ILF or EIF" [Garmus and Herron 1996, pp. 46–47]. These correspond to the individual attributes and relationships in your UML classes. You count one DET for each attribute/relationship; you don't vary this by the number of objects of the class or the number of related objects. You just count the attributes and relationships. If you have a relationship to a class with an explicit OID consisting of more than one attribute, you count one DET for each of the attributes rather than just one DET for the relationship. The explicit OID means that you are using a user-recognizable attribute to identify an object, and therefore each contributes to complexity. You can ignore attributes that appear only as implementation techniques. You also should collapse repeating attributes that are identical in format, a common implementation technique. Usually these are arrays or structures (or embedded classes); sometimes for reasons of clarity you break them out into separate attributes, such as a series of bit flags or a group of monthly amount fields. Ignore these extra attributes and count a single DET.

RETs "are user recognizable subgroups (optional or mandatory) of data elements contained within an ILF or EIF. Subgroups are typically represented in an entity relationship diagram as entity subtypes or attributive entities, commonly called parent-child relationships" [Garmus and Herron 1996, p. 47]. The RET thus corresponds to either the generalization relationship or to the composite aggregation association or to the parent-child recursive relationship in UML persistent object diagrams. The idea is to count a single RET for a single object, and an object consists of its class and its superclasses as well as the objects it owns through aggregation. You count one RET for an object with no generalization or aggregation association, or you count one RET for each such relationship.

For a real-world example, consider the criminal organization in Figure 8-9, reproduced here and labeled for your convenience as Figure 9-1. The commonplace book lets the operative query information about the criminal organization; other parts of the Holmes PLC system maintain the information. Therefore, all of the classes in Figure 9-1 are EIFs or RETs. In a data entry application for criminal organizations, they would be ILFs and RETs. The RET/DET determination is the same, however. The EIFs appear with the «EIF» stereotype and the RETs appear with the «RET» stereotype, just to be completely compatible with the UML notational world. You show the DET counts as tagged DET values on the classes.

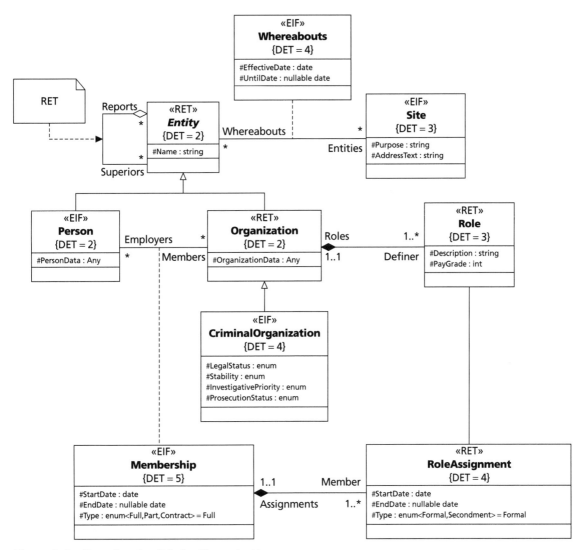

Figure 9-1   *Counting the CriminalOrganization*

There are five EIFs with five RETs and 29 DETs in Figure 9-1. It's not quite that simple, however, because you need to associate the RETs and DETs with the EIFs of which they are a part. This lets you factor in the complexity of the EIF or ILF in counting its function points. The example shows the kind of decisions you need to make.

> *Note: Figure 9-1 shows how you can use the UML notation in a completely different way, in this case to count function points more easily. If you are using a diagramming tool that permits multiple views of models, you can use the various different stereotypes and tags to great effect in this way. Such tools are hard to come by, however; I know of none that currently support this kind of modeling.*

The first decision you must make is what class in a class hierarchy to use as the EIF. In this case, our application focuses on CriminalOrganization, so that becomes the first EIF. If you're counting a standalone database design, you start with the root class as the EIF. You then make the subclasses RETs. In this case, we make the CriminalOrganization class an EIF and the rest RETs.

The Entity class provides a second decision. It has a recursive, parent-child relationship to show how entities relate to one another. This association becomes an RET.

The Role class provides a third decision. Because it relates to the Organization class as a composite aggregate, it becomes an RET rather than an EIF. That is, you consider the Role a part of the Organization object rather than thinking about it separately. The Role is a part of the Organization.

Finally, the Membership class owns the RoleAssignment class, so that is in turn an RET rather than an EIF. Again, the RoleAssignment is a part of the Membership (which in turn is a relationship between a Person and an Organization, just to be totally confusing).

How do you convert the raw function point count (in this case, five EIFs) into the unadjusted function point count? Use Table 9-3 to determine the ordinal value for the complexity given the number of RETs and the number of DETs for a given EIF.

Let's consider the EIFs one by one. The first one is CriminalOrganization, the center of the web. It has two generalization RETs, Organization and Entity, its superclasses. Organization has in turn the RET for Role, making three RETs. Leave the RoleAssignment to its owner, Membership. Entity has a RET for the parent-child recursive relationship. Thus the CriminalOrganization EIF has four RETs and a total of eight DETs from the various classes, leading to a low complexity.

Person has a single RET, its superclass Entity. It has two DETs itself and two for Entity. That leads to a low complexity. You don't count the RET for the

Table 9-3 *File Complexity Ordinals*

RETs	1–19 DETs	20–50 DETs	51+ DETs
1	Low	Low	Average
2–5	Low	Average	High
6+	Average	High	High

parent-child recursive relationship again, as you've already accounted for that in the Organization count.

Site has no RETs, which means you count one RET for the class itself. It has three DETs. That leads to a low complexity.

Whereabouts has no RETS (1) and four DETs, two for its attributes and two for the foreign keys of the association class, leading to a low complexity.

Membership has one RET (RoleAssignment) and five DETs, three for the attributes and two for the foreign keys of the association class, leading to a low complexity.

Given these ordinals, you calculate unadjusted function points with Table 9-4.

Since all of the complexity ordinals are low, you multiply the number of EIFs by five to get a total of 25 unadjusted function points (five EIFs multiplied by complexity multiplier five). The CriminalOrganization application that uses these classes thus has 25 function points relating to the database. There are, of course, other function points coming from the EI, EO, and EQ calculations for the transient software subsystems; these contribute to effort estimates just as much as the data calculations.

The final step in counting function points is to adjust the total by the "general system characteristics." It is at this point that function points become a bad metric. You evaluate your application according to an ordinal scale on various characteristics, such as data communications, performance, transaction rate, online data entry, reusability, installation ease, multiple sites, and online update. You rate each item on an ordinal scale of 1 to 5, then sum these to get the total degree of influence. You then calculate the value adjustment factor by multiplying this number by .01 and adding 0.65 to it. This calculation, unfortunately, completely destroys the validity of the measure by converting it from an ordinal scale to a ratio scale, resulting in a meaningless fractional number such as 4.356.

Fortunately, for most database systems using the client/server model and destined for a real-world commercial environment with a decent number of users, the value adjustment factor comes surprisingly close to unity (1). For the most

Table 9-4 *Function Point Count Multipliers*

Type	Low	Average	High
ILF	×7	×10	×15
EIF	×5	×7	×10

part, I recommend using the unadjusted function point count as your size measure for this reason.

> *Note: You should consult the IFPUG documentation for complete details on adjusting function points. If your situation differs significantly from the normal commercial database application, you may need to adjust your function point count. Don't put too much faith in the exact nature of the number, however, since you've abrogated the mathematical validity of the scale by moving to a ratio scale.*

Complexity Measures

Function points give you a measure of the size of your information system, but they don't tell you much about how complex it is. Although you adjust your functions for complexity, the result is still a weighted size measure.

Most of the work on complexity relates to programming complexity, but even then the problem with the term is its vague meaning [Fenton and Pfleeger 1997; Henderson-Sellers 1996]. In the context of the data model, it is definitely less than clear what you mean when you say you want to measure complexity. The dictionary defines "complex" as "made up of related parts" or "complicated," which in turn means "difficult, confused, intricate, or complex." The complexity of a model is of interest because of the assumed relationship between such complexity and the difficulty in building the system.

The first distinction you need to make is between problem complexity and solution complexity. Data modeling generally models the problem, and thus the problem complexity is of more interest here than the solution complexity. On the other hand, the data model is the first cut at the design of the system, and design complexity is solution complexity. If you spend any amount of time working with designing databases, you very quickly realize that there are different ways to model the problem—some more difficult and some less difficult. Which is more appropriate depends usually on the use to which you are going to put the model.

Solution complexity breaks down a number of different ways. One breakdown divides complexity into algorithmic (efficiency of the system), structural (architectural elements and relationships), and cognitive (effort required to understand the system) [Fenton and Pfleeger 1997, p. 245]. Another approach breaks complexity into computational (algorithmic), psychological (cognitive, structural, and problem), and representational complexity [Henderson-Sellers 1996, pp. 51–52]. Most research focuses on structural complexity, with some research devoted to cognitive complexity. Unfortunately, most of this work relates to procedural design, not to database design.

An example is the most frequently used complexity metric, *cyclomatic complexity,* or the McCabe metric [McCabe and Butler 1989]. This metric takes a model of a procedure as a connected graph (a graph where all nodes are reachable from every other node):

$$V(G) = e - n + 2$$

where e is the number of edges in the graph, n is the number of nodes in the graph, and 2 has to do with the number of paths in a strongly connected graph. $V(G)$ measures the number of linearly independent paths through graph G [Fenton and Pfleeger 1997, p. 293]. Unfortunately, there are significant limitations in the metric as a measure of complexity, and it applies to procedural structure, not to data structure.

> Note: For tools that let you apply McCabe's metric to a variety of programming languages, consult the McCabe Associates Web page at www.mccabe.com/vqt/.

There is no widely accepted measure of database schema complexity. Nevertheless, database designers intuitively know when they are complicating their lives with their design. The best I can do at this point is Occam's razor, turning complexity into simplicity: make the data model as simple as possible. This does not mean fewer classes; you can combine a bunch of classes into a single class and have a much more complicated system because the result is harder to use and maintain. Another test is the idiot test: explain the model to any idiot off the street (who understands UML) and see where he or she fails to grasp what's going on. The problem with the idiot test is that you're assuming that you understand the model well enough to make up questions that reveal lack of knowledge on other people's parts, a rather subjective assumption at best. It's also kind of rude.

Cohesion Measures

There are two types of cohesion of interest to the database designer: the abstract cohesion of a classifier and the structural cohesion of a set of related classifiers. It's important to realize that cohesion is a central aspect of reusability. The more cohesive your classes, the more likely you are to be able to reuse the classes under different circumstances. The later section "Reuse Potential" addresses this issue in detail.

Abstraction Cohesion

The *cohesion* of an individual classifier (class, interface, package, subsystem) is "the extent to which its individual components are needed to perform the same task" [Fenton and Pfleeger 1997, p. 312]. The data model classifier requires a slight modification of this definition: the extent to which it needs its individual components to maintain its *abstraction*.

The data model as a UML static structure model is a set of abstract classifiers and the relationships between them. You should therefore be able to use standard measures of abstraction cohesion to measure the cohesion of your model. One such metric is the *lack-of-cohesion metric* [Chidamber and Kemerer 1993]. This metric relates the class methods to its attributes on a pairwise basis. You systematically compare all pairs of methods and classify them as good or bad: a good member function pair is one that shares at least one attribute or relationship of the class. You don't compare the method to itself, nor do you distinguish pairs based on the order of the operations in the pair.

The biggest problem with this measure of cohesion is that it requires at least partial implementation of the system's methods. You could estimate this at the data model stage by listing the attributes or relationships you think a method that implements an operation will use. This is just an estimate until you get through the coding. Most of the examples in the last two chapters don't even have operations specified, as they aren't critical to data modeling.

Another problem with this metric is the emphasis on abstraction as a data concept rather than as a semantic concept. You really want to measure how well the class hangs together conceptually, how integral the various components are to the meaning of the class. We do not as yet have any direct way to measure this. Again, using your intuition can be the best way to estimate the cohesion of a class. Are the attributes and relationships meaningful aspects of some underlying thing you are modeling? If you think you can spot clusters of attributes that relate to different things, you can try to split up the class to see whether the different components can work as separate classes. This is often successful in creating inheritance hierarchies, as you separate individual elements that apply only under certain circumstances. A classic example of this is the undefined null value, where an attribute is null by definition when a certain logical condition is true. Creating a subclass and moving the attribute into it often removes the need to make the attribute null. This is a good example of abstraction cohesion.

Structural Cohesion

If you consider a set of related classes as a system comprising the classes and their relationships, you can think about the cohesion of that system directly rather than just the cohesion of the individual classes. This structural cohesion is the extent to which the objects' structure yields meaningful results in queries.

A *dependency* is an implication constraint on a set of attributes. A *functional dependency* is a single-attribute implication: if you know the value of attribute A, then you know the value of attribute B. A *multivalued dependency* is a two-attribute constraint: if you know the values of A and B, then you know the value of C. More generally, a *join dependency* is an *n*-valued constraint. Dependencies are the basis for the process of normalization in relational databases. See Chapter 11 for a complete discussion of these concepts.

Normalization provides you with the assurance that

1. you can update or delete a value in a table with a single command

2. you can join any tables without losing information

These assurances are also a good definition of structural cohesion, at least to the extent that they apply to the underlying structures. The problem with using strict normalization as a measure of OO cohesion of a set of classes is that its formal requirements are a bit *too* strict for the very flexible OO world. First normal form, for example, requires that all attributes have a single value, whereas multivalued attributes such as arrays, structures, and nested classes are possible in OR and OO systems. The join operation is meaningless on such attributes, as it depends on a single-valued comparison operator. That is, you can't join two sets of objects on an array attribute; the whole notion is meaningless.

On the other hand, you can make a pretty good argument that a database with such things in it is going to be difficult to use, at best, if your query language has a join operator in it. If you use arrays, for example, as attributes of a persistent class, and you are designing a relational database, you're going to have problems using ANSI SQL to form queries of that data. Since relational databases don't have the concept of an array, you're going to have problems mapping the UML design into your relational schema at all.

Given this fact, it should be clear that unless your target schema data model is an OR or OO model, you should not use structured data in your classes. To do so reduces structural cohesion. Instead, you should break out structured data into separate classes and use relationships to represent the multivalued structure. This solution, of course, maps directly to normalization.

You thus can evaluate the structural cohesion of your system on a five-point ordinal scale:

- *First normal form:* No class contains an attribute of a structured data type.

- *Second normal form:* No class contains an attribute that is not fully dependent on an OID of the class.

- *Third normal form:* No class contains a functional dependency that is not from a full OID of the class (really Boyce-Codd normal form).

- *Fourth normal form:* No class contains a multivalued dependency that is not from a full OID of the class.

- *Fifth normal form:* No class contains a join dependency that is not from a full OID of the class; put another way, you cannot join any tables in such a way that you lose information.

The use of normalization status as a proxy for cohesion shows promise, but it definitely restricts your design choices in interesting ways. By "interesting," I mean likely to cause arguments among knowledgeable people. You will find those who adamantly believe that "good" database design has nothing to do with normalization, and those who believe that unless the data is in at least third normal form the design is evil and degenerate in the extreme. You will also find those who regard normalization irrelevant to OO design [Blaha and Premerlani 1998, p. 273]. I prefer to think about normalization more gently as a cohesion metric. I strive to be more cohesive and use cohesion as a rationale for decision making, but it does not constrain my application of common sense to data model design. I will say that using entity- or class-based design methods such as UML, you tend to get fully normalized, fifth-normal-form databases because they tend to reflect semantically meaningful objects and relationships.

Coupling Measures

Coupling is "the degree of interdependence between modules" [Fenton and Pfleeger 1997, p. 310; Yourdon and Constantine 1979]. As with cohesion, design theory says it is easier to modify and to reuse systems that minimize coupling. Yourdon and Constantine defined six kinds of coupling between two modules in an ordinal scale. This metric refers to the way in which a module uses data in another module, which (in a regular program) either happens through direct reference or by passing data on the stack.

1. *No coupling:* The two modules are totally independent of one another.

2. *Data coupling:* The two modules pass data (not control) through parameters on methods.

3. *Stamp coupling:* The two modules pass data of the same structured type through parameters on methods (they both depend on a third structure).

4. *Control coupling:* One module passes data that controls a decision point in the other module (control data, or flag parameters that a conditional statement checks before doing something).

5. *Common coupling:* Both modules refer to shared global data.

6. *Content coupling:* One module refers directly to data inside the other.

Translating these ordinal values into the database world is reasonably straightforward. The database provides more connections, however. You can refer to data through associations, through generalization and inheritance, or by reference in operational code (SQL, OQL, or procedural code in stored procedures or methods).

No coupling in the database means that a given class does not have any associations to other classes and does not inherit from another class. Methods on the class do not refer to data in other classes in any way. They refer only by calling methods on other classes, executing stored global procedures that refer to data in other classes, or directly through SQL or variable references.

Data coupling limits access to persistent data values (not objects, just primitive data types) by encapsulating them all in methods. A class that accesses such data through method calls, but not by association or inheritance or direct reference and not any other object data, exhibits data coupling to the other class.

A class that gains access to structured data (record types, arrays, or objects) through methods exhibits *stamp coupling.* In a relational database, this means accessing data through stored procedures that return cursors or structured data (record types or some other structured object). In an OR database, stamp coupling means having methods that pass in or return objects, such as the Oracle8 object view. In an OO database, stamp coupling can additionally mean using OQL constructs that refer to objects. For example, you can have expressions that return a set or bag of objects or expressions that use functions taking arguments of class types.

Control coupling is by definition procedural, not data oriented. To the extent a database language supports procedural control, you can have control coupling in your language statements. In the relational database, for example, a correlated subquery exhibits control coupling. This is where a nested SELECT refers outside itself to a value in the outer select (a parameter) to limit its return. Even more directly, creating a parameterized SQL statement that uses the parameter in a WHERE clause, or building an SQL statement using data passed in by parameter in a transient method, both exhibit control coupling. Boolean flags in methods are still the most common control coupling in OR and OO databases.

Turning this around, if you find yourself creating Boolean flags in your tables or classes, are you going to use these to make control decisions, or do they just represent true/false data? If it's the former, you should consider a subclass to represent the different control choice. For example, consider Criminal-Organization in the commonplace book. You can add a Boolean value to indicate whether the organization is active or not. If the intent is to represent information for query purposes, this is just fine. If the intent is to support a method that returns a different value if the caller sets the flag, that's control coupling. The same logic applies to invalid nulls—null values that represent not missing data but invalid attributes. Breaking the attributes out into a separate table eliminates the nulls and the control coupling they require.

Another way to look at this decision is to decide whether your flag is part of the object state or whether it represents a different kind of object. The best way to decide this is to think about what happens when the flag's value changes. Does the object need to mutate into a different kind of object? If it does, it's a strong indication that the flag represents state. Once you create an object, you generally shouldn't be converting it into another object because of some control transition in your system. It's better design to change the internal state of the object through an internal flag.

Common coupling refers to the use of global data. In a sense, using a database at all means you are using global data, and hence you raise your coupling level to common for any class that refers to data in the database. Global data is data that is visible to all parts of a system. To get access to data in a database, you connect to the database server, then use SQL, OQL, or some other access mechanism to manipulate the data. What little visibility control exists is part of the database security mechanism, not the programming visibility mechanism.

> Note: It would be interesting to design a feature into an RDBMS or ORDBMS to provide visibility control for just this reason. Your application could declare visibility of a particular schema, reducing your coupling to data/stamp coupling. I often use security mechanisms to achieve this effect by splitting up the integrated schema into subsystems stored in different areas (users, roles, databases, authorizations, or whatever the security construct in the particular DBMS). I then use security access mechanisms, usually either privilege grants or database links, to make data selectively visible. This limits the global impact, but it's not very portable and requires quite a bit of database administration on the server side. Another approach I've used is to encapsulate tables within stored procedures, or in the case of PL/SQL, with packages. I hide the tables in a user that owns everything but just grants access to the procedures, not to the underlying data.

With a relational schema, you don't have much choice but to access the data globally. OR schemas, unfortunately, do not encapsulate their data for the most part, so again you must access data globally. OO schemas, on the other hand, offer fully encapsulated access to data, so in an OO database you have full visibility control.

Similarly, with *content coupling,* you refer directly to data rather than referring to it only through methods. The relational and object-relational database do not encapsulate the data, and the SQL refers directly to it. You can use views and stored procedures to emulate encapsulation in relational and OR systems. The view is a way of encapsulating access to a schema by creating a stored SQL statement that looks like a table, at least for query purposes. Similarly, you can create stored procedures (in Oracle, stored packages) that emulate classes and methods with some limitations already discussed in Chapter 7. With OO databases, you should never make your data visible directly but rather you should create accessor and mutator operations that provide access, thus reducing coupling to data/stamp coupling.

Coupling intimately relates to maintainability and reusability. The lower you are on the coupling scale, the easier it is to maintain your system, and the more likely you are to be able to reuse it under different scenarios. The less strongly coupled your classes are, the less impact do changes to any given class have on the rest of the system.

In OO design, there are three specific ways to limit coupling.

First, observe encapsulation. If you make your attributes public, you allow other classes to move all the way to content coupling, the worst variety. If you change your class, all the classes that use it must also change. The more you can conceal, the better. For example, do not just create get/set methods for all your attributes by rote. This is, strictly speaking, better than content coupling (it's data or stamp coupling), but you will find that changing the internal structure without changing the interface is quite difficult. Create an interface that is meaningful rather than just exposing your internal structure. A nice way to remember all this is to observe the Law of Demeter: any object should access directly only objects directly connected to it through association or generalization [Lieberherr, Holland, and Riel 1988].

In persistent terms, this means that you should encapsulate your data attributes as much as possible. If you use SQL or OQL in your coding, encapsulate it in the appropriate classes. SQL, almost by definition, is a global-variable programming language with no encapsulation at all. This leads naturally to a programming style that uses common and content coupling. As just mentioned, there are ways around this using stored procedures and functions to encapsulate tables, and you can also use views to limit your exposure. Extended OR SQL is better, and OQL is better still, in that they give you more direct encapsulation techniques by integrating operations and methods into the programming language.

Second, use inheritance sparingly. If a subclass refers directly to a member in a superclass, that's content coupling. If you change the superclass, you have to change all the subclasses that use it. If you can, make your data members private and use superclass member functions to access superclass features.

Persistent inheritance is a bit more difficult to control. Avoid joins of super- and subclasses where possible; instead, break access to the tables into their logical parts and place those parts into super- and subclasses in your transient code. Pass data from one query result into the query of the super- or subclass. This reduces the common coupling to data coupling. In OR and OO databases, use the private access declaration to limit access as much as possible.

Third, avoid control coupling by using polymorphism where possible and feasible. Control coupling is where you pass in data that you use to make some choice about the flow of control in your code. Passing in a Boolean flag is the most common example of this. You can usually avoid this kind of control by subclassing and defining virtual or polymorphic functions for the alternatives. There are certain circumstances, however, where this leads to difficulties.

For example, consider a system of currency conversion. You can create a class hierarchy with one class for each currency you support, adding conversion methods for each other currency and a common set of virtual methods for addition, subtraction, and the like. Using double-dispatching, you can construct arbitrary currency expressions that always return the right result no matter what currency you use where. In operation, and in concept, this sounds great. In practice, you've traded one kind of coupling for another.

The alternative to this is to have a single currency converter class that has a table of conversions. You pass in an amount and a currency flag (the control data), and you get back an amount in dollars or some other common currency. You can have another method in which you pass in dollars and a currency, and you get back the amount in the currency.

The second approach is definitely at the level of control coupling. The function uses the currency flag to decide where to look in its internal tables (or the database) for conversion factors. The first approach avoids this by distributing the table across a class hierarchy. However, now each class knows about each other class, which is minimally stamp coupling and maximally content coupling if you use friend access or some other direct mechanism to get at internal data. Stamp coupling is better than control coupling; however, in this case you have created a monster by creating dozens of classes all coupled together using stamp coupling. Add a new currency, and you literally must change all the classes in the currency system. The second approach, control coupling, is definitely preferable.

In the database, this translates to similar structures. A currency conversion table is preferable to spreading the conversion information among many separate tables, one for each currency. It would never occur to a relational database designer to think that way, for better or worse.

Reuse Potential

Reuse is the ability to use a database again outside the task or application system that created and used it. The *potential for reuse* is the probability that you will reuse the database. This depends on three reusability factors [Goldberg and Rubin 1995; Karlsson 1996]:

- *Inherent reusability:* The probability of reuse due to *internal* properties, such as the completeness of the database and its programming interface or domain model with respect to use cases, or with respect to the lack of coupling of the database elements to other elements (degree of encapsulation), and especially elements in other databases or in the transient classes that make up the application system

- *Domain reusability:* The probability of reusing the database because its content and structure will support meeting the *requirements* of future systems; another way to say this is the probability that you will have similar requirements (domains) in the future

- *Organizational reusability:* The probability of reuse due to *organizational* factors such as repository facilities, communication, and reuse policies

The relative impact of each probability on reuse potential depends on the kind of system. If, for example, the system is heavily domain-dependent, such as a specialized manufacturing database, you should weight the domain reusability probability higher. If the system depends less on a particular domain and more on its inherent structure, such as a pattern-oriented database of generic organizations and people, you should weight inherent reusability higher. The weight for organizational reusability depends on the overall impact of organizational factors on reuse; if you want to focus efforts on organizational aspects, weight this factor more heavily. You can calculate a weighted reuse potential measure using this formula:

$$\text{Potential} = w_i P_i + w_d P_d + w_o P_o$$

where $w_i P_i$ is the weighted probability of inherent reuse, $w_d P_d$ is the weighted probability of domain reuse, and $w_o P_o$ is the weighted probability of organizational reuse. Weights by default are all $\frac{1}{3}$, so the probabilities contribute equally, but you can vary the weights to emphasize one type of probability over another if that makes sense for the system, as long as the weights sum to one.

Certain characteristics of OO design techniques make more general kinds of reuse easier. The emphasis on encapsulation, for example, emphasizes the internal properties that lead to inherent reusability. The availability of inheritance makes it more likely that you will meet at least some future requirements even though you need to override certain features and add others. The focus of OO design on modeling domains leads to a high level of domain reusability in databases. The cohesion you introduce with OO design is easier to communicate and document, leading to higher organizational reusability. Even a "global" database, such as a relational one designed with OO techniques, is often easier to make sense of for organizations needing its features.

In developing reusable databases, you need to consider the potential reusers and their requirements. As with any kind of development project, you can never identify all the requirements or stakeholders, as there will always be something new. What you can do is apply general OO design principles and patterns that make your system extensible and adaptable:

- Parameterize the system.

- Let users set options through persistent data stores.

- Make classes easy to reuse through inheritance.

- Don't make too many assumptions about what people want to do.

If you give reusers a chance, they will want to reuse your database and its design.

Reuse Certification

Certifying the database as reusable requires a certification policy to establish trust in the system. Trust is essential for reuse; if you don't trust a system, you won't use it.

First, you have to establish the risk level of the system. This means certifying that the system can achieve its mission within a certain level of risk (the risk tolerance of the reusing systems). To do this, you need to use the appropriate risk control approaches, such as design reviews and database tests, to reduce the database risk to the certified level. The reuser determines their risk tolerance, which in turn determines whether they can reuse the system at its indicated risk.

Second, you must provide a clear statement of the goals and structure of the system. Generally, this requires the publication of the vision, mission, and operational objectives of the database components. Those attributes of the system should be useful for potential reusers in determining whether to trust the system in a particular situation. Besides the mission, reusers also want to know precisely what the system does, and to what domain or domains it does it. The operational objectives show reusers how the system approaches its mission and how it measures success, but there may be additional components of the system that provide useful information. In particular, publishing the data model and the schema design provide potential reusers with a complete description of the database. As well, if you have a database test bed for exercising the database, making that available will raise the comfort level of reusers a good deal.

Third, you must provide a clear statement of responsibility for the database and its components. That is, by publishing the system as reusable, you are offering a kind of "contract" to the reuser. Part of any legal contract is the promise you make regarding quality, quantity, performance, or legal title to a system. This warranty may range from the typical "as is" warranty (no express or implied warranties including implied warranties of merchantability or fitness for a particular purpose) to a complete, express warranty of some promise. The warranty means that you accept responsibility for the problems of the system. The level of warranty often determines the level of trust the system user places in the system. For example, if you provide a reusable database schema "as is," you take no responsibility for its problems. This almost guarantees that no one will reuse the schema. You can make some express warranties by guaranteeing some level of maintenance or by providing the reuser with enough detail that they can do the maintenance themselves if they so desire. This usually means providing the data model and all the scripts or programs the reuser needs to recreate the database. Table 9-5 lists some standard warranties of responsibility.

> *Warning: All of this sounds like soulless legal claptrap, and that's exactly what it is. You can incur definite legal responsibilities and liabilities if you make reusable software available for use by others, even inside your company. You should consult an attorney without fail about the implications of your warranties and even your extended reuse certification as a whole, just so that you're aware of what risks you're taking.*

Certification must state for the reuser exactly what responsibility the source of the system assumes and what actions that source will take in what time frame if there is a problem. You are informing the reuser of your accountability and thus establishing the third plank of trust in your system. You need to tell the user, for example, who the domain experts are that can answer questions about how the system fits into its intended domains. You need to supply experts and maintainers to keep the system operational.

Certifying a reusable database establishes trust, but only for those in the know. That is, if a potential reuser does not know about the existence of the database and its design, it really doesn't matter how well you have certified it. The sharing step communicates the availability of the system to its potential reusers. The focus of the sharing step is the reuse repository, the storage facility in which you keep the design. Usually this will be some kind of database with a set of associated browser and search tools. You need to classify and index the reusable systems to support these tools.

But the repository is a passive communication tool at best. If you want to emphasize reuse as an approach to improving productivity, you need to sell your

***Table 9-5**   System Warranties for System Reuse Certification*

Warranty	Description
Performance	The database will function at a certain level of risk, and it will do what it claims to do in the domains you've specified for it.
Title and infringement	The creator of the database has the right to let reusers use it, usually with respect to intellectual property rights or exclusive use agreements. You need to reassure users they are not infringing your copyrights, for example, by using your test plans.
Disablement	There is no feature of the system that will disable the database.
Compatibility	The database will function in a particular environment stated in the description of the system. For example, you can designate a design and a schema for use with a particular DBMS only or certify it for use with any DBMS for which an ODBC level 3 driver with specific extended features exists. You must also specify any third-party software required to use the system, such as Microsoft Access, OLE controls, or any other software your system requires for reuse.

database actively. You can do this with communication meetings, in which people familiar with what's available work with potential reusers to identify reusable systems of interest. You can use training classes to train people in the systems they may want to use. Typically, project managers and architects get the most benefit from training. You can also use organizational structures to transfer knowledge. For example, you can train resources in what's available for reuse, then assign those resources as reuse experts to work groups on projects. This cross-pollinates the work groups with resources that know what is available in the reuse repository.

The maintenance step is the final task you perform for the reusable system. Maintenance supports the warranties of your system certification with live bodies. You must provide the appropriate maintenance services to fulfill your responsibilities. Usually this involves revising the reusable database in some way. But you can't stop there; you must propagate the changes to the reusers of the database. You must maintain a list of the systems who reuse your system to be able to inform those systems of changes. The model for reusable systems uses the system class relationship to other systems to represent this list.

Note: It may be easier to maintain a database that has only a single instance reused by many applications. This is the promise of the enterprisewide database. On the other hand, developers may want more control over the database than this gives them, as often an enterprisewide database puts a real straightjacket on new application development. Certification is always full of trade-offs.

Summary

The chapter started out with an overview of how to transform your measurement goals into actual metrics, or yardsticks that you can use to take measurements. To do that effectively, you must both understand the concept of scale from measurement theory and you must know how to validate your metric using the several different areas of validation criteria.

Specific metrics measure various aspects of databases and data models:

- *Size:* Database size (number of classes and objects) and schema size (function points)

- *Complexity:* Metrics of problem and solution complexity, including the McCabe metric and the idiot test

- *Cohesion:* Metrics of how well the system hangs together; abstract cohesion and structural cohesion

- *Coupling:* Metrics of the degree of interdependence between modules, including coupling type and the logical horizon

- *Reuse potential:* Metrics of how easy it will be to reuse the database or data model

In this chapter, you've seen a range of methods for measuring your database and data model. Now, it's time to start designing the actual database schema at the conceptual level, the subject of the next four chapters.

Choosing Your Parents 10

If men could learn from history, what lessons it might teach us! But passion and party blind our eyes, and the light which experience gives is a lantern on the stern, which shines only on the waves behind us!

Samuel Taylor Coleridge, December 18, 1831

N ot everyone can choose their parents; most of us must do the best we can with the hand we're dealt. This is no less true with database design. Most of the databases I've designed over 15 years did not emerge full-blown from my head like Athena. Rather, they emerged out of existing systems, other designers' work, and the various corporate cultures in which I was working.

In moving from data modeling to database design, you must first confront the impact of previous design decisions on your schema. As with children, those decisions can have been good or bad in their own context and might be equally bad or good in the new context you are providing for their growth. All of this happens in an organizational culture that heavily influences your decisions. Your job is to migrate the existing schema (and probably the existing data) into your new schema and database. The section "Software Development Cultures and the Legacy System" helps you through some of the political, cultural, and technical perils you will encounter. It covers the issues with replacing or reusing legacy schemas.

When you start fresh, you can look at it as incredibly fortunate or particularly ill-favored, depending on the situation. It is often easier to begin with an existing schema than to try to imagine—or worse, determine—the nature of the reality your business needs to model. The section "Starting Fresh" goes through the issues specific to creating a completely new schema, including the choice of database technology.

There are a series of problems you face when you must start from a database that is "wrong" in some sense. Issues of trust and legitimacy arise to undermine the political support you need to make things happen. The section "Starting from Scratched" helps you navigate these issues and gives you some tips for moving your design forward.

The next section, "The Structure of Schema Design," summarizes the structure the following chapters will use to present specific transformations of your data model into relational, object-relational, and object-oriented schema design. This structure establishes a framework for schema design that you can use regardless of your target database technology.

The final section, "Integrating Data Model Views," brings the last few chapters together to discuss the integration of your data modeling into a complete system model. With that done, you can begin to consider the transformation of your model into a schema design.

Software Development Cultures and the Legacy System

Every software development project proceeds in the context of a development culture. The nature of your culture structures the way you go about the design and construction of your database. This culture has a large impact on how you deal with legacy systems.

Cultural Events

Your development culture is possibly the most robust reusable system you will find in your workplace. It's there, you can't ignore it, and it's not going away, unlike most of your reusable code. The *cultural system* is the collection of socially transmitted systems that make up your way of doing things. Besides the simple process of learning technology, your main task when you join an organization is to learn how it does things—to become part of the culture.

First, here is the summary from Anthropology 1A: there are five major systems that make up the culture of a software development organization [Simons 1997; Hohmann 1997]:

- Norms
- Values, attitudes, and beliefs
- Rituals
- Folklore (stories and symbols)
- Shared Language

Norms

Norms are the shared policies and standards that the organization uses to set boundaries on what behavior it does or does not allow. Boundaries exist to avoid or mitigate risks, either external or internal. Some norms are formal, set explicitly by those in authority. Some norms are informal, set by interacting social leaders in the organization. Here are some examples of norms that range from very formal (enforced by law) to very informal (not enforced at all):

- HR policies about discrimination and sexual harassment
- Travel expense policies
- SQL coding standards
- Mandatory design methods and tools such as UML or ERwin
- SEI capability maturity level
- Process models and development life cycles
- Delivering systems on schedule
- The "usual" number of hours worked per week
- Anti–dress codes (that is, nobody can wear a tie on pain of social ostracism or at least ridicule)
- Starting meetings on time
- Not playing computer games during the workday (the Suit Culture)
- Requiring playing computer games during the workday (the T-Shirt Culture)

All norms relate to some kind of risk. Your culture is more or less useful depending on how well it addresses your business mission. For example, you may spend all your time figuring out how to enforce on-time delivery. Your management may spend most of its time on figuring out how to stuff more bodies into cubicles. If your business mission focuses on quality, not budget or schedule, your culture doesn't support your mission. That means you are at high risk of not achieving that mission. Norms help your organization focus on managing such risks.

How does forcing everyone to participate in joint computer games address risk? Mostly, it manages the risk of cultural drift. It is a ritual designed to bring people together into a functioning team, even if they're busy killing each other through simulations. The point is not blasting simulacra, it is doing so *with everyone else.* This reduces the risk that people who aren't a part of the group culture will introduce Dilbertian nonsense into the development process. On the other hand, they may blast you, but a game reset takes care of that!

Also, it's important to realize that norms establish trust. If your market expects you to deliver high-quality products on time, but you have no internal norms relating to quality and schedule, your stakeholders will not trust your organization. I have participated in presentations to customers that had no other purpose than to reassure the customer that the organization and its culture were trustworthy. Having standards and policies can go a long way toward garnering external support. Having a good delivery record is even better.

Similarly, a shop with no standards often makes developers uncomfortable. A completely anarchic shop is too hard to deal with on an ongoing basis. Instead, most developers prefer to stabilize the process around authoritative decisions and policies, however informal. Picking a standard database, for example, in a large, diverse organization dramatically simplifies the lives of the database designers and engineers. It allows more exact planning and execution of plans. Sometimes too much creativity is as much of a problem as too little, particularly when it turns into thrashing around decisions and people not being productive. This is a balancing act for management, which must find the right mix of formal and informal norms and encourage a productive, mission-directed culture.

Values, Attitudes, and Beliefs

Values are the social principles of the organization, the things people care about. *Attitudes* are the ways people think about organizational facts. *Beliefs* are the things you think are true about your organization or about the world it inhabits.

Here are some common values, attitudes, and beliefs in software organizations:

- A vision statement

- A mission statement

- A values statement

- It's so hard to get anything done around here during the workday. That's why I come in at 10 PM.

- How's the pig doing today? (This in reference to the financial database system you're about to deliver to 10,000 slavering customers.)

- That's marketing's job, not ours. (This is in reference to someone requesting a requirements model for a new product.)

- The market won't buy anything but software that runs under Microsoft Windows (UNIX, the Mac, whatever).

- The market insists on software that runs on any operating system (presumably including RSX-11M).

- My manager wants us all to work weekends.

- We succeeded beyond our wildest dreams with this latest system!

- We can do better than that [expletive deleted] system you bought!

Reflect on these examples for a moment. What is their common thread? Purpose. Without values, attitudes, and beliefs, the members of your organization must be very uncertain about what they *should* achieve, much less what they *can* achieve. Core values of an organization, as represented by vision, mission, values, and objectives statements, are vital in establishing a set of values aligned with the goals of the organization as a whole.

Most database people have very strong belief systems, having gone through extensive preparation for their priesthood. This is, of course, a metaphorical stretch; nevertheless, database designers and programmers have a strong set of beliefs that qualifies them for their profession. Some are adherents of the main-stream relational religion, while others belong to smaller cults such as OO data-bases or dBase worship, an almost extinct religion that pops up every now and again in odd places. Anyone who has ever confronted an Oracle DBA with the need to denormalize a database schema understands the religious nature of these values and beliefs. Moving to design using UML is, to a certain extent, a challenge to these values and beliefs, so I'm trying to make it as easy as possible to say, "It's really the same thing, just a different notation."

Rituals

A *ritual* is a repeated pattern of social behavior. Related to norms, rituals establish routines that you follow. Sometimes rituals exist to channel behavior that might otherwise violate norms, such as expressing less-than-serious visions of your boss. The formality of the ritual comes from its source (upper management, teams, or other level of authority). Here are some examples of rituals in a software organization:

- Christmas parties
- Team lunches
- Communication meetings
- "Open door" meetings
- Friday breakfasts
- Casual days
- Development method processes
- Quality assurance system tests
- Structured walkthroughs
- Dunking the boss on carnival day

In modern American software organizations, you can divide rituals into three types: outlet, purposive, and magical. An *outlet ritual* is one that serves as a way to blow off steam or to integrate out-of-the-ordinary elements of life into the organization, such as a party. A *purposive ritual* is one done for a reason—the reason being empirical in nature, such as a structured walkthrough or a system test. A *magical ritual* is one that serves a protective or instrumental purpose without the benefit of empirical evidence, such as a management review or communication meeting. Regardless of type, the main point of a ritual is to repeat the behavior, usually in the hope of achieving some goal, whether real or magical.

Database rituals are everywhere. In design, the normalization process is such a ritual. As Chapter 11 discusses in detail, it is very easy to put your database into fifth normal form with a simple, direct design (strongly related to the OO design methods). Because the usual ritual proceeds very differently, however, I've found it difficult to persuade some DBAs to do this. Instead, they insist on going through the stages of normalization (first, second, third, BCNF, fourth, fifth) and arguing Talmudic points the whole way. Pilpul aside, normalization is a ritual, and often not a particularly useful one. Nevertheless, it's one you have to deal with in large organizations.

Another ritual is optimization. As they gain experience (go through ritual torture), DBAs and database designers create small rituals that exist to propitiate the database performance gods. Creating a bitmap index here, enabling dirty reads there, using unique column names even though SQL scopes names to the table, not to the database, and so on—these are all rituals with the purpose of developing shields against "doing it wrong." Usually, there is little or no empirical evidence for the value of these. Sometimes, the DBA will go so far as to say that it is just the "right thing to do" and leave it at that. As your organization moves from a ritualistic, magical culture into a feedback culture, you see measurement start to appear. As an anthropological observer, you can distinguish these cultures by their actions: Do DBAs benchmark their databases and change them based on the results? Or do they simply assert that using VARCHAR is slower than CHAR and you shouldn't do it? Magic rituals work as long as you don't have the time to tie your system to empirical reality, but eventually the problems and scope of the database expand beyond this kind of ritual.

There are useful rituals too, of course. As you experience, you learn; as you learn, you ritualize. You begin to understand how to install Oracle reliably through a sequence of very specific steps repeated many times, hopefully not all on the same weekend. You learn that translating a data model consistently into a schema requires specific transformations in a certain sequence. You learn that using single-attribute surrogate keys is often preferable to using multiattribute primary keys, so you ritualize the design in a pattern that you apply to most tables. As you gain experience, you sediment and abbreviate the rituals into processes or actions that become second nature—until someone challenges them and you must expand them again. As you ritualize, you create folklore to support your rituals, and it's that folklore that emerges on demand when you get a challenge to your rituals.

Folklore

Folklore is a set of symbols and stories about the organization. Folklore often transmits organizational or personal values and norms as part of the socialization structure of the organization. One major purpose is to show status. Another is to show achievement. Yet another is to represent some value the organization holds in high regard. Here are some symbols and stories common in software organizations:

- The product T-shirt or coffee mug
- Stories about the early days of the company
- Stories about other parts of the organization (sometimes known as "rumors")
- War stories about past projects at the company and elsewhere that caution against something
- Fables that promote some behavior as good
- Slogans and mottoes ("Sooner is better than later.")
- Meeting minutes
- Functional specs (a special kind of fable, with or without the implication of being imaginary)
- Team award trophies
- Project wall charts
- Window offices
- Corner window offices

Folklore is all about transmitting other aspects of culture. Without folklore, you have no way to communicate the culture without depending on dry, academic descriptions of the anthropology of the organization (such as this section).

Database work is full of folklore, both good and bad. Anyone who has worked in databases more than a year has war stories about Oracle, Informix, Sybase, or whatever system they've used. Most designers have a repertoire of analysis patterns (see Chapter 8) with accompanying stories about how the patterns worked in practice on various jobs. Most people have their DBMS vendor coffee mugs prominently displayed, or T-shirts from the last users' conference. Some of us have even worked at DBMS companies and thus have a good range of war stories and fables to explain some of the quirks of the products we worked with or built.

Most people don't realize, for example, that PL/SQL (Oracle's built-in programming language) comes from Ada, the 1980s' military software engineer's choice. The architect of PL/SQL was an Ada guru hired into Oracle to manage development projects and grew into the role of language guru for the company. The Ada story tells people why certain things are there (packages, for example, with overloaded procedures, and exceptions), putting the language in a broader context than just a database programming one. Folklore contributes in a big way to shared language by providing common symbols and stories using that language.

Shared Language

Shared language is the special language that evolves in the organization to describe things of interest to its members. Here are some examples of shared language in a software organization:

- Technical jargon from the tools you use
- Method-speak
- Puns or coinages on the company name ("license plate words")
- Derogatory references to products, groups, or people
- Culturally or geographically related references to products, groups, or people
- Abbreviated terms for common tasks or things
- Catch phrases that aren't quite slogans or mottoes

Shared language establishes a linguistic boundary around the organization, or around parts of the organization. Language is possibly the most important aspect of a social group because it is the mechanism by which people communicate. A good deal of the social content of a software organization resides in the software it builds; virtually everything else except the coffee mugs is language.

The database world has its own technical jargon, from normalizing relations to pinning objects to cost-based optimizations. The various techniques (bitmap indexes, outer joins, pointer swizzling, and so on) account for much of the linguistic acculturation that people must go through to become effective database designers and developers.

As you develop your data models, and especially at the enterprise/global level, you also build a shared language to describe your business objects. You make countless decisions about what to call things, particularly abstract things such as relationships. You develop standard abbreviations and start using them in everyday speech to refer to your objects. All this is part of the linguistic culture of your organization.

What's interesting about the shared language is the way it focuses the values and beliefs of the organization. If the words you develop about the product, for example, are negative ("pig," "trash," and so on), the organization clearly believes the product is poor, and the implications are dire for motivation. If all you hear is high-tech jargon, clearly the organization values technology. If all you hear is language about motivation ("rowing harder," "Work smarter, not harder"), look for (1) a belief that people, not technology, are central to getting work done, (2) a lack of motivation, and the reasons behind such a lack, or (3) a strong belief that people need pushing to get their jobs done. You can tell a lot about an organization from the language its managers use.

Culture consists of people interacting with one another. A development culture centers on software systems that are the focus of this interaction. Culture is at its most important when you are creating new software in the presence of old software: the legacy system.

Replacing or Leveraging Legacy Systems

A *legacy system* is a system created long enough ago that it no longer represents the best practices in technology or design but still provides value to the business. It may involve older database technology, such as mainframe IMS databases or personal computer dBase systems that now must grow up. With your new data model, you are providing a framework for replacing the legacy schema with a new one using new technology. This may be the right way to go, or it may not.

The viability of the existing technology is the prime driver for your decisions about a legacy system. Just because new technology exists doesn't mean you have to use it. Existing technology becomes a problem under various circumstances:

- When the vendor abandons all or part of the technology, refusing to maintain it or enhance it further because of lack of market demand

- When the underlying technology, such as hardware platforms or operating systems, changes enough to render the technology useless or obsolete

- When the nature of your business problems changes enough to make the original technology useless because it does not have the scalability or features to solve the changed problem

- When new technology appears that delivers massive improvements over a range of different requirements (performance, scalability, access, security, recoverability, or whatever)

- When new methods emerge that focus your attention on solutions quite different from the original technology (adopting OO design across all your applications, for example, can render much of older PC or mainframe technology irrelevant and harmful)

- When the risk of change becomes too great for the older technology to handle effectively

All of these situations lead to the need to replace the legacy system. Certainly, if you are in a crisis situation where you simply cannot continue to use the old technology, your decision is made for you. Often, however, the situation is not so cut and dried:

- The vendor may not be enhancing the technology, but they're still signing maintenance contracts and fixing bugs.

- You may be able to keep running an older version of an operating system by adding compatibility software or making other changes to accommodate the older software.

- While massive improvements may be available, you may not really need them in your application.

As a metaphor, consider the difference between the Public Broadcasting System's two popular builder's shows, *This Old House* and *Hometime* [O'Day 1998]. The premises of *This Old House,* as the title expresses, are that (1) old houses are valuable in themselves, and (2) you restore an old house, while improving it with modern materials and techniques. The premises of *Hometime,* on the other hand, are that (1) new houses are wonderful, and (2) building a new house gives you the opportunity to use the best of modern materials and techniques. These approaches are not conflicting; they simply apply in different situations. When you have an old house that works, you restore it. When you have an old house that sort of works but not really, you renovate it. When you have a nice piece of land with potential, or when you have an old house that isn't working and can't work, you build a new house.

Extending the metaphor to culture, the two shows express a very different culture. The culture of *This Old House* places tremendous value on restorative techniques and ways of integrating modern materials and technology into an existing context. The culture of *Hometime* emphasizes modern materials and technology and focuses on the techniques and processes by which you use it, lots of advice on dealing with contractors and architects, and tips for clever shopping. Again, these are not conflicting cultures. *Hometime,* for example, does restoration work occasionally and usually places more emphasis on existing quality in those situations. *This Old House* sometimes strays into renovation when pushed by owner's needs, neighbor or planning commission requirements, or a really cool new technology such as groundwater-based heat pumps. Sound familiar?

If you do a return-on-investment (ROI) analysis on the work involved in replacing the legacy system versus adding to it, you may find the latter significantly outperforms the former. To do this, estimate the amount of work involved in the new solution, not forgetting the maintenance costs over a certain time period, such as five years. Then estimate the maintenance costs over the same period for your legacy system. Estimate the additional revenue you will gain through the advantages of the new system and the benchmark revenue you get with the legacy system. Plug these cash flows into a standard ROI algorithm using discounted cash flow techniques, and you can see the internal rate of return or net present value of both solutions. Easy, right?

Unfortunately, while ROI analysis gives you a nice, clear, hardheaded set of numbers that you can use to impress your friends and bosses, these numbers aren't very realistic. Estimation weaknesses aside, ROI ignores much of the real-world impact on your decision. Is your organization one that values leading-edge technology? Or do you hear the term "bleeding edge" used in most meetings on such decisions? Perhaps people bring up stories about previous jobs where management made the wrong decision (one way or the other). Perhaps someone in the decision meeting is ostentatiously fiddling with an Oracle8 coffee mug or is wearing a CORBA T-shirt. Technology is important in such decisions, but beliefs about technology, values, and symbols relating to technology are often more important. In other words, you need to take culture into account when making decisions about legacy systems.

Design is all about satisfying the project stakeholders. If those stakeholders have a lot invested in their organizational culture, you ignore it at your peril. Add up the stories, folklore, values, norms, and other aspects of culture. If they tell you a story about how well the legacy system has worked, or conversely about how appalling the situation is, you know where the organization wants to go, and very probably where it needs to go. Help it get there.

Actually getting there is half the fun. Once you've plumbed the depths of your organizational culture, your job as a database designer is to figure out how to best represent your data model given your legacy requirements.

> *Note: It's probably worthwhile for large legacy systems to use metrics to evaluate the reliability and stability of the system. Using reliability measures such as mean time to failure can tell you how your system is performing in the hands of its users. Using stability measures [Schneidewind 1998] can tell you whether your efforts to maintain the legacy system are successful or whether the system is degrading.*

Starting Fresh

You've just convinced the chief financial officer of your company that the legacy IMS database from the 1960s is ready for the scrap heap. You've contracted for demolition and site grading, and you're ready to start designing the new house. What are the key things you must worry about in replacing the legacy system?

Using Your Legacy

Even though you are developing your design from scratch, you should not just ignore what went before. First and foremost, the old system constitutes an intellectual asset of the company. It represents work-years of effort to distill and reify the knowledge of customers, developers, and company management. The needs may have changed, but the legacy system obviously relates in some way to those needs or it wouldn't be legacy, just junk. This corresponds to materials or features you can save from the old house you're demolishing. What's more, the legacy system may be more than just an intellectual asset; it may be intellectual property.

While an *intellectual asset* represents knowledge realized in some permanent form such as software, *intellectual property* is a legally protected form that has a specific value to your company. Patents, copyrights, trademarks, and trade secrets are all intellectual property. You should do your utmost to preserve intellectual property rather than just throwing it away. Reuse the property as much as possible. For example, even if you demolish the house, you usually try to save the important features of the landscape, such as ancient but viable oak trees. Some features, such as lakes, are a key part of the value of the land. Perhaps you can't use the actual software, but you can use the patented processes, the trademarks, or the trade secrets that represent the knowledge embedded in the software.

Another kind of intellectual asset that the legacy system represents is the know-how accumulated in the company through work done on the old system. Much of this know-how may not be in realized form but rather in the heads of people who have worked on the system. As you develop your use cases, data model, and schema designs, consult people associated with the legacy systems.

Database systems in particular have a value that goes beyond just intellectual property. The data in the database is often valuable in itself—not as the bits that make up the data, but the information that it represents. Minimally, a business database contains the sedimented organizational knowledge of your business. It represents transaction histories, people, events, processes, and a truly infinite array of other systems on which your business runs. It represents both operational parameters of your business (process specifications, manufacturing models, and other business systems) and history (accounting databases, product databases, contact management databases, and so on).

Regardless of whether you are intending to reuse the software of the legacy system, you will almost certainly have to use the data. You've decided not to reuse the database, and that means you have to move the data into the format of the new database. With any luck, your new database manager will provide tools capable of moving the data with minimal configuration information. Possibly you may be able to find a third-party tool to do this; there are several such tools, ranging from generic file readers such as Data Junction or Cambio (*www.datajunction.com*) to higher-end DBMS-oriented data migration tools such as Powermart (*www.informatica.com*) or Data Navigator (*www.platinum.com*). At worst, you may have to write a program to export the data from your old system into a format that your new system can load. This is a good job for an independent consultant because one can do it with very little interaction or reference to other parts of your project.

The key issue in reusing legacy data is data quality. How well can you trust the legacy data? Answering this question tells you how much work you'll have in reusing the data. This is, of course, what reuse certification is all about. If you haven't certified your legacy database for reuse, formally or informally, you have work to do to determine just how much you can trust the data. Part of the process of transferring the data into your new schema uses the standard constraint tools such as referential integrity constraints, triggers, and validation methods. You should be sure that all of the data that comes in through the import process goes through the same constraints as the data that users will enter through your application system.

You should also audit or test the data, either by random sampling or census techniques, to determine its quality according to the criteria your requirements set. This is a relative measure of quality, not an absolute one. You don't need perfect data in this best of all possible worlds; you need data that satisfies the needs of your application users. Your requirements should express all these data-related needs.

> *Warning: Data quality is almost certainly the biggest problem you're going to have in a legacy-bound project. If your schedule doesn't include a big chunk of time for analyzing, fixing, and testing the data from the legacy system, your schedule is wrong.*

Having dealt with the data, how about the functionality? This is where culture comes in. You need to unearth the rituals, folklore, and other aspects of culture that have grown up around the old system over the years. Ask customers how they used the old system and what they'd like to see as a result in the new one. What's worth keeping, and what didn't you use? What did they hate about the old system? What did they love about it? What new things have cropped up in their work that the system might address? Get them to relate the folklore of the system.

Ask developers on the old system, those that haven't ascended to corporate heaven, about complex algorithms or relationships. Often, it isn't obvious what led to these decisions in the old system. You need to distinguish hacks—temporary solutions to problems—from innate complexity of the problem. Someone may have developed a large amount of code to work around a bug in version 3 of your DBMS. Since you are replacing it with an OODBMS, you don't need to worry about that. On the other hand, you may not have realized just how complicated certain financial transactions can be. Probe the ritual solutions to figure out exactly what function they perform.

> *Tip: You may find it possible to use deassemblers, decompilers, or similar tools for reengineering your data. For an example, see the tools offered by McCabe and Associates (www.mccabe.com). While these tools can help you understand existing legacy code, they aren't infallible. Don't depend on any tool to translate legacy code into modern systems because this is an almost impossible task.*

You can also reuse the legacy schema to some extent. Someone may have worked with customers to solve a broad array of complex problems with a particularly ornate set of tables and relationships. You can use that knowledge to structure your class model more effectively, perhaps improving on the design by reducing complexity, decreasing coupling, and increasing cohesion. Again, the schema may reflect hacks and not innate complexity. Probe into the folklore and norms of the schema system and its culture to understand why it developed the way it did.

Even though you're starting afresh, you can make strong use of what went before.

Scoping the System and the Culture

When you're building your new database application from scratch, you have the opportunity to get the scope right that you might not have when you're expanding an existing system. Make the most of it.

System Requirements

Chapters 3 and 4 went into detail on gathering requirements and building a requirements model with use cases. When you have a set of use cases that describe your system, you've scoped your project. The techniques of Chapter 3 in gathering requirements are an essential part of this process because they force you to question the scope of the system. Starting fresh with the technology, you should also start fresh with the requirements.

Don't assume that the legacy system expresses the requirements of the users. It may only reflect the development culture that produced it. Investigate the norms and values of that culture if you're not already a part of it. If you find a strong value system around satisfying the customer's needs, fine. That means you can look at the legacy system for the roots of customer satisfaction. The development culture that built the legacy system may be one that places value on technology—or worse, places little value on anything but getting the job done. If so, you can't use the legacy system as your starting point because of the potential for data quality problems. You'll need to evaluate and audit the data first. You'll also need to evaluate the requirements that the legacy system expresses to validate them against current needs.

You should also look beyond your application requirements. Your business may be planning to add other applications to the system that uses your database. Though you need not take these requirements into account, and though it may be difficult to state these requirements, it's in your best interest to make a stab at it. The best approach to getting the big picture is generalization and certification for reuse, discussed in Chapter 9. Work on the inherent, domain, and organizational reuse potential of your requirements and design. Conduct tests and risk analysis to certify them for reuse under appropriate conditions.

System Culture

You may find that the scope of your new system is broader than just the technical issues involving software and data. It may be that the environment has changed enough that you must initiate cultural changes as well. To evaluate this, look at three statistics: system size, customer satisfaction, and delivery failure [Muller 1998, pp. 532–536]. If the system you're proposing to build is an order of magnitude greater in size than ones you've built previously, it's a good bet your culture isn't capable of doing it. If the last few projects your culture has undertaken resulted in relatively low customer satisfaction (many complaints and defect reports, a lot of database maintenance and availability problems, for example) or were very late or over their budgets or canceled, you've definitely got a culture problem.

The capability of a given culture to achieve project missions depends on the level of risk and the stakeholders' expectations for the projects the organization undertakes. As risk grows, and as expectations become more complex and demanding, the culture must adapt and grow. Beyond a certain risk or expectation level, a culture may become incapable of delivering on its promises. It must change to incorporate better processes, feedback, and anticipation of problems [Weinberg 1992].

In database work, the big size transition comes with projects involving more than about 100 classes. This size indicates that the expectations for the system are relatively complex because of the inherent nature of the business problems it is proposing to solve. Increased risk in database systems comes from technical difficulty or feature mismatch. Again, we're discussing systems you are building from scratch, not legacy systems you're maintaining or enhancing.

Technical difficulty in the database arena comes from using leading-edge technology that more readily fails under loading. Pushing down to root causes, you tend to use such technology when you have business problems that require the technology. You can easily manage the risk associated with using technology you don't need by just not using it. You can't easily manage risk that comes from hard problems. As your business becomes more willing to take on such problems, you begin to strain the limits of existing technology, and you take on a lot more risk. Terabytes of data, thousands of simultaneous transactions, huge interactive queries—all of these are business issues that put strain on the safe technology you've used in the past. These very problems may be the reason you've decided to abandon the legacy system and move to a completely new one.

Feature mismatch comes from using technology that is not appropriate to the purpose. You may be using a personal database manager to create a sophisticated multiuser application, or you may be using a complex, distributed-object application development system to develop an address database. A fundamental problem is choosing the type of database manager. Many database projects choose RDBMS technology, for example, rather than moving into ORDBMS or OODBMS technology. You might do this because of corporate standards, or because of money concerns, or because it's what you know. If the problem involves objects with many behavioral requirements, or if the problem involves a lot of navigation, tree building, or the like, choosing relational technology is likely to increase your risk dramatically. The software can't deliver the features you need.

Given this kind of situation, you may need to move your culture into a more capable set of values, norms, and rituals. Introducing feedback through measurement, data collection, and data evaluation usually is a big culture shift for most software companies. Once you have the rituals in place, you can build your organization's capabilities for building larger, more complex database applications.

Starting from Scratched

Every database designer has war stories about finding the entire schema in first normal form instead of third normal form, or of discovering that half of the attributes in the schema are keywords in the new database system you've spent three weeks installing, or of wandering through a maze of cryptic abbreviated column names like YRTREBUT, B_423_SPD, or FRED. As stories, these provide us all with something to talk about while waiting for people to show up at meetings. As reality, finding a database with these kinds of problems is the start of a rather nightmarish process of spring cleaning if you're lucky, and building a patched-up monster if you're not.

We're now in the culture of *This Old House*. This section assumes that you are building your application as an enhancement to the existing system, which may or may not be a legacy system. That is, you are extending what already works. In the ordinary way of things, this is the same thing as developing a new system except that you have to identify where to put your new data based on new requirements. This section also assumes that the system you're extending is not perfect—in fact, it is far from perfect, and you've just acquired a huge problem. The floor's sagging, or the roof leaks and has damaged the upper story irreparably. You can't ignore the problem, however, because for one reason or another your organization has decided that the existing system is too important. Your culture, in other words, values the old house for itself. They've declared it a national landmark, and you're stuck with making it safe for tourists.

War Stories and Shared Language

First of all, pay attention to the particular war stories and language in your culture. Understanding where other people think things have gone wrong is a great way to identify risky places in your system. For example, I worked with one application system that used a batch process at night to deal with massive updates to a financial institution's portfolio of securities. The data requirements were huge, and doing it interactively would slow down the system to a crawl. Interestingly, the acronym for this program was the PIG, short for Principal and Interest Generation. I never found out whether this was fortuitous or intentional, but it was clear that this was a problem area in the system. When we looked at the database design behind this, we found several problems relating to invalid assumptions about customer needs, poorly organized data, and poorly developed application code. One project rewrote the application code using structured techniques to improve memory-based performance, and other projects restructured the requirements and the database to improve performance on the back end. It was still the PIG, but it didn't run for 36 hours to do daily batch processing anymore.

Language translation can also lead to problems. Are you well versed in OO design theory, but your culture only knows relational SQL? This kind of language mismatch mirrors the underlying conceptual mismatch between the needs of your system and the existing database. Although the database may reflect a relational culture, it probably won't reflect the kind of suggestions that Chapter 11 of this book makes. You'll find table structures that are less than optimal for reuse.

For example, I worked on a database done by some pure relational database people. A new manager was introducing object-oriented design techniques similar to those in this book. I designed a class hierarchy around some of the geographical concepts in the system to extend it with new requirements by adding new geographic classes. The translation of this class hierarchy into multiple tables with relationships proved to be almost too much for the system to handle. The problems didn't come from any technical issue with the database technology but with the language with which the developers and designers talked about the system. Introducing generalization relationships confused them by introducing a new language and a new set of structure requirements into the system. They were constantly missing the need to update the superclass tables, for example, and not putting in the triggers and/or application code needed to do that.

Norms, Values, and Beliefs

Second, consider the norms, values, and beliefs of your culture. People make bad technical decisions often because they believe something that isn't true. The existing system often reflects such beliefs and poor decisions. These come in two flavors, the hack and the bug.

A *hack* is a solution to a specific problem that has some kind of unfortunate side effect. This is classic *This Old House*. You're always finding carpenter's tricks that may have held up for years but worked their damage unseen. The database code may not be portable, such as using an SQL Server–specific feature to solve a very specific problem. It may involve a performance trade-off under different conditions. It may use a feature of the programming language or of SQL that is harder to understand.

For example, many Oracle applications have code reaching back to version 3 of Oracle that uses the DECODE built-in function. That function lets you use conditional logic in your SELECT expressions or WHERE clause to achieve things that might otherwise require program code. This is a hack, especially when you have DECODE expressions nested to three or more levels. This hack comes from a value: the belief that it is better to express a solution in a single SQL statement than in multiple ones embedded in program code. Often this value comes from the belief that such program code is hard to write, expensive, and hard to debug, while SQL is not. Anyone who has tried to maintain a six-level DECODE statement would disagree with this, and all but the most hardened SQL advocates don't believe it. If you must, for some reason, extend this kind of hack, you should seriously consider throwing it away and rewriting it. The DECODE, for example, you can better express these days as a PL/SQL function, with the conditional logic expressed as it should be with IF statements in a clear flow-of-control logic.

The *bug* is a solution that once worked but no longer does. Again, classic *This Old House*. This is where you poke the screwdriver into the beam holding up the first floor, and it goes all the way through, disturbing the termites unwarrantably. These are the things that you have to fix or the house will fall down. For example, Year 2000 problems are this kind of bug. At some point, a database encoded data in a format that did not consider the millenium change. Most database products handle this, but for some reason the tool you were using did not. Another classic example is a system that has no integrity constraints defined because the database developers had not upgraded their schema scripts to use the referential integrity features when they became available. Bugs come from two basic cultural areas: beliefs and values.

Beliefs often persist beyond the point where they are useful, and they actually become harmful because of changing business requirements. I knew one database designer who absolutely refused to normalize his designs because he knew that performance would suffer. When a new version of the DBMS came out with a cost-based optimizer that did away with the problem, he ignored it and kept designing unnormalized databases, causing all kinds of problems with update code. Usually, the answer to this kind of problem is training.

Values-based bugs are harder to manage. The developer who loves coding but thinks documentation is a waste of time is usually a source of major bugs in the system. They value the coding process so much relative to everything else that they lose track of their impact on the overall system. They check code in without testing it, for example. They put schema changes into production databases that require you to recompile and reinstall all the code. Egregious examples like this usually only happen once or twice because their impact is so great that it forces management, even hands-off management, to step in. It's usually the more subtle memory and schema design bugs these people introduce that cause you problems when you're updating a legacy system.

A special case of values-based impact on legacy systems comes from the assumptions underlying a reusable framework. The original architect of a house generally imposes a values-based view of how the house will adapt to the people that live in it. That's the source of the patterns movement led by the famous architect Christopher Alexander, now being adopted as a model for object-oriented system design (see Chapter 8). If those assumptions are wrong, or a changing environment makes them less than valid, you may have to tear down the house and replace it rather than restoring or renovating it.

One framework developer, for example, assumed that every application that used the general GUI framework he was designing would use the standard file open dialog. I came along with a database application that opened databases, not files. It turned out that it was impossible to substitute a different dialog box for the standard open dialog. The framework designer coupled the classes involved into other parts of the system to such an extent that replacing the standard dialog crashed the system with a pointer error. We wound up having to "open" the database file rather than being able to use a standard connect login box.

Rituals

Third, consider the rituals of your culture. Processes alone contain tremendous potential for blocking your ability to modify an existing system. You might find, for example, that the smallest change to a legacy system requires reams of supporting documentation and change bureaucracy. If you run into problems with the legacy database design, or with the legacy application architecture based on that design, you may well discover that the cultural rituals are effective in preserving the current system regardless of its adequacy and quality.

Even harder than simple process blocking is the situation where you must work with a priesthood. A priest, in database design, is a team member who mediates the relationship between you and the gods, with the database schema and content being the physical manifestation of the gods on earth. By definition, the priesthood that created it (with the help of the Gods, of course) controls the legacy system. To modify the database, you must get the priest to understand what you want, then the priest tells you what the gods will deliver. As with all Oracles, this can be very ambiguous.

One can carry metaphor too far. In any event, there is usually somebody associated with the legacy system who has to go through some process to make what you are doing legitimate. The level of ritual varies depending on the culture. Do make sure that there is no human sacrifice involved before getting in too deep.

I've worked with large companies that are very bureaucratic, with many rituals around the legacy application. For example, one large contract administration system I worked with needed to migrate to a different fourth-generation language. The group that maintained the database in Oracle was in another building from the group that was charged with developing the new application system. To make any changes to the database, the application group needed to meet with the database group, then file change requests and get them approved. This applied to new tables as well as to changes to existing tables. As you might imagine, this slowed down application development considerably. As well as processes, there were corporate politics involved. There was a reuse organization (in yet another building) that needed to have a say in making sure everything was reusable, or was at least contributing to the concept of reuse. The head of this organization did not like the head of the application organization, so nothing ever got done.

Working culture is full of challenges to the database designer working on a system with problems. Many of these challenges come down to the way the designer must gain the support of the culture for needed change. Gaining support is all about negotiation and the way you create legitimacy in the culture. Often, it requires gaining support for change by making the change legitimate through positive organizational politics and strong technical leadership. You may find it easier to convince legacy gatekeepers to change, for example, if you demonstrate the benefits of OO design and development on smaller, prototype projects. Having measures of success, you can build legitimacy and begin to convince adherents of the current culture that change can be beneficial.

Whatever choices you need to make with respect to developing new systems or adapting legacy systems, the transition from your data model to your schema is a critical process of designing databases.

The Structure of Schema Design

At some point, you make your choice as to the exact nature of the database management approach you will take. The rest of the book, Chapters 11 to 13, shows you the process of transforming your data model into a schema in one of the three approaches. The rest of this section outlines the pattern of this transformation, which is the same in all three cases. The next section then wraps up data modeling with a discussion of integrating views and systems.

Structures

Every database schema contains a series of structures that represent in some way the classes of your data model. A structure groups the data attributes as the data architecture permits: with simple structures in the relational architecture, and with more complex structures in the OR and OO architectures.

The structural section in each chapter shows you how to transform the basic structures of the UML data model into schema structures:

- Packages
- Subsystems
- Classes
- Interfaces
- Attributes (including visibility)
- Domains and data types, including nullability and initialization
- Operations and methods (including polymorphic operations, signals, and visibility)
- Object identity

After transforming the data model structures into schema structures, you have the start of your schema design.

Relationships

The UML data model contains two kinds of relationships, the association and the generalization. Transforming the UML relationships is the area in which the competing architectures differ the most, especially in transforming generalizations.

There are certain interactions between the relationships and the schema structures in the different architectures. "Creating a relationship" is not always creating a relationship: it may involve creating a structure in place of, or in addition to, a relationship. Also, certain relationships have characteristics of structures; sometimes a relationship role is an attribute, for example.

Each of these UML elements has a transformation for each data architecture:

- Generalizations (abstract and concrete classes, multiple and single inheritance)
- Binary associations
- Roles
- Shared and composite aggregations
- Multiplicities
- Association attributes
- Ternary and higher-cardinality associations
- Qualified associations
- Ordered associations

Business Rules

The previous sections deal with many of the classic business rules. Primary keys, foreign keys, multiplicities—all are part of structures and relationships. There are certain constraints, however, that exist outside these structural elements.

When you express an explicit UML constraint, you are usually expressing a business rule that is beyond the capability of the standard modeling language of classifiers and relationships. Most database management systems have a way to express these constraints. The transformation of your data model into a schema must also transform these constraints. You have two choices.

First, you can transform the constraints into a set of transient behaviors. That is, you can build the constraints in your application (or application server) rather than in your database (or database server). In the extreme, you build the constraint into your client. Unfortunately, client constraints are seldom reusable. You must implement the constraint anew in each application, and possibly in each subsystem of your application.

Second, you can transform the constraints into a set of persistent behaviors. In a relational database, this means triggers and stored procedures. In an OR database, it means the same thing, or possibly type methods. In an OO database, it means adding methods or asserts in methods to enforce the constraints.

Design Guidelines

Whatever your target data architecture, you will need guidelines for design. Every architecture has a different set of informal or formal patterns, such as normalization for relational databases. In OR systems, you must decide between many different ways of doing the same thing. In OO systems, you have very specific guidelines for inheritance, encapsulation, and other aspects of the object-oriented design that relate to persistence.

Data Definition Languages

Each database architecture has its own data definition language. The following chapters give you a brief introduction to the language of the architecture (SQL-92, SQL3, and ODL, respectively).

Integrating Data Model Views

Data modeling hardly ever proceeds in a vacuum. Most large databases support multiple views of the data, different ways of using the data in a single database. By using the techniques in this book, you can produce data models that are highly reusable. Why do this? Because in a real-world domain, there are usually multiple uses for any information subsystem.

Chapter 2 introduced one of the earliest logical architectures for database systems, the ANSI/SPARC three-level architecture. The highest level is the view taken by the applications that use the data. The job of the conceptual data model is to map different user views into a single conceptual data model that serves all the application views. As modeling has grown more sophisticated, the underlying structure of the conceptual and physical schemas has grown more complex. Multiple reusable subsystems replace monolithic enterprise data models, and multiple, highly specific optimizations replace a monolithic access path model. You can even integrate heterogeneous collections of databases into a fully distributed object architecture.

At the highest level in the logical architecture sit the applications. You have described these applications with a set of use cases and a corresponding data model that describes the objects to which the use cases refer. Each use case represents a view of the persistent data. The mapping between the use case and the persistent data model is the view database, the schema that represents just the data the use case needs.

As you move down in the architecture, your use cases become part of a subsystem, and your subsystems eventually combine into a working system, or application. Each subsystem maps to the data model, as does the full system. The mapping models the database for that system. Finally, as you move down toward the conceptual schema, your working systems combine into a global system of applications working against a global, or enterprise, database. The data model at this level integrates all the views of the enterprise into a single model. The next job is to translate that data model into a conceptual schema. The next few chapters move from the data model to the conceptual schema and its derivation from the data model. At the end of that process, you have integrated the disparate and competing user views into a single, global database that supports all applications. Or, at least, that's the theory.

You may find it exceedingly difficult to reconcile all the competing views of the system. Once you win or lose the arguments over the structure of the logical data, you then need to work out the competing needs for physical storage and performance. Databases that consume huge amounts of resources often cause plenty of concurrency and reliability problems to support just one user view. Other users of the database will not be especially receptive to their being told that their application must take second place to another, larger one. You may find it easier to set up several separate databases at the global level to support these users, always assuming you can work out and enforce the constraints across these databases.

The integration process achieves these goals:

- Accurate representation of functional needs through structures and constraints, including ones between high-level systems or applications

- Controlling redundancy

- Resolution of inconsistency

Representational accuracy sounds easy to achieve, but it requires a very clear understanding of all the domains you are modeling. Accuracy, consistency, and redundancy often are all aspects of the same thing—the interaction of constraints on the data. In the process of working out the use cases, you consult with users and potential users of the system, domain experts, and anybody else that can give you information about the domain. As an analyst, you integrate all this detailed information into your use cases and develop the class model to support the data requirements of those use cases. In the end, you must rely on your own understanding to develop the correct structures and constraints. A user can tell you whether a use case describes what they want to do. They will not necessarily understand the database structure and constraints, especially when you are trying to integrate different user and application views.

For example, Holmes PLC has several different users interested in various aspects of the commonplace book system. One group in Switzerland, for example, liaises with Interpol. They want to make sure that they can get the information that Interpol wants when they want it. To do that (this is purely a made-up example, not how Interpol really works), they need data about criminal events and suspects with certain specific international data about those things. The particular structure of the several classes conflicts with the more general pattern of people, organizations, and events that the main set of users of the commonplace book system will use. The conflicts are in different multiplicity constraints on the relationships and different attribute constraints on the classes. By working through the details, you understand the differences and how you might make the two sets of requirements compatible with one another. A judicious blend of negotiation and interfacing (creating separate subclasses, for example, and integrating the results into the class model) will bring the two views together into a database that makes sense for both users. You might discover one or two things (or more, in a complex application) that make no sense. On investigating further, you find that you misinterpreted some requirements. For example, the Interpol requirement might have originally sounded like a many-to-many relationship, but when you investigate further to resolve a conflict, you discover that it's really one-to-many.

You can make your integration approach as formal as you wish. If you are in an environment where you must be able to roll back changes selectively or to trace changes to the individual schemas, a formal transformation approach is appropriate [Blaha and Premerlani 1998, pp. 210–222]. A transformation is a specific change that you can make to a data model, such as subtracting an element, partitioning a class, and factoring multiple inheritance. As you find integration issues, you transform the source schemas into the merged schema using these transformations. At any time, you can see exactly how you got from the source schema to the merged one. This lets you understand the rationale for the merged schema, and it lets you selectively reverse the transformations to get back to a valid schema state if you run into trouble.

Most database designs don't need this level of formality, however, and can proceed keeping the basic goals in mind through a few key strategies:

- Merge classes with similar structures.

- Use generalization as appropriate to integrate structures and constraints.

- Use specialization as appropriate to differentiate structures and constraints with shared characteristics.

- Use generalization and association to eliminate unneeded redundancy in structure and relationships between classes; replace derived attributes created by merging with operations that derive the values.

- Make all constraints, especially complex ones, consistent with one another.

- Look for and add any missing relationships.

- Place the classes into loosely connected subsystems with a minimal number of relationships.

- Evaluate the big picture from the design perspective and redistribute any components for better cohesion and coupling.

Structural Integration

The first step in integrating two different data models is to compare them for overlaps. You can take at least two approaches to this. First, look for structural similarities—similar class names, similar attribute names, and similar class and relationship structures. Compare the object identifiers for the classes you think are the same to ensure that basic identity requirements are correct. Second, use your now-extensive domain knowledge to compare the two models for overlaps in meaning. This means looking for concepts that are similar, then looking for similar structure within the classes and relationships. You may be able to resolve superficial differences by adding or subtracting attributes or rearranging relationships.

The commonplace book system, for example, uses Person as a central table for representing all the individual people that are the subjects of interest to operatives. Holmes PLC also has a contact management application that it wants to integrate into the same global database as the commonplace book. Figure 10-1 shows the two original schemas for Contact and for Person.

You can see in comparing the Person and the Contact that there are certain structural similarities. Person links to Name and Address, Contact links to Name and Contact Method, and the key is a standard object identifier. Semantically, the comparison is even more similar. A contact is a kind of person, and there is really no distinction between them except for the purpose of the data. A Contact in the contact management application is a person along with the various ways to communicate with that person. A Person in the commonplace book is a biographical entry that tracks a personal history and the various personal characteristics for identification and investigation requirements. Merging the two is not hard, as Figure 10-2 shows.

To merge the two classes into a single Person class, the Person class acquires a link to the Contact Method class, replacing the link to Address. Address becomes a subclass of Contact Method (discussed later in "Generalization Integration"). You will need to recode the three Address methods (Add, Get, and Remove) as more general methods for handling contact information. You might add

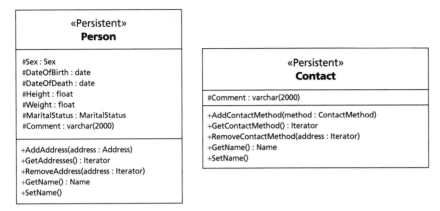

Figure 10-1 *People and Contacts in Their Original Form*

a specific GetAddress method to simplify programming in the commonplace book classes if that makes sense.

> *Tip: In standard database design, structural integration centers on primary keys and attributes. In the OO model, you're much more likely to find similarities based on the relationships and operations, though attributes do play a role. Using primary keys for discovering similarities is less likely because of assumptions about implicit primary keys. If you can determine that a primary key (object identifier) shares a domain with another class in another application, that's a good candidate for merging the two classes.*

Generalization Integration

Two classes or clusters may diverge in structural requirements only a little, having much more in common than not. This is a classic situation for using generalization. Generalize the shared attributes into a superclass and keep the differences in subclasses. More directly, you may find concepts that fit directly into generalization hierarchies in other systems; the system in which they appear just didn't need the rest of the hierarchy.

For example, one Holmes PLC application implements a detective work flow system. Each process type in the work flow is a different subclass of the class hierarchy of processes. Often, two or more processes share a set of attributes because they're conceptually similar. You abstract these common attributes from

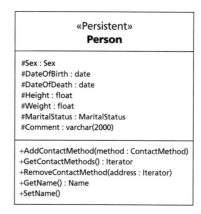

Figure 10-2   *The Merged Person and Contact Classes*

the different process types into a single superclass. This generalizes the concept but provides the concrete subclasses for specific work flows.

Another system models people and organizations to represent criminals, criminal organizations, and other people and organizations of interest to operatives. Again, because of structural characteristics they share, the application data model abstracts people and organizations into a common superclass, Entity.

Business Rule Integration

There are many different business rules in a global data model for a large business. Logic being what it is, and people being what they are, you can almost guarantee that any two applications merging into a single model will have conflicts in their logic. Relationships will have different multiplicities, some attributes will be nullable in one application and not in the other, or complex constraints will simply be logically irreconcilable with one another.

For example, Holmes PLC has an application that manages checking account security for banks. A federal regulation requires that a bank check the customer's picture identification when they open an account. The Bank Account class links to a Person class with the relationship including a PictureID class that represents the individual ID used to establish the account. When this data model integrates with the commonplace book, which has a much more extensive identification model, the Bank Account links to the already existing Person class, but the PictureID is harder. Figure 10-3 shows the conflict.

In this case, linking PictureID is a bit more difficult than just figuring out a new generalization or association link. The whole notion of a picture ID is out of place in the commonplace book model, which models specific identification vari-

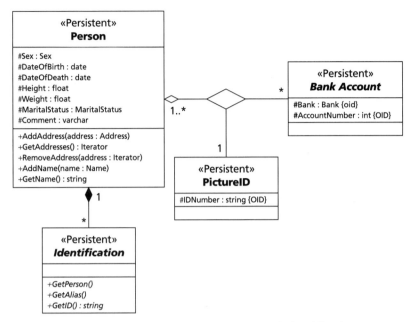

Figure 10-3   *The Conflict between PictureID and Identification*

eties. Moving PictureID into the Identification class hierarchy won't work, because the picture ID objects (Driver's License, NationalID, or whatever it might be) will overlap with objects of another class. There are some alternatives:

- Link PictureID to the specific (as opposed to abstract) subclasses that are in fact picture IDs. This introduces multiple inheritance into the schema and clearly makes things more complex.

- Create a PictureID interface and add it to the specific subclasses that are in fact picture IDs. This is a good solution for the short term. It allows merging the two schemas without any change to the underlying schema structure other than the addition of a single interface and the implementation of a few methods (not shown in Figure 10-3) in the specific subclasses that support it.

- Rethink the Identification class hierarchy to include an abstract PictureID class. Reorganize the specific classes under it. This is going to disrupt the commonplace book system a good deal, depending on how much work designers have already done using the current hierarchy.

- Rethink the PictureID class and replace it with an association to Identification. Add constraints that require the Identification to exist when there is a Bank Account for the person and that require the ID to have a picture. Add that polymorphic feature to the relevant interfaces of Identification. This generalizes the relationship nicely, reducing coupling by use of polymorphism, but it also introduces more complexity through the additional constraints required to express the complex requirements of Bank Accounts for identification.

The choice is yours. Each choice trades off advantages with disadvantages. For maximal reuse of the schema, the last choice of generalizing PictureID is probably best, despite the added complexity. You can encapsulate that. The interface solution is a great short-term solution if you need to merge the two systems and get them working quickly. You'll run into trouble the next time, however, because of the slightly jury-rigged nature of the relationship. If it seems to you that picture IDs are more important than the original breakdown of expiring IDs and so on, then the third choice may be best. Everything depends on your project goals in this case, or on your long-term goals.

Big Picture Integration

Beyond just looking at short- or long-term goals, though, you really need to step back from your design and look at the big picture before you finally accept the choices you need to make. Work through the scenarios from your use cases and from the use cases in the systems you are merging into your schema to see how the schema actually supports them. As you do that, you'll emerge with a bigger and bigger picture of the merged schema as a whole rather than as a collection of parts. The synergy of the whole system and its interrelationships is the key to the final set of strategies for integrating schemas.

The first thing to look at is whether there are any missing relationships. If you want to do this systematically, you can create a spreadsheet matrix for each subsystem with all the subsystem classes along the top and down the side. Fill in the cells with a value if there is a relationship. The value itself can be "True," or you can use the relationship type (such as generalization or association), or you can use the multiplicity. Don't forget the recursive relationships along the diagonal of the matrix, where classes relate to themselves. You can leave the cells above the diagonal (or below, whichever you wish) blank if you think of the relationships as symmetric. If you use directed arrows, on the other hand, you need to represent the different directions of the relationship in different cells. Also, include transitive generalizations, where a class is a subclass of another indirectly at a lower level. Below this matrix, you can list the relationships to classes outside the subsystem, which you'll use later.

Now look at the blank cells. First, consider each association that isn't there. Would it make sense in any potential application to associate the classes? Is the association meaningful? Is it useful enough to add some complexity to the data model? If you can answer "yes" to all these questions, create a new association.

Second, consider each generalization that isn't there. Would connecting the classes as superclass-subclass be meaningful? Again, is it worth adding the complexity? The comments on the various design choices in the previous section on "Business Rule Integration" show you some of the trade-offs here. If it makes sense, reorganize the class hierarchy to include the new class at the appropriate place in the hierarchy.

After you've gone through this exercise for each subsystem, step out another level and consider the relationships between subsystems. If it helps, draw a package diagram and annotate the package dependencies with the exact relationships you've listed at the bottom of your various spreadsheets.

First, find any cycles. A cycle in the package diagram is where a dependency from a package leads to a package on which the first package is dependent, directly or indirectly.

Second, find any relationships that are composite aggregations (the black diamond that establishes a class as contained within another class). Without a really strong reason, you should not have such relationships between packages. Composites are tightly coupled, usually with overlapping object identity. Therefore, they belong in the same unit of cohesion in the system.

Third, find any generalization relationships between packages. Again, subclasses are tightly coupled to their superclasses, as an object contains an instance of both classes. There are, however, certain situations that justify putting a superclass in a different subsystem.

For example, you can reuse a packaged component such as a framework through "black box" reuse, which requires subclassing the component class to make it specific to your domain. That means by definition that the superclass is in a different package, as the "black box" nature of the situation means you can't modify the reused component package.

Another example: you can have class hierarchies with disjoint subtrees that relate to completely different parts of the system. The joint superclass may exist only for implementation or very general feature inheritance. This is the case, for example, in systems that have a single root object (CObject, ooObject, and so on). The hierarchical nature of UML is somewhat inhibiting in this regard. It might be better to treat packages as overlapping, with some classes being part of a generalization tree package as well as an association-related package. One represents the entire class hierarchy starting at an arbitrary root, while other packages represent the use of those classes. The more overlaps you have, though, the more difficult it is to understand everything that's going on because of the increasing complexity of relationships between packages.

Fourth, and finally, look at the number of dependencies between each package and the other parts of the system. The objective in decomposing your system into subsystems is to uncouple the subsystem from the rest of the system to the highest possible degree. The fewer dependencies you have, the better. On the other hand, each dependency represents a form of reuse. If a subsystem is highly reusable, it almost certainly means that more than one other system will depend on it for its features.

To understand the trade-offs, you should measure the dependencies with the coupling and reuse potential metrics from Chapter 9. If a subsystem has a low reuse potential, you should have a relatively low coupling metric for each dependency and a low number of dependencies. The higher the reuse potential, the more dependencies the package can support. On the other side, a package that depends on more than just a few other packages should not have a particularly high reuse potential because of its strongly coupled nature. If you find this combination, go back and understand why you have rated the reuse potential so high. Should the entire set of subsystems be part of a larger reusable subsystem (a "framework"), for example?

> *Note: Another method for evaluating the cohesion of your subsystems is to use the logical horizon of classes. The* logical horizon of a class *is the transitive closure of the association and generalization relationships from the class that terminate in a multiplicity of 1..1 or 0..1 [Blaha and Premerlani 1998, pp. 62–64; Feldman and Miller 1986]. Walk all the paths from the class to other classes. If an association to the other class has a multiplicity of 1..1 or 0..1, that class is in the logical horizon, but the path ends there. You can walk up a generalization relationship to the class's superclass, but not down again to its siblings. The classes with the largest horizons are usually at the center of a subsystem that includes most of the logical horizon of that class. As with most mechanistic methods, however, using a logical horizon approach can be misleading and does not guarantee a highly cohesive subsystem, particularly if the associations are incomplete or wrong (never happens, right?).*

Because you are changing the subsystem relationships, you may want to make one more pass through the subsystem analysis to see if anything has changed because of moving classes between subsystems.

Summary

Not everyone chooses their parents wisely. Developing data models around legacy systems brings into sharp focus the culture of the organization that created those systems. This culture has a large impact on your legacy development and maintenance efforts through several mechanisms:

- Norms
- Values, attitudes, and beliefs
- Rituals
- Folklore
- Shared language

Given these elements of your organizational culture, you may or may not be able to leverage existing data and technology in your legacy system to provide the basis for your system development. Sometimes it's better to start fresh; sometimes its better to renovate the old house. Part of your job is to develop the scope of the new system based on both the system requirements and the system culture. On the other hand, if you renovate, you need to pay a lot more attention to culture to understand both the scope of the old system and the scope of your changes to it.

The next three chapters (the rest of the book) show you how to transform your data model into one of the three schemas: relational, object-relational, or object-oriented. Each chapter follows a similar structure, showing you the transformation of the following elements:

- Structures
- Relationships
- Business rules
- Design guidelines
- Data definition languages

Finally, the last stage of building your data model is the integration of all the different views into a single shared conceptual model. You integrate different structures into a unified and well-structured whole. You generalize concepts brought together into class hierarchies. You integrate business rules and resolve any logical conflicts between them. Lastly, you step back and look at the big picture to optimize the total view of the system.

You are now at the point where the rubber meets the road. Unfortunately, you are in a computer game where the road changes its character depending on where you are and what tools you are carrying. Moving from the data model to the schema is a tricky process. You must find your way through the maze of culture, you must understand the tools available, and you must understand how to leverage what you are carrying with you. Good luck, and do watch out for the human sacrifice in Chapter 12.

Designing a Relational Database Schema 11

Thou shalt prepare a table before me against them that trouble me: thou hast anointed my head with oil, and my cup shall be full. But thy loving-kindness and mercy shall follow me all the days of my life: and I will dwell in the house of the Lord for ever.

Church of England Prayer Book, 23:4

Transforming a data model into a database schema is not easy, but it's not going to put another person on the moon either. The techniques for turning an ER model into a relational model are well understood [Teorey 1999, Chapter 4]. Transforming a UML data model into a relational database uses these techniques and adds some more to take some of the expanded features of such models into account. The first three sections of this chapter go into detail on the structures, relationships, and constraints of your UML data model and their transformation into the relational schema.

The next section of the chapter discusses the concept of data normalization. You really can't talk about relational databases without talking about normalization. If you approach it from the OO perspective, though, you can eliminate much of its complexity and detail. It is still important to understand how your database structure meets the "normal" requirements of the relational world, but it's much easier to get there from an OO data model.

The last section summarizes the sequence of steps you take to transform the OO data model into an SQL-92 schema. It also shows you some of the specialized things you can do by using the nonstandard elements of a database manager, in this case Oracle7.

Turning the Tables

The structures of a relational database are very simple. You have tables, and you have tables. Unless you want to create a table, of course. This simplicity has one negative effect: it complicates the process of representing complex objects. The trick in moving from a UML data model to a relational schema is to make the simplicity of the relational table work for you instead of against you.

To illustrate the process, Figure 11-1 shows a UML model for the Person subsystem of the commonplace book, and Figure 11-2 shows a UML model for the Organization subsystem. Both of these subsystems are part of a third subsystem, the Entity subsystem. Figure 11-3 shows the architecture for the package.

The Person subsystem contains the Person class and the Identification hierarchy that belongs to it. I've chosen to use the inheritance version of Identification rather than the interface version. People connect to organizations through a three-way relationship to the Role class in the Organization package. The scope notation (Organization::Role) identifies classes that are not a part of the Person subsystem.

The Organization subsystem contains the Organization hierarchy, which includes the CriminalOrganization class. It also includes the Role class and the relationships between Role and Organization. Organizations connect to people through a three-way relationship to Role.

The Entity subsystem contains three elements: the two subsystems Person and Organization plus an abstract class, Entity. The Person and Organization classes in their respective packages inherit from that class. In the future, Entity will have relationships to other subsystems such as Contact Method, Geographical Location, and Image.

Packages, Subsystems, and Name Spaces

The package and its specialization, the subsystem (see Chapter 7), provide organizing name spaces for your system architecture. The objective is to design a system in reusable chunks that are as independent from one another as possible.

Packages are a new concept to the relational world. Most database designers think about relational schemas as a kind of global data repository, or even as a single name space. This approach comes from technological limitations in the past and from cultures that built up around these limitations. For example, you will still find DBAs who insist on global column names, or on names that include all kinds of identifying information. CMN_ID_ID_NO_NUM, for example, might represent such an excessive naming convention: The commonplace book (CMN) ID table (ID) ID number (ID_NO) column, which is a numeric data type (NUM). I prefer IDNumber in the Identification table, taking full advantage of the name space established by the schema and the table.

> *Note: Don't confuse the UML package that I discuss here and in Chapter 7 (and later in this chapter put to use designing a database) with the Oracle PL/SQL package. PL/SQL took the package idea from the Ada programming language, where a package is a compilation*

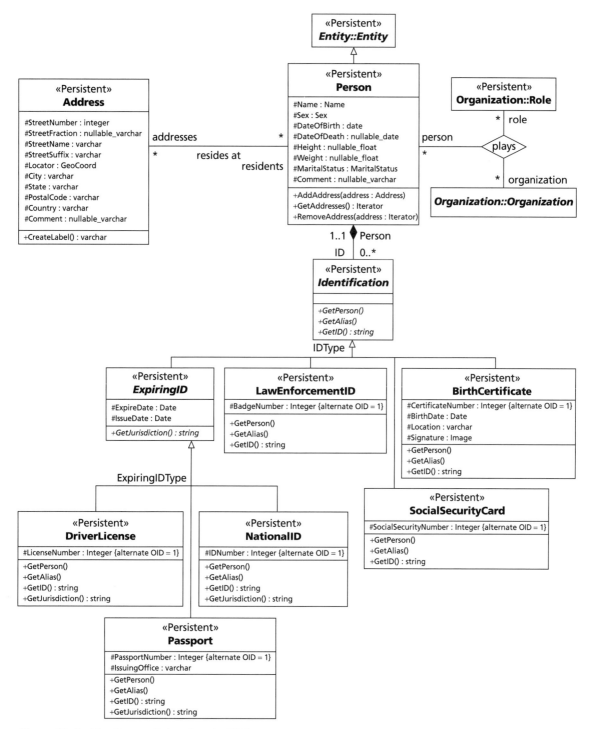

Figure 11-1 The Person Subsystem in UML

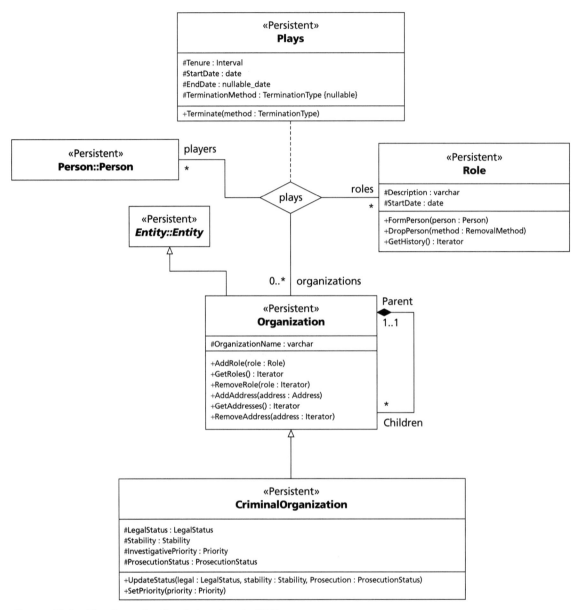

Figure 11-2 *The Organization Subsystem in UML*

> *unit that collects a number of different elements into a single ob-*
> *ject. It's really more of a module or a class than a subsystem, al-*
> *though the concepts are related by the concept of the name space.*

The problem with schemas as sets of global names is precisely the problem that packages address: reusability through encapsulation and uncoupling. Most

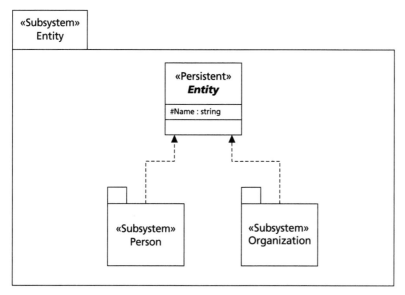

Figure 11-3   *The Entity Subsystem in UML*

database designers have at some point confronted the need to integrate more than one database into a seamless whole. In reality, you should think about the problem as integrating multiple packages into a system. Each package provides its contribution as required in an encapsulated, uncoupled way. Using OO techniques, you don't use the lowest common denominator approach of raising all the names up to the top as global; you use name spaces to carefully organize access.

Standard SQL provides a very basic name space capability with the schema name [Melton and Simon 1993; ANSI 1992]. An ANSI schema is a descriptor that includes a name, an authorization identifier, a character set name, and all the descriptors of a set of components (tables, views, domains, assertions, privileges, character sets, collations, or translations). No major DBMS of which I am aware implements this schema capability precisely. IBM's SQL/DS and DB2 systems established a de facto standard by setting up a system of users in a single database. Oracle and Informix followed suit, as did a host of smaller DBMS vendors. This concept of user corresponds to the ANSI concept of authorization identifier. In the earlier SQL standard, schema name and authorization were the same; the 1992 standard uncoupled them.

> *Note: As an aside, I have to express my opinion (repeat, opinion) at this point in a small sermon about the unfortunate way in which the major relational vendors have ignored the ANSI standard. Not one of the major vendors even comes close to implementing the full features of that standard, despite the dramatic improvements it makes*

to the SQL language in areas ranging from date-time processing to character sets and internationalization [Melton and Simon 1993]. The schema name space capabilities are just another example of the major vendors' inability to move forward. You should pressure the vendors to implement the complete standard as quickly as possible. You can remind vendors that complain about the difficulty of implementing the standard that people are paying huge amounts of money for their software design and implementation skills. Also, having a complete ANSI SQL provides a tremendously strong value proposition for customers. A vendor who provides this will have a very strong competitive position in the RDBMS market.

The user corresponds to the authentication identifier and to the schema name. These databases do not have a "schema" object, although they implement the CREATE SCHEMA statement from the standard. Instead of establishing a schema name space, these systems establish a user name space. Each user can run multiple CREATE SCHEMA statements without any implication about the relationships between the sets of objects the various statements create other than that they all belong to the named user.

Users are really part of the standard SQL security mechanism, which security theorists call *discretionary access control*. This kind of security system establishes an owner for each object, such as a table, and a set of privileges granted on that object to other users. Users must refer to objects owned by other users by prefacing the object with the name of the owning user. Again, this corresponds to the SQL standard's authentication identifier and schema name.

Note: Microsoft has integrated its SQL Server security system with the security system of the underlying operating system, Windows NT. This makes it easier to administer the database by using the NT user and password to authenticate access to the database as well. You don't have to define separate users for the database and the operating system. The database name space thus becomes part of the larger name space established by operating system security.

Various DBMS vendors extend this system with an additional concept: the *synonym* or *alias*. You can create an alias for an object that belongs to another user. You can then refer to the alias without prefacing it with the name of the owning user. Using synonyms, you can create names in your user name space that make a database with multiple name spaces look like a single, global name space. A public synonym makes the name global to all users to provide a truly global name.

But what about multiple databases? The SQL standard is totally silent on the concept of database; its only concern is to establish the schema name space. This omission has resulted in an array of different approaches to having multiple databases. Oracle and Informix have added the concept of a database link. This is essentially a synonym you establish that refers to a foreign database within the database in which you create the link. You then prefix the name of an object in the foreign database with not only the name of the owning user but the database link name as well.

Sybase and its cousin Microsoft SQL Server take a different and more complex approach. These systems have multiple databases as objects registered on a server. Databases and users are completely separate. You also have logins, the username and password with which a user authenticates themselves, and these are also completely separate. You can give a user access to any object in any accessible database. You then refer to an object by prefacing it with the database name and the name of the owning user, which may or may not be the name of the login. At the moment, the name space extends only to the boundaries of the server on which the databases reside due to the way these systems identify the server. There is an administrative login (sa) with full access to everything. There is for each database a publicly owned set of tables (the standard user dbo, database owner, owns these tables) that any user with access to the database can see.

> Note: Again, SQL Server version 7 integrates the security system
> with operating system security.

Bringing all of this diversity to bear on the problem of implementing persistent UML packages is an interesting exercise. First, forget a standard approach—there is none. Second, spend some design time establishing how your applications will refer to the different name spaces. Ideally, a subsystem or package should refer to a well-defined set of other packages, and it should be able to ignore any relationships between those packages.

To see an example of implementing an approach to name spaces in Oracle7, see the section "Packaged Subsystems" toward the end of this chapter.

To summarize, you can establish separate package and subsystem name spaces and encapsulation using a combination of different aspects of your relational database manager. You still don't get a complete representation of the package, but you get more encapsulation than with a more usual implementation of the system.

Types and Domains

Once you've established your name spaces, you can start thinking about the kinds of data you want to put into the database. Before you start transforming your UML classes into tables, you need to establish the types that you will use to declare the table columns.

Recall from Chapter 7 that you can easily build a set of basic data types in a separate package of classifiers defined with the «Type» stereotype. You have at least four alternatives to structuring this package:

- You can build a set of types corresponding to the types your RDBMS makes available; for example, if you're using Oracle7, you might define types for NUMBER, VARCHAR2, CHAR, DATE, LONG, RAW, and LONGRAW.

- You can build a set of types corresponding to ANSI standard types: CHARACTER, CHARACTER VARYING, BIT, BIT VARYING, NUMERIC, DECIMAL, INTEGER, SMALLINT, FLOAT, REAL, DOUBLE PRECISION, DATE, TIME, TIMESTAMP, and INTERVAL.

- You can build a set of types based on OO programming types, such as the C++ types: int, string, char, array of type, struct, enum, and so on.

- You can build a set of types based on the OR and OO database standards for maximum portability between different kinds of database managers. The ODMG types that the "Domain Constraints" section in Chapter 7 defines are an example of this.

There are two aspects to transforming these types into a relational database schema: creating ANSI standard domains and establishing a transformation table.

ANSI Domains

The ANSI SQL-92 standard added the concept of domain to standard SQL. An SQL *domain* is "a set of permissible values. . . . The purpose of a domain is to constrain the set of valid values that can be stored in SQL-data by various operations" [ANSI 1992]. Melton and Simon give a slightly more practical definition [Melton and Simon 1993]: "A domain is a sort of macro that you can define to pull together a specific data type (and, if applicable, size), as well as some characteristics [including] defaults, constraints, and collations. You can then use the name of the domain to define columns that inherit the data type (and other characteristics) of the domain."

Figure 11-4 gives the syntax of the ANSI CREATE DOMAIN statement.

Note: These syntax diagrams are "railroad diagrams" because you follow the tracks, tracing along the lines from the start to the finish. You start at the arrow with nothing at the starting point and finish at an arrow which points to nothing, following the arrows between syntax elements. If you can trace a line that skips a box, it means the element is optional, such as <default clause> and the other options

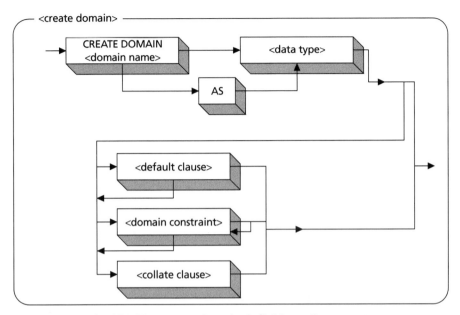

Figure 11-4   *The SQL-92 <create domain definition> Statement*

in Figure 11-4. Splits like the one between <data type> and <domain name> in Figure 11-6 (the <column definition> clause) are alternatives: *you can go one way or the other. If a line links back to a box, it means repetition or looping, such as with the <domain constraint> in Figure 11-4. You can have zero or more domain constraints following one another in a CREATE DOMAIN statement. In constructing the statement, you can go directly from the data type to the end of the expression, or you can put in the default clause, the column constraint(s), or the collation clause. Elements in angle brackets <> indicate elements with definitions in other diagrams. You separate elements in different boxes with at least one space. Some boxes combine several elements for readability, but you can put any number of spaces between the internal elements of a box if one space appears there.*

The <default clause> corresponds to the initial-value specification in the UML attribute definition (see the later section on "Attributes"). Figure 11-5 shows the syntax for the default clause.

The ANSI standard specifies several possible values for <default option> that most of the RDBMS products don't implement, and most provide possibilities that the standard does not. You can use the standard values in your UML, but you

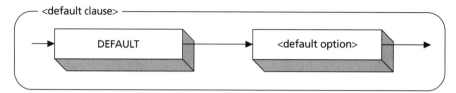

Figure 11-5   *The SQL-92 <default clause> Syntax*

will need to transform them into the system-dependent values that your target RDBMS provides. Similarly, you can define your own set of possibilities to use in UML, as long as you provide a transformation table for the target RDBMS.

The <collate clause> in Figure 11-4 defines the collating sequence if the <data type> is a character type. Since none of the major vendors implement this syntax, don't worry about it.

Now, all that being said, forget it. Let me repeat my sermon about database vendors and the ANSI standard: none of the major database vendors implement the CREATE DOMAIN statement in their systems. The newer ORDBMS products from these vendors add capabilities that look suspiciously like this, such as CREATE TYPE, but even they don't implement the CREATE DOMAIN from the standard. Therefore, although you can dream about the transformation of types into domains, in practice it's hopeless.

The Transformation Table

Even if you could create domains in RDBMS schemas, you would still need a way to relate your UML types to your domains and data types. Before transforming classes, you should have a table in some form that shows how to map UML type expressions into the SQL of your target DBMS. If you have multiple targets, you should have multiple tables. For optimal reusability, you should package your UML type package diagram and the table together in a reuse repository for use in multiple data models and schema designs.

The transformations may be simple ("if UML type is string, then SQL type is VARCHAR(254)," for example), but usually you will find various ifs, ands, or buts that make your job more complex. For example, does a string translate into a VARCHAR(254), or can you specify a shorter size? Do you sometimes want a CHAR instead of a VARCHAR?

Enumerated types pose a real problem. If there is a way to define domains, you can encode the CHECK constraint that corresponds to the list of values into the CREATE DOMAIN statement:

```
CREATE DOMAIN Boolean AS CHAR(1) NOT NULL DEFAULT 'T'
  CONSTRAINT Bool_Constraint CHECK (Boolean IN ('T', 'F'));
```

If you don't have domains, and mostly you don't, you must put the CHECK constraint (and probably the DEFAULT and NOT NULL clauses as well) into each attribute that uses the type. Alternatively, you can create a type table and put the values into it, then create a foreign key constraint to that table. You would definitely do that if you thought you might add new values to the enumeration over time. For a Boolean type, that isn't true; for other enumerations, it is often true.

You may also want to specify some display values to use in your programs. For example, if your user interface presents a field that takes a value of an enumerated type, you might want to make it a dropdown list. It can then display full-word natural language values such as "True" and "False" for a Boolean type. You can encode this into a type table, a single table for each type with the following structure:

```
CREATE TABLE <Name>Type (
  Value <Data Type> PRIMARY KEY,
  DisplayString VARCHAR2(50) NOT NULL,
  Description VARCHAR2(2000))
```

In this parameterized CREATE TABLE statement, <Name> is your UML type name and <Data Type> is the SQL data type that corresponds to your enumerated values. The type is usually either CHAR(n) for character code representations or NUMBER for numeric code representations. You insert one row of data for each enumeration value. For example, the possible states of the legal status of a criminal organization include Legally Defined, On Trial, Alleged, and Unknown. The following Oracle7 SQL creates a type table for the UML LegalStatus Type:

```
CREATE TABLE LegalStatusType (
  Value CHAR(1) PRIMARY KEY,
  DisplayString VARCHAR2(50) NOT NULL,
  Description VARCHAR2(2000));
INSERT INTO LegalStatusType (Value, DisplayString)
VALUES ('L', 'Legally Defined');
INSERT INTO LegalStatusType (Value, DisplayString)
VALUES ('T', 'On Trial');
INSERT INTO LegalStatusType (Value, DisplayString)
VALUES ('A', 'Alleged');
INSERT INTO LegalStatusType (Value, DisplayString)
VALUES ('U', 'Unknown');
CREATE TABLE LegalStatusTypeDefault(
  Value CHAR(1) PRIMARY KEY);
INSERT INTO LegalStatusTypeDefault (Value)
VALUES ('U');
```

This series of SQL statements sets up the table, inserts a row for each enumeration value with an alphabetic code, and sets up a singleton table containing the default code. The advantage in this approach is that you can add to or modify the value set by inserting or updating rows in the type table. You can use the default table to modify the default value. An alternative way to indicate defaults is with a Boolean tag column in the type table, IsDefault or something like that. The singleton table is clearer in most cases and is easier to maintain from your application.

> Note: Sometimes you see type tables in relational database designs
> that merge several types into a single table. This is a bad design idea
> for two reasons. First, the Value column must have the type of value
> that is correct for the enumeration. It may be NUMBER, it may be
> CHAR, or it may be a DATE. Your choice is either to use the wrong
> type by choosing one of these or to add a column for each type and
> make it null for enumerations that are not of that type. Neither of
> these is good design. The first approach is bad because it doesn't do
> the job. The second approach is bad because you introduce a com-
> plex constraint into the table. The second reason is that you intro-
> duce control coupling into your database unnecessarily. By adding a
> discriminator column, usually the type name, to distinguish just
> those rows that apply to a given type, you force applications to add
> control logic to their SQL retrieval.

Classes

A UML class contains attributes and operations. The transformation is easy, at least for the attributes: each class becomes a table in a relational database, and each attribute becomes a column in the table. For example, in the Person subsystem from Figure 11-1, you create a table for each of the classes in the diagram: Person, Address, Identification, ExpiringID, LawEnforcementID, and so on. For example, here is the transformation of the Person class and attributes into a standard CREATE TABLE statement:

```
CREATE TABLE Person (
  PersonID INTEGER PRIMARY KEY,
  Sex CHARACTER(2) NOT NULL CHECK (Sex IN ('M', 'F')),
  BirthDate DATE NOT NULL,
  Height FLOAT,
  Weight FLOAT,
  MaritalStatus CHARACTER(1) NULL
    CHECK (MaritalStatus IN ('S', 'M', 'D', 'W')),
  Comment VARCHAR(200))
```

The trick to producing CREATE TABLE statements is in transforming the attribute types into SQL data types and single-attribute constraints. See the following sections on "Attributes" and "Domains and Data Types" for details on these decisions. There is also the problem of the primary key attributes; see the section on "Constraints and Object Identity" for details on producing a PRIMARY KEY constraint.

> *Warning: A small worry is the length of your class name. Standard SQL-92 limits the length of table names to a maximum of 128 characters, including schema name qualifier, but you'll be lucky if your system gives you anything like that. All the systems I've used limit you to 31 or 32 characters (Oracle, Informix, Sybase, and SQL Server) or even 18 characters (DB2).*

But what about the operations? There is nowhere in the CREATE TABLE statement for these. In most relational databases these days you have at least some possibilities for representing behavior as well as structure. See the following section on "Operations and Methods" for some suggestions.

Attributes

Each attribute in a UML class becomes a column in a table. Again, you must worry about name length; this is 18–32 characters depending on your target DBMS. Most of the transformation of attributes has to do with creating suitable data type and constraint declarations, however.

Recall the UML attribute definition syntax from Chapter 7:

```
stereotype visibility name : type-expression =
    initial-value { property-string }
```

There are no attribute stereotypes, and visibility in relational databases is always public (+), so you can ignore these parts of the attribute definition. See the section on "Operations and Methods" for a way to pretend that your attributes are private, however.

Figure 11-6 presents the SQL-92 syntax for the column definition.

The <data type> or <domain name> corresponds to the type-expression you've associated with the attribute in UML. See the following section on "Domains and Data Types" for details. The <column constraint definition> is one of the several types of integrity constraint you can specify or the NOT NULL constraint. This corresponds to the tagged values in the property-string. See the following section on "Constraints and Object Identity."

Domains and Data Types   Your type-expression may include two kinds of type: a type that directly corresponds to a basic SQL data type or a more complex

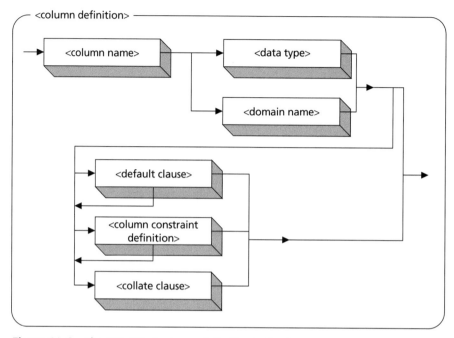

Figure 11-6   *The SQL-92 <column definition> Syntax*

domain based on such a type (see the previous section "Types and Domains"). You use your type transformation table to determine a reasonable SQL data type for the attribute. Beyond that, things get complex.

For enumerated types, you should build a type table (see "Types and Domains"). You can then specify a foreign key constraint to map the column to that table:

```
LegalStatus CHAR(1) NOT NULL DEFAULT 'U'
  REFERENCES LegalStatusType(Value),
```

This column definition links to the LegalStatus Type table's Value column to get the set of possible values for the LegalStatus column in the Criminal Organization table. You use the same data type as the type table defines (CHAR(1)). The NOT NULL is optional, as is the DEFAULT clause. You may want to depend on a default table approach in which the application queries the default value rather than using a DEFAULT clause.

For the kind of subtyping available in SQL, you can specify character size, numeric precision and scale, and any other such restrictions available in your target RDBMS.

For ranges and other subtypes of that sort, you must use a CHECK constraint:

```
IDNumber NUMBER(10,0) CHECK (IDNumber > 999999999),
```

This column definition specifies a 10-digit integer number, a number between 1,000,000,000 and 9,999,999,999. Notice how the numeric precision combines with the check constraint to enforce the range. You can also specify the range directly:

```
IDNumber INTEGER CHECK (IDNumber BETWEEN 1000000000 AND 9999999999),
```

To exclude noninteger values, this definition uses the INTEGER data type. This is not a native Oracle7 data type but rather an internal synonym for NUMBER with a scale of 0.

To summarize this example, you can go quite far to satisfying most subtype constraints using the SQL built-in types and the CHECK constraint mechanism. Unfortunately, you must specify the entire mess each time you use the UML type, because current RDBMS products do not yet implement the ANSI SQL-92 domain. If your vendor does, by all means use the domain to represent subtypes, as this greatly enhances reusability and consistency in your schema.

> *Note: Relational schemas cannot represent structured or multi-valued data types such as records or arrays. If your UML design includes attributes with these kinds of types, you must treat them as though the type were a class. Create a separate table for the data, then link the table back to the owning table with a foreign key relationship.*

Constraints and Object Identity   The series of property strings in curly braces in the UML attribute definition includes the following extended tagged values:

- *{OID}*: An explicit primary key
- *{alternate OID}*: An explicit candidate key
- *{nullable}*: A specification that the attribute can be null instead of having a value

The Chapter 7 section on "Object Identity and Uniqueness Constraints" goes into detail on the UML approaches to explicit and implicit object identity. Relational databases rely entirely on explicit identity. Relational theorists raise this feature to a principle, stating that "all information in the database at any given time must be cast explicitly in terms of values in relations and in no other way" [Date and Darwen 1998, pp. 145–146]. The consequence of this principle is that there can be no such thing as an object identifier that is not a value in a table column, nor can there be pointers to values or rows (see Chapter 12 for the OR concept of "reference," for example).

Most DBMS products support some kind of identification "under the covers." For example, Oracle7 provides a ROWID that uniquely identifies a row in a table. That ROWID can change, however, if the DBMS moves the row to a different location on disk. It is a physical identifier, not a logical identifier, and you should not consider it to be an object identifier. You thus can't store off a ROWID value in another table and use it later to retrieve the original row, as the internal value may change. Also, Oracle reserves the right to change the ROWID structure from version to version, as they did in Oracle8. Thus, both as a practical matter and in theory, you should restrict yourself in RDBMS schemas to explicit identity.

> *Note: SQL Server version 7 provides an OID data type to represent object identity explicitly. This moves SQL Server one step in the direction of the object-relational databases discussed in Chapter 12. It also integrates the concept of object identity directly into the relational model. Whether this constitutes a "value" according to Date's definition is unlikely.*

Taking the explicit approach, you must figure out how to transform implicit and explicit UML identity into explicit relational identity. Starting with explicit {OID} attributes is much easier: you just create your columns from the attributes and put a PRIMARY KEY constraint on them. If it is a single column, you can just add the words PRIMARY KEY to the column definition as a <column constraint definition>. If there are multiple attributes with {OID} tags, you must add a <table constraint definition> to specify the PRIMARY KEY.

Transforming implicit UML object identity to explicit relational identity is a bit harder because the tools vary widely from system to system. Usually, the simplest approach is to add an integer column to the table. The variance is how you assign values to that column. Oracle7, for example, has the SEQUENCE object that you can use to supply monotonically increasing integer values. This corresponds directly to a primary key domain that any number of tables can share. SQL Server and Sybase, on the other hand, let you add the keyword IDENTITY to the attribute, and it then generates a monotonically increasing number as part of the INSERT operation. This does not correspond to a domain because you can't share the value across tables.

> *Tip: You should think about the identifier domain from the perspective of the required integer size. Computers limit integer values by the memory architecture of the machine. Many DBMS products limit integers to 4 billion or so (2^{32}), or half that for signed integers (-2 billion to 2 billion). If you will have fewer than 2 billion (4 billion) objects, that's fine, but think about it carefully. Your application code should understand the limitation as well and decline gracefully to produce more objects when it nears the limit.*

Another alternative is to add code, either as a stored procedure or in your application, to generate these numbers. I've encountered three ways of doing this.

One approach is to create a table that has one row for each domain; you increment the number and store it as the "current" number, emulating the SEQUENCE. The only problem with this approach is that you lock the row (or in SQL Server and Sybase, even worse, the page). Locking can dramatically impact concurrency if you create many rows very quickly from many different connections (the OLTP scenario).

A second alternative is to query the maximum value of the column from the table, increment that by one, and use that number as the new value in an INSERT statement. This approach may or may not perform very well depending on the optimization available from the DBMS; at worst, it can scan all the rows in the table. It also has various impacts on locking the rows in the table (and locking the index pages for the table if the query uses them).

A third alternative is to generate a unique number in some way. Variants on this include hashing (using a simple MOD transformation on the current date and time, for example, or some kind of random number generator) or GUID (globally unique identifier) generation. A GUID is also known as a uuid (universally unique identifier) [Leach and Salz 1997]. You generate it using a standard algorithm based on hardware identity and timestamp. The hashing approach works 90% of the time (the real number actually depends on the hash function you use), so you need to check the number or add code to generate a new number if the INSERT fails because of duplicate values in the primary key. The GUID approach works fine as long as you're willing to accept all keys using 36 bytes of fixed-length character space in the table and in the primary key index. For very large tables, this space can really add up compared with a single integer value.

> *Tip: GUIDs are the method of choice for identity domains that you want to be able to handle virtually any number of objects, as is likely for Holmes PLC. If it concerns you that integer values may be too limiting, you should definitely look into GUIDs [Leach and Salz 1997]. The Win32 application programming interface contains functions that generate GUIDs, as part of the remote procedure control library (rpc.h).*

The candidate keys require some additional SQL syntax. Recall that each {alternate OID} tag specifies a number identifying the particular candidate key. This lets you have multiple candidate keys that comprise multiple columns. For each unique number in such a tag, you should generate a UNIQUE constraint, either as a <column constraint definition> or as a <table constraint definition>. Since these candidate keys are always explicit, you just create the attribute(s) as columns, then put in the constraints.

The UML {nullable} tag corresponds to the NOT NULL constraint, at least in its absence. That is, you attach {nullable} to the attribute in UML if you do not want a NOT NULL constraint in your relational database. If there is no tag on the attribute, you must add the keywords NOT NULL to your column definition. Most RDBMS products let you add a null constraint, the reverse of the NOT NULL constraint, though that isn't part of the ANSI standard for the column definition.

Operations and Methods

Creating your columns only gets you part of the way to having a complete application. Table columns comprise the static part, but what about the dynamic part? UML classes have operations as well as attributes. How can you leverage these operations in a relational database environment?

The major relational databases limit you to stored procedures and functions as objects in your schema. For example, Oracle7 lets you define stored functions or procedures. If your functions don't have side effects, you can use them in standard SQL expressions wherever you can use a scalar value. With a little creativity, you can often represent your class behavior as stored procedures or functions that you can call either in SQL expressions or as part of a larger stored procedure. You can also call these from your application programs using various nonstandard APIs. Whether this makes sense depends on the nature of the behavior, the larger system architecture of which the database is a part, and the requirements for reuse across applications.

First, however, it's important to realize the distinction between the database server and the application code. This division is not arbitrary; some things make sense as database server behavior, while other things do not. This is the art of application partitioning.

Partitioning   There are whole classes of operations that you don't want to see on the server. *Partitioning* is the process of deciding whether to put the behavior on the database server, an application server, or the client.

> *Note: The world is full of partitions. With respect to computers, in different contexts you can partition any number of different things. The consequence so far as this book is concerned is to confuse you with using the same word for different things. In particular, don't confuse* application partitioning, *the division of the application between client and server, or server and server, with* data partitioning, *the division of a table or other collection of data into different physical chunks for physical input/output optimization.*

First, you don't want operations that handle transient issues. Any operation that requires a reference to an in-memory address or an in-memory object is not suitable for the database server, since that server has no access to such things.

Second, you don't want client-called operations that access data attribute by attribute. Recall from Chapter 7 that you can create operations with the {query} property, here called accessors or observers, that simply return an attribute's value (usually as a constant reference in C++, for example). Database servers don't work that way; they return records, not values. Visualize a very large tunnel filled with a huge cargo train that contains a single grain of corn for each trip. It's going to take a lot of resources to get even a single bag of corn to market. Moving data value by value across a network is not a good idea. You can extend this logic to any of the operations on single attributes. For example, simple mutators (set operations) often change a single attribute value. Instead, you should leave these on the client or application server side, then submit changes as entire rows of data when you're ready to commit the transaction. If you can group several attributes for a single update, that's better, but still has limitations.

> Note: If you intend the operations only for use within the database server (that is, by other stored procedures), then you can probably get away with accessors and mutators as stored functions. If you choose to do this, don't make the functions available to applications.

Third, you don't want to put operations on the server that need to refer back to the transient client in any way. It's not good design to require the server to maintain behavioral state across calls. It has enough to do managing transaction state. This is not to say that you can't do it; PL/SQL packages, for example, let you set data values and keep them in a special shared buffer across as many calls as you like. This can have very strange effects as you scale up to many clients accessing the data at once. Generally, you want your server code to be *reentrant*: you want a session to be able to access and run the behavior without worrying about anything that happened before. That means not relying on any state left over from previous invocations of the operation (static data or data from tables). Keep these kinds of operations on the server.

Also, some operations do extensive error checking in memory, aborting the operation if things don't work out. Do this checking on the client or application server side, not on the database server side. The only error handling you want to do on the server side is error handling related to database structures—business rule checking, physical data storage errors, DBMS errors, and so on. This especially applies to code you think belongs in a trigger. Because triggers execute when the DBMS raises an event, you don't really have control over trigger execution. Choose code you put into triggers wisely. You should code trigger operations that make sense for the event that runs the trigger (AFTER INSERT and so on). If you find yourself creating trigger code to work around some problem with a stored procedure, consider other alternatives. If you find yourself creating trigger code to work around other trigger code, bail out fast! Keeping it simple works nicely with triggers.

Finally, you want to evaluate the performance of your remaining operations. It may be cheaper to run your operation in a compiled language on the application server rather than in an interpreted, slow PL/SQL stored procedure.

So what kind of operations does this leave?

- *Query a result set:* Return a set of records to the client

- *Insert/update/delete:* Modify data for a single row (not a single value)

- *Rule checking:* Enforce business rules with triggers or procedures (for example, you can handle special constraints on foreign keys using triggers or add code that evaluates complex procedural constraints on an input row or rows)

- *Derived values:* Calculate a value from database data with an algorithm you can't specify as an SQL expression in your target DBMS version of SQL

- *Encapsulating operations:* Operations that call other database operations such as stored procedures provided by the vendor or data dictionary accesses related to the data in the table (for example, a stored procedure to retrieve the primary key column definition of the table)

- *Error checking:* Operations that check various error states and raise exceptions (or whatever method by which errors return to the client)

Stimulus and Response: Behavior and Side Effects   Much in the relational database world depends on the nature of the behavior you intend to put into your persistent classes. Oracle7, Informix, and Sybase all provide server-side programming facilities, but there are various subtleties about structure and use that depend directly on what's happening inside the black box of the operation.

Oracle7.3 provides both stored procedures and stored functions. You can use the functions in your SQL statements, but only if they have no side effects. In UML terms, the operation must have a {query} tag. This permits the Oracle7 parser to call the function and return a value with the knowledge that the function won't be doing anything to upset the internal processing of the DBMS.

On the flip side, if the operation has no {query} tag, you cannot use it as an SQL function. You can, however, add it to your set of database objects as a stored program unit for use by other program units or by the client through some kind of API for calling stored units from programs.

The SQL security system introduces another factor: privileges. One frequently asked question in the Usenet newsgroups for Oracle is "I've coded a stored procedure and I have access to all the data it uses, but I can't run it from my program." This is usually because the user logs in under a user name different from the owner of the stored procedure and has not granted EXECUTE privilege on the procedure to that user. There are various quirks and subtleties in the different RDBMS products with respect to stored program unit privileges.

A third factor is the external access required by the operation. Many programmers want to open or write to files or print things or display things on the screen from a stored program unit. The RDBMS permits all of these things. What it does at runtime is not, however, very easy to understand in a client/server context. Generally, if you try to do things outside the DBMS, the code executes on the server. You thus print to the printers attached to the server, not to those attached to your client. You write files on disks accessible to the server, not your client hard disk (unless of course that disk is accessible to the server and you identify it and write to it using parameters). Sending mail, running devices, synchronizing with other applications—all of these operations make for much more complexity in your operations if you make them stored procedures.

Another form of access is to in-memory data. Often, programmers want to refer to data in their running program in their stored program unit. Since they are running in different processes and potentially on different machines, this is not possible. All such references must be to parameters of the stored procedure. In its ultimate form, this leads to *stateless programming:* ensuring that the stored program unit gets everything it needs through its parameters and makes no assumptions about prior calls or actions in the database. You will often find such procedures with embedded transaction commits and rollbacks, as being stateless implies not carrying transactions across server access calls.

That leads to a final behavioral factor: transaction requirements. If your transactions are at all complex, you will have to decide at some point where those transactions happen. Generally, transactions happen in the application, not on the database server. In other words, you generally do not put transaction commands (COMMIT, ROLLBACK, SAVEPOINT) into your stored program units. Instead, the application server (or client in a two-tier system) issues these commands separately because it is the center for the transaction semantics. Whichever you decide is appropriate, you then must stick to that: mixing is forbidden. If some stored procedures have transaction logic and others don't, programmers get terminally confused about whether they must code commits and rollbacks. Programmers are quite surprised if (in Oracle7) they attempt to roll back data that a stored procedure has already committed. They are surprised (in SQL Server or Sybase) when they get an exception or database error when they commit because there is no active transaction because a stored procedure committed or rolled back earlier.

The transaction logic issue leads into the next topic: system architecture.

A Pattern Language: Architecture and Visibility   The system architecture determines quite a lot about your approach. Given that your UML design is OO, and given that relational databases are not, you need to shift one architecture toward the other. It's better to make the relational system look more object-oriented than to mess up your OO system architecture to make it look relational. I've done both, and the latter approach is definitely bad for the digestion.

Unfortunately, RDBMS products are not chock-full of OO capabilities. This lack is part of what led to the primary justification for OODBMS products—the "impedance mismatch" between the OO and relational structure. You have a number of different ways to overcome this mismatch, none totally satisfactory.

On the database side, you can use stored procedures and packages to encapsulate your objects. In Oracle7, for example, you can create packages that correspond to the classes in your UML data model; in other systems, you can just use a collection of stored procedures. You implement the operations that make sense for the database server as packaged program units. You create the underlying tables and the packages in a schema belonging to a specific user, the "owner" of your application schema. You don't grant access to the tables, though; instead, you just grant the appropriate privileges such as EXECUTE to the users that need access to objects of the class. The procedures provide the database server interface (API) for the class. When an application logs on as an enabled user, the code calls the procedures rather than using SQL to query or manipulate the underlying tables.

This approach reduces the mismatch in two ways. First, it packages the underlying tables as classes rather than as tables. This permits you to use OO structure rather than forcing you into the flat table model of programming. Second, the approach eliminates the SQL programming interface, reducing every database access to a procedural call. Such calls are much closer to the OO way of thinking, though they don't get all the way there. You must still pass the object identifier (that is, the primary key or row identifier) to most of your procedures as a parameter, as the package doesn't let you create an instance for each object in your program. That is, procedures are independent of the state of any individual row or rows in the underlying tables, so you have to pass in primary keys or other identifiers to operate on the correct data.

Also, this approach provides full encapsulation of your data. No application can access the data in the tables directly. You can thus protect the data from accidental or deliberate damage through unauthorized access to the table data. Everything goes through the packaged procedures. This provides the same visibility control that an OO language gives you through access control and operational visibility restrictions. It's kind of all or nothing, however: you must hide all your table data, not just some of it.

The limitation to this approach is the mismatch hypothesis itself: the lack of SQL. SQL is a declarative language. In using it, you specify what you want, not how to get it. Your stored procedures, on the other hand (and OO languages) are procedural: you tell the computer exactly how to navigate around the data by procedure calls. The whole reason for the existence of SQL is that it is much easier to use a declarative language to specify complex data requirements. By eliminating SQL, the procedural approach eliminates all the advantages that SQL gives you. You may be fully OO, but you'll be much less efficient at creating the code that manipulates the data. For simple data access, that usually isn't a problem. If you find yourself adding more than a few lines of code to a packaged procedure, however, you may want to reevaluate your approach.

Gray Water Applications: Portability and Reuse   "Gray water" is water you recycle from household uses such as baths to reuse in irrigation or other applications that don't require "clean" water. Many jurisdictions wrongly ban the use of gray water on the assumption that dirty water is evil. Gray water is a useful metaphor for relational database operations. Each gray water application uses a different technology, which makes it difficult to develop a standard approach. Consequently, people use clean water for purposes for which they could be using gray water, and the gray water goes down the sewer without reuse. The end result is that you waste a lot of water.

Similarly, different RDBMS products have completely different approaches to database behavior. The SQL-92 standard says nothing whatever about it, leaving it up to the database vendors to be creative. Many shops outlaw the use of stored procedures and other behavioral constructs such as triggers on the theory that it makes the database less portable. I'll take a position on this: it's wrong. It's not wrong because the code is portable; it's wrong because it arbitrarily removes a tool you can use effectively to get reuse on the database server. You are essentially flushing your reuse potential down the sewer.

The holy grail of portability is to reduce the amount of code that requires work to move to another system to zero. Having achieved the grail, you can move your system from platform to platform with no effort—the ultimate in code reuse.

The trick with grails is that very few people can see them or reach them, and it's a whole lot of work to do so even if you are pure of heart, body, and soul. Usually, full database portability implies both a level of performance and a level of coding productivity that are close to unacceptable. Many managers think that by insisting on full portability they will be saving themselves millions in maintenance and porting costs. This is nothing but magical thinking in a shaman culture.

For example, different DBMS products have radically different transaction processing architectures. Some support page-level locking; others support row-level locking. Some support read consistency (Oracle7); others don't. Some RDBMS products have automatically maintained temporary tables (Sybase, SQL Server, Informix); others don't (Oracle7). Some RDBMS products support UNICODE for standard international language support (Oracle7); others don't (SQL Server). Don't even get me started on SQL optimizers. Portability? Only if you don't have transactions, don't use temporary tables, and don't need to retrieve data in a hurry.

I believe it is foolish not to take the limitations of your targeted range of platforms into account. It is also foolish not to take advantage of the major productivity and performance features of your target DBMS. In the best of all possible worlds, you would have a standard to which all vendors adhere. That doesn't exist, and will not exist, for relational databases, particularly with respect to optimization and transactions, but also for things like globalization and character strings. Economics is against it, the installed base is against it, and Microsoft/IBM/Oracle are against it. I won't say I'm against it, but you must bow to reality occasionally.

The best way to proceed in this situation is to evaluate rationally which parts of your application can benefit from using a portable, reusable approach and which would benefit most from coding as stored procedures in your database server. It's not going to be 100% one way or the other. As with gray water, you'll find that using dirty stuff is fine if you do it in the right place.

Special Issues

Having dealt with the basic operations-related issues, there are still some specific things to discuss: polymorphism, signals, and interfaces.

Polymorphic Operations   Recall from Chapter 7 that some operations are polymorphic: they use the same name for different behavior. *Overloading* uses the same operation name but a different signature (parameters), while *overriding* uses the same signature in a subclass. Overloading is mostly cosmetic, giving you a way to make commands look the same even though they differ based on the objects. Overriding works with dynamic binding to provide a real advantage: the ability to call an operation without knowing what kind of object you're calling. Figure 11-7 shows a portion of Figure 11-1, from the Person subsystem, that illustrates overriding operations.

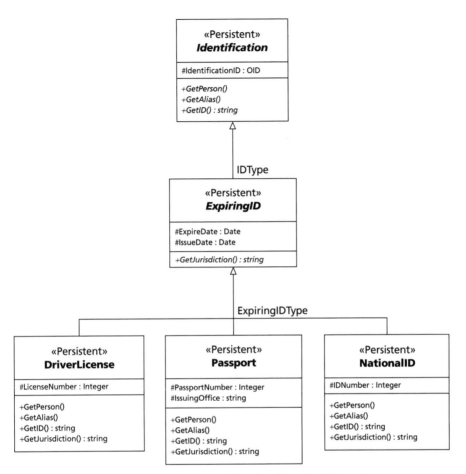

Figure 11-7 *Overriding Operations in the Identification Hierarchy*

The abstract classes Identification and ExpiringID both specify abstract operations. The leaf classes implement these operations, overriding the abstract operations with concrete ones. This lets you create a leaf object but refer to it as an Identification or ExpiringID, then to call GetJurisdiction or whatever without needing to know which specific, concrete class the object really is.

Most relational databases do not support any kind of polymorphism, with one exception of which I'm aware. Oracle7 PL/SQL supports overloading in the procedures of a package. You can provide several procedures with the same name as long as the types of objects you pass through parameters are different in type or order (that is, a different type *signature* for the operation). The primary reason for designing these kinds of overloaded program units is to provide alternative parameter lists for slightly different behavior while maintaining the same name. Using overloaded procedures, you can leave out "optional" parameters, or you can reverse the parameters so that the programmer doesn't need to remember the order. Again, these are cosmetic changes that don't yield a tremendous amount of productivity increase, but it's a nice feature.

For example, say the commonplace book image processing subsystem has the ability to compare fingerprints, handwriting, and facial images to libraries of fingerprint and handwriting records and mug shots. This service provides consulting detectives with the ability to use evidence gathered at the crime scene to identify people that might have something to contribute to a solution to the problem.

> "Having once spotted my man, it was easy to get corroboration. I knew the firm for which this man worked. Having taken the printed description, I eliminated everything from it which could be the result of a disguise—the whiskers, the glasses, the voice, and I sent it to the firm, with a request that they would inform me whether it answered to the description of any of their travelers. I had already noticed the peculiarities of the typewriter, and I wrote to the man himself at his business address, asking him if he would come here. As I expected, his reply was typewritten and revealed the same trivial but characteristic defects. The same post brought me a letter from Westhouse & Marbank, of Fenchurch Street, to say that the description tallied in every respect with that of their employee, James Windibank. *Voilà tout!*" [IDEN]

The parameters to the Compare operation on these classes will be wildly different. For example, the Compare operation for fingerprints might specify that the print is a thumbprint or a fingerprint, or it might specify that the image contains two or more adjoining prints. A typewriter image might contain parameters that identify the text of the image or the probable make of the typewriter. The facial image might contain a list of features to ignore in the comparison, to eliminate disguises. All the classes have several Compare operations, none of which have the same parameter types or signatures. When the calling operation compiles the Compare call, the compiler decides which method to call based on the parameter signature.

True overriding, dynamic binding, or virtual operations simply don't exist in the relational world. If your UML model depends on these, what do you do in your relational program units to implement your model?

The issue with overriding behavior is that the runtime system needs a lookup table to decide which procedure to execute. In C++, every class with virtual methods has a *vtable,* a table of function pointers that permits the C++ runtime system to call the overriding method rather than a single method that the compiler determines when you build your system. You have a simple choice in relational systems: either build a dynamic binding capability in your procedural language or just ignore it. My advice: keep it simple. I've seen many work hours spent on systems to emulate OO dynamic binding and inheritance in the context of C programming, for example. It usually works, sort of, but always at a cost—the cost of maintaining outrageously complicated code, the cost of explaining what that code does, and the cost of telling your boss why this is really a good thing even though it reduces productivity.

So, where does that leave you with your UML design? You have to rename your overriding operations with unique names and call them in the appropriate places. That usually means more ornate conditional code such as case statements or if-then-else conditionals that test the types of the objects involved and decide which procedure to call.

Take the GetJurisdiction operation, for instance. That operation returns different information for each class, as the type of jurisdiction varies widely with the classes. Counties issue birth certificates, nations issue passports and national IDs, and states issue driver's licenses. In an OO system, all these operations override the same abstract parent. In Oracle7, that's not possible, so you must provide different stored procedures for each operation. The DriverLicense package has its GetJurisdiction, and the Passport package has its jurisdiction. In this case, you use the package name space to distinguish between the two functions. When you refer to it in PL/SQL code, you preface the operation name with the package name: DriverLicense.GetJurisdiction().

In other procedural languages that don't have packages, you would have to use a naming convention to distinguish the procedures. You could, for example, preface the operation name with the class name: DriverLicense_GetJurisdiction(). Often it is advisable to come up with a unique abbreviation for the class name to shorten the total name to get it within the limitations of SQL identifier length for the RDBMS: DrL_GetJurisdiction, for example.

> Note: You should realize that despite your creation of these methods, you are not getting any of the benefits of polymorphism. Your SQL or PL/SQL code must know exactly what kind of object you are dealing with in order to call the method, so you don't get the benefits of dynamic binding through inheritance.

Signals If you design a UML operation with the «signal» stereotype, it means that the operation responds to an event of some kind. This corresponds to a trigger, as long as you limit the events to the specific set of trigger events. Most RDBMS products now support triggers, though there is no standard ANSI syntax for them in SQL-92. The SQL3 standard defines the CREATE TRIGGER statement (Figure 11-8).

The event that fires a trigger is some point in a database system operation. Figure 11-8 defines the standard events for «signal» operations in a database as the various combinations of the <trigger action time> and the <trigger event>:

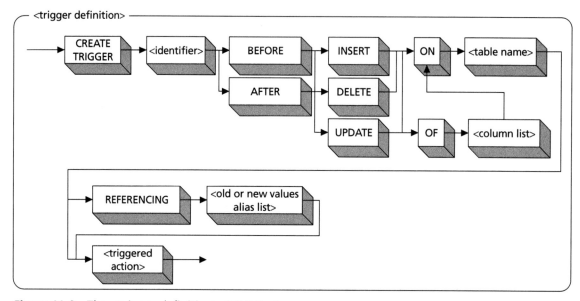

Figure 11-8   *The <trigger definition> SQL3 Syntax*

- BEFORE INSERT
- AFTER INSERT
- BEFORE DELETE
- AFTER DELETE
- BEFORE UPDATE
- AFTER UPDATE

You can therefore define «signal» operations in your persistent classes with these names, suitably transformed into whatever naming convention you use: "BeforeInsert," for example. The "before" operations execute before the corresponding database operation (insert, delete, or update), while the "after" operations execute after them.

> *Note: When you transform the «signal» operation into a database trigger, you will need to use the procedural language available in your system, such as Transact/SQL for SQL Server and Sybase, PL/SQL for Oracle7 and Oracle8, or a programming language such as C for DB2. Each system has its own tips and tricks relating to triggers, such as how to refer to old data versus the changed data in an update trigger, so use the documentation for your system to figure out the best way of moving the code from your data model into your database schema. As with any operation, you can use the procedural language from your target DBMS or some neutral pseudocode or pro-*

gramming language to represent the trigger implementation in your data model.

The other parts of the trigger definition syntax vary from product to product. The SQL3 standard contains the REFERENCING clause that lets you refer to both the old values and the new values in an UPDATE action. The action itself is an SQL procedure sequence. In Oracle7, the equivalent is a PL/SQL block, for example.

Interfaces   Interfaces are a special case of class—a class with no attributes, just operations. A persistent interface is thus somewhat of a contradiction in terms, particularly for a relational database. You should consider an interface a simple notation for polymorphism (see the previous section on "Polymorphic Operations"). That is, if a persistent class realizes an interface (see Chapter 7 for the notation), you need to implement stored procedures corresponding to the interface operations if they are appropriate for DBMS-server execution.

So, for example, if you design the Identification hierarchy as an interface hierarchy as in Chapter 7 (Figure 7-9), you need to implement the GetID operation for each table you generate from the classes that realize the Identification interface. Again, you don't get the benefits of full dynamic binding using interface realization, but you do get to implement the design to the fullest given the relational tools at your disposal.

Foreign Affairs

In a relational database, there are no relationships. Everything is a table. That means that you must build your relationships into the tables through special columns. The way in which you go about this based on a UML design is somewhat different than if you used standard entity-relationship designs, but there are more similarities than differences. The key differences have to do with generalization (inheritance) and with the special features of UML, such as aggregations and qualified associations.

Binary Associations

A binary association is a relationship between two classes, with each end of the association being a role and having multiplicity (Chapter 7, "Associations, Containment, and Visibility"). The role is the role that the class at that end of the association plays in the relationship. The multiplicity is the constraint on the number of objects that can play the role in a single link. A *link* is an instance of an association, a relationship between objects as opposed to between classes.

Transforming a binary association into a relational schema is reasonably straightforward and strongly resembles the transformation of the ER relationship. To make the transformation, you must first understand the idea of the foreign key constraint in a relational database.

Foreign Keys

A foreign key is one or more columns of a table that share their joint domain with the primary key of another table. It is the relational data model's way of representing the association and its data semantics, a fact stating that one row (object) relates to another row (object) in a well-defined, easy-to-use way. Relational databases let you join tables on these foreign keys as the primary way of retrieving data that is semantically meaningful given the relationships between objects. Relational database theory refers to the whole area of primary and foreign keys as *referential integrity*—the idea that foreign keys must at all times refer to valid primary keys to be consistent.

SQL provides the REFERENCES and FOREIGN KEY constraints as a way to enforce referential integrity in the database server. The REFERENCES clause (Figure 11-9, illustrating the <references clause>) is a column constraint that lets you link a single column to a single-column primary key in another table. The FOREIGN KEY clause (Figure 11-10, illustrating the <foreign key constraint>) is a table constraint that lets you link more than one column to a primary key in another table.

The table constraint syntax uses the <references clause>. In the context of the column constraint, the <references clause> can have only one column in its <reference column list>.

When you put this constraint on a table, you are asserting that if you insert a row with the foreign key columns not null, the values must correspond to primary key values in the other table. If you update the foreign key column values, the new values must correspond to primary key values in the other table. You can also have referential triggered actions; see the later section "Shared and Composite Aggregations" for details on this syntax and where to apply it.

Given all these capabilities for expressing foreign keys, now we can move on to understanding how to transform binary associations into such expressions.

Roles, Multiplicity, and Foreign Key Columns

A binary association is a relationship between two classes that implies that one or both classes are visible to the other. This corresponds exactly to the concept of the foreign key in relational database theory. As you might expect, the transformation is straightforward: you convert each binary association into a REFER-

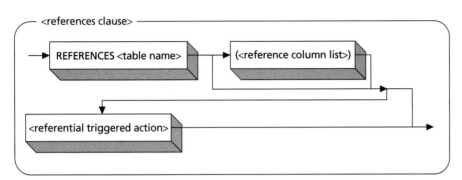

Figure 11-9 *The <references clause> SQL Syntax*

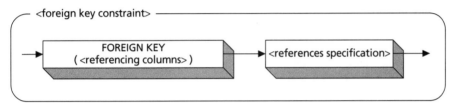

Figure 11-10 *The <foreign key constraint> SQL Syntax*

ENCES or FOREIGN KEY constraint in your table definitions. The interesting part of this isn't creating the constraints; it's creating the foreign key columns onto which you place them.

Your UML design does not specify the foreign key attributes. It represents these as the binary association. That association in turn has two roles (one for each class participating in the association) and two multiplicities (ditto). The roles and multiplicities control the specific transformation you make to add foreign key columns.

To determine the structure of your transformation, you need to consider both the individual multiplicities and their combination between the two roles.

Individual multiplicities can have a number of different configurations:

- *0..*:* Zero or more objects
- *0..1:* No more than one optional object
- *1..*:* At least one object
- *1:* Exactly one object
- **:* Zero or more objects
- *2..6:* At least two but no more than six objects
- *1, 3, 5–7:* At least one object but possibly three, five, six, or seven objects

The characteristics of these multiplicities break down into two components of interest in the relational transformation: columns to produce in which table, and how to produce the NULL/NOT NULL constraint on the column(s).

If the multiplicity contains a maximum of 1 (0..1 or 1 from the above list of possible multiplicities), then that role corresponds to a foreign key column or columns. First, determine the object identity in the class attached to the other role. If the class has implicit object identity, it usually has a single primary key column, usually an integer-generated sequence of some kind. There are some variations on this, such as in a table with a primary key that depends on another class's primary key. This results in two columns (the original primary key and the additional column that identifies the specific row in the dependent table).

For example, in the Person subsystem in Figure 11-1, the Person class has a binary association to the Identification class. That binary association is a composite aggregation, as the person owns the identifications that identify him or her. The Person class has implicit object identity and a PersonID column in the Person table that is a unique number for each person. The Identification class has implicit identity but is an aggregation. It acquires both the PersonID column, which identifies all those Identifications that apply to a single person, and the Identification ID column, which identifies each unique Identification within a person's set of Identifications. The PersonID column in Identification is a foreign key to the Person table.

```
CREATE TABLE Identification (
  PersonID Integer REFERENCES Person,
  IdentificationID INTEGER,
  CONSTRAINT Identification_PK PRIMARY KEY (PersonID, IdentificationID))
```

If an Identification object were independent of the Person, it would not need the PersonID column but just the single unique identifier Identification ID. If each identification belonged to a single person at a time, there would be a multiplicity of 0..1 on the Person role in the association, so Identification would get a PersonID column that was not part of the primary key.

```
CREATE TABLE Identification (
  PersonID Integer REFERENCES Person,
  IdentificationID INTEGER PRIMARY KEY )
```

If the multiplicity contains a 0 or implies it (0..*, *, 0..1), then you can have nulls as foreign key values.

The role is the name you give to one side of an association. It is the role the associated class plays in the association. In OO programming, it becomes the name of a variable holding an item or collection of items of the other class. In tables, roles accompanied by a multiplicity with a maximum of 1 can become the name of the foreign key. You actually have a choice in this; you can either use the role name or the name of the identity attributes in the other class. Some examples can show you the alternatives more clearly.

The classic example where you use the role name is a recursive association. Figure 11-2 illustrates the Organization class with its representation of the organizational hierarchy, a recursive composite aggregation association that relates an organization to its parent and a parent organization to its children. When you transform this association into a relational database schema, you confront a basic naming problem. The obvious way to represent this association produces this Organization table:

```
CREATE TABLE Organization (
  OrganizationID INTEGER PRIMARY KEY,
  OrganizationName VARCHAR2(100) NOT NULL,
  OrganizationID INTEGER REFERENCES Organization)
```

The problem with this table specification is the duplicate column name for the foreign key that refers to the parent organization. The biggest problem is the name space: you can't have duplicate column names in a single table. The next biggest problem is that "OrganizationID" doesn't really convey the purpose of the column to the user. Renaming this column using the role name is a good solution:

```
CREATE TABLE Organization (
  OrganizationID INTEGER PRIMARY KEY,
  OrganizationName VARCHAR2(100) NOT NULL,
  Parent INTEGER REFERENCES Organization)
```

With associations that aren't recursive, you don't have the name space problem, but you may find the primary key name less than clear in your foreign table. In this case, it's your judgment as to whether to use the role name or the primary key column name as the name of the foreign key column. One candidate for such treatment is when you have a large hierarchy of classes, all of which share a single primary key name. For example, the multimedia document archive in the commonplace book system standardizes the hierarchy around the abstract document class with its DocumentID column as the primary key. Video clips are documents with a DocumentID, as are sound clips, digital photographs and images, and scanned document images. The Driver License class might refer to a digital photograph document as a foreign key. Using "DocumentID" as the column name doesn't help the user of the Driver's License class understand what's going on. Instead, use the role name, "Photograph," in the Driver License table:

```
CREATE TABLE DriverLicense (
  PersonID INTEGER NOT NULL REFERENCES Person,
  IdentificationID INTEGER NOT NULL,
  LicenseNumber INTEGER NOT NULL,
```

```
Photograph INTEGER REFERENCES DigitalPhotograph,
CONSTRAINT DriverLicense_PK PRIMARY KEY (PersonID, IdentificationID))
```

There are doubtless many other situations where using a role name is clearer than using the name of the primary key column, but generalization provides the best examples I've found.

Generalizations

Chapter 7 went into some detail on generalization relationships and their implications for attributes and operations. In this section, you'll see how to transform generalizations into relational tables. The specific situations you must consider include single inheritance, inheritance from abstract classes, and multiple inheritance.

Single Inheritance

Single inheritance occurs when you relate a class to a single parent through generalization. The more specific class inherits attributes and behavior from the more general class.

To transform this situation into a relational table, you can take one of two approaches: mapping the classes *directly,* or mapping them through *spreading* the attributes and behavior to the subclasses.

Direct Mapping   To map classes directly, you create a single table for each class in the inheritance hierarchy, then create a foreign key relationship for each generalization relationship. Figure 11-11 repeats Figure 7-6, the Identification inheritance hierarchy.

To transform the hierarchy in Figure 11-11 into tables, you create a single table for each of the classes in the diagram, including the abstract classes. Following the guidelines in the previous section on "Classes," you create a primary key out of explicit or implicit object identifiers. Identification has implicit object identity, so you create a primary key column for the Identification table, usually an integer column that gets a value from an automatic sequence number generator. We'll name this column IdentificationID, meaning that it identifies an Identification object. Because the Identification class also has a composite aggregation association to the Person class, the primary key also contains the primary key of the Person table, PersonID.

```
CREATE TABLE Identification (
  PersonID INTEGER NOT NULL REFERENCES Person,
  IdentificationID INTEGER NOT NULL,
  Constraint Identification_PK PRIMARY KEY (PersonID, IdentificationID))
```

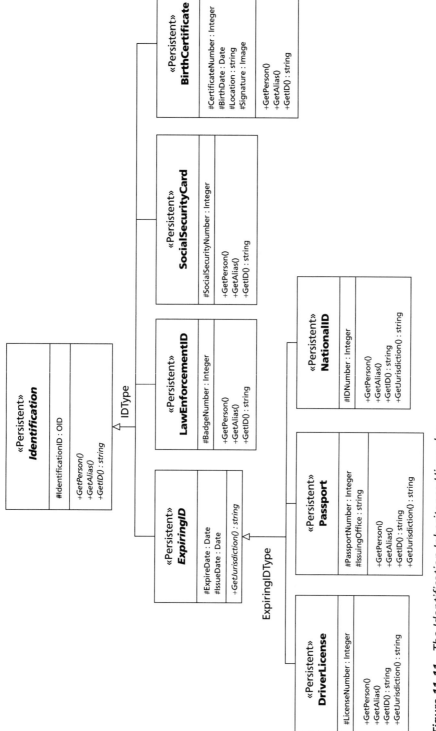

Figure 11-11 The Identification Inheritance Hierarchy

For each subclass of the root parent, you create the class, then create the
same column for each subclass as the primary key for the superclass. If you created multiple primary key columns in the superclass for some reason, you create
the same columns in the subclass. With LawEnforcementID, for example, you
create the same primary key columns, PersonID and IdentificationID.

```
CREATE TABLE LawEnforcementID (
  PersonID INTEGER NOT NULL REFERENCES Identification,
  IdentificationID INTEGER NOT NULL REFERENCES Identification,
  BadgeNumber INTEGER NOT NULL UNIQUE,—candidate key
  Constraint LawEnforcementID_PK
    PRIMARY KEY (PersonID, IdentificationID))
```

In addition to making the column a primary key using the PRIMARY KEY
column or table constraint, you must also make it a foreign key with a REFER-
ENCES column constraint or a FOREIGN KEY column constraint. In the example, PersonID references not the Person table but the Identification table. See earlier in this "Foreign Affairs" section for some perspectives on these constraints.
This foreign key constraint partially represents the generalization relationship,
but not necessarily fully. If you insert a row in LawEnforcementID, the PersonID
and IdentityID of that row must match a row in Identification. The foreign key
constraint enforces this restriction. However, if you insert an Identity row, there
is nothing that links the IdentityID of that row to any subclass table. Even conceptually, this makes no sense, because SQL has no way to tell what kind of table
you mean to create, as it doesn't understand generalization. You can't put another
foreign key constraint on Identity, as it would mean a circular dependency.

> Note: This situation applies when your parent class is an abstract
> class. If the class is concrete, then you can create an object of that
> class without worrying about subclasses. This analysis suggests that
> an abstract class needs a trigger that enforces its abstractness. The
> trigger must ensure that if you insert a row in a table corresponding
> to an abstract class that you also insert a row into one of the several
> subclasses of the abstract class. If you use this approach, step back
> and evaluate your overall system complexity before adding the trig-
> ger. You may find that it makes less trouble to maintain the integ-
> rity at the application level, particularly for smaller databases. Once
> your stable of applications grows to a decent size, though, you want
> to enforce as much integrity on the server as possible, as the next
> application could foul things up.

Spreading   The basic idea behind generalization is inheritance, where
each subclass inherits the attributes and operations of the superclasses. You can
represent the classes directly as in the prior section on "Direct Mapping," then

you can use joins and unions to represent the inheritance. Alternatively, you can do the inheritance up front by creating the attributes and operations in the subclasses, which I call *spreading*.

Spreading has the main advantage that you no longer need to refer to the superclasses for data values or existence. This eliminates many joins and unions and triggers and thus reduces complexity in both your schema and in your application code. So, why wouldn't you want to do this? The downside of this advantage is denormalization of the database schema design. You get a good deal of unnecessary redundancy in your data, leading to insert, update, and delete anomalies (see the later section on "Normalizing Relations").

Consider the Passport class from Figure 11-11. Using the direct approach, you get this schema design:

```
CREATE TABLE Passport (
  PersonID INTEGER NOT NULL REFERENCES Identification
    ON DELETE CASCADE,
  IdentificationID INTEGER NOT NULL REFERENCES Identification
    ON DELETE CASCADE,
  PassportNumber INTEGER NOT NULL UNIQUE,—candidate key
  IssuingOffice VARCHAR2(100) NOT NULL,
  Constraint Passport_PK
    PRIMARY KEY (PersonID, IdentificationID))
```

Using the spreading approach, you get this design instead:

```
CREATE TABLE Passport (
  PersonID INTEGER NOT NULL REFERENCES Identification,
  IdentificationID INTEGER NOT NULL REFERENCES Identification,
  ExpireDate DATE NOT NULL CHECK (ExpireDate > IssueDate),
  IssueDate DATE NOT NULL,
  PassportNumber INTEGER NOT NULL UNIQUE,—candidate key
  IssuingOffice VARCHAR2(100) NOT NULL,
  Constraint Passport_PK
    PRIMARY KEY (PersonID, IdentificationID))
```

Instead of referring to the ExpiringID table for the ExpireDate and Issue Date, this design copies the columns down the hierarchy into the Passport table (and into all the other subclasses of ExpiringID as well). Passport stands alone as a useful table with all its data available to users. A use case that needs passport information need only access the one table. However, whenever you update the ExpireDate or IssueDate of a passport, you must also update the same columns in the superclass row that corresponds to the passport. That means an additional trigger or code in your application.

As with any design decision, you must consider the broad impact of the decision on overall system quality. Does the increased complexity from the trigger balance well against the reduced complexity in the application code that accesses passport information? For example, if the hierarchy is quite deep, you could wind up accessing several classes by joins rather than a single table that provides all the data. However, the trigger processing contributes little to the maintenance of the system, because once done you leave it alone. In this case, with a single level in the hierarchy, it's probably not worth it.

It's also worth noting that you can mix the two approaches in your system. You can spread certain deep hierarchies while leaving other, more shallow hierarchies to use the direct approach. Any time you mix design approaches, you risk confusing those who come after you. If you do it, you should carefully document what you're doing, preferably in the database itself using table comments or some kind of repository documentation.

Multiple Inheritance

Multiple inheritance occurs when a class has generalization relationships to more than one superclass. The subclass inherits all the attributes and operations of its superclasses.

There is really no good way to represent multiple inheritance in a relational database schema. You are usually better off if you can restructure your design to avoid multiple inheritance, either through the use of interface types or through factoring the elements into separate but conceptually redundant classes. The "elegance" of multiple inheritance forces you to pay too high a price in the semantics of the relational table and its foreign keys [Date and Darwen 1998, pp. 299–315].

As an example of a poor transformation and its problems, consider the approach of building a subclass table that includes the primary keys of two superclasses. As an example, what if you decided to have a Digital Photograph be both a Document and an Image (Figure 11-12)?

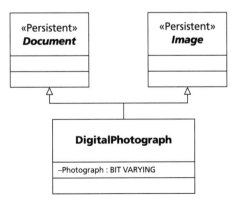

Figure 11-12 *Multiple Generalizations*

You might create the Digital Photograph table this way:

```
CREATE TABLE DigitalPhotograph (
  DocumentID INTEGER NOT NULL REFERENCES Document,
  ImageID INTEGER NOT NULL REFERENCES Image,
  Photograph BIT VARYING (65536))
```

Now you need to choose a primary key. Do you choose DocumentID or ImageID? Both are unique identifiers, but you can only have one primary key to use as a foreign key in other tables, such as in the Driver License example in the section on "Roles, Multiplicity, and Foreign Key Columns." As well, you want the primary key to represent *the* generalization relationship, but since you can only have one, you can't.

When you get into some of the standard conundrums of representing multiple inheritance, such as the diamond-shaped hierarchy in which the two superclasses refer in turn to a common superclass, you get into even more trouble (Figure 11-13). You could potentially have two separate objects in the common superclass with different primary keys. Which primary key do you use in the subclass row? If you use the spreading approach, do you create two attributes for each one in the common superclass? Worse and worse.

In C++ and other programming languages, the language designers have built various contorted solutions to this problem, such as virtual base classes in

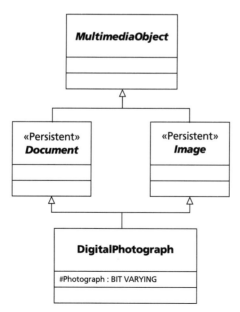

Figure 11-13   *Multiple Generalizations with a Common Superclass*

C++. You don't have that option in the relational schema and its standard language SQL-92.

The Digital Photograph is better done as an interface realization:

```
CREATE TABLE DigitalPhotograph (
  DigitalPhotographID INTEGER PRIMARY KEY,
  DocumentID INTEGER NOT NULL REFERENCES Document,
  ImageID INTEGER NOT NULL REFERENCES Image,
  Photograph BIT VARYING (65536))
```

The object (the row) stands alone with a primary key unique to the Digital Photograph table. There are references to the document and image, and the table conceptually inherits the interface behavior and behaves as a realized document and image. Semantically, this is comprehensible, if strained, in the context of a relational schema.

Alternatively, you can recast the relationship between the classes as an association instead of a generalization or realization. From the OO design perspective, the main difference is that you abjure the possibility of treating the photograph itself as a document or image. Instead, you "get" a document or image related to the photograph. The Document and Image classes thus encapsulate a photograph (where that applies) and the Digital Photograph class in turn encapsulates a document and an image. Since all these classes directly relate, you must create a ternary association rather than a binary one; see the later section on "Ternary and Higher-Cardinality Associations" for details on transforming ternary associations. The results in this case look like this:

```
CREATE TABLE DigitalPhotograph (
  DigitalPhotographID INTEGER PRIMARY KEY,
  Photograph BIT VARYING (65536))

CREATE TABLE PhotoUsedAs (
  DigitalPhotographID INTEGER,
  DocumentID INTEGER NOT NULL REFERENCES Document,
  ImageID INTEGER NOT NULL REFERENCES Image,
  CONSTRAINT PhotoUsedAs_PK (DigitalPhotographID, DocumentID,
    ImageID))
```

The obvious difference is that you now have two tables instead of one, with the Photo Used As table corresponding to the ternary association. That table has as its primary key the three primary keys of the participating tables. This constraint implies the restriction that there can be only one combination of any particular photo, document, and image in the database. You may also need a multiplicity constraint if there can be only one document and image associated with the photo. That means a UNIQUE constraint on the DigitalPhotographID. Since this implies a functional dependency that is not on the primary key, you may want to normalize this back to the single table. Make DigitalPhotographID the primary key to get it into fourth normal form.

> *Note: This seems to be a rare case where standard OO design techniques yield a schema that is not in fourth normal form. You can recognize these situations fairly easily and deal with them with standard normalization techniques, which you should always have in the back of your mind. See the later section on "Normalizing Relations" for details. Alternatively, this is probably yet another justification for avoiding multiple inheritance.*

Special Situations

Associations and generalizations give rise to some special situations that you need to consider when transforming your data model into a relational schema: ternary associations, association classes, composite aggregations, qualified associations, and ordered associations. Earlier sections have mentioned some of these situations in their usual context; this section discusses them in themselves.

Ternary and Higher-Cardinality Associations

A binary association is the most common kind of association. The cardinality of the association (how many classes participate in the association) may be three or higher, in which case you create a separate class for the association.

In Figure 11-2, the Plays association is a diamond that links the Role, the Person, and the Organization. The Person plays a Role in an Organization. This translates directly into the Plays table.

```
CREATE TABLE Plays (
   PersonID INTEGER REFERENCES Person,
   OrganizationID INTEGER REFERENCES Organization,
   Role INTEGER REFERENCES Role,
   CONSTRAINT Plays_PK PRIMARY KEY (PersonID, OrganizationID, RoleID))
```

The table consists entirely of the primary key columns from the associated tables. If a primary key has multiple columns, all of those columns migrate into the association table.

Association Classes and Attributes

Any association can have an association class and attributes, properties of the association itself. Any such association class gets its own table.

Looking back at Figure 11-2, you see the Plays class connected to the Plays association diamond. This association class contains the attributes of the association: how long it lasted, its start and end dates, and the way in which the organization terminated the relationship.

> *Note: Once you get into the CriminalOrganization subclass of Organization, these attributes get a lot more interesting, especially the termination method.*

You thus extend the table with the association attributes and their constraints:

```
CREATE TABLE Plays (
  PersonID INTEGER REFERENCES Person,
  OrganizationID INTEGER REFERENCES Organization,
  Role INTEGER REFERENCES Role,
  Tenure INTERVAL DAY NOT NULL,—your DBMS probably won't have this
    type
  StartDate DATE NOT NULL,
  EndDate DATE,
  TerminationMethod INTEGER REFERENCES TerminationMethod
    CHECK (TerminationMethod IS NOT NULL OR
           (TerminationMethod IS NULL AND EndDate IS NULL))
  CONSTRAINT Plays_PK PRIMARY KEY (PersonID, OrganizationID, RoleID))
```

Shared and Composite Aggregations

An aggregation is an association between two classes that represents a part-whole relationship between the classes. See the section "Aggregation, Composition, and Ownership" in Chapter 7 for details. Shared aggregation is irrelevant for relational schema design, but composite aggregation has an interesting side effect.

Composition says that the composing object owns the other object and that no other object can link to it. This strong form of aggregation corresponds directly to a foreign key with update and delete actions. Figure 11-2 shows a composition association between Person and Identification. As the previous section demonstrated, the Identification class gets the PersonID primary key of Person as part of its primary key. This gives direct meaning to one name for a multiattribute primary key: a *composite key*. The composition relationship applies to all the subclasses in a class hierarchy as well, though the composition is implicit. The Passport class, for example, inherits both the primary key of the Person table and the additional key column IdentificationID. The foreign key PersonID references the ExpiringID table, however, not the Person table. It still represents a composition, however.

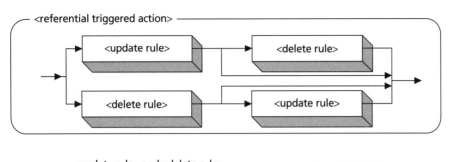

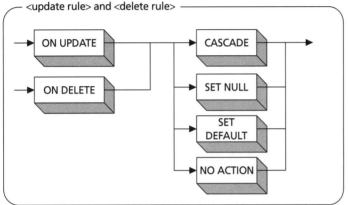

Figure 11-14   *The <referential triggered action> SQL Syntax*

The special syntax in the <referential triggered action> clause in the referential integrity constraints lets you control some actions that happen when you update or delete the row with the primary key in the owning table [ANSI 1992; Melton and Simon 1993, pp. 221–227]. Updating or deleting the primary values directly implies a change to the foreign keys in dependent tables. The ON clause tells the DBMS what exactly to do. Figure 11-14 shows the syntax of this clause.

The CASCADE action updates the value in the dependent table when you update the value in the primary key in the owning table. Alternatively, it deletes the row in the dependent table when you delete the row with the primary key to which it refers. Since your foreign key is part of the primary key of the dependent table as well, the CASCADE may cascade to other tables that have foreign keys to that primary key.

The Passport table serves as an example of this action:

```
CREATE TABLE Passport (
  PersonID INTEGER NOT NULL REFERENCES Identification
    ON DELETE CASCADE ON UPDATE CASCADE,
  IdentificationID INTEGER NOT NULL REFERENCES Identification
```

```
   ON DELETE CASCADE ON UPDATE CASCADE,
PassportNumber INTEGER NOT NULL UNIQUE,—candidate key
IssuingOffice VARCHAR2(100) NOT NULL,
Constraint Passport_PK
   PRIMARY KEY (PersonID, IdentificationID))
```

If you delete or update a PersonID, the DBMS will also delete or update the corresponding Passport PersonID.

SET NULL sets the foreign key values to NULL instead of updating or deleting them when you update or delete the primary key row. The SET DEFAULT action sets the foreign key values to the value in the DEFAULT clause of the column.

NO ACTION is the default action. This "lack of action" choice tells the DBMS to do nothing to the foreign key. If you don't handle it with other SQL statements in the transaction, you get an error, and the whole update or delete rolls back.

Instead of using this syntax, you can also code your integrity maintenance in triggers linked to the UPDATE and DELETE events. See the earlier section on "Signals" for details on designing in and using triggers.

Now that I've said all this, now forget it. The key assumption behind all these actions is that you are changing a primary key value. This is not a good idea under most circumstances, with certain exceptions. Object identity should generally be unchanging; there are more implications to changing key values than just cascading an update or delete. Many figurative lives have been lost in the battle to maintain databases that allowed changing primary keys. This is not a good strategy.

If you are using implicit object identity in your design, you should have no reason at all to change your primary key values. PersonID, for example, should not change through your applications. There is no reason to allow it. You may want to change the name, but not the identifier. Some designers don't even expose the identifier through their user interface; it stays encapsulated in their internal objects. The integer keys you generate, by whatever methods, can stay the same forever—as long as you don't run out of integers. You do need to concern yourself about the long-term number of objects you are going to create if you can't change the keys.

There are a couple of situations where this restriction doesn't apply. First and foremost, when you delete a row in a table that owns rows in other tables, you must cascade the delete. This ownership corresponds to composite aggregation in your UML design. There is a degenerate case of this situation in which you order the association to the child table, resulting in a two-part primary key for that table that includes an integer order number. If you allow changing the order of items in the association, you must be able to change the order number in the primary key. This degenerates when other tables depend on that primary key in their turn.

Second, if you are using explicit identity, you will encounter pressure to allow changing primary key values, as they correspond to information that may change in the real world. Ideally, you pick attributes of real-world items that don't change, but you don't always have that luxury. A good general strategy is to move to implicit identity and integer generated keys when you have a candidate key that might change.

Qualified Associations and Discriminators

A *qualified association* is a kind of shorthand for a combination of enumerated data type and an association. It says that the qualified object has one link for each type value (see the details in Chapter 7, "Qualified Association"). You thus usually convert what would have been a to-many association into a to-one association qualified by the qualifier attribute. The example in Figure 11-15 (reproducing Figure 7-12) shows the Identification-Person association as a qualified association, meaning that a person has several different kinds of ID documents, structured by a qualifier attribute. That is, every person has a birth certificate, a driver's license, and a passport, for example.

The mechanics of producing the relational schema from the qualified association require a combination of a foreign key and a qualifier column that specifies the type of object.

```
CREATE TABLE Identification (
    PersonID INTEGER NOT NULL REFERENCES Person,
    IdentificationID INTEGER NOT NULL,
    IDType INTEGER NOT NULL REFERENCES IDType,
    Constraint Identification_PK PRIMARY KEY (PersonID, IdentificationID))
```

If there are specific requirements for the qualified class, you need to add a trigger or other constraint that enforces them. For example, if a person must have a birth certificate and a passport, you would need a trigger that checked that there are two Identification objects with the Birth Certificate IDType and the Passport IDType.

Figure 11-15 *The Qualified Association*

Tip: I've never liked qualified associations as a modeling tool. They seem to obscure more than they elucidate for me (this is an opinion, not an assertion). They can simplify a complex relationship, but usually don't. I don't use them.

You can also transform a qualified association into parallel columns in the qualified table. For example, you could add two columns to Person, Birth Certificate and Passport, which in turn are foreign keys to the Birth Certificate and Passport tables. Modelers call this structure *parallel attributes*. A common example is when you create a table with seven columns, one for each day of the week, or a table with three address columns to support up to three addresses for a person. The limitations of this design are reasonably obvious: if you have the potential for an unknown number of objects, you will have to add columns. With days of the week, that's not really a problem. What is a problem is that you can't easily use SQL to gather information over multiple parallel attributes. For example, if you wanted to average some number for each day of the week, it would be very difficult to do it with parallel day columns. It would be easy if you had the data in a separate table with a single day column to identify the day [Blaha and Premerlani 1998, pp. 287–288].

Note: Parallel columns are not "repeating groups." See the later section on "Normalizing Relations" for a discussion of first normal form and repeating groups. However, even though you can be fully normalized using parallel columns, they are not generally a good way to design relational tables.

The *discriminator* is a type attribute you associate with a generalization relationship. The IDType in the Identification example of a qualified association could also serve as a discriminator associated with the Identification class generalization from its subclasses. The type does not have the potential for constraints of a qualified association, nor does it imply multiple links.

You need a column of this type when you navigate to the subclasses by way of the superclass. For example, in the transient domain model, a person has a set of identifications. The query you use to build this set retrieves the rows from the Identification table. Without a discriminator attribute, it is difficult to write the queries that retrieve the object-specific information from the subclass tables. The discriminator column lets you fetch the Identification row with a Passport IDType column value, then query the Passport row that corresponds to it. Without the discriminator column, you would not know enough to query the Passport table; you'd have to try all the subclass tables in turn. In terms of patterns, the discriminator supports the Abstract Factory or Factory Method pattern for building subclass objects in a class hierarchy [Gamma et al. 1995].

You have to balance this need, however, with the additional complexity that maintaining discriminators adds to your code. For example, if a superclass is concrete (can have instances), then your discriminator must include a value that identifies the object that is of that class with no subclass. For example, say the Driver's License had a subclass Trucker's License (a kind of driver's license that permits you to drive a truck in addition to driving other vehicles). You can have driver's licenses and trucker's licenses. The discriminator in Driver's License would have to have two possible values, "Driver" and "Trucker." The first identifies an object that is of type Driver's License, while the second identifies an object of the subclass Trucker's License. Maintaining this gets moderately complex. What happens if you upgrade your license from a general to a trucker's license? What happens when you add another subclass? Do you need to check or use the discriminator when retrieving the driver's license? Do you need to retrieve the subclass objects if you are just interested in driver's licenses? You may find it easier to deal with the tables directly rather than using the discriminator to navigate.

Ordered Associations

Another special case is the *ordered association*—an association with a to-many multiplicity role that has the {ordered} tag on it. In OO design, an {ordered} tag means you need some kind of sequenced collection, such as a list or vector, to represent the association. In transforming this kind of association to a relational database, you must convert the structural representation (a list) into a data representation (an order attribute).

The typical order attribute is an integer value that goes from 1 to <n>, where <n> is the number of links to the associated object. Two major uses for ordering of this type include the display order of items in a user interface and the ordering of details in a master-detail relationship. User interfaces often display lists of objects. If you want them to appear in the same order, or if you want the user to control the order across instances of the program, you need to store the order in a table. An order column on the table corresponding to the displayed data does that. Similarly, if you have purchase orders and lists of items for each order, you usually want them ordered in some way.

In this last case, the order serves more than one function in the detail table: it is also part of the primary key. This is because a master-detail combination is a composite aggregation association (see the prior section on "Shared and Composite Aggregations"). If you add the {ordered} tag to the composite association, you generate a counter for the second part of the composite key. For example, if for some reason you ordered the Identification-to-Person association, say, for display in the user interface, you would implement the table slightly differently:

```
CREATE TABLE Identification (
  PersonID INTEGER NOT NULL REFERENCES Person,
```

```
OrderNumber INTEGER NOT NULL,
IDType INTEGER NOT NULL REFERENCES IDType,
Constraint Identification_PK PRIMARY KEY (PersonID, OrderNumber))
```

Instead of IdentificationID as the second part of the primary key, you now have an OrderNumber column. Your application or constructor methods in the database server must set the number to the correct order number, usually the index of the item in an in-memory list. This requires some additional code for updating because you must update the entire set of objects with new order numbers when you change the order.

Living by the Rules

Rules are everywhere in a relational database; they're just hard to see. When you create a column with a certain data type, you're imposing a domain constraint. When you add a PRIMARY KEY clause, you're enforcing an object identity constraint. When you make a column refer to another one in a REFERENCES clause, you're imposing a foreign key constraint. When you add an AFTER INSERT trigger, you're adding a complex integrity constraint or business rule.

The first part of this chapter has dealt with many of the basic constraints:

- *Domain constraints:* Types, domains, CHECK constraints, and NOT NULL constraints

- *Primary key constraints:* Implicit and explicit object identity

- *Uniqueness constraints:* Candidate keys and alternate OIDs

- *Foreign key constraints:* Associations, multiplicity, and aggregation

There are other business rules you need to enforce in your database besides these structural ones. These constraints appear in your UML data model as constraint boxes associated with the appropriate things you want to constrain. See the Chapter 7 section "Complex Constraints" for details on expressing constraints in the UML OCL or in SQL.

Class Invariants

When you have a constraint on a class, it is usually an expression that asserts a class invariant over the attributes of the class. A *class invariant* is a logical expression that an object of the class must satisfy at all times (the truth of the expression does not vary with the state of the object).

Transforming your class into a table creates a need to express your class invariants in your schema. You have two choices: CHECK constraints and triggers.

A CHECK constraint lets you attach an SQL expression that evaluates to true, false, or null to a column or table. The basic syntax is very simple—a search condition that evaluates to a truth value. In the SQL language, there are three truth values: true, false, and unknown (null) [ANSI 1992, pp. 188–189]. Standard logic is two-valued: true or false. Most constraints you conceive in data models reflect this standard.

When you use SQL to express constraints, you move into the world of quasi-modal logic—three-valued logic that adds a new factor to truth, the *unknown* truth value. Your Boolean search condition must take into account the situation in which the values have nulls that cause the expression to evaluate to null. The ANSI standard has syntax that lets you test the expression against a truth value: <search condition> IS [NOT] <truth value>. None of the RDBMS vendors implement this expression; therefore, your search condition must not evaluate to false to satisfy the constraint. Read that last sentence again, carefully: what happens if the search condition evaluates to null? Answer: the table satisfies the CHECK constraint. You must therefore ensure the correct handling of nulls in the expression, usually by converting them to a value (the NVL() function in Oracle7, for example, does this) or by checking for them with IS NOT NULL as part of the search condition. Using a three-valued logic thus introduces considerable complexities into your constraint checking, and SQL is by no means correct in the way it uses null values [Date 1986, pp. 313–334]. Understand the limitations of your tools and take care here.

There are some restrictions on the SQL you can use in your search condition. You cannot use an aggregation function such as AVG or SUM unless it is in a subquery, a nested SELECT statement within the expression. You thus can't express a constraint that checks a sum or average against a column value directly. You can't refer to session-specific or dynamically changing information, such as CURRENT_USER (ANSI) or SYSDATE (Oracle7), for example. This also means you can't call a user-defined function in a CHECK clause. You could change the function, and the CHECK constraint would no longer necessarily evaluate to true for the data already in the database.

The full ANSI syntax lets you use subqueries in your expression, but the intermediate form of the standard excludes these. This reflects the industry norm. None of the major RDBMS vendors implement a complete expression syntax for CHECK constraints. Oracle7, for example, does not allow subqueries. You thus can't enforce any constraint that refers to data outside the table or in rows other than the current row on which the constraint is being checked.

Finally, there are two forms of the CHECK constraint: using it as a column or domain constraint, and using it as a table constraint. The column constraint generally checks a single column; the table constraint may check more than one column to represent complex class invariants over several attributes. In either case, the RDBMS evaluates the constraint when the SQL statement, such as an

INSERT statement, completes. There is no actual distinction between the two forms; you can refer to multiple columns in a column constraint or to a single column in a table constraint. Some systems, such as SQL Server, warn you when you refer to a column other than the column to which you've attached a column CHECK constraint. This is just a warning, however, not an error fatal to creating the table.

Given these limitations on the CHECK constraint in principle and in practice, you will probably have to build many of your class-invariant constraints as triggers rather than as CHECK constraints. A trigger is a stored procedure that the RDBMS executes when a certain event occurs. See the earlier section "Signals" for details.

System Invariants

There is another class of constraints that go beyond a single class. A system invariant is a logical expression that must always be true for the system as a whole. In this case, by "the system as a whole," I mean the collection of database schemas and the data contained in the tables defined by those schemas. If you define your system across multiple schemas, you sometimes have constraints that extend beyond the boundaries of a single schema into another. The most common variety of this sort is the foreign key constraint that makes one subsystem dependent on another. See the earlier section on "Packages, Subsystems, and Name Spaces" for a complete discussion of multiple-subsystem design for database schemas. You can build triggers that enforce these constraints, as single tables (the table containing the foreign key) drive them.

> *Note: No current systems let you use a REFERENCES or FOREIGN KEY constraint across schemas. There are also some restrictions on distributed databases with multiple servers, often constraining you as to what you can do across servers. Check your target system carefully in this regard if you have system invariants of this kind.*

A second variety of system invariant is the constraint that refers to two or more tables in a single logical expression. You can't express this kind of constraint as a CHECK constraint because it is not a class invariant on a single table.

The ANSI standard defined this kind of system constraint as an *assertion* and gave it a new DDL statement, the CREATE ASSERTION statement. This statement is essentially a CHECK clause for a schema instead of for a table. Although the standard lets you use subqueries in table or column CHECK constraints, you really want the DBMS to evaluate system invariants at a higher level. Changes to any of the tables involved should result in constraint checking.

Tip: A table or column constraint on an empty table is always satisfied (think about it). If you want to ensure that a table has data in it, you must use an assertion. An assertion is satisfied if and only if the condition returns true, regardless of the presence of data in any of the tables involved.

The major problem with the assertion is that no RDBMS vendor implements it. In current systems, you must build stored procedures or even application code that your application system runs at the appropriate point in each transaction. This requires additional code and complexity in your system, but you really have no choice at this time.

Normalizing Relations

Normalization is the process of structuring the tables and columns in your schema to avoid having certain dependency constraints (functional dependencies, multivalued dependencies, and join dependencies).

It is possible to write an entire chapter or book on normalization [Dutka and Hanson 1989], though hard to make it fun to read. The odd thing about normalization is that it is really a state, not a process. The progress from first to second to third and so on is illusory ordering of a much more straightforward approach: find and eliminate structural dependencies that cause problems. There is no benefit at all to working through the various normal forms. Instead, you should understand the mathematics of dependencies, then focus on the practical design techniques that eliminate them as a whole.

Before getting into the dependencies, you should note that an OO design, as reflected in the UML data model, pretty much automatically removes most dependencies. The whole idea of object identity and the construction of cohesive hierarchies of classes tends to structure your data into related tables rather than into jumbled-together single tables with lots of interdependencies between the columns. Starting with OO (or even ER) design is much more likely to yield a normalized database than not. This fact impresses some designers so much they believe you can dispense entirely with the theory of normalization [Blaha and Premerlani 1998, pp. 273–274]. While I wouldn't go that far, it's fair to say that normalization is not really a worry if you start with an OO design.

Atomic Values

Next, I'd like to address a very common misconception about first normal form: atomic values. First normal form says that each value must be atomic. Consider this example table:

```
CREATE TABLE Atomic (
  NuclearProgramID INTEGER PRIMARY KEY,
  Reactor1 VARCHAR2(50),
  Reactor2 VARCHAR2(50),
  Reactor3 VARCHAR2(50))
```

The three Reactor columns represent values for the three reactors in the nuclear program.

If you're a practicing DBA familiar with normalization, here's a quiz: What normal form does this table satisfy?

Most DBAs, apparently, believe that this table is *not* in first normal form. To be direct: *they are wrong.* This is a perfectly fine, fully normalized relation in fifth normal form. Each value is atomic, and there are no dependencies of any kind in this table. The arguments start when you define what "atomic" means, and part of the problem is the confusion with the concept of "repeating groups." This latter concept is an old programming concept that lets you repeat a structure within another structure. It has nothing whatever to do with either atomicity or first normal form.

Atomicity is very simple. All it says is that each column can have only one value for each row in a table. In the Atomic table example, each Reactor column has a single value for each row in the table: it is therefore atomic and in first normal form. What would a table that is not in first normal form look like? It's a bit of a problem, since in standard SQL you can't define it. Looking ahead a chapter, however, consider this definition from the Oracle8 SQL syntax:

```
CREATE TYPE ReactorArray AS VARRAY(3) OF VARCHAR2(50);
CREATE TABLE NotAtomic (
  NuclearProgramID INTEGER PRIMARY KEY,
  Reactors ReactorArray);
```

The VARRAY, or variable array, is a multivalued data type that holds a specified number of objects of a single-valued data type. The table Not Atomic is not in first normal form because the Reactors column holds more than one value for each row of the table.

I'd like to stress that *it is not possible* to create nonatomic tables using standard, relational SQL. That language does not have multivalued data types such as VARRAY. Therefore, whenever you are designing tables in a standard relational schema, your tables are in first normal form. Period.

> *Note: The design of the Atomic table has problems, but they aren't normalization problems. Because the solution is similar to the kind of decomposition you find in normalization, many DBAs equate it with the normalization process, but it's totally different. The main limitation in the design is the lack of flexibility about the number of reactors each program can have. The other major limitation is when*

you want to search or compute aggregations over the different val-
ues; it's much easier when you have each value in a separate row.
Also, all of this analysis about first normal form notwithstanding, if
you have more than one piece of data repeating (reactor plus on-
line date plus operating time, for example, instead of just the reac-
tor name), then you introduce functional or multivalued dependen-
cies, which means you are not in fifth normal form but rather in
second normal form. But that's a different issue from the atomicity
requirement of first normal form.

Dependencies and Normalization

Now, on to the heart of darkness in normalization: dependencies. Explaining dependencies is best done by example, so I will manipulate some of the examples of
this book into examples of dependencies. The ones you've seen so far have no un-
wanted dependencies.

First, some background. Codd developed the original approach to normalization in some very early relational theoretical articles [Codd 1970, 1972]. The
basic idea those articles developed was to provide guidance for relation design in
the presence of certain data manipulation anomalies caused by poor structure.

Note: The whole normalization approach starts with a complete da-
tabase design in place. You need to have all your attributes defined
somewhere to be able to normalize the tables in which they appear
through analyzing the dependencies. While this is a very formal,
consistent, and mathematical approach, it provides little guidance
to the database designer creating a database. UML and the meth-
ods that use it, on the other hand, guide you the whole way
through the process with design methods, prescriptions, patterns,
and metrics (one of which is the degree of normalization).

When you determined that a dependency between data elements existed,
you would break out the dependent data into a separate table, eliminating the dependency. Codd called this process *decomposition* and structured it as a series of
normal forms. As the computer scientists and mathematicians began developing
these early ideas, they grew into ever-more generalized forms. Ultimately, this results in the end of history: the proof that the "join" dependency is the most general form of dependency, and that therefore fifth normal form is the highest form
of normalization [Fagin 1979]. Which is just as well, since people who could explain fourth normal form barely adequately began having real trouble with fifth
normal form. Having admitted my limitations, let's forge ahead.

A *functional dependency* occurs when a column value determines the value
of another column in the same table. You've already seen the most common functional dependency: the key. A primary key determines the values of the other

columns in its table, as does every candidate key. So every table you create with object identity, implicit or explicit, exhibits a functional dependency.

A slightly more subtle but very common functional dependency occurs when you represent a to-many relationship in a single table along with all the related data. For example, take the relationship between Person and Identification in Figure 11-1. If you've been following along, you know that the standard way to represent this relationship is to create two tables, a Person table and an Identification table (and all the subclasses as separate tables as well). Instead, consider what a single Person table might look like if you included the information in the Driver License and Passport tables in it.

```
CREATE TABLE Person (
  PersonID INTEGER PRIMARY KEY,
  Name VARCHAR2(100) NOT NULL,
  Sex CHAR(1) NOT NULL CHECK (Sex IN ('M', 'F')),
  DateOfBirth DATE NOT NULL,
  DateOfDeath DATE,
  Height NUMBER,
  Weight NUMBER,
  MaritalStatus CHAR(1) CHECK(MaritalStatus in ('S', 'M', 'D', 'W'))
  Comment VARCHAR2(2000),
  DriverLicenseNumber NUMBER,
  LicenseIssueDate DATE,
  LicenseExpirationDate DATE,
  PassportNumber NUMBER,
  PassportIssueDate DATE,
  PassportExpirationDate DATE,
  IssuingOffice VARCHAR2(100))
```

Intuitively, you can see what's happened: you've combined three objects into a single table, the person, the driver's license, and the passport. Mathematically what's happened is that you've introduced five functional dependencies: LicenseIssueDate and LicenseExpirationDate both depend on DriverLicenseNumber. The three passport-related columns depend on PassportNumber, assuming that the two numbers are unique.

This is a subtle example of a functional dependency because the structure assumes that there is a one-to-one relationship between person and driver's license and between person and passport. Therefore, PersonID is still the key of the Person table, and you don't have any serious problems with updating or removing data. If a person gets a new passport, you just update those columns, for example. However, consider the more general model that Figure 11-1 represents, and what would happen if you tried to represent it directly. Since a person can have a varying number of multiple IDs, the best way to combine all this information in one table is to have one row for each combination of person and ID:

```
CREATE TABLE Person (
  PersonID INTEGER NOT NULL,
  Name VARCHAR2(100) NOT NULL,
  Sex CHAR(1) NOT NULL CHECK (Sex IN ('M', 'F')),
  DateOfBirth DATE NOT NULL,
  DateOfDeath DATE,
  Height NUMBER,
  Weight NUMBER,
  MaritalStatus CHAR(1) CHECK(MaritalStatus in ('S', 'M', 'D', 'W'))
  Comment VARCHAR2(2000),
  IDNumber NUMBER,
  LicenseIssueDate DATE,
  LicenseExpirationDate DATE,
  PassportIssueDate DATE,
  PassportExpirationDate DATE,
  IssuingOffice VARCHAR2(100)
  CONSTRAINT Person_PK (PersonID, IDNumber))
```

I'm going to stop at this point because we're already far down a road that you don't want to travel. This table is a mess. You've mixed together all kinds of data at varying multiplicity. This is a terrible way to represent the world you're trying to model. It results in, for example, two Person records for each person with a Passport and Driver's License. In the Passport-related row, all the Driver's License columns are null. In the Driver's License–related row, all the Passport columns are null. More importantly, you duplicate all the Person data in each of the two rows. When you add in identifications of different sorts along with their specific columns, it just gets worse. Now, when you update a Weight, for example, you have to update it in two different rows. This is Codd's update anomaly.

You solve this problem by representing the objects in a straightforward way in separate tables, which is third normal form or Boyce-Codd normal form (BCNF), depending on the exact structure. Normalization theory starts with one huge table and decomposes it into pieces using the functional dependencies, which represent the clusters of facts around object identity and relationships between objects. You can now see why OO and ER design, which represent objects and relationships directly, tend not to need much normalization. You directly represent your functional dependencies and structure your model from the start into decomposed relations because you represent associations directly.

But I digress. It gets worse.

A *multivalued dependency* occurs when a table is the join of two of its projections having a shared subset of columns [Fagin 1981, p. 390]. The functional dependency is a special case of the multivalued dependency. Again, let's explore the concept by example rather than focusing on the relational mathematics. Consider the CriminalOrganization in Figure 11-2, and consider what might happen if you modeled the particular criminal operations that the people in the organization conducted (their "businesses"). The following code adds a Business Type table that contains the kinds of businesses a criminal organization might operate, and the Criminal Business table lists the people and the businesses they run.

```
CREATE TABLE CriminalOrganization (
  OrganizationID INTEGER PRIMARY KEY REFERENCES Organization,
  LegalStatus CHAR(1) NOT NULL,
  Stability CHAR(1) NOT NULL,
  InvestigativePriority CHAR(1) NOT NULL,
  ProsecutionStatus CHAR(1) NOT NULL);
CREATE TABLE BusinessType (
  BusinessTypeID INTEGER PRIMARY KEY,
  TypeName VARCHAR2(100));
CREATE TABLE CriminalBusiness (
  OrganizationID INTEGER REFERENCES CriminalOrganization,—the mob
  PersonID INTEGER REFERENCES Person,—the mob member
  BusinessType INTEGER REFERENCES BusinessType,—the criminal business
  PRIMARY KEY (OrganizationID, PersonID, BusinessID));
```

There is nothing obviously wrong with this model until you understand the underlying semantics of the data. Businesses are run by *organizations*, not by individuals within the organization. The Criminal Business table represents this, but it throws in the person as well. Table 11-1 presents the data for the Criminal Business table (I've replaced the implicit object-identifying integers with the relevant names for clarity; the names refer to several Holmes stories):

The multivalued dependency here stems from the fact that the PRIMARY KEY constraint on the Criminal Business table is the full set of primary keys from

Table 11-1   *The Criminal Business Table*

Organization Name	Person Name	Business Type Name
Moriarty Organization	Fred Porlock	Extortion
Moriarty Organization	Fred Porlock	Burglary
Moriarty Organization	Col. Sebastian Moran	Extortion
Moriarty Organization	Col. Sebastian Moran	Burglary
Clay Gang	John Clay	Bank Robbery
Clay Gang	John Clay	Burglary
Clay Gang	Archie	Bank Robbery
Clay Gang	Archie	Bank Robbery

the three related tables Person, Criminal Organization, and Business Type. However, if you know the organization, you know the businesses it operates, and you know the people in the organization. But people and businesses are independent of one another. Thus, you have two columns that depend on one other column but are independent—a multivalued dependency that is not on the primary key of the table. The Business Type table is a join of two projections, the Organization-Person projection and the Organization–Business Type projection.

Table 11-2 presents the Party table, which contains the Organization-Person projection along with the person's role in the organization. In this case, although the three columns constitute the primary key, each person plays just one role; this is purely for illustration in this case.

Table 11-3 presents the Criminal Business table revised to include just the organizations and business types, which better represents the underlying meaning of the data:

You can see that joining the new Criminal Business table with the Party table yields the result in the first try at the Criminal Business table in Table 11-1. You can also see that keeping the data in the form of Table 11-1 is fraught with peril. The second most dangerous man in London becomes a threat to your database integrity because you must update his redundant businesses in four separate rows when an organization changes businesses. That's the update anomaly for the multivalued dependency. Decomposing into the projections eliminates the redundancies and the anomalies.

A *join dependency* takes the multivalued dependency and expands it to the general case of joining three or more projections having a shared subset of columns. If there were another set of columns in a separate table aggregating objects to an organization, joining it in would produce a very redundant series of rows. The join dependency decomposition is called fifth normal form and is very hard to define. Basically, you must find the set of projection tables (decompositions) that, when joined together, eliminate any spurious rows produced by the join of any two tables. That usually means at least three decomposition tables. It's

Table 11-2 *The Party Table*

Organization Name	Person Name	Organizational Role Name
Moriarty Organization	Fred Porlock	Executive
Moriarty Organization	Col. Sebastian Moran	Second most dangerous man in London
Clay Gang	John Clay	Fourth smartest man in London
Clay Gang	Archie	Pal

Table 11-3 *The Revised Criminal Business Table*

Organization Name	Business Type Name
Moriarty Organization	Extortion
Moriarty Organization	Burglary
Clay Gang	Burglary
Clay Gang	Bank Robbery

usually quite hard to see these constraints until you encounter a problem in a particular join [Date 1998b].

> *Note: To follow up on join dependencies, the best articles on the subject are Fagin's two articles [Fagin 1979, 1981]. Date has a good two-part article on the subject [Date 1998a, 1998b], which is a modified version of the material in his seminal book on database theory [Date 1995]. William Kent's classic article is also an easy-to-understand source for the theory of join dependencies [Kent 1983].*

The general rule is thus to decompose the tables in your database without losing any information about data relationships until you have no dependencies that are not onto the full primary key of each table. Fifth normal form also requires having enough tables to represent all the primary keys you need to get correct data when joining these tables back together (that's the nonloss part of the definition, really).

If you follow the basic rule and eliminate any of these dependencies that are not dependencies on a key of the table, you will always have a database that is in fifth normal form.

Denormalizing Your Schema

If you spend any time around relational database administrators at all, you will hear heated arguments about "denormalizing" the data. Some believe religiously in keeping all data in fifth normal form; others believe, just as religiously, that fifth normal form is for zealots and serves no useful purpose.

Both of these positions are extremes to avoid. It should be obvious from the examples in the earlier section on "Dependencies and Normalization" that eliminating multivalued and join dependencies is a good thing. If you don't decompose your tables right to get rid of join dependencies, your joins can yield invalid results because of the loss of information. Similarly, the complexity of the data resulting from a multivalued dependency and the simplicity of the normalized form (fourth normal form) is pretty clear.

Why do DBAs consider denormalizing data? In a word, performance. The most expensive operation with a relational database is the join (aside from buying the thing in the first place, of course). By prejoining projections into a single table, DBAs eliminate the need to join the tables in application SQL code. That can increase performance dramatically. Does it in fact do so? The best answer that any DBA who is telling the truth can say is, "It depends." Because of the separation of the physical schema from the logical, any change to the logical schema to facilitate physical operations is of necessity indirect. Depending on storage requirements, for example, a prejoined table can take up more than one physical page. This results in more I/O for the query than a join of two separate tables stored on separate disks might [Date 1997b, p. 24].

Relational database performance tuning requires good data analysis, a strong understanding of the target DBMS and its physical operations, and a clear understanding of the trade-offs in denormalizing data. You should consider denormalizing data only when you confront a performance problem. You should almost certainly look at alternative SQL expressions and alternative physical structures first, as these solutions don't have the deleterious trade-offs of denormalization. It should be a last resort, especially if there are many applications that share the data structures in question.

It's also important to realize that "denormalization" is not a process any more than is normalization. Yes, if you are not in third normal form, you are not in fifth normal form. However, you can eliminate all the nontrivial join and multivalued dependencies in your database and still have a few functional dependencies in prejoined, denormalized tables. Your goal should be to eliminate as many of the nonkey dependencies as possible and to get as close to modeling the real objects as possible.

Finally, many DBAs think they are denormalizing when they are really just introducing redundancy [Date 1997b]. Often, this isn't true.

First, go back and read the section on "Atomic Values." Many DBAs think that introducing "repeating groups" into the table structure, such as Address1, Address2, and Address3, or Monday, Tuesday, Wednesday, Thursday, Friday, Saturday, and Sunday columns, is denormalization. Unless you introduce a dependency not onto the full primary key, your table remains fully normalized. The DBA will usually argue that these are "repeating groups" and that therefore the table is no longer in first normal form. As the earlier section demonstrated, this is nonsense. First normal form is about multivalued columns, not a sequence of columns with single values. When you introduce sequences of multiple columns that imply a functional dependency you could get rid of by storing the projection of those columns with its own primary key in a separate table, you can get a dependency. For example, say you wanted to add the monthly income for each person in each role to your schema. You could add the columns JanIncome, FebIncome, MarIncome and so on to the Party table. That table is still in fifth normal form. However, if you add two columns, both dependent on the month, you introduce a functional dependency—JanIncome, JanPayDate, Feb Income, FebPayDate, and so on.

Second, storing aggregates doesn't denormalize the database. For example, you could store the total number of people in an organization in the Organization table. This introduces a constraint that the number is the count of the number of distinct people related to the organization through the Party table. While this constraint is complex, it is most definitely not a functional, multivalued, or join dependency. Therefore, storing the count does not move your Organization table out of fifth normal form.

Third, you often encounter a situation where your tables contain null values for things that can't logically exist. This is a result of combining a super-class and subclass. For example, if you combined the Organization and Criminal Organization tables, the LegalStatus column would have null values for any row corresponding to an organization that is not a criminal organization. While this is perhaps not ideal, it is also not denormalization because there are no functional dependencies—or any other kind of dependency. This comes from a *union* of projections rather than a join of projections; you are combining the objects of two exclusive subclasses into a superclass table with a set union operation rather than with a join operation. Normalization, however, depends on the join of projections, not on the union of them.

Fourth, creating a star schema for a data warehouse (see the Preface for a definition) does not denormalize the database. What you are doing in a star schema is creating a very complex, *n*-ary relationship table (the fact table) with many related tables (the dimension tables). You are not introducing dependencies or even redundancies; you are simply representing the multidimensional characteristics of the data using the Star Design pattern (see the section "Modeling with Reusable Design Patterns" in Chapter 8).

There are probably many other cases of decomposition and composition that do not affect normalization. Your guide should be to consider the dependencies rather than being fooled by the composition process. Again, normalization isn't really a process, it's a state.

The Language of Peace

SQL-92 provides a comprehensive schema definition language. The section "Conformity Rules" shows you the steps you take to transform your OO model into that language using the techniques presented in the previous sections in this chapter. The next section, "Nonconformity Rocks," departs from the standard language to show you some techniques in Oracle7, as an example, that provide alternatives to the standard process.

The transformation process uses the example data model from Figures 11-1, 11-2, and 11-3.

Conformity Rules

There are two basic steps to creating an SQL-92 conforming database from a UML data model: creating tables from persistent types and creating tables for many-to-many and ternary associations. Each step has various choices to make. The preceding parts of this chapter have discussed each of these choices in the context of the UML constructs; this section guides you through a complete transformation, connecting everything.

Persistent Classes

As the first transformation, create a table for each class in your UML data model that has the «persistent» stereotype, including association classes and classes that inherit from other classes. Name the table with the name of the class. From Figure 11-1, the Person subsystem, you create 10 tables: Person, Address, Identification, Expiring ID, Driver License, Passport, NationalID, Law Enforcement ID, Social Security Card, and Birth Certificate.

> Note: You may merge the association class into another table later if that proves feasible. For now, leave it as a separate table in your emerging schema.

Within each table, now add a column for each attribute in the attribute section of the class. As an example, for Address, add StreetNumber, StreetFraction, StreetName, StreetSuffix, Locator, City, State, PostalCode, Country, and Comment.

You should at this point have a transformation map that shows how to transform each data type in your data model into an ANSI SQL data type. The commonplace book system uses the basic ANSI types extended to include a series of "nullable" types for each ANSI type, so the mapping is trivial. There are certain special types that correspond to object identity (OID) or enumerated types (Sex, for example). Certain of the types, such as VARCHAR, need refinement with the addition of a size specifier. If you need the maximum number of characters available for a size, use the least-common-denominator approach. Look at all your target DBMS products and take the maximum from the one that supports the lowest number, such as SQL Server's support for only 254 characters in a character varying field. Still other types correspond to references to other tables through foreign keys; hold off on these columns, which we'll add a bit further on in the process. The end result for this stage for the Address table looks like this:

```
CREATE TABLE Address (
  AddressID INTEGER PRIMARY KEY,—OID type
  StreetNumber NUMBER,
  StreetFraction VARCHAR(5),
  StreetName VARCHAR(100),
  StreetSuffix VARCHAR(25),
  City VARCHAR(100),
  State CHAR(2),
  PostalCode CHAR(20),
  Country VARCHAR(100),
  Comment VARCHAR(250));—size for worst case, SQL Server
```

If there is a {nullable} tag on the attribute, add a null constraint; otherwise, add a NOT NULL constraint. In the case of the commonplace book, the data model uses the nullable types to represent null constraints, and all of the columns in Address except for StreetFraction and Comment are not null:

```
CREATE TABLE Address (
  AddressID INTEGER PRIMARY KEY,—OID type
  StreetNumber NUMBER NOT NULL,
  StreetFraction VARCHAR(5) NULL,
  StreetName VARCHAR(100) NOT NULL,
  StreetSuffix VARCHAR(25) NOT NULL,
  City VARCHAR(100) NOT NULL,
  State CHAR(2) NOT NULL,
  PostalCode CHAR(20) NOT NULL,
  Country VARCHAR(100) NOT NULL,
  Comment VARCHAR(250));—size for worst case, SQL Server
```

You'll find an example of the {nullable} tag in Figure 11-2: the Plays association class contains the TerminationMethod column, which has an enumerated type. Instead of creating a separate nullable_TerminationType type, this diagram uses the {nullable} tag to specify nullability.

You should also at this point construct any type-checking utility tables for enumerated types. For example, you need a Termination Type table:

```
CREATE TABLE TerminationType (
  TerminationType CHAR(1) PRIMARY KEY,—character code
  DisplayString VARCHAR(25));—string to display in UI and reports
```

If there is an initial value for a column, add a DEFAULT expression to the column definition.

Now it's time to construct the primary key and the things that depend on it. To start with, find the root class of each generalization hierarchy (classes to which a generalization arrow points but from which no generalization arrow emerges). Also consider all classes with no generalization relationships.

If the class has implicit object identity, add a column to the table. Name the primary key column with the class name suffixed with _ID, such as Person_ID, and add PRIMARY KEY as a constraint. PRIMARY KEY implies NOT NULL, so you don't need that constraint on the primary key column. Usually, you should give the column a NUMBER data type and use a sequence or the equivalent to generate numbers for it.

> *Note: If the class has a composite aggregation association to another class, and the other class is the aggregating class, hold off on creating the primary key until you are creating foreign keys. Composite aggregation keys are a combination of the primary key of the related class and another attribute.*

All the classes in Figures 11-1 and 11-2 have implicit object identity. Consider the Identification class, which is a root class with implicit object identity:

```
CREATE TABLE Identification (
  IdentificationID INTEGER PRIMARY KEY);
```

If the class has explicit object identity (an {OID} tag), add a PRIMARY KEY constraint clause to the table and put all columns with the {OID} tag into the constraint. If there is only one column in the explicit identifier, just add the PRIMARY KEY column constraint to that column.

If the class has subclasses, add a column to represent the discriminator, and create a CHECK constraint with the appropriate enumerated values to represent the subclasses.

Now proceed on to the subclasses. If there is a single superclass for the class, add a column to the table named either with the name of the primary key in the superclass or with a new name more appropriate to the subclass. Add PRIMARY KEY as a constraint, and add a REFERENCES clause to relate the column to the primary key of the superclass table as a foreign key. Use PRIMARY KEY and FOREIGN KEY table constraints instead of the column constraints if there is a multiple-column explicit identifier in the superclass.

The LawEnforcementID class adds a column, BadgeNumber, to the Identification attributes. It gets the primary key of its superclass:

```
CREATE TABLE LawEnforcementID (
  IdentificationID INTEGER PRIMARY KEY REFERENCES Identification,
  BadgeNumber INTEGER NOT NULL);
```

If there are multiple superclasses (multiple inheritance), add a column to the table for each column in each primary key of each superclass. Add a PRIMARY KEY clause with all the columns, and add a FOREIGN KEY clause with the columns for each superclass primary key. Consult the earlier section in this chapter on "Multiple Inheritance" for examples.

Association classes are slightly special with respect to primary keys. Instead of creating a new key to represent object identity, give the association class the primary keys of all its related classes. For example, the Plays class in Figure 11-2 represents a ternary association between three classes. Therefore, Plays gets a primary key comprising the three primary keys of its associated classes. Each key in turn is a foreign key back to the role-playing table, so it gets a REFERENCES constraint for single-valued keys and a FOREIGN KEY table constraint for multivalued keys.

```
CREATE TABLE Plays (
  PersonID INTEGER REFERENCES Person,
  OrganizationID INTEGER REFERENCES Organization,
  RoleID INTEGER REFERENCES Role,
  Tenure INTERVAL YEAR TO MONTH,
  StartDate DATE NOT NULL,
  EndDate DATE,
  TerminationMethod CHAR(1),
  PRIMARY KEY (PersonID, OrganizationID, RoleID));
```

Next, find any candidate keys. If there are any {alternate OID = <n>} tags, add a UNIQUE constraint to the table for each unique <n> identifier and put all columns with the same <n> identifier into the constraint. Again, LawEnforcementID serves as an example, as BadgeNumber has the tag {alternate OID = 1}:

```
CREATE TABLE LawEnforcementID (
  IdentificationID INTEGER PRIMARY KEY REFERENCES Identification,
  BadgeNumber INTEGER NOT NULL UNIQUE);
```

Next step: add any simple table constraints. If there are constraint boxes in the diagram, convert them into CHECK clauses if you can express the constraint in an SQL expression that contains only references to columns in the table you are defining. If there are data type constraints such as enumerations or ranges, add a CHECK clause to the column to represent the constraint. For enumerations with utility tables that list the possible values in the type, wait for creating the foreign keys, the next step.

Now, add any foreign keys. At this point, all tables should have a primary key. If there are any binary associations to the class you are defining with a multiplicity of 0..1 or 1..1 on the role attached to the other class, and the association has no association class, create a column to represent the association. As you go through the tables, of course, you will reach the other end of each binary association. If it's a 1..1 or 0..1 association, and you've already created a column for it in another table, don't create the foreign key in both tables. Creating two foreign keys for a relationship is not only circular and hard to maintain, it can seriously confuse developers using the tables. You can optimize your decision by thinking about how applications will use the tables. If one side of the association seems more natural or more likely for a developer to use, put the column in that table. If the multiplicity on the role is 1..1 rather than 0..1, add a NOT NULL constraint to the foreign key column(s).

You will already have created the foreign keys to superclasses through generalization relationships in the prior step for creating primary keys.

There are a couple of alternatives for creating foreign keys, depending on the number of columns in the primary key to which they refer. If the primary key of the associated table has a single column, create a single column with the same data type and the role name in the current table. Add a REFERENCES clause as a column constraint to relate the column to the primary key of the associated table. For example, the Locator attribute in the Address table refers to a table in another system called GeoCoord (geographical coordinate) with an implicit object identifier, GeoCoordID:

```
Locator INTEGER NOT NULL REFERENCES GeoCoord(GeoCoordID),
```

If the primary key of the associated table has multiple columns, create the same number of columns with the same data types in the current table. Name the columns using both the role name and the column names in the associated table (converting the names as appropriate or required by column name length restrictions). Add a FOREIGN KEY table constraint to relate the columns to the primary key of the associated table.

If you've added a foreign key from a composite aggregation association with a to-one multiplicity to the other class, add the foreign key column(s) to the primary key (a parent-child class pair). Add the appropriate CASCADE constraint to the FOREIGN KEY clause in the other table. Then create a second column for the primary key that uniquely identifies the object. Often this will be either an explicit {OID} column or a sequence if the association is {ordered}. If not, then create an integer value to uniquely identify the children of the aggregate.

Finally, optimize your association classes. If there are any binary associations with role multiplicity greater than 1 on the role played by the class you are defining, and the association has an association class, add the attributes from the association class to the table with data types and constraints as above. Remove the table you created for the association class from the schema.

The schema is nearing completion, but there are still some special associations for you to handle.

Many-to-Many and Ternary Associations

You may have many-to-many or ternary associations that do not have association classes. If they did have, you would have already created a class for the association. Now, you must create such a class if it doesn't already exist.

A many-to-many association has two to-many multiplicities (0..*, 1..*, *, 1..5, 10, and so on). A ternary association has three classes participating in the association linked through a diamond shape. You can of course have quaternary or higher associations as well.

Find all the many-to-many and ternary associations in your data model. Create a table for each many-to-many or ternary association that does not have an association class to represent it. Add columns to the table for the primary keys of each of the participating tables just as you would for the association class.

If the primary key of the associated table is a single column, add a column with the name of the role or of the primary key column (depending on semantics). Use the data type from the primary key column and add a REFERENCES constraint to relate the column to the primary key.

If the primary key of the associated table has multiple columns, add a similar number of columns to the association table using the role name and the column name. Add a FOREIGN KEY constraint to relate the column to the primary key.

Add a PRIMARY KEY constraint to the table and add all the columns representing the primary keys of the participating tables to that constraint.

For example, the association between Address and Person is *, *, indicating a many-to-many association. Create an association table for it:

```
CREATE TABLE PersonalAddress (
  AddressID INTEGER REFERENCES Address,
  ResidentID INTEGER REFERENCES Person,
  PRIMARY KEY (AddressID, PersonID));
```

Notice the adaptation of the role name "residents" to the ResidentID column name. This better conveys the meaning of the column than "PersonID" would.

If a multiplicity of a role has a minimum value greater than 0, add a stored procedure that checks that a row in the association table exists if a row in the associated table exists. You will need to execute that stored procedure as the last step in a transaction involving an INSERT into the associated table. You may be able to do this as an AFTER INSERT trigger, but not necessarily if more than one associated table has such multiplicities.

If you go through this process a few times on moderately complex designs, you'll begin to find the transformations second nature. Again, this produces a schema in ANSI standard SQL. Now, let's consider using some of the features of the target RDBMS that go beyond the standard.

Nonconformity Rocks

The decision to go "off the board" depends on many things, mostly cultural. If your clients only use a certain DBMS, or if your organization does not particularly value standards conformance, you may have the freedom to consider innovative ways to transform your model into a specific relational database. A key reason to do this is to get closer to the OO model and hence to the benefits of that model: ease of maintenance, fewer bugs, and a higher reuse potential. Unfortunately, standard SQL has many benefits, but they do not include innovative architecture and OO features.

That having been said, however, relational databases are not OO systems in any way. You can move closer to the OO model by using some of the standard features and some of the extending features of the RDBMS, but you are not using an OO database. The following transformation, for example, uses the features of Oracle7 as an example to add to the standard model from the "Conformity Rules" section. The objectives are to get a higher level of encapsulation than is possible with standard SQL and to model as much behavior as possible on the server rather than in the application. You can't do this using standard SQL because it doesn't have the behavioral features that most RDBMS products have.

To illustrate some interesting ways to abandon conformity, this section looks at two areas: how Oracle7 can implement the packaged subsystems of your data model, and how it can implement your class operations.

> *Note: As I said in the Preface, most of my working experience is with Oracle. Please forgive the focus on Oracle in this section. Each RDBMS has its own set of extensions that you can use in similar ways. I'm most familiar with Oracle, so my examples are Oracle examples.*

Packaged Subsystems

Subsystems, also known as name spaces, do have a representation in standard SQL: the ANSI SQL-92 schema concept. Virtually no RDBMS represents this concept directly, and all provide facilities that go beyond the standard in this area, particularly in their support of distributed databases (databases with multiple servers in different locations).

You can use one of two approaches to this problem in Oracle7. You can implement a UML subsystem package as either a different name space in a single database or as different databases. This means either creating the schema for the package in a separate user or in a separate database.

First, here's how you would set up the users if you want to create the name spaces in a single Oracle7 database:

```
CREATE USER Entity IDENTIFIED BY xxxxx;
CREATE USER PersonIDENTIFIED BY xxxxx;
CREATE USER Organization IDENTIFIED BY xxxxx;
```

These users define three schemas corresponding to the persistent packages in the commonplace book data model (see Figures 11-1 to 11-3). Next, you create the objects with CREATE TABLE, CREATE VIEW, or whatever is appropriate. Then, if you want to hide the tripartite database division, you create synonyms for each object; otherwise, you need to preface object names with their schema name in your SQL code.

To use the schemas, it's usually a good idea to create users other than the package users. It's those users that need the synonyms. You can create public synonyms, but again that's not the best for encapsulation of the name spaces. Once you've created a login user for your application, you must grant the appropriate privileges (SELECT, INSERT, UPDATE, and/or DELETE) on the objects the application will use. Keeping the privileges to the minimum helps ensure you get a reasonably high level of encapsulation. You can also create a view to further encapsulate the underlying objects.

This approach combines the security, data independence, and schema definition elements of Oracle7 SQL to achieve at least partial encapsulation. It isn't complete, but you gain assurance that no application can get access to the underlying data beyond what you've explicitly granted.

An alternative to the user approach is to create separate databases. This is a bit more involved from the perspective of the DBA. You must identify the database files, size the database, and take care of all the physical database loose ends such as redo logs and rollback segments. Once you've created the databases through the CREATE DATABASE command or through the Enterprise Manager, you then create the same system and application users as in the previous approach. You still have to grant privileges to all the tables, but instead of doing so directly, you must first establish links to the databases:

```
CREATE DATABASE LINK PersonLink;
CREATE DATABASE LINK IdentificationLink;
CREATE DATABASE LINK OrganizationLink;
```

Now, you can grant access to the objects in each schema by adding the link name to the object name:

```
GRANT SELECT ON Person.Person@PersonLink TO AppUser;
```

The only benefit to this separate database approach is that you can reuse elements of the system without any concern for the underlying physical connections between the schemas. You would have to concern yourself with these if they were all in the same database. There really isn't that much advantage over the single-database approach unless you have some physical optimization of your separate databases that makes sense. This happens mostly in the context of fully distributed systems in a wide-area network.

Operations

The simplest way to represent operations in Oracle7 is to create a stored procedure or function for each operation you've defined in the data model. Using this approach, it's up to you to get your applications calling the right operations. As an example, consider the CriminalOrganization class from Figure 11-2. That class exports two operations: UpdateStatus and SetPriority, both "mutators" that change the state of a particular criminal organization object.

PL/SQL, the programming language that Oracle7 provides, is a computationally complete programming language that embeds the SQL data sublanguage for database access. Technically, you can use only SELECT, INSERT, UPDATE, and DELETE commands using embedded SQL, but you can issue any SQL through special program units that Oracle provides (the DBMS_SQL package) to create or alter tables, grant privileges, and so on. Oracle is moving in the direction of adding a second language for programming, Java, to its stable, jumping on the OO bandwagon with a vengeance. Perhaps this will be available in time for the second edition of this book. But I digress once again.

You can transform an operation on a class into a stored PL/SQL procedure. The method (remember, a method is the implementation of an operation in UML) has at least one input—something that identifies the row of the table (the object) on which you want to operate.

Without making this small section a lengthy treatise on PL/SQL and its myriad capabilities, I can't go into detail on the many options you have for representing specific concepts. PL/SQL has something for everyone and can usually provide some way of handling a given UML notation. In this case, we have two requirements: enumerated data types and updating a row.

The first requirement, an enumerated data type, is an example of something that is hard to do in PL/SQL. The PL/SQL type system closely models the SQL type system, which has no concept of enumerated type. At least an SQL column definition can have a CHECK constraint; this is not true of a PL/SQL variable definition, unfortunately. So, you'll have to jump through a couple of hoops to represent your enumerated type.

A classic approach is to build a lookup table of enumeration values. The section "The Transformation Table" earlier in this chapter demonstrated how to do this for the LegalStatus type:

```
CREATE TABLE LegalStatusType (
  Value CHAR(1) PRIMARY KEY,
  DisplayString VARCHAR2(50) NOT NULL,
  Description VARCHAR2(2000));
```

```
INSERT INTO LegalStatusType (Value, DisplayString)
VALUES ('D', 'Legally Defined');
INSERT INTO LegalStatusType (Value, DisplayString)
VALUES ('T', 'On Trial');
INSERT INTO LegalStatusType (Value, DisplayString)
VALUES ('A', 'Alledged');
INSERT INTO LegalStatusType (Value, DisplayString)
VALUES ('U', 'Unknown');
```

To use the type, you pass the value code into the procedure, then use the table to check the value:

```
CREATE OR REPLACE PROCEDURE SetStatus(p_Self IN INTEGER,
                                       p_Status IN CHAR) IS
  v_TypeOK INTEGER := 0;
BEGIN
  SELECT 1
    INTO v_TypeOK
    FROM LegalStatusType
  WHERE Value = p_Status;
  IF v_TypeOK = 1 THEN
    UPDATE CriminalOrganization
      SET LegalStatus = p_Status
      WHERE OrganizationID = p_Self;
  END IF;
EXCEPTION
  WHEN NO_DATA_FOUND THEN—Couldn't find the status
    DBMS_OUTPUT.Enable(100000);
    DBMS_OUTPUT.Put_Line(to_char(sysdate, 'dd-Mon-yy hh:mm')||
      ' SetStatus: '||p_Status||
      ' is not a valid legal status for a criminal
        organization.');
END SetStatus;
```

This PL/SQL procedure checks the enumerated type against the table of values, and if it is there, updates the criminal organization you've specified (p_Self) with the new status. If it isn't there, PL/SQL raises the NO_DATA_FOUND exception and passes control to the exception handler, which writes the error message out on the server-output log. Having this mutator procedure in place, you now no longer need to code update statements in your code. Instead, you call the stored procedure, perhaps from a Pro*C embedded SQL C++ program:

```
exec sql execute begin SetStatus(:self, :legalStatus); end; end-exec;
```

You could encapsulate this code, for example, in the SetStatus member function of the CriminalOrganization class.

In this case, the code for updating the row is a simple SQL statement, but the code for checking the enumerated value type is quite extensive. This is typical of database coding in relational (and object-relational) database management, which doesn't give you much in the way of programming tools for error handling. The exceptions in PL/SQL are actually a big improvement over the return code approach that prevailed in earlier environments. As with any kind of exception handling, though, you must be careful to isolate the exception handling on the server. You don't want exceptions trying to propagate to the client crashing the server process.

A more systematic approach to operations is to add another step to the algorithm in the "Conformity Rules" section.

Create a PL/SQL package for each class with a «persistent» stereotype. Name the package with the name of the class, adding a _pg suffix to distinguish the package from the table you define for the class (this is a single name space). Add a RECORD type for the underlying table and its columns, which you use to define a SELECT cursor later. Add a RECORD type for the columns in the primary key. Add subprograms to INSERT, UPDATE, DELETE, and LOCK rows to the underlying table. Add a subprogram to return a cursor to all the rows in the table (a general query of the table). Add subprograms for each operation you've specified in the behavior section of the class box, naming the methods with the name of the operation.

For the CriminalOrganization class, the resulting PL/SQL package looks like this:

```
CREATE OR REPLACE PACKAGE CriminalOrganization_pg IS
  TYPE tCriminalOrganization IS RECORD (
    rOrganizationID CriminalOrganization.OrganizationID%TYPE,
    rLegalStatusID CriminalOrganization.LegalStatus%TYPE,
    rStability CriminalOrganization.LegalStatus%TYPE,
    rInvestigativePriority
      CriminalOrganization.InvestigatePriority%TYPE,
    rProsecutionStatus CriminalOrganization.ProsecutionStatus%TYPE);
  TYPE tCriminalOrganizationKey IS RECORD (
    rOrganizationID CriminalOrganization.OrganizationID%TYPE);
  TYPE tCriminalOrganizationCursor IS REF CURSOR
    RETURN tCriminalOrganization;
  TYPE tCriminalOrganizationTable IS TABLE OF tCriminalOrganization
    INDEX BY BINARY_INTEGER;
  TYPE tCriminalOrganizationKeyTable IS TABLE
    OF tCriminalOrganizationKey INDEX BY BINARY_INTEGER;

  —Operations
  PROCEDURE SelectCursor(pCursor IN OUT tCriminalOrganizationCursor);
```

```
    PROCEDURE SelectRows(pTable IN OUT tCriminalOrganizationTable);
    PROCEDURE InsertRows(pTable IN tCriminalOrganizationTable);
    PROCEDURE UpdateRows(pTable IN tCriminalOrganizationTable);
    PROCEDURE DeleteRows(pKeyTable IN tCriminalOrganizationKeyTable);
    PROCEDURE LockRows(pKeyTable IN tCriminalOrganizationKeyTable);
END CriminalOrganization_pg;
```

This approach lets you fully encapsulate the underlying table in the package in a very general way. The first type sets up the table columns in a record type. The second type lets you represent the primary key value in a single record. The third type gives you a "ref cursor" that lets you query all the data in the table. The fourth type gives you a "result set" PL/SQL table that lets you store multiple criminal organizations in a single variable. The fifth type gives you a similar capability to store multiple primary keys. The procedures then use these types to give you standard select, insert, update, and delete capabilities. The SelectCursor procedure returns a cursor that you can use to iterate through the table. You can add parameters to this procedure to pass in WHERE clause qualifiers to return subsets. The SelectRows procedure returns a complete result set from a single call rather than returning the cursor. The InsertRows and UpdateRows procedures insert and update rows from a set of records in a table. The DeleteRows procedure deletes any rows identified in a table of primary keys. The LockRows procedure lets you lock a set of rows identified by their primary keys for update. These generic procedures give you all the capabilities you need to maintain your database. You can, of course, add specific operations such as SetStatus:

```
PROCEDURE SetStatus(pKey IN tCriminalOrganizationKey,
                    pStatus IN CHAR);
```

Again, you specify the object to update with a key and the status to update it with as a parameter. You could also provide a bulk update procedure using a key table:

```
PROCEDURE SetStatus(pKeyTable IN tCriminalOrganizationKeyTable,
                    pStatus IN CHAR);
```

If you now grant EXECUTE privilege on the package to application users but do not grant privileges on the underlying table, the application must program to the package interface instead of selecting data directly from the table. Using this combination of SQL security and PL/SQL packaging lets you fully encapsulate your database table within a programming API.

> *Note: Developer/2000, the Oracle application generation system,*
> *uses this kind of package as an alternative to direct table access.*
> *You can thus provide much more control over your tables using*

Table 11-4 *Summary of Relational Schema Transformation*

Step	Transformation
1	UML class becomes table.
2	UML attribute in class becomes column in table.
3	UML attribute type in class becomes column type in table through type transformation table.
4	If {nullable} UML attribute tag, attribute has NULL constraint; otherwise, NOT NULL constraint.
5	If UML attribute has initializer, add DEFAULT clause to column.
6	For classes with no generalization (root or independent) and implicit identity, create integer primary key; for {oid}, add {oid} tagged columns to PRIMARY KEY constraint; ignore composite aggregation and association classes.
7	For subclasses, add the key of each parent class to the PRIMARY KEY constraint and to a FOREIGN KEY constraint.
8	For association classes, add primary key from each role-playing table to PRIMARY KEY constraint and FOREIGN KEY constraint.
9	If {alternate oid = <n>} tag, add columns to UNIQUE constraint.
10	Add CHECK for each explicit constraint.
11	Create FOREIGN KEY columns in referencing table for each 0..1, 1..1 role in association.
12	Create PRIMARY KEY for composite aggregation with FOREIGN KEY to aggregating table (with CASCADE option); add additional column for PRIMARY KEY.
13	Optimize binary association classes by moving into to-many side table where appropriate.
14	Create tables for many-to-many, ternary associations with no association classes.
15	Create PRIMARY KEY, FOREIGN KEY constraints from keys of role-playing tables in many-to-many, ternary associations.

Developer/2000 applications because no other application of any kind can access the tables directly without authorization. This gives you a rapid application development facility with highly encapsulated RDBMS data access.

Summary

This has been a long chapter, and it is impossible to summarize it in a couple of paragraphs. The real trick to transforming your UML data model into a relational database is being very, very systematic about your approach. If you understand how each UML concept maps into a relational concept, you can easily represent most aspects of your model. The biggest decision you must make is whether to conform to ANSI SQL for portability or to make use of the capabilities of your target DBMS that go beyond the standard. Taking the latter approach lets you get much closer to a real OO implementation of your system.

For convenience, Table 11-4 summarizes the process. FOREIGN KEY and PRIMARY KEY mean either a table constraint or a REFERENCES column constraint depending on whether the key is multivalued.

The standard approach is thus very limiting but very safe in terms of interacting with the relational database. With the next two kinds of database manager, you don't have the issue. While there are nascent standards for OR and OO databases, in practice you must adapt to the target DBMS implementations, which largely do not conform to any standards.

Designing an Object-Relational Database Schema 12

Ex umbris et imaginibus in veritatem. "From shadows and types to the reality."

Cardinal Newman's motto

Object-relational databases extend the capabilities of the relational database toward representing objects. Although there are no standards yet in this arena, a clear picture emerges from the competitive landscape and from the ongoing standards efforts of SQL3.

So What's New?

ORDBMS products are also known as "universal" servers or database managers, presumably because they can handle any kind of data, or possibly because vendor marketing would like their customers to adopt the new technology universally (very small joke). ORDBMS products add several basic things to a relational system:

- Large object data types
- Extended data types
- Multivalued data types
- Object identity
- Extensions that aid in using the above new features

Features

First, ORDBMS products add extra types to the type system to represent objects of arbitrary complexity: BLOBs, CLOBs, FLOBs, and so on. LOB stands for "large object," and these data types represent objects by giving you access to the computer representation of the object as SQL data. On reflection, though, this makes it sound like more than it is. In reality, LOB data types let you put some arbitrary set of bits or characters into a database—and that's it. The more advanced databases let you get the bits or characters out again, but it's up to you to make sense of them. The ANSI SQL3 standard specifies three kinds of large object: the CHARACTER LARGE OBJECT (CLOB), NATIONAL CHARACTER LARGE OBJECT (NCLOB), and the BINARY LARGE OBJECT (BLOB). Since these types have no built-in capabilities, ORDBMS products also provide a way to add behavior to the system to make these objects come alive. Unfortunately, this is the least standardized part of the extension. Oracle8, Informix Dynamic Server, and DB2 Universal Data BAse (UDB) all support these kinds of types, though with differing syntax and features.

Second, ORDBMS products extend the typing system to allow SQL to deal with user-defined types (UDTs), abstract data types (ADTs), or object types. The emerging SQL3 standard has the CREATE TYPE statement for creating these extended types, for example, mirrored by Oracle8's CREATE TYPE and IBM UDB's distinct types. SQL3 includes generalization of types into an inheritance structure. Oracle8 and UDB don't support inheritance, while Informix does. Many ORDBMS products also provide ways to externalize type representations, such as Oracle8 NCA cartridges, Informix DataBlades and opaque types, or UDB distinct types and stored procedures. The key difference between these extensions and the similar features in relational systems is the close integration of the extensions into the SQL typing system. This makes the data available within the context of SQL as well as in application programs. The older relational database technology simply stored the data in unstructured BLOBS and forced you to retrieve it into your programs to do anything with it.

Third, many (but not all) ORDBMS products relax the constraints of first normal form to let you nest tables within tables, to have arrays as column values, and to link tables through pointers or references rather than through data. The ANSI SQL3 standard has arrays but not nested tables. UDB provides table types, external programs that materialize tables that you can then use in FROM clauses to further process with SQL. Oracle8 has nested tables and variable arrays. Informix has three collection data types: set, multiset, and list.

Finally, accompanying all these other changes, ORDBMS products enhance the rest of the system to help you use those changes more effectively. Cast operators, a part of the ANSI SQL-92 standard, extend easily to act as constructors for UDTs. Oracle8 attaches methods to its new TYPE objects, including construction and indexing methods. Informix and UDB also provide ways of adding conversion functions to the system. The SQL3 standard has a complex system of "observer" and "mutator" functions for each type that work with the CAST feature to produce a comprehensive approach to typing in the context of complex SQL queries. DB2 UDB implements the SQL CAST operator, while the other ORDBMS products have not yet done so.

The Downside

While all this technology is fascinating, you should bear in mind the lessons of the SQL3 standard [Melton 1998]. The sheer complexity of adding serious typing to the SQL language has proved almost beyond the capabilities of our current technological understanding. Everyone has a solution; it's just that everyone has a *different* solution. Compromise is in the air, but there's still much disagreement over the important details. Some authors disagree over the entire approach the vendors are taking [Date and Darwen 1998].

The complexity of standardizing the OR capabilities is far worse because of the tremendous array of different capabilities in ORDBMS products, many of which do not conform to the emerging standard. I believe that no database vendor will even come close to implementing the SQL3 standard during the next 10 years, if you extend the lessons learned from the SQL-92 standard to the new standard.

This jungle of features makes it very difficult to advocate a generalized approach to transforming a UML data model into an ORDBMS schema. This chapter takes the approach of relying on basic principles rather than on specific technology. Without an accepted standard, and with the very real possibility that the standard will not practically exist for a long, long time, you have to base your approach on the quirky tools you have at hand. This leads to three major recommendations.

First, understand your technology before you decide to apply it. The choice of technology in this jungle can mean the difference between a successful project and an abysmal failure. Spend the time up front to learn about the specific features you think will solve your problems, and don't believe vendor claims—benchmark with your type of application.

Second, be flexible in your design approach. Don't lock in design decisions before you have prototyped and understood their implications for production applications. For example, nested tables may seem the ideal solution to a complex design full of composite aggregation. In practice, you may find the details of the SQL you have to write very complex and the performance of the system you build very slow.

Third, if you have any concern whatsoever about portability, don't even bother reading the rest of this chapter. Certainly don't expect to be able to develop portable OR schemas any time in the near future. The equivalents of ODBC and JDBC or even ADO simply don't exist in this kind of database, and the sheer complexity of the problem means they won't exist for a long time to come. I hope the ORDBMS vendors prove me wrong on this one, but I seriously doubt it.

Therefore, this chapter goes into less detail on specific technologies than it could. The focus here is on basic transformational principles that you can apply to your data model in the context of the various kinds of features that OR products provide. Take the principles and apply them in detail to the technology of your choice.

The Transformation Process for ORDBMS Products

This chapter covers the SQL3 draft standard schema language for object-relational systems [ISO 1997]. It gives examples of schema choices in the Oracle8 database manager using Oracle SQL and PL/SQL [Koch 1998]. Where they are relevant, it provides a look at the syntax that Informix Dynamic Server [McNally 1997] and the DB2 UDB using DB2 SQL [Chamberlin 1998] provide. While the SQL3 language is illuminating, its differences from emerging technology and the difficulties associated with its acceptance as a formal ISO standard [Melton 1998] mean that you shouldn't spend too much time over its details.

To illustrate the process, this chapter uses the same design as Chapter 11, reproduced here for convenience. Figure 12-1 shows a UML model for the Person subsystem of the commonplace book, and Figure 12-2 shows a UML model for the Organization subsystem. Both of these subsystems are part of a third subsystem, the Entity subsystem. Figure 12-3 shows the architecture for the package.

The Person subsystem contains the Person class and the Identification hierarchy that belongs to it. I've chosen to use the inheritance version of Identification rather than the Interface version. People connect to Organizations through a three-way relationship to the Role class in the Organization package. The scope notation (Organization::Role) identifies classes that are not a part of the Person subsystem.

The Organization subsystem contains the Organization hierarchy, which includes the CriminalOrganization class. It also includes the Role class and the relationships between Role and Organization. Organizations connect to people through a three-way relationship to Role.

The Entity subsystem contains three elements: the two subsystems People and Organization plus an abstract class, Entity. The Person and Organization classes in their respective packages inherit from that class.

Considering just these packages, though, you won't see much benefit from moving to an ORDBMS. So, let's add to the mix a package for handling images and a package for handling geographic locations.

Figure 12-4 illustrates a simple hierarchy of images. The design comes directly from the Oracle8 Visual Information Retrieval data cartridge [Oracle

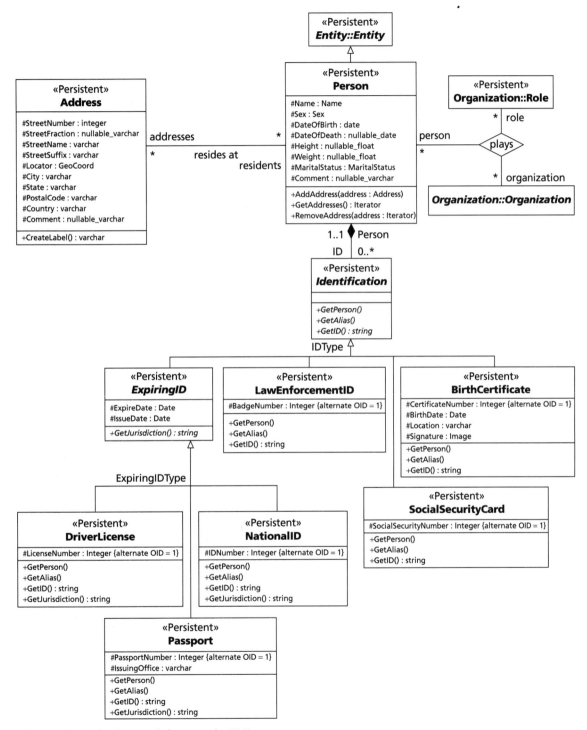

Figure 12-1   *The Person Subsystem in UML*

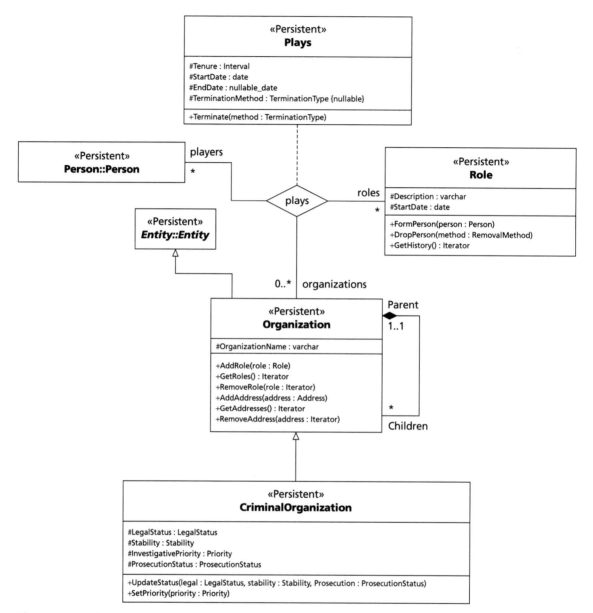

Figure 12-2   *The Organization Subsystem in UML*

1997b]. The subclasses reflect some of the options that Holmes might like to see in the commonplace book system: cigar ash images, facial images, and images of collected evidence. You can relate these images to other classes, such as the relationship between the Person subsystem's Person class and the Facial-Image class.

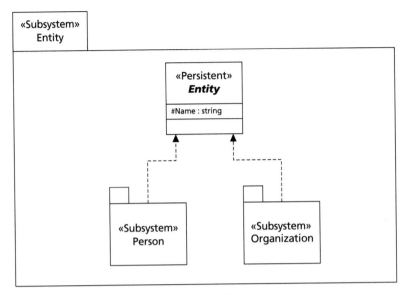

Figure 12-3   *The Entity Subsystem in UML*

To motivate the Image hierarchy, consider these situations in which Holmes found himself. In an early case, the issue of cigar ash identification came up.

> "I gathered up some scattered ash from the floor. It was dark in colour and flakey—such an ash is only made by a Trichinopoly. I have made a special study of cigar ashes—in fact, I have written a monograph upon the subject. I flatter myself that I can distinguish at a glance the ash of any known brand either of cigar or of tobacco. It is just in such details that the skilled detective differs from the Gregson and Lestrade type." [STUD]

With a searchable image of cigar ashes encoding texture and color, any Scotland Yard detective could have done the job using a photograph of the ash sample.

In a much later case during his retirement from the profession, Holmes used photography in his investigation:

> "Finally, there is the question of the instrument with which these injuries were inflicted."
> "What could it be but a scourge or flexible whip of some sort?"
> "Have you examined the marks?" I asked.
> "I have seen them. So has the doctor."
> "But I have examined them very carefully with a lens. They have peculiarities."
> "What are they, Mr. Holmes?"
> I stepped to my bureau and brought out an enlarged photograph. "This is my method in such cases," I explained.

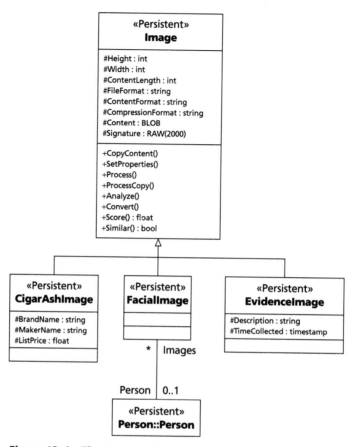

Figure 12-4   *The Image Subsystem in UML*

"You certainly do things thoroughly, Mr. Holmes."

"I should hardly be what I am if I did not. Now let us consider this weal which extends round the right shoulder. Do you observe nothing remarkable?"

"I can't say I do."

"Surely it is evident that it is unequal in its intensity. There is a dot of extravasated blood here, and another there. There are similar indications in this other weal down here. What can that mean?" [LION]

Using photographic comparisons to medical case histories, a detective could potentially have identified these characteristic weals of the Lion's Mane. Certainly making the photograph available digitally would make it easier to engage the help of a consulting forensics expert who might be more likely to notice the odd characteristics of the wounds on the victim's back.

Holmes could be dramatic when he chose:

He slipped his key into the lock, and we all very quietly entered the cell. The sleeper half turned, and then settled down once more into a deep slumber. Holmes stooped to the water-jug, moistened his sponge, and then rubbed it twice vigorously across and down the prisoner's face.

"Let me introduce you," he shouted, "to Mr. Neville St. Clair, of Lee, in the county of Kent."

Never in my life have I seen such a sight. The man's face peeled off under the sponge like the bark from a tree. Gone was the coarse brown tint! Gone, too, the horrid scar which had seamed it across, and the twisted lip which had given the repulsive sneer to the face!

. . . "Great heavens!" cried the inspector, "it is, indeed, the missing man. I know him from the photograph." [TWIS]

Had Scotland Yard been using a system of facial identification, the computer could possibly have turned up Mr. Neville St. Clair based on the photograph of the subject: the man with the twisted lip. The similarities in facial characteristics would very probably have been great.

A final example will help to clarify the close relationship between technology and requirements that occurs when you start to use OR approaches. Consider the problem of the Priory School:

"This case grows upon me, Watson," said he. "There are decidedly some points of interest in connection with it. In this early stage, I want you to realize those geographical features which may have a good deal to do with our investigation.

"Look at this map. This dark square is the Priory School. I'll put a pin in it. Now, this line is the main road. You see that it runs east and west past the school, and you see also there is no side road for a mile either way. If these two folk passed away by road it was *this* road."

"Exactly."

"By a singular and happy chance, we are able to some extent to check what passed along this road during the night in question. At this point, where my pipe is now resting, a country constable was on duty from twelve to six. It is, as you perceive, the first cross-road on the east side. This man declares that he was not absent from his post for an instant, and he is positive that neither boy nor man could have gone that way unseen. I have spoken with this policeman to-night, and he appears to me to be a perfectly reliable person. That blocks this end. We have now to deal with the other. There is an inn here, the Red Bull, the landlady of which was ill. She had sent to Mackleton for a doctor, but he did not arrive until morning, being absent at another case. The people at the inn were alert all night, awaiting his coming, and one or other of them seems to have continually had an eye upon the road. They declare that no one passed. If their evidence is good, then we are fortunate enough to be able to block the west, and also to be able to say that the fugitives did *not* use the road at all."

"But the bicycle?" I objected.

"Quite so. We will come to the bicycle presently. To continue our reasoning: if these people did not go by the road, they must have traversed the country to the north of the house or to the south of the house. That is certain. Let us weigh the one against the other. On the south of the house is, as you perceive, a large district of arable land, cut up into small fields, with stone walls between them. There, I admit that a bicycle is impossible. We can dismiss the idea. We turn to the country on the north. Here there lies a grove of trees, marked as the 'Ragged Shaw,' and on the farther side stretches a great rolling moor, Lower Gill Moor, extending for ten miles and sloping gradually upwards. Here, at one side of this wilderness, is Holdernesse Hall, ten miles by road, but only six across the moor. It is a peculiarly desolate plain. A few moor farmers have small holdings, where they rear sheep and cattle. Except these, the plover and the curlew are the only inhabitants until you come to the Chesterfield high road. There is a church there, you see, a few cottages, and an inn. Beyond that the hills become precipitous. Surely it is here to the north that our quest must lie."

"But the bicycle?" I persisted.

"Well, well!" said Holmes impatiently. "A good cyclist does not need a high road. The moor is intersected with paths, and the moon was at the full." [PRIO]

In the midst of a case involving this kind of geography, a detective would find a geographical location database of great use, both as a reference and as a search tool. The Geometry subsystem in Figure 12-5 illustrates one such design.

An element is a point (latitude and longitude), a line (two points), or a polygon. A geometry is a collection of elements that make up a geographical object (the moor, for example, or the two inns). A layer is a collection of related geometries. You could have a land feature layer, a road layer, and a building layer to describe the entire map with which Holmes solved his problem. The GeometryElement class supports all the behavior of the system, including construction of the element (InitElement and AddNodes), validation of the internal characteristics of the element (ValidateGeometry), and searching (Interact and Relate to test whether elements overlap or relate to one another through containment or other relationships).

With this kind of design, you confront a fact of life. Using a specific technology means your database design must use the schema that technology imposes on you. If you are up to the task of writing your own geographical information system (GIS), you can use any design you wish, as long as it works. In this case, Figure 12-5 uses the design from the Oracle8 Spatial Data Cartridge [Oracle 1997a], a technology developed by a third party and integrated into Oracle that uses line and polygon computational geometry to represent and process geographical information. This cartridge is a completely proprietary and unique approach to geographical information systems that is not compatible with other such systems. It indexes geographic elements using a tiling approach called tessellation. Tessellation breaks the space into tiles containing pieces of the geogra-

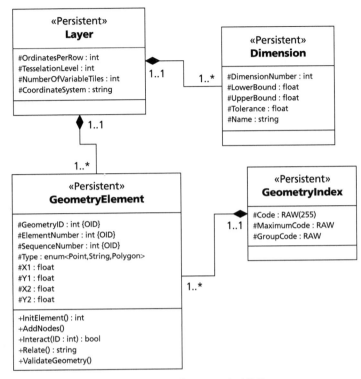

Figure 12-5   *The Geometry Subsystem in UML*

phy down to a fine resolution. Using the data cartridge means installing a number of tables that the system requires to store information that it needs, such as the Layer and Geometry tables. These, then, become the basis for your data model. The technological requirement thus dominates the functional requirement and couples you to a particular solution in your design. This situation wasn't so bad in the Image design in Figure 12-4.

In this case, the design is not what an OO designer would like to see. First, the Spatial Data Cartridge does not use object types or any of the more interesting OR additions to Oracle8. It is a simple transference of the relational implementation of the "Spatial Data Option" to Oracle7. Also, presumably for performance optimization, the designers of the Spatial Data Cartridge have broken most of the design rules.

First, each layer in the system gets a unique set of tables identified by name. That is, if you have a road layer, you have four tables for that layer named Road_SDOLayer, Road_SDODim, Road_SDOGeom, and Road_SDOIndex. This makes the Layer table a singleton table, with the single row describing the layer. There really isn't any reason for a singleton except to avoid a join, and in this case it's far too limiting. Instead, you should have a series of layers identified by ID and Name. The Dimension table is a doubleton, if there is such a thing, with two rows corresponding to the two dimensions that the Spatial Data Cartridge supports. Neither of the two tables contains a primary key because of the singleton approach.

The Geom table is not, as you would think, a geometry table; rather it represents the individual elements that make up a geometry. Worse, the designers used a "repeating groups" pattern that lets you configure the table differently for each layer. One layer could have Geom rows with two coordinates, while another layer could have six. Worse still, an individual element can span objects, with one real geometry element (a polygon) stretching over several rows with multiple coordinate pairs. Standard design techniques would add a real Geometry table to store geometry information, an Element table to store element information, and a Coordinate table to store coordinate pairs. Broadening this a bit, you could support more than two dimensions with a Coordinate class that keeps constant-sized vectors of coordinates. This will be very difficult to do with the current schema.

The Index table contains the tiles for a geometry that the tessellation scheme computes. The table links to the Geometry. Unfortunately, there is no such object in the data model, since the tables don't represent it directly, only in an aggregate form through the multiple-row element table.

This design is really painful to an OO designer. It does, however, have the simple fact of existence. It contributes value to an Oracle8 application developer because it allows that developer to do geographical representation and searching, however inflexibly, without writing the code to do it. Existence, in the reusable software arena, is nine-tenths of the law. The law can be harsh at times.

You thus have a choice between design and reuse. The usual answer to this situation is layering: building packages to contain packages. To make the Spatial Data Cartridge approach more general, you could encapsulate these persistent classes in an emollient layer of abstraction that presents the structure more directly without layers and geometries and elements. You can package common queries. (For example, in a given bounded area, what roads provide exits? Or, how many paths exist between two fixed points in the road layer?) Unless you write a full-scale graphical query system, however, you are likely to decrease the flexibility of the underlying technology a great deal by such layering. Giving consulting technologists access to the spatial database and training in spatial queries using first- and second-order filtering may prove much better when the requirements call for a more flexible style of query. That usually means exposing the underlying technology and therefore making your design more specific to that technology.

You can usually expand the information these designs include with little effort. Unlike a compiled reusable component, the server-based extended types permit you to add your own columns to the tables, or to add your own tables that map to the tables that support the type. In the case of the Spatial Data Cartridge, for example, you can add a Geometry table that has the GeometryID as its primary key. The standard Element and Index tables link to that with foreign keys. You could also create a History table, again for example, that contains records of incidents at that location. This is the equivalent of taking a standard map and sticking pins in the locations where incidents have occurred. The reusable component supplies the map, and you supply the pins.

The problem with this comes from the lack of true OO features in the ORDBMS. Your basic data type is only subject to black-box reuse: that is, you can't change the type, you can only subclass it or add additional classes. Since Oracle8 doesn't have subclassing, that means you can only add classes, and the original type and its behaviors don't know anything about them. You have to add your own behaviors (stored procedures or methods) to the new classes. You can't really leverage the behaviors in the extended type, just use them by reference.

This choice becomes more common with OR schemas than with relational schemas. The OR approach encourages the use of reusable components through extended data types such as the spatial and image types that Oracle8 provides.

Object Diversity—Types

The key advantage to universal servers is their ability to represent a wide variety of data. As is usual in the software marketplace, ORDBMS products also manage to represent that wide variety of data in a wide variety of ways. The real trick to designing an OR database is to take advantage of the right OR structures for your particular problem, choosing among the multitude of possible structures.

Many of the innovations in the ORDBMS world center on the type. In OO design, the type plays a central role. Chapter 7 discussed in detail the different aspects of packages, classes, types, and interfaces, all of which the UML treats as classifiers, a general concept at the center of the design approach and notation.

In a relational database, a type is one of the basic data types you associate with columns, such as NUMERIC, FLOAT, VARCHAR, or TIMESTAMP. There are no structured types of any kind.

> Note: Programmers like to think of tables as the "equivalent" of record types in their programming languages. Unfortunately, SQL as a programming language does not treat tables or rows as types—or at least SQL-92 doesn't, nor should it [Date and Darwen 1998]. Chapter 11 showed you how to transform your class and type definitions into schema tables, but they really aren't the same thing. It's that flexibility that lets you UNION ALL across multiple tables without worrying about the underlying record types, for example,

just the structure of the columns. It's that flexibility that is at the ba-
sis of many of the criticisms of SQL as well [Codd 1990; Date 1986;
Date and Darwen 1998]. SQL-92 is the Basic of database program-
ming languages; SQL3 is shaping up to be the C++ of such lan-
guages, for better or worse.

In OR databases, the situation is completely different. The SQL3 standard, for example, defines several new data types, ranging from the user-defined type (UDT) to the row type:

- *User-defined type:* A type that you define using the CREATE TYPE state-ment that you can use with reference types, in generalization (subtyping) relationships, in returning values from user-defined functions, in the secu-rity system (privileges for using the type), in casting (type conversion) op-erations, and probably most importantly as the basis for defining a table; the distinct UDT refers to a built-in type, while the structured UDT lets you define a complex structure.

- *Row type:* A type that represents the structure of a row of data

- *Reference type:* A "pointer" to a user-defined type, used for referring to a structured type from a single-valued column

- *Collection type:* A multivalued type, currently limited to the ARRAY, a col-lection of items of the same type arranged in a sequence

- *(CLOB):* An implementation-defined storage area for characters that can be very large

- *(NCLOB):* A CLOB that stores multibyte characters as defined by one of the SQL3 character sets

- *(BLOB):* An implementation-defined storage area for binary data that can be very large

There are two kinds of UDTs, the distinct type and the structured type. A *distinct type* is a UDT that refers to a predefined or built-in type as its source. For example, you can define a MONEY UDT that is a distinct type of NUMERIC, for example. A *structured type* is a UDT that contains a user-defined set of data attri-butes rather than referring to a single-valued built-in type.

The SQL3 UDT includes the OO features of encapsulation and inheritance by defining methods for data access. When you refer to a column name in an SQL3 SELECT statement, for example, you are really calling a function that re-turns the column value, not directly referring to the value. The UDT also sup-ports subtyping, which is a major reason for this apparent fiction, as it allows the subtypes to refer to the column values of the supertypes through a well-defined set of functions on the type. These features are still quite controversial in the SQL standards community, and the details may change [Melton 1998].

The ORDBMS vendors implement parts of these standards, but no one vendor comes close to offering the full array of SQL3 types. Informix Dynamic Server is the only vendor to offer inheritance of any kind at this time, for example, and none of the vendors support full encapsulation of table or type attributes. Most vendors now have a full complement of LOB types, as vendors can easily build them and they have no semantic impact on their database languages or access methods (indexes, clusters, and so on).

If the OR world was as orderly as the UML world, you would have no problems constructing an OR schema from a UML data model. Unfortunately, that's not the case. The ORDBMS vendors and the SQL3 standardization effort have developed a complex array of competing structures. There are some common themes that run through all of them, however: object types, large object types, collections, references, and behavior.

User-Defined and Object Types

The user-defined type started life as the more theoretical abstract data type (ADT). Oracle8 has changed the name of the UDT to "object type," a much more euphonious appellation that this chapter will cheerfully adopt. This labeling focuses attention on the contribution of the UDT to OO representation. The key innovation in OR systems is to separate the concept of type from the table rather than trying to redefine the table as a kind of type.

> *Warning: It is very dangerous to attach any real meaning to terms such as "ADT" or "object type" when in the presence of a database theorist [Date and Darwen 1998]. Serious damage is likely to result, either to the theorist from apoplexy or to you from the resultant explosion. Treat these terms as operationally defined by the products that use them, not as theoretical concepts.*

In the SQL3 world, a type is a description of data. The type tells you what the data means, such as that a character string is a sequence of characters defined by a character set with an order defined by the collation of the character set, or that a timestamp with time zone has characteristics defined by timekeeping standards. The type also has a set of operations (arithmetic operations, string operations, date operations, for example). Finally, the type tells you what kinds of values you may compare or convert to what other kinds of values. With an object type, the semantics and operations are totally up to you; the comparison, however, requires that the types be related. You can compare two objects only if they are of the same base type (have the same superclass at some level in the class hierarchy). You can define conversions between types that don't meet this strong typing convention, usually as operators on the object type.

The section in Chapter 7 on "Domain Constraints" discusses the use of the UML type classifier. The UML defines the semantics of the data type this way:

> A *data type* is a type whose values have no identity, i.e. they are pure values. Data types include primitive built-in types (such as integer and string) as well as definable enumeration types (such as the predefined enumeration type boolean whose literals are false and true). [Rational Software 1997b, p. 22]

There are three subclasses of the DataType classifier in the UML metamodel: Primitive, Structure, and Enumeration. These are stereotypes you can use to qualify the classifier (class box) that you set up to represent the type and its operations. If you define classifiers with the «type», «primitive», «structure», or «enumeration» stereotypes, you convert these classifiers to distinct types in your ODBMS.

Class and interface classifiers in UML static structure diagrams correspond to the structured type. In relational systems (Chapter 11), you convert classes into tables and interfaces into stored procedures of some kind (if at all). In OR systems, you can translate all classes and interfaces into structured types through the CREATE TYPE statement.

> *Note: You don't actually need to translate all classes into types, just those you intend to use as types in SQL statements. You use a class as a type when it is the target of an association (a foreign key, reference to an object, or nested table in the ORDBMS), when you make it the parent of another class, or when you define multiple tables based on the type. In most systems, that covers just about all the classes. You may have some classes that you just use as lookups or that have some other reason for being completely isolated in the system; singleton objects are an example of this. Adding the complexity of having some tables without types may complicate your life unnecessarily, however, especially as you extend your system.*

To illustrate the varieties of OR object types, consider these versions of the concept:

- SQL3 user-defined type
- Oracle8 object type
- DB2 UDB distinct type (similar to SQL3 and Informix Dynamic Server distinct type)

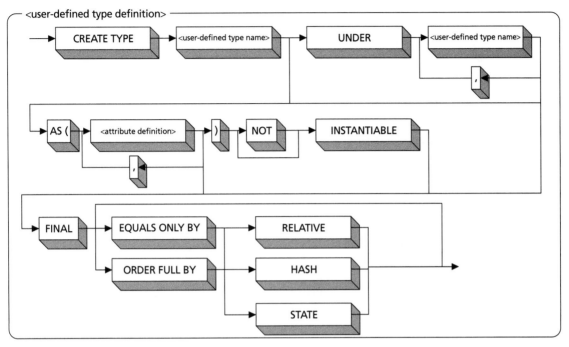

Figure 12-6   *The SQL3 CREATE TYPE Syntax*

The SQL3 UDT

The user-defined type from the pending SQL3 standard is the most complete definition of an object type. It also doesn't exist in any of the major ORDBMS products. Figure 12-6 shows the syntax of the SQL3 CREATE TYPE statement that creates a structured UDT.

> *Note: The complete syntax of the SQL3 CREATE TYPE statement con-*
> *tains several more options, particularly those that let you define a*
> *distinct type, including the cast operators.*

The UNDER clause identifies the superclasses of the type you're defining in a comma-separated list of type names. You thus convert UML generalizations to other classes into type names in the UNDER clause list.

The AS clause defines all the attributes of the class. If you don't have an AS clause, you must have an UNDER clause that identifies attributes from the superclass. You translate the attributes from a UML class directly into attribute definitions in the AS clause using the same transformations you would use to produce column definitions in a relational table.

> *Note: That is, except for the constraints. The type defines attributes, but it does not define their connections to other types, nor does it define their primary key or business rules (CHECK constraints). You must place those constraints directly on the tables you create using the type with the CREATE TABLE statement. That means that in the OR model, you do not have a complete design implementation until you create both the types and the tables that instantiate those types. Unfortunately, the SQL3 syntax seems ambiguous on the constraints you can place on a table you construct from a structured type.*

If the UML class is an abstract class, specify NOT INSTANTIABLE. Otherwise, specify INSTANTIABLE. In the SQL3 database, you can create rows in tables of the type only if the type is INSTANTIABLE. The NOT FINAL clause, which the standard requires for structured UDTs, doesn't have any semantics in the standard, so I'm not sure what purpose it serves.

The final clause specifies an ordering method for objects of the type. The EQUALS ONLY clause limits ordering comparisons to equality comparisons, while ORDER FULL lets you define a complete order for the extension of the type. The RELATIVE and HASH ordering methods use relational comparison (greater than or less than) or hashing to order elements using functions that you supply as stored functions. The STATE option is valid only for EQUALS ONLY comparisons and does the equality comparison based on the attributes of the type. You may be able to specify equivalents in your UML operations list for the class and transform them into stored functions, if that makes sense in your context.

> *Note: The syntax and semantics of the CREATE TYPE statement are among the most contentious issues still to be resolved in the SQL3 standardization process [Melton 1998]. You can probably count on changes here.*

The Oracle8 Object Type

The object type in Oracle8 is at the heart of the object extensions to the relational Oracle database. Object types serve as the basis for nested tables, let you reference objects in other tables, and provide well-defined ways to integrate behavior with table rows. They do have two major limitations from the OO perspective: a complete lack of any form of inheritance and a complete lack of encapsulation. These limitations make them much harder to use from the UML perspective, but at least they provide a structured type and object identity you can use creatively in your Oracle8 applications. Figure 12-7 shows the syntax of the Oracle8 CREATE TYPE statement that creates an object type.

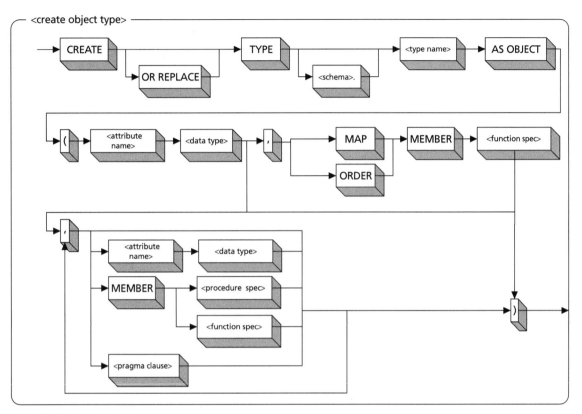

Figure 12-7   *The Oracle8 CREATE TYPE Syntax*

The Oracle8 CREATE TYPE statement has a type name in it, but other than that, bears little resemblance to the SQL3 statement. This syntax is one of the three variations in Oracle8, which also include creating a VARRAY type (see the later "Collections" section) and a nested table type. The syntax in Figure 12-7 creates an Oracle8 object type, which you can then use to create tables of those objects. The CREATE TYPE statement contains a list of members. You can supply either a MAP or ORDER member to support indexing and sorting. If you don't supply one or the other, you can only do equality comparisons. This corresponds to the ORDER FULL and EQUALS ONLY syntax in SQL3. You must supply at least one data attribute with a type, and optionally more data attributes and types. You can also supply a series of member subprogram (function or procedure) declarations that represent the operations of the object type. There is a separate CREATE TYPE BODY statement that separates the implementation of the operation from its declaration in the CREATE TYPE statement. The PRAGMA clause lets you restrict side effects on database and PL/SQL package state in the methods, a requirement to use the methods in SQL statements.

The Oracle8 type thus supports easy transformation of several of the UML constructs in ways that the SQL3 type does not. Each class in your UML static structure diagram transforms to an object type, and each attribute and data type to an object type attribute and data type.

Although you can't refer directly to an object type for an attribute, you can define a REF to such a type (see the later section on "References"). That means that you can define to-one associations as attributes of the object type, with 0..1 multiplicity transforming to a REF type that allows nulls and 1..1 or just 1 being NOT NULL. Since one kind of object type is a VARRAY, you can also define an attribute with a VARRAY of REFs to another object type to handle to-many multiplicities. Similarly, you can define an object type for a nested table. If you have a composite aggregation association, you can define a nested table object type for the child class, then include a REF to that object type to nest the data within each row of tables based on your parent object type.

> *Warning: For several reasons, I don't recommend using nested tables or VARRAYs of anything but REF to another type. First, using these features leads to the sort of normalization problems that we've known about for almost 30 years. I don't see any pressing need to forget the basics of database design to go back to the days of hierarchical database management and all its complexity. Second, OO design reduces complexity by encapsulation. Oracle8 nested tables and VARRAYs do precisely the reverse by exposing all the structure and making your life difficult with new and more complex SQL syntax (the THE function, if you want to look it up).*

Operations map to member subprograms and the method implementations of operations to member subprogram bodies in the CREATE TYPE BODY statement. If an operation has a {readonly} tag, or if it has a {query} tag, you can add a PRAGMA clause that restricts references using the WNDS, WNPS, and RNPS purity levels (write no database state, write no package state, and read no package state, respectively). Specifying WNDS lets you use the function as an SQL function.

> *Note: The actual meaning and use of Oracle purity levels is complex. If you intend to make extensive use of purity levels in your schema, either with object types or with PL/SQL packages, you should consult the Oracle8 Application Developer's Guide [Oracle 1997c] for its discussion of the ins and outs of side effect restrictions in PL/SQL.*

As an example of creating an object type and using it, consider the Image example in Figure 12-4. Oracle8 provides this class through its Visual Information Cartridge. However, if you wanted to develop your own object types, you could create an Image object type to facilitate your representation and processing:

```
CREATE OR REPLACE TYPE Image AS OBJECT (
  ImageID NUMBER,
  Height NUMBER,
  Width NUMBER,
  ContentLength NUMBER,
  FileFormat VARCHAR2(64),
  ContentFormat VARCHAR2(64),
  CompressionFormat VARCHAR2(64),
  Content BLOB,
  ImageSignature RAW(2000),
  MEMBER PROCEDURE copyContent (destination IN OUT Image),
  PRAGMA RESTRICT_REFERENCES (copyContent, WNDS),
  MEMBER PROCEDURE setProperties (SELF IN OUT Image),
  PRAGMA RESTRICT_REFERENCES (setProperties, WNDS),
  MEMBER PROCEDURE process (SELF IN OUT Image,
  command IN VARCHAR2),
  PRAGMA RESTRICT_REFERENCES (process, WNDS),
  MEMBER PROCEDURE processCopy (command IN VARCHAR2,
  destination IN OUT BLOB),
  PRAGMA RESTRICT_REFERENCES (processCopy, WNDS)
);
```

The SELF argument is an explicit declaration of the current object as the first argument to each method. If you don't supply this, Oracle8 assumes a parameter type of IN (read only). So, for example, the first member procedure, copyContent, gives read access to the current Image object, while the second procedure, setProperties, gives both read and write access to it.

You can now set up tables of images, and you can refer to images from other tables:

```
CREATE TABLE CrimeSceneImages OF Image (
  ImageID PRIMARY KEY);
CREATE TYPE ImageArray AS VARYING ARRAY (50) OF REF Image;
CREATE TABLE CrimeScene (
  SceneID NUMBER PRIMARY KEY,
  Description VARCHAR2(2000) NOT NULL,
  Images ImageArray
);
```

> *Note: The CREATE TABLE statement based on the Image type contains the primary key declaration. You can add a constraint for each of the attributes you've defined in the type, and you can add table constraints that involve more than one attribute.*

Depending on how you intend to access the images, you may find it better to create the set of image references in a separate table, which permits indexing and joining. The varying array permits only navigation to the specific image through program loops or (very ornate) SQL statements. You may also want to consider a nested table structure, with or without indexes. This can lead to very complicated maintenance and SQL statement access, especially if you wind up storing images in more than one nested table.

This example leads to a major point about Oracle8 and its OR friends: you truly have an enormous array of choices to make when you use these systems. You can create structures in a bewildering variety of forms, each of which has advantages and disadvantages. If you intend to target an ORDBMS as your object repository, you should count on a steep learning curve as you acquire the knowledge of what works and what doesn't. This is complicated by the lack of standards, of course.

You may have noticed one big difference between the SQL3 CREATE TYPE statement and the Oracle8 object type creation statement: you cannot use the latter to create a distinct type, just a structured type. Again, a distinct type is a type you derive from one of the built-in SQL types. SQL then enforces strong typing, which increases your assurance that you're using the right kind of data in your SQL statements. The consequence, as far as transforming UML static structure diagrams is concerned, is that if your target is Oracle8, you cannot translate your «type» classifiers directly into distinct types. Instead, you must use a transformation table just as in the relational system (see Chapter 11). Distinct types can do more for you, however, as their use in the DB2 UDB product shows.

The UDB Distinct Type

DB2 UDB provides no structured types, but it does include the concept of distinct types with the syntax in Figure 12-8.

The UDB CREATE TYPE statement is thus much simpler than the SQL3 or Oracle8 statements. All it needs to do is to name the new type, relate the name to the source built-in type, and optionally specify the inclusion of default comparison operators ($=$, $<$, $<=$, $>$, $>,=$ and $<>$). If you leave off WITH COMPARISONS, you cannot compare the values of the type.

A key use of distinct types in UDB is to encapsulate LOBs as distinct types [Chamberlin 1998]. For example, to provide the Image class from Figure 12-4 in a relational table, you would create a BLOB column:

```
CREATE TABLE Image (
  ImageID INTEGER PRIMARY KEY,
  Height INTEGER,
```

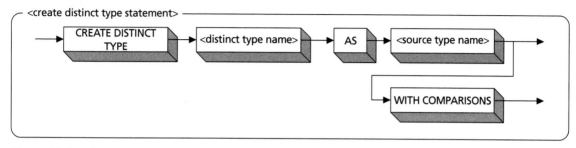

Figure 12-8   *The UDB CREATE DISTINCT TYPE Syntax*

```
Width INTEGER,
ContentLength INTEGER,
FileFormat VARCHAR(64),
ContentFormat VARCHAR(64),
CompressionFormat VARCHAR(64),
Content BLOB(2M),
ImageSignature BLOB(2000))
```

This is fine as far as it goes, but there is no way to tell an SQL statement that the Content column contains an image or that the Signature column contains a signature. To achieve this effect, you can use distinct types:

```
CREATE DISTINCT TYPE Image AS BLOB(2M);
CREATE DISTINCT TYPE Signature AS BLOB(2000);
CREATE TABLE Image (
  ImageID INTEGER PRIMARY KEY,
  Height INTEGER,
  Width INTEGER,
  ContentLength INTEGER,
  FileFormat VARCHAR(64),
  ContentFormat VARCHAR(64),
  CompressionFormat VARCHAR(64),
  Content Image,
  ImageSignature Signature)
```

The two distinct types define specific varieties of BLOBs as Image and Signature types, and the CREATE TABLE statement then uses those types to declare the columns. Now when you refer to those columns, UDB SQL will treat them as special types and will not allow you to assign them or to call functions on them. You can then define external functions in a programming language that accepts arguments of the distinct type. For example, you can define the CopyContent, Analyze, and Similar functions as C functions and declare them as UDB functions taking arguments of Image and/or Signature. You can then call them on any given Image or Signature, being assured that the data is of the correct type.

Associations

Creating associations in an OR system is difficult, not because of the lack of technology, but because of too many choices. You can stick with the tried and true techniques of Chapter 11 using foreign keys, or you can venture into the OR world of object types, references, and collections. My own preference is to use the OR features only where they make obvious sense and directly and easily implement the object structure in the UML design.

> *Warning: As always, what is obvious to one person may be opaque to another; I am expressing opinions, not facts.*

First, you need to understand the concepts of the object attribute, reference, and collection types to make sense of these new ways of associating objects. You can also still have foreign keys, but you have to declare them in tables, not in the object types.

Object Attributes

An *object attribute* is an attribute of an object type that is itself an object instead of a value with a built-in data type such as NUMBER or VARCHAR. If you're confused after reading that sentence, I'm not surprised. Take it piece by piece. In relational tables, you have columns that you declare with built-in data types such as NUMBER, CHARACTER VARYING, or LONG. Values in such columns are indeed *values:* they have no separate identity outside the row they are in. Objects always have identity as separate, individual things. When, in an OR system, you create an attribute with a user-defined or object type, you are creating the possibility of an object embedded within a table, each row of which constitutes yet another object with identity. In a UML diagram, this is an association with a 1..1 or 0..1 multiplicity to the class that represents the embedded object.

For example, in Figure 12-1, the Identification class associates with the Person class with a 1..1 multiplicity: every identification identifies precisely one person. In Oracle8, for example, you can create an object type for Identification that embeds a single Person object. Once you are looking at the Identification object, you also know the Person object that the Identification identifies. But this isn't a very good example for the embedded object, since a Person has more than one identification. The embedded object, or object attribute, is a clear example of composite aggregation, where the object owns the embedded object. But in the case of Identification, the ownership is the other way around: a Person owns several Identifications.

Given this logic, you should use object attributes or embedded objects only when you have an association that is a composite aggregation with the 1..1 multiplicity on the side of the aggregated object rather than the aggregating object. This is reasonably rare in practice, as most composite aggregations are master-detail relationships with multiple details for each master. It only occurs when there is a one-to-one mapping or an even rarer one-to-many with aggregation on the one side (one detail to many masters with the master owning each detail, and if you can figure out what this means semantically, you're welcome to it).

References

A *reference* is a logical pointer to an object you store somewhere other than in the current table. The "pointer" in this case is the object identifier, or OID. The ORDBMS constructs an OID for each object of a structured type you create. You can then refer to the object by putting the OID into a column value in the referring table. The reference is a way to break the strong ownership model, meaning that the attribute no longer implies a composite aggregation association but rather a simple association to a single object. This arrangement is much more common in practice than embedded objects.

You thus have the choice in an ORDBMS of representing associations as either foreign keys or as references. If you use foreign keys, you must join the tables in your queries. If you use references, you can navigate to the referenced object through SQL expressions, avoiding the join. There are a couple of other issues with references: scope and dangling references.

Both the SQL3 standard and Oracle8 provide a mechanism that scopes a reference to a particular table or tables. Each object type may be the genesis of several tables. If you refer to an object of the type, by default there is no constraint on what table may store the object to which you are referring. Adding the scope qualifier to the reference lets you specify a list of tables. When you insert a new row with a reference or update the reference, that reference must refer to an object of the appropriate type in one of the tables you've specified as the scope of the reference.

There is a bit of a problem with references, however. As implemented by the various ORDBMS products, and as specified in the SQL3 standard, references do not enforce referential integrity. If you delete an object, any references to it remain just as they are. Also, you cannot constrain operations such as DELETE to fail if there are outstanding references to an object. If you use references, you should encapsulate the objects to which they refer within a set of operations that maintain the references. You can do this through triggers on the referenced tables, or you can use a stored-procedure encapsulation scheme to deny direct access to tables, as Chapter 11 outlines.

Given the referential integrity problems, you should use references as a performance optimization only. Your usual course with associations should be to establish foreign keys. If the join performance of the tables is poor for some reason, consider using references instead, but realize that you will then need additional code to maintain referential integrity.

> *Note: C. J. Date discusses the concepts behind references (he calls them "pointers") extensively and decisively rejects them as incompatible with the relational model [Date and Darwen 1998].*

Collections

Thus far, the discussion has focused on the to-one side of associations. What about the many?

A *collection* is a multivalued attribute of some kind, such as an array, a set, or a table. SQL3 provides the ARRAY as the only kind of collection. Oracle8 provides the VARYING ARRAY and the nested table. Informix provides the SET, MULTISET, and LIST. The objective of all of these types is to collect several objects into a single column value. This is just what you need to represent the * multiplicity side of an association. Or is it?

Take the Person-Identification association in Figure 12-1, for example. Each person has some number of identification documents. This is a composite aggregation association, so we should be able to get away with storing the Identification objects as part of the Person object to which they belong, as they do not share the objects.

As a varying array in Oracle8, the identification documents would be part of an array-typed column of the Person table. One limitation occurs right away: you must specify a limit on the number of elements in the array when you create the array type. In the original UML diagram, the multiplicity is 0..*, meaning there is no limit. You could replace the * with 20, say, to accommodate the implementation limitation. Your type would look like this:

```
CREATE TYPE IdentificationDocuments_t
  AS VARYING ARRAY (20) OF Identification;
CREATE TYPE Person_t AS OBJECT (
  PersonID INTEGER,
  . . . ,
  IDs IdentificationDocuments);
```

If the multiplicity were 1..20, you would need to qualify the IDs attribute when you create the table with a NOT NULL constraint and perhaps a CHECK constraint that the size of the array must be >= 1. Notice that there is a difference between a null array and an array with no elements (an empty array). In the first case, the column value is entirely null; in the second case, the row has storage for the VARRAY but there are no elements in the array. This distinction can complicate your programming slightly.

For associations that are not composite aggregations, varying arrays of references are a better choice. For example, each person can have some number of addresses (Figure 12-1). On the person side, you could represent this as a varying array of references to Address objects. Again, references do not enforce referential integrity, so if a house burns down or somebody goes to jail, you have to clean up the references in your application code or in triggers.

You might also have noticed in this last example that, although the collection represents the person side of the association, it doesn't do a thing for the address side. To take care of that, you need to create another collection, this time as an attribute of Address, that keeps references to Person objects. Your application code or triggers will need to ensure that these two collections stay synchronized.

Given these limitations of the association as collection, you should use this technique only for one-way associations (associations with an arrowhead showing one-way visibility with no need to maintain both sides of the association). This makes navigation slightly less flexible but improves your code maintainability dramatically.

Finally, consider the ternary, many-to-many association, such as the Plays association in Figure 12-1. A Person plays a Role in a CriminalOrganization. Could you use a collection to represent this association?

In a word, no. Each element of the varying array must be a single object of another type. You can have an array of people in the criminal organization, but you can't bring their roles with them. You can create a type for Plays, giving it references to the three other kinds of objects, then create an array for the Plays objects in each of the three other types. Because of dangling references and presumably other internal issues, Oracle8 (for one) does not permit you to create a primary key on a reference, so the tables of references would have no way to enforce uniqueness constraints on the association links—a major headache.

To sum up, then, if you have a composite aggregation association, you can consider a collection as its representation. If you have a one-way, to-many association, you might consider an array of references as its representation. For referential integrity reasons, however, you should consider this an option only to improve performance when needed. Finally, using collections in other association situations is not advisable.

Behavior

In relational databases, you transform operations into stored procedures or triggers as appropriate. Of course, these elements are completely nonstandard, so there is no portable way to represent behavior in relational systems.

Object-relational databases vary this theme only slightly by providing some additional ways to attach behavior to objects. The behavioral elements are still completely nonstandard, leaving you with the unsatisfying choice between lack of portability and an inability to have your behavior where it belongs on the database server. Once you move to an ORDBMS, you have to commit yourself to nonstandard solutions with respect to behavior. For example, although Oracle8 adds methods to the object type, the SQL3 standard does not. What it does do is to define the operations on the structured type in terms of functions that the system generates, such as get and set functions (observers and mutators, in the language of the standard) corresponding to the attributes of the type, constructors, and casting functions.

> *Note: For a somewhat different logical model of this area, consult Date's book [Date and Darwen 1998, pp. 104-122]. Date's model places constructors, observers, and mutators in a much different position relative to the underlying types. The constructor, which Date calls a "selector," selects existing data rather than allocating storage. Date defines THE_ operators that act as pseudovariables to provide both retrieval and updating of the possible representations of his types. You can use nested operator calls to navigate through complex representations, for example, instead of using dot notation on the attribute names. All these operators are globally scoped, not tied directly to the type. This approach has some benefits, logical and practical, but you must adopt the entire RM model to realize them, and I doubt any of the major vendors will do that in the near future.*

If you are using Oracle8, you can create all the operations on your UML classes as methods on your object type. As previously mentioned, each operation has an implicit, read-only SELF parameter that you can use as a reference to the current object. If you want to change the current object, you have to declare SELF as IN OUT in the method parameter list. You should create such methods only for operations that make sense as database server operations. Operations that work on in-memory objects are not candidates for transformation to the server side.

Who Makes the Rules?

With respect to business rules, there is very little difference between a relational system and an object-relational system. You use the same constraints, the same assertions, and the same kind of procedural code to enforce the rules.

One difference is the presence of the object or structured type versus the tables you build with such types. Types do not have constraints, only tables have constraints. Therefore, if you build multiple tables for a given type, you must constrain both tables separately. You must have separate foreign key declarations, separate check constraints, and so on.

> *Note: The logic of how constraints apply to data is somewhat con-*
> *fused in SQL3. As Date points out, there is no way in SQL3 to add a*
> *type constraint—a constraint that applies to a type definition rather*
> *than to the underlying relations or values that use it [Date and*
> *Darwen 1998, pp. 159–168, 389–390]. This will condemn SQL3 pro-*
> *grammers to years of maintaining multiple CHECK constraints and*
> *value lookup tables that should go away with a decent typing*
> *system.*

The Language of War

It would be nice to have a cut-and-dried, easily understood way to produce an effective object-relational schema. Until there is a standard, that is unlikely to happen, and as mentioned earlier, the standard is having real problems [Melton 1998]. Worse, those problems center on the precise parts of the standard with which this book is most concerned, the object features.

This section nevertheless tries to summarize how you can best go about creating an object-relational schema, focusing not on the relatively impractical SQL3 standard but on the very practical Oracle8 feature set. The structure and language of this section mirrors the similar section in Chapter 11, "The Language of Peace." It thus includes the relational techniques for transforming a schema, modified by the object-relational possibilities that the prior sections of this chapter have discussed. You should consult Chapter 11 for examples and details on the relational transformations; this section focuses on the object-relational additions to the transformation process. The transformation process uses the example data model from Figures 12-1 through 12-5. It uses Oracle8 OR syntax rather than SQL3 because there is no product that implements the SQL3 standard at this time.

Just as with the relational schema, you create an object-relational schema in two basic steps: creating types and tables from persistent types, and creating tables for many-to-many and ternary associations. This section guides you through a complete transformation, connecting everything previously discussed into a transformational whole. Conformity, in this case, is in the eye of the beholder. You can think about the SQL-92 requirements, with which SQL3 is compatible, while you are deciding which OR extensions to use to best advantage. Conforming with those features is not possible at the moment, but you should give some attention to the forthcoming SQL3 standard and its way of looking at these features.

Persistent Classes

Before starting the transformation process, you will have already identified the classes that correspond to object-relational extensions in your target ORDBMS. Figures 12-4 and 12-5, which respectively show the Image and Geography subsystems for the commonplace book system, directly correspond to Oracle8 cartridges that extend the Oracle8 RDBMS. The first task is to build the object types, tables, and other elements that the extension requires to do its job.

> *Note: Again, I use an Oracle8 example because I'm most familiar with that system. Informix DataBlades and DB2 UDB table types with their external C programs provide similar features and have similar problems with design and reuse. I would not like to see teachers using any of these technologies as examples of how to go about designing modern software systems to budding computer scientists and software engineers.*

In the case of the Image class, the basic image type already exists in Oracle8 as the ORDSYS.ORDVIRB object type. All you need to do in this case is use that type as an attribute type in the classes that encapsulate image data. In this case, the type is really more of an interface, though it does include the data attributes that represent the image. Instead of treating the ORDSYS.ORDVIRB type as a root class for the image class hierarchy, it is probably better to create a new Image class with an internal attribute of the ORDSYS.ORDVIRB type:

```
CREATE TYPE Image_t AS OBJECT (
  ImageData ORDSYS.ORDVIRB;
);
```

You could add methods to pass through the behavior on the Image class in Figure 12-4. Alternatively, you could design an interface for the Image object type that is more useful for your particular needs. Then you could implement the operations with the underlying ORDSYS.ORDVIRB methods.

The Geometry class is more complex, given its somewhat difficult design. Oracle8 provides a couple of SQL scripts that you run in SQL*Plus or another SQL command tool. The crlayer.sql script creates the various layer tables for a particular layer, naming the tables with the layer name. These tables would correspond to subclasses of the base types in Figure 12-5. Because there is no automatic updating of superclasses in Oracle8, it is probably counterproductive to create tables for the abstract superclasses in Figure 12-5. The subclass tables that crlayer.sql creates lack primary key and foreign key capabilities, making it very difficult to integrate them into an OO design. The Geometry example is a clear case of a legacy system that you want to reuse. As with any legacy system, you have the choice of exposing the legacy design or encapsulating it in your own classes. In this case, if you decide to encapsulate, you should add a facade layer that presents the Geometry interface that fits your requirements. You then implement this interface with the underlying Oracle8 Spatial Cartridge tables, preferably in a way that makes them completely invisible to application programmers developing against your schema.

As the first transformation, create an object or structured type for each class in your UML data model that has the «persistent» stereotype, including association classes and classes that inherit from other classes. Name the type with the name of the class, adding a suffix of "_t" to indicate that the object is a type. This lets you create a table based on the type using the name of the class, as most ORDBMS products place types and tables in the same name space, thus requiring unique names. From Figure 12-1, the Person subsystem, you create 10 object types: Person_t, Address_t, Identification_t, Expiring_ID_t, Driver_License_t, Passport_t, National_ID_t, Law_Enforcement_ID_t, Social_Security_Card_t, and Birth_Certificate_t.

> *Note: You may merge the association class into another type later if that proves feasible. For now, leave it as a separate type in your emerging schema.*

Within each type, now add an object attribute for each attribute in the attribute section of the class. As an example, for Address_t, add StreetNumber, StreetFraction, StreetName, StreetSuffix, Locator, City, State, PostalCode, Country, and Comment.

You should at this point have a transformation map that shows how to transform each data type in your data model into an SQL3 data type. These data types consist of the built-in types, including BLOBs, CLOBS, and so on; distinct types you derive from those built-in types; and user-defined types or object types, including references to those types.

Now you come to your first OR choice, other than using the type instead of creating a table for each class. If your object identity is implicit, you now need to decide whether to use the built-in object identity of the ORDBMS to represent identity or to create a primary key attribute as in a relational schema. The primary key attribute lets you specify referential integrity constraints. If you are going to have any foreign keys directed at the type, you must have a primary key attribute. If, on the other hand, you intend to use object references instead of foreign keys, you can dispense with the primary key attribute. Of course, by doing this, you also dispense with the ability to join to the table based on a primary key match, a critical relational feature. On balance, I believe you should always add a primary key attribute to preserve flexibility in the schema design and to make it easier to adopt relational referential integrity where it is advisable. Name the primary key column with the class name suffixed with ID, such as AddressID, Usually, you should give the column a NUMBER data type and use a sequence or the equivalent to generate numbers for it.

The end result for this stage for the Address_t type looks like this:

```
CREATE TYPE Address_t AS OBJECT (
  AddressID INTEGER,
  StreetNumber NUMBER,
  StreetFraction VARCHAR(5),
  StreetName VARCHAR(100),
  StreetSuffix VARCHAR(25),
  City VARCHAR(100),
  State CHAR(2),
  PostalCode CHAR(20),
  Country VARCHAR(100),
  Comment VARCHAR(250));
```

> *Note: There are no constraints on the attributes. You constrain tables, not types, in an ORDBMS. In SQL3, you can have a DEFAULT clause that corresponds to the UML initial value, and that's it. Oracle8 is much the same. See the section "Who Makes the Rules?" in this chapter for details.*

You now have a set of types related only by the use of types in attribute declarations, if any. Now you need to create tables based on those types and add constraints. For each type, create at least one table. If there is a reason to partition the objects of a given type into two or more collections, create additional tables with different names. I generally regard this as a physical schema design issue, not a logical one.w

If there is a {nullable} tag on the attribute, add a null constraint; otherwise, add a NOT NULL constraint. In the case of the commonplace book, the data model uses the nullable types to represent null constraints, and all of the columns in Address_t except for StreetFraction and Comment are NOT NULL:

```
CREATE TABLE Address OF Address_t (
  AddressID PRIMARY KEY,—OID type
  StreetNumber NOT NULL,
  StreetName NOT NULL,
  StreetSuffix NOT NULL,
  City NOT NULL,
  State NOT NULL,
  PostalCode NOT NULL,
  Country NOT NULL);
```

You still need to create type-checking utility tables for enumerated types in an ORDBMS, as their typing system still does not include this kind of type (see the previous section in this chapter, "Who Makes the Rules?").

Now it's time to construct the primary key constraint and the things that depend on it. To start with, find the root class of each generalization hierarchy (classes to which a generalization arrow points but from which no generalization arrow emerges). Also consider all classes with no generalization relationships.

If the class has implicit object identity, you will have already made a choice about whether to include a primary key attribute. If you chose to add one, add PRIMARY KEY as a constraint to that column in the CREATE TABLE statement. PRIMARY KEY implies NOT NULL, so you don't need that constraint on the primary key column.

> *Note: If the class has a composite aggregation association to another class, and the other class is the aggregating class, hold off on creating the primary key until you are creating foreign keys. Composite aggregation keys are a combination of the primary key of the related class and another attribute. As well, you may decide to represent the composite aggregation association with a varying array or other collection instead of a foreign key.*

If the class has explicit object identity (an {OID} tag), add a PRIMARY KEY constraint clause to the tables you've created from the type and put all columns with the {OID} tag into the constraint. If there is only one column in the explicit identifier, just add the PRIMARY KEY column constraint to that column.

If the class has subclasses, add an attribute to the type to represent the discriminator. Create a CHECK constraint in the tables you create from the type with the appropriate enumerated values to represent the subclasses. If your ORDBMS supports inheritance (Informix Universal Server, for example, supports inheritance either through its ROW TYPE hierarchies or through table inheritance for tables based on those row types, and SQL3 supports inheritance directly with the UNDER clause in CREATE TYPE), use the appropriate syntax to link the types. Otherwise, you need to use the same primary key method that Chapter 11 recommended.

> *Note: I agree with Date that inheritance is a type feature, not a table feature [Date and Darwen 1998, pp. 373–378]. You should avoid using the Informix table inheritance features, as they will add nothing but confusion to your model-schema relationships.*

In SQL3, for example, you can create the LawEnforcementID class as a type, adding the BadgeNumber attribute to the attributes and behavior of the Identification abstract class:

```
CREATE TYPE LawEnforcementID_t UNDER Identification_t (
  BadgeNumber INTEGER);
```

If there are multiple superclasses (multiple inheritance), you have to fall back on the schemes of Chapter 11 for dealing with multiple superclasses. SQL3 lets you define multiple superclasses in the UNDER clause, but the semantics of the standard are very weak and don't address even basic problems such as duplicate attribute names in different superclasses. This should either prevent the definition of the ambiguous subclass or should involve the kind of complex ambiguity resolution mechanisms that languages such as C++ implement [Stonebraker and Brown 1999]. Again, your best bet is to avoid multiple inheritance if you can. The lack of support for it in your chosen DBMS may make this choice for you.

Association classes represent associations with attributes, many-to-many associations, and *n*-ary associations that link two or more classes together. The association class transforms into a table that contains the primary keys of all its related classes. You can create an object type that contains the key and other attributes, then define a table based on it, though this doesn't buy you much. Compare the object type Plays_t with the Plays table that Chapter 11 defines:

```
CREATE TYPE Plays_t AS OBJECT (
  PersonID INTEGER,
  OrganizationID INTEGER,
  RoleID INTEGER,
  Tenure INTEGER,—Oracle8 doesn't have interval types
  StartDate DATE,
  EndDate DATE,
  TerminationMethod CHAR(1));
CREATE TABLE Plays OF Plays_t (
  PRIMARY KEY (PersonID, OrganizationID, RoleID),
  PersonID REFERENCES Person,
  OrganizationID REFERENCES Organization,
  RoleID REFERENCES Role,
  Tenure NOT NULL,
  StartDate NOT NULL);

—Here is the relational table for comparison
CREATE TABLE Plays (
  PersonID INTEGER REFERENCES Person,
  OrganizationID INTEGER REFERENCES Organization,
  RoleID INTEGER REFERENCES Role,
  Tenure INTEGER NOT NULL,—Oracle doesn't have interval types
  StartDate DATE NOT NULL,
  EndDate DATE,
```

```
TerminationMethod CHAR(1),
PRIMARY KEY (PersonID, OrganizationID, RoleID));
```

If you choose the type approach, you gain the ability to create more than one table to contain link objects, which may or may not be valuable. Most systems see these associations as unique; if split between tables, the primary key can't enforce that uniqueness. You should choose the type approach only if you have a real need to have two or more tables of links with the same structure and the same linked classes.

Next, find any candidate keys. If there are any {alternate OID = <n>} tags, add a UNIQUE constraint to the tables you've created from types for each unique <n> identifier and put all columns with the same <n> identifier into the constraint. Again, LawEnforcementID serves as an example, as BadgeNumber has the tag {alternate OID = 1}:

```
CREATE TABLE LawEnforcementID OF LawEnforcementID_t (
  BadgeNumber NOT NULL UNIQUE);
```

Next step: add any simple table constraints to the tables you've created from types. If there are constraint boxes in the diagram, convert them into CHECK clauses if you can express the constraint in an SQL expression that contains only references to columns in the table you are defining. If there are data type constraints such as enumerations or ranges, add a CHECK clause to the column to represent the constraint. Again, all of these constraints are on tables, not types. For enumerations with utility tables that list the possible values in the type, wait for creating the associations, the next step.

At this point, all tables should have a primary key. Find the binary associations to the class you are defining with a multiplicity of 0..1 or 1..1 on the role attached to the other class. If the association has an association class, ignore the association for now. To represent the to-one association direction, you either create an attribute to represent the association as a foreign key or create a reference to the other class. If you create the foreign key, you need to create the appropriate constraints (REFERENCES or FOREIGN KEY) in the tables you base on the type. If you create the reference, you need to add the code to maintain the reference in the face of object deletion or other referential integrity issues.

As you go through the tables, of course, you will reach the other end of each binary association. If it's a 1..1 or 0..1 association, and you've already created an attribute for it in another table, don't create the foreign key or reference in both types. Creating two foreign keys for a relationship is not only circular and hard to maintain, it can seriously confuse developers using the types. You can optimize your decision by thinking about how applications will use the tables based on the type. If one side of the association seems more natural or more likely for a developer to use, put the attribute in that type. This corresponds to an association with an arrowhead pointing to the other type. If the multiplicity on the role is 1..1 rather than 0..1, add a NOT NULL constraint to the foreign key column(s) in the table.

You will already have created any foreign keys to superclasses through generalization relationships in the prior step for creating primary keys.

For composite aggregations with only one object being aggregated, you should consider the alternative of embedding the object in the type rather than creating foreign keys or references. If the composite aggregates multiple objects, you can represent this as a collection of child objects. If you choose not to tie the child object so closely to the parent type, add the primary key attributes to the child object type. Then create a second attribute for the primary key that uniquely identifies the object. Often this will be either an explicit {OID} column or a sequence if the association is {ordered}. If not, then create an integer value to uniquely identify the children of the aggregate. Make the attributes from the parent table a foreign key to the parent table in the table constraints on the tables based on the child type. Add the appropriate CASCADE constraint to the FOREIGN KEY clause in the tables as well.

Now optimize your one-to-one association classes. Find any binary associations with role multiplicity greater than 1 on the role played by the class you are defining. If the association has an association class, add the attributes from the association class to the type rather than creating a separate type for the association class.

Create many-to-many and ternary associations using foreign keys just as in the relational transformation. The OR collections and referencing techniques do not apply to these kinds of associations.

Operations

The simplest way to represent operations in Oracle8 is to create a member procedure or function for each operation you've defined in the data model. As an example, consider the CriminalOrganization class from Figure 12-2. That class exports two operations: UpdateStatus and SetPriority, both "mutators" that change the state of a particular Criminal Organization object. In this case, we have two requirements: enumerated data types and updating the current object.

The first requirement, an enumerated data type, is still hard to do in PL/SQL. The PL/SQL type system has no concept of enumerated type. At least an SQL column definition can have a CHECK constraint; this is not true of a PL/SQL variable definition, unfortunately. You need to build the same lookup table you would build for a relational system (see Chapter 11). The code in the

Table 12-1 *Summary of Object-Relational Schema Transformation*

Step	Transformation
1	Create any types, tables, or ancillary objects that you need to create to make use of reusable ORDBMS extensions, such as Oracle8 cartridges, Informix DataBlades, or DB2 UDB extensions.
2	UML class becomes object (structured) type, usually with a corresponding table of that type to hold the object rows, but possibly with more than one such table.
3	UML type becomes distinct type if based on built-in type or object type if it has attributes.
4	UML attribute in class becomes attribute in object type.
5	UML attribute type in class becomes attribute type in object type through type transformation table and/or object and distinct types.
6	If {nullable} UML attribute tag, attribute has NULL constraint; otherwise, NOT NULL constraint.
7	If UML attribute has initializer, add DEFAULT clause to column.
8	For classes with no generalization (root or independent) and implicit identity, create integer primary key; for {oid}, add {oid} tagged columns to PRIMARY KEY constraint; ignore composite aggregation and association classes.
9	For subclasses, add the key of each parent class to the PRIMARY KEY constraint and to a FOREIGN KEY constraint; for fully SQL3 compliant ORDBMS products, you can use an UNDER clause to represent the relationship instead, but for all others you'll have to put the foreign key constraint in the tables you define with your object type.
10	For association classes, create an object type and add primary key from each role-playing table to PRIMARY KEY constraint and FOREIGN KEY constraint.
11	If {alternate oid = \<n\>} tag, add columns to UNIQUE constraint.
12	Add CHECK for each explicit constraint.
13	Create FOREIGN KEY columns in referencing table for each 0..1, 1..1 role in association; alternately, use a reference to an object type to declare the object as an attribute in its own right for single objects or a collection such as an array of references for multiple related objects.
14	Create PRIMARY KEY for composite aggregation with FOREIGN KEY to aggregating table (with CASCADE option), add additional column for PRIMARY KEY; alternately, use an object type to store the aggregate in the table itself, either through an object attribute (for a single object) or a collection such as an array or as a nested table (not recommended without extensive experimentation to determine whether it's more trouble than it's worth).
15	Optimize binary association classes by moving into to-many side table where appropriate.
16	Create tables for many-to-many, ternary associations with no association classes using foreign keys.
17	Create PRIMARY KEY, FOREIGN KEY constraints from keys of role-playing tables in many-to-many, ternary associations.
18	Create methods on object types for operations on the corresponding UML classes; use the appropriate "purity level" formats for {readonly} or {query} tagged operations.

UpdateStatus member procedure then looks up the appropriate value to use in updating the object.

Summary

For convenience, Table 12-1 summarizes the transformation to an object-relational database. FOREIGN KEY and PRIMARY KEY mean either a table constraint or a REFERENCES column constraint depending on whether the key is multivalued. This table greatly resembles Table 11-4, which describes the relational transformation.

Object-relational databases thus give you a broad array of alternative representations for your data models, perhaps too many. The next chapter moves into the fully object-oriented world, in which you have fewer choices but they map better to the concepts of UML.

Designing an Object-Oriented Database Schema 13

Work without hope draws nectar in a sieve, and hope without an object cannot live.

Samuel Taylor Coleridge, *Work without Hope*

The final stop in this trip through the world of database design is the object-oriented (OO) schema. Mapping a UML data model to an OO schema is straightforward, though there are as always a few issues to consider. Many issues arise because OODBMS vendors do not adhere to any schema definition standard. Other issues arise out of the inherent nature of persistent object design, appearing in all OODBMS products and in the ODMG standard as well.

The Transformation Process for OODBMS Products

This chapter covers the ODMG 2.0 Object Definition Language (ODL) for object-oriented systems [Cattell and Barry 1997]. It gives examples of schema choices in the POET database manager using the POET ODL precompiler and the C++ language binding [POET 1997b, 1997a].

The ODMG 2.0 standard is a comprehensive benchmark for the capabilities of an OODBMS. Unfortunately, the OODBMS community does not yet provide schema definition facilities that conform to the standard. Some, like POET and Versant, provide variations on the standard; others, such as ObjectDesign and Objectivity, have a completely different way of defining their schemas. I use ODL because it provides a generic set of features that map well to the different vendors' software. I use POET here because it provides a full-fledged but incomplete ODL schema definition facility based on ODMG 1.5 ODL. ODL is in turn based on the OMG's CORBA Interface Definition Language (IDL), a language for defining distributed-object interfaces for use with CORBA distributed-object systems.

Note: Interestingly, POET adopted the ODL interface in addition to the C++ and Java language bindings to support language-independent interfaces for use with distributed object technology such as COM and Visual Basic. The language independence of ODL thus provides value in the world of distributed objects, illustrating at least one of the fallacies of the "impedance mismatch" rationale for object databases.

Almost all OODBMS products started out using OO programming languages as their schema definition languages. Most used C++, though at least one (Gemstone) used Smalltalk. By adding language elements or by adding class libraries to support persistence, these products turned C++ interface definitions into schema declarations. Most have added support for Java schemas as well. The examples in this chapter use the C++ language binding of POET [POET 1997a] to illustrate the language-specific approach to schema definition.

Ultimately, the process of defining an OO database schema with UML comes down to the same kind of transformation you make between a UML design and an ODL or C++ implementation of that design. This is the simple part of the transformation, mapping from the UML OO concepts into those of C++ or some other OO programming language.

Complexity emerges when the OODBMS vendor's language comes into play either through ODL or OO programming language extensions that enable use of persistent objects. Each language has different features and different approaches to modeling OO concepts. No OODBMS provides support directly for many-to-many or *n*-ary associations, for example, nor do they offer association classes, so you need to do some transformation work on these UML concepts. Also, most OO programming languages don't provide any way of representing null values, so it's a challenge to represent nullable attributes.

To illustrate the process, this chapter uses the same design as Chapter 11, reproduced here for convenience. Figure 13-1 shows a UML model for the Person subsystem of the Commonplace book, and Figure 13-2 shows a UML model for the Organization subsystem. Both of these subsystems are part of a third subsystem, the Entity subsystem. Figure 13-3 shows the architecture for the package.

The Person subsystem contains the Person class and the Identification hierarchy that belongs to it. I've chosen to use the inheritance version of Identification rather than the interface version. People connect to Organizations through a three-way relationship to the Role class in the Organization package. The scope notation (Organization::Role) identifies classes that are not a part of the Person subsystem.

The Organization subsystem contains the Organization hierarchy, which includes the CriminalOrganization class. It also includes the Role class and the

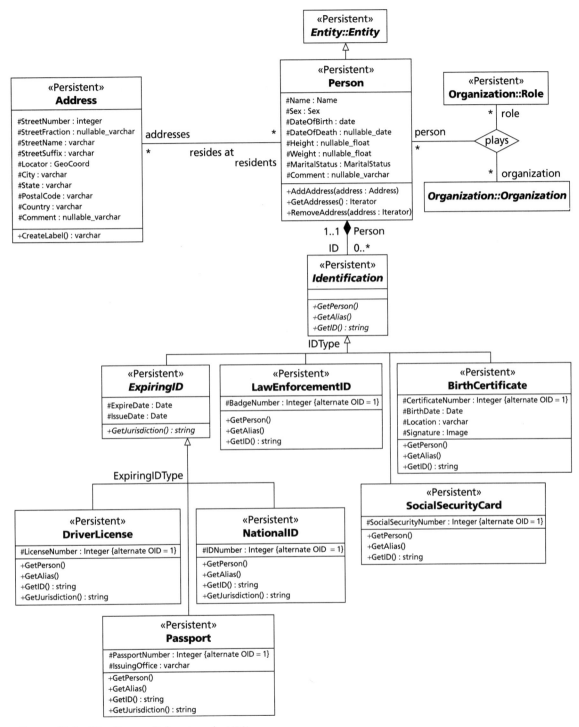

Figure 13-1   The Person Subsystem in UML

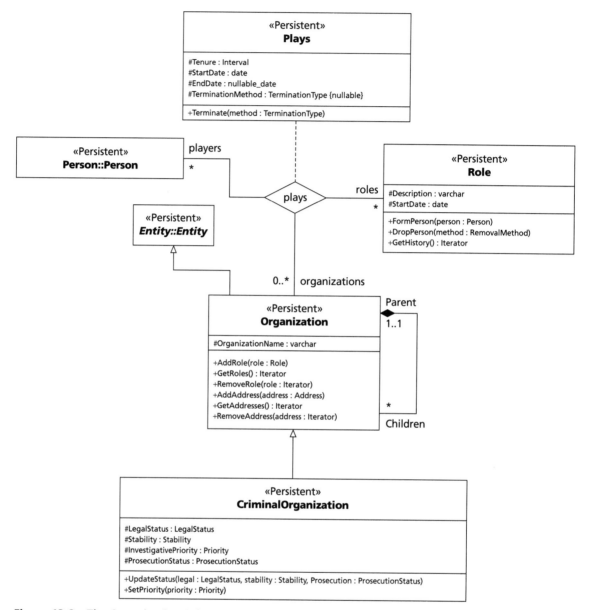

Figure 13-2   *The Organization Subsystem in UML*

relationships between Role and Organization. Organizations connect to people
through a three-way relationship to Role.

The Entity subsystem contains three elements: the two subsystems People
and Organization plus an abstract class, Entity. The Person and Organization
classes in their respective packages inherit from that class.

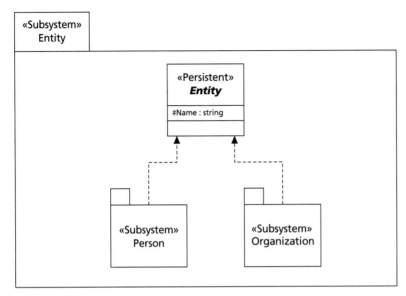

Figure 13-3 *The Entity Subsystem in UML*

Objective Simplicity?

Recall from Chapter 2 that the primary rationale for object-oriented databases is to reduce the impedance mismatch between the programming language and the database. Instead of having to map between the application views and the conceptual schema with yet another language (SQL), you just make your classes persistent and run your application.

While the promise of OO transparency and application simplicity is alluring, in practice the OODBMS does not really deliver when you look at schema generation. Overall, the mapping process is simpler than for relational databases, but there are still a fair number of issues that arise to complicate your life. Where the transparency succeeds and succeeds well is in the area of inserting, updating, and deleting objects.

The primary set of issues comes from the lack of standardization between OODBMS products. There is a standard, ODMG, but it really only covers the OQL query language and the basic features that an OODBMS must provide. The ODMG standard does not provide interoperability, nor does it help much in reconciling the very different programming interfaces of the various OODBMS products.

The remaining issues come from the same impedance mismatch that motivates the OO database in the first place. Transactions, client/server caching, complex associations, keys, and extents are all concepts foreign to the popular OO programming languages but essential for databases. OODBMS products cannot ignore these issues, so they all provide mappings to them in different ways.

A third component of transformation complexity comes from the old shibboleth of "portability." With the increasing popularity of OO programming, new languages are emerging that challenge the market leaders. OO programming languages started with Smalltalk and C++, two very different programming paradigms. Now Java is increasing in popularity, bringing as much Smalltalk as C++ to the programming equation and adding new elements such as interfaces to the mash. Languages with broader appeal such as Visual Basic are gaining object-oriented features. More importantly, with distributed object technology, such languages are able to make use of objects written in any language through CORBA and COM interfaces. To write a "portable" program in this context is quite tough; to write a portable OO database application is even tougher. For example, consider the ODMG standard Java binding: it does not support relationships, keys, extents, or access to the ODMG metaschema [Cattell and Barry 1997, p. 230]. I'll let you decide how useful a standard that doesn't handle associations, keys, or extents is to the Java database application programmer.

Thus, it is by no means easy to transform a UML data model into an OODBMS schema. The following sections cover some of the basic issues that arise for most such transformations, but individual products will always produce surprises.

Classes

The class is at the center of the object-oriented transformation, just as the table is at the center of the relational transformation and the object type is at the center of the object-relational transformation. The quirks that the OODBMS world contributes to class definition include persistence, use of interfaces, differing data types, null-value handling (or the lack thereof), object identity, and extents.

Persistent Classes and Interfaces

Mapping a class into an OODBMS schema is easy: create a class. It goes downhill from there.

The first thing you need to worry about is how to make your classes persistent. There have been quite a few interesting schemes for this. ODL 2.0 simply assumes that your classes are persistent. POET requires the use of the persistent keyword before the class keyword:

```
persistent class CriminalOrganization : public Organization { . . . };
```

There are at least two other schemes. ObjectDesign's ObjectStore, for example, uses the C++ storage class to indicate object persistence as opposed to class persistence. This enables the feature of ObjectStore that lets you query over an extent that includes both persistent objects and transient objects. By creating persistent objects instead of tying the type definition to the database, ObjectStore makes querying independent of persistence. This addresses the second major thrust of the OODBMS community: making data types orthogonal to, or independent of, persistence.

The ODMG standard supports this with its C++ binding concept of persistence-capable classes—classes that can have both persistent and transient instances. The standard then overloads the new operator in C++ with a Database object argument. This gives you the ability to declare a database to be *transient* (in memory, not persistent), so that you can declare transient, persistence-capable objects. This approach nicely integrates class persistence and object persistence.

The Objectivity/DB system used a different approach: inheritance. That system provided a class library with the ooObject class. To make a class persistent, you inherited from ooObject. This approach eliminated the need for pre- or post-processing and relied directly on C++ to handle everything. The dark side of this approach was the coupling of your classes to the Objectivity class and thus the need for multiple inheritance and a greater complexity in the class interface.

Broadening the picture a bit, there are two standard ways to make objects persistent: declarative persistence and persistence by reachability, also known as transitive persistence. *Declarative persistence* is the approach in the systems thus far introduced: you declare that a class (or object) is persistent, and only those classes (or objects) persist. *Transitive persistence* declares some root object persistent, then makes all objects to which that root object refers persistent. This is more in line with the way the Smalltalk and Java languages work and is thus part of the standard ODMG bindings for those languages [Cattell and Barry 1997]. As those languages provide garbage collection, you don't actually delete objects, just eliminate references to them. The database then cleans out any objects to which nothing refers (persistent garbage collection, a metaphor that boggles the mind).

If you program in Java, you will doubtless define many interfaces in your UML data model rather than relying exclusively on classes and class generalization. Interfaces do not possess state, just abstract behavior specifications. As a consequence, interfaces are not persistent objects. The Java ODMG binding, for example, specifies that interfaces are not persistent and that the DBMS does not store interfaces in any way. Similarly, abstract classes do not correspond directly to objects; any object must therefore be a concrete class, and no OODBMS needs to make abstract classes persistent. Thus any UML interface, or any class with an {abstract} tag, does not translate into a persistent database class for Java programs. The C++ binding, on the other hand, is silent with respect to abstract classes [Cattell and Barry 1997].

Your best bet at transforming UML interfaces into a C++ OODBMS schema is to define an abstract class for the interface, making all the operations pure virtual (= 0 initializer for the method and no implementation) and having no data members at all. You can then use multiple inheritance to represent realization. This requires that (as with Java interface implementation) you must implement all the operations you've defined as pure virtual in the abstract base class in the subclass that inherits from it. Using multiple inheritance may or may not be possible with any specific OODBMS, nor may it be advisable given its theoretical and practical problems, so you should research and experiment with your target OODBMS before committing yourself to a particular transformation strategy.

Attribute Data Types

In tune with their underlying philosophy, most OODBMS products define their basic types as the types of the programming language, unifying the programming and database type systems. Because databases have some additional requirements for data, these products also usually define additional types.

The ODL defines a set of basic types that it terms atomic literals. A *literal* in the ODMG standard is a value that has no object identity, as opposed to an object, which does. These types are for the most part quite standard: long, short, unsigned long, unsigned short, float, double, boolean, octet (byte), char, string, and enum<>. This last type is a type generator that creates a type based on the list of element names you supply. There are also a set of collection literal type generators (set, bag, list, array, and dictionary) and structured literals (date, time, timestamp, interval, and structure<>). The ODL also specifies a nullable literal type for each literal type (nullable_float, nullable_set<>, nullable_date, for example) [Cattell and Barry 1997, pp. 32–35].

Null values are somewhat problematic in OODBMS products, as most OO programming languages have no concept of a null value. C++, Smalltalk, and Java bindings for ODL do not support the nullable literal types, for example, nor do they support nulls for objects. In practice, most OODBMS products do not support null values either. If you use a {nullable} tag in your UML data models, you will often find that you cannot transform this into a corresponding nullable data type in your OODBMS schema. If you can't represent nulls, you'll have to find a standard value that means null if you can't find a way to eliminate nulls entirely.

The ODMG collection types let you collect literals or objects:

- *Set:* An unordered collection of elements with no duplicates

- *Bag:* An unordered collection of elements that may contain duplicates

- *List:* An ordered collection of elements indexed by relative position
- *Array:* An ordered collection of elements indexed by numeric position
- *Dictionary:* An unordered sequence of key-value pairs with no duplicate keys (an object of type Association)

The collection can be either an object with an object identifier or a literal with no identifier. You use the latter types mainly to define relationships between classes. For example, to define the relationship between Person and Address in Figure 13-1, you use the following syntax fragment:

```
relationship set<Address> addresses inverse Person::residents;
```

The set<> literal collection type tells you that each person may have zero or more addresses, that the relationship is not ordered (no {ordered} tag), and that there are no duplicate addresses. If you have an {ordered} tag on the relationship, use a list<> or array<> type. You use a dictionary if you want to be able to do indexed lookups on some value that you can use as the index. Finding a use for the bag<> is hard, since UML relationships assume that there are no duplicate links. You may find the bag<> literal type or its object cousin Bag more useful in holding collections of transient objects or pointers.

> Note: See the section "Associations" for more details on relationships and how they depend on object identity.

The *typedef* is a C and C++ concept that lets you create an alias for a type. It does not define a new type. Nothing in UML notation corresponds to the typedef.

An *enum* is a literal type with a name. A value typed with the enum can take on one of the specific, enumerated values you list in the enum declaration. You can define an enumerated type with a UML «type» classifier that lists the value elements. This then transforms into a C++ or ODL enumeration that you can use to define attributes and operation parameters:

```
enum LegalStatus{LegallyDefined, OnTrial, Alleged, Unknown};
attribute LegalStatus status;
void SetStatus(LegalStatus status);
```

Class Extents and Subextents

The ODMG standard defines the extent of a type as "the set of all instances of the type within a particular database" [Cattell and Barry 1997, p. 16]. If CriminalOrganization is a subtype of Organization, then the set of all criminal organization objects in the database is the extent of CriminalOrganization and each criminal organization object is also a member of the extent of Organization.

In relational databases, an extent corresponds to all the rows in a table. In object-relational databases, an extent corresponds to a table scope, which may include several tables. In object-oriented databases, the database can automatically maintain the extent set regardless of the ownership or location of objects of a given type. You tell the OODBMS to do this by some kind of keyword or other schema definition mechanism. In ODL, you specify the extent keyword and a name:

```
class CriminalOrganization extends Organization (extent Mobs)
   { . . . }
```

The OODBMS may index the extent automatically to speed up queries if you specify that. You could always maintain the extent yourself in a collection; the problem is that this reduces concurrency by locking the collection object. Having the database do the job eliminates unnecessary object locks that can block readers and writers. You use the extent in queries when you want to search over the set of all objects of a type and its subtypes. Some systems even let you restrict the search to a type without its subtypes [Jordan 1998]. You can also create a reference to the extent dynamically using the d_Extent<> template, which constructs the extent with a supplied pointer to a database object [Jordan 1998, pp. 107–108]:

```
d_Extent<CriminalOrganization> mobs(pDatabase);
```

The UML has no concept of extent. If you wish, you can add a class tag to your UML static structure diagrams to specify the extent name, such as tagging CriminalOrganization with the tag {extent=Mobs}. You can then transform this into the appropriate schema definition for your target OODBMS.

An interesting application of extents comes in the next section with the discussion of keys.

Object Identity

The ODMG standard and most OO systems distinguish between two kinds of data: values and objects. Systems make this distinction by defining objects as data elements that have object identity, that the system can uniquely identify relative to all other objects in the system. In the case of the OODBMS, the "system" is the database storage domain. You will usually have some way to test whether two objects are the same by identity comparison: ODMG provides the same_as() operation on all persistent objects, for example. Many OODBMS products let you compare objects for equality by comparing attribute values; most also provide a way to compare objects by identity, usually through operations on references to objects (the OODBMS equivalent of pointers).

Object identity renders the concept of the primary key both redundant and unnecessary. References to an object refer to it through the object identifier, not the values of attributes within the object. Thus there is no concept of either a primary key or a foreign key in an OODBMS. Instead, the {OID} and {alternate OID} tags that you define transform into constraints on the extent of the class. ODMG even provides a way to specify the key values—the key clause:

```
class LawEnforcementID extends Identification
    (extent Badges key BadgeNumber){
  attribute unsigned long BadgeNumber;
. . .
};
```

Alternatively, the target DBMS may provide some kind of unique indexing, as POET does [POET 1997a, p. 114]:

```
persistent class LawEnforcementID : public Identification {
  unsigned long BadgeNumber;
  useindex BadgeNumberIX;
};

unique indexdef BadgeNumberIX : LawEnforcementID
{
  BadgeNumber;
};
```

Another aspect of object identity is global naming. The original OODBMS products did not support OQL or any similar kind of query language. Instead, they let you start at a root object, then navigate through relationships to find other objects. To make this easier, OODBMS products introduced the concept of global object names within the database name space. You could thus create your own object identifier alias and use it to name the root object of your navigational network. You then retrieve that object directly by its global name and start navigating [Jordan 1997, pp. 87–88].

> *Note: Query languages provide a more general and easy-to-use way to achieve the same effect as global naming, which also has the disadvantage of increasing data coupling through linking to global names in your programs. If your OODBMS provides a query language, use it instead of global naming if at all possible.*

You may want to define these global objects using the UML object notation, as in Figure 13-4, which shows the various key criminal organizations of interest to commonplace book applications. This particular naming setup names five criminal organizations. You can retrieve each CriminalOrganization object

Figure 13-4   *Criminal Organization Object Names*

directly, then start navigating to its members and related criminal organizations through the relationships on the CriminalOrganization class.

To look up the status of the members of the Worthington Bank Gang, for example, you would retrieve that object by its object name, then navigate to the collection of people that played roles in the gang.

If you have such an object diagram, you can transform it directly into global object names in your target DBMS.

Generalizations and Realizations

The ODMG standard distinguishes two kinds of object type, the class and the interface. The class defines abstract behavior and state for an object type. The interface defines only abstract behavior. These concepts map directly to the UML concepts of class and interface (see Chapter 7 for details).

The ODMG standard divides inheritance into two varieties, inheritance of behavior and inheritance of state. These concepts correspond more or less to the UML concepts of realization and generalization relationships, but the subtleties between the two object models make them different. A quotation from the standard may or may not clarify the relationships for you:

> Classes are types that are directly instantiable, meaning instances of these types may be created by the programmer. Interfaces are types that cannot be directly instantiated. For examples, instances of the classes Salaried_Employee and Hourly_Employee may be created, but instances of their supertype interface Employee cannot. Subtyping pertains to the inheritance of behavior only; thus interfaces may inherit from other interfaces and classes may also inherit from interfaces. Due to the inefficiencies and ambiguities of multiple inheritance of state, however, interfaces may not inherit from classes, nor may classes inherit from other classes. [Cattell and Barry 1997, p. 15]

The upshot of all this abstraction is that ODL provides two kinds of inheritance. *Behavioral* inheritance appears in interfaces and class specifications following a colon-separated notation resembling C++ base class specifications. This is the is-a relationship that corresponds to UML realization or to generalization depending on whether you are inheriting from an interface or a class. *State* inheritance appears in classes in a separate extends clause and corresponds to generalization without the behavioral component. You may thus have interfaces inheriting from other interfaces (but not classes), and classes inheriting both from interfaces and other classes.

The ODMG distinction between behavioral and state inheritance has not yet migrated into the realm of the working OODBMS, for better or worse. C++ APIs for OODBMS products use the C++ model of inheritance that combines the two forms with all the ambiguities that result from multiple inheritance. Thus, for practical purposes, OODBMS products support UML generalization. If you are programming with Java, which supports the interface and class concepts separately, you may find that the Java OODBMS API maps more closely to the ODMG 2.0 standard. Nevertheless, the Java model differs from the ODMG model, more closely resembling the UML concepts of generalization (class or interface inheritance using the extends keyword) and realization (interface implementation using the implements keyword).

The practical transformation of your UML data model's generalization relationships into an OODBMS schema thus usually comes down to translating your UML diagram into your chosen OO programming language. This will usually be a one-to-one mapping, as UML was explicitly designed with this kind of transformation in mind. Interfaces throw something of a wrench into the situation, but unless you're using Java, you don't need to worry about it. If you are using Java, there should be a one-to-one transformation of generalizations and realizations into the corresponding Java syntax (the extends and implements clauses, respectively). If you're using C++, you must produce abstract classes and use multiple inheritance to represent realization (see the previous section on "Persistent Classes and Interfaces" for a complete discussion of interface transformation).

Associations

The association is where OODBMS products will give you trouble in generating your schema. Associations—relationships between objects—are at the center of the services that an OODBMS provides. Storing data, transaction management, and even recovery and integrity are standard database operations. Being able to navigate between objects is what OODBMS products bring to the table as their main advantage.

Variations on a Theme

You can represent a link between two objects in a number of different ways, even in the ODMG standard. This section presents you with the basic alternatives, and the following section shows you how you can best represent the various kinds of UML associations using these structures.

- *Attribute:* Directly embedding a single related object as a member of the relating object, which owns the related object. In C++, this means declaring a data member using the object type with no pointer or reference. For OODBMS schemas, this translates to an object that has no object identity but rather consists entirely of values embedded within the relating object. When you activate the relating object, you get all its embedded data, including the related object. There is no referential integrity directly, but deleting the relating object also deletes the related object.

- *Reference:* Embedding a single related object as a reference member of the relating object using the d_Ref template or its equivalent (a *handle* or *persistent reference*). This corresponds to a C++ data member declared as a pointer, but persistent data must have a reference, not a pointer, as pointers aren't persistent. The related object has a life cycle separate from its containing object, and the reference can be null. When you activate the relating object, you do not necessarily activate the related object, though you may with the right options set. The system does not maintain referential integrity; your application must manage dangling references.

- *Collection of objects:* Embedding a collection template of objects as a member of the relating object. This corresponds to a collection of objects allocated directly by the collection in C++, and the system treats it exactly as such. The related objects are part of the collection object and have no separate object identity. When you activate the embedding object, you get the collection and all its data as part of the value. The system does not maintain referential integrity; the collection manages the objects as their owner.

- *Collection of references:* Embedding a collection template of object references as a member of the relating object. This corresponds to a C++ collection of object pointers, but the references enable the objects to persist. The related objects have life cycles separate from the containing object, and each reference can be dangling (to a nonexistent object) or null. The collection can be empty. The system does not maintain referential integrity, and your application must maintain the objects, deleting them explicitly and removing dangling references.

- *Relationship:* Embedding a special collection template of object references as a member of the relating object. This corresponds again to a C++ collection of object pointers, but the template collection maintains referential integrity on both sides of the relationship, so there are no dangling references. References can be null, and the collection itself can be empty. In some OODBMS products, references also permit lazy activation of objects, letting you retrieve the object from the server only when you need to use it. Other systems activate all the objects that you can reach from an object you activate (a transitive closure activation).

Figure 13-5 presents the ODL syntax for a relationship. The first identifier (or collection class) is the type of the relationship. The second identifier is the name of the relationship. If you use a collection, you put the type of the relationship inside angle brackets after the collection class name (set, list, or bag).

The ODL syntax requires that the relationship contain an inverse clause, which means that the relationship is always bidirectional: the relationship is visible from both classes. Since only relationships maintain referential integrity, you can have automatic referential integrity only for bidirectional associations. The inverse clause contains two identifiers: the name of the target class and the name of the relationship in that class, separated by the scope operator (::).

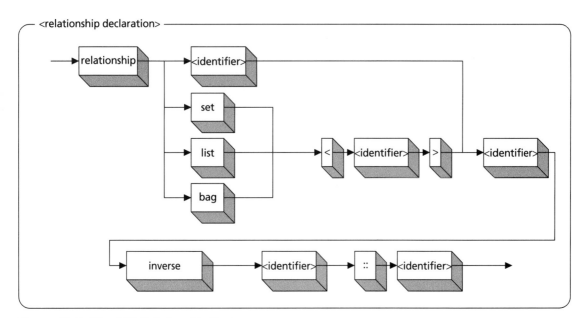

Figure 13-5 *The ODL Relationship Syntax*

The following sections show you how to transform the various kinds of UML association configurations into ODL and C++ OODBMS schemas.

Directed Associations with Multiplicity 1

A UML *directed association* is an association with an arrowhead pointing to a class. Adding direction to the association establishes one-way visibility. The pointing class can see the target class to which it points, but that class cannot in turn see the pointing class. The advantage in specifying a directed association comes from encapsulation and the consequent limiting of coupling. Since the target class knows nothing about the class that uses it, its contents are completely unaffected by any changes to the pointing class. Also, in this section, the association is not an aggregation but a simple association. That means that neither class owns the other class.

If the multiplicity on the target class role is 0..1 or 1..1, it means that the pointing class object refers to only one object of the target class. The transformation thus requires a single-valued attribute for the pointing class. The specific nature of this attribute depends mainly on the OODBMS types available. The generic ODL provides for declaring an attribute of a class type, and this translates into get-and-set methods, hiding the underlying data structure implementation. The C++ ODL provides for two specific kinds of declarations: an embedded object declared as part of the data structure and a persistent reference to an object. The embedded object has no object identity; it becomes part of the data structure of the embedding object, not a separate object in the database. That's appropriate for a composite aggregation association, but not for a regular association. That leaves just the reference, a smart-pointer class that lets you declare the reference and point it to the target object with an object identifier after creating or activating the object.

If the multiplicity is 0..1, the reference can be null, and your methods should check for null or catch the null reference exception as appropriate. If the multiplicity is 1..1 or just 1, you must enforce the constraint that the reference must always point to a valid object in your methods. That means your constructor must associate an object with the reference, and no method may leave the reference as null or dangling.

You will find this situation more common with a 0..1 multiplicity, as the 1..1 multiplicity usually comes with a composite aggregation instead of a regular association. The only real reason to have a regular association with a single target instead of a composite aggregation is to allow the association to be null. This corresponds to a C++ data member that needs to be a pointer because the object may not always exist.

Note: This very point illustrates a major difference between writing a C++ program and porting a C++ program to an OODBMS-based persistent data model. You can't use pointers, which are memory objects; instead, you must use some kind of reference or handle or smart pointer to refer to persistent objects. The consequence: you can't just take a C++ program, mark certain objects as persistent, and go. You have to convert your pointer members, pointer parameters, and pointer return arguments to persistent references. This doesn't sound like much, but in reality this can result in quite a lot of work in converting the code.

As an example, consider the specialized need for an optional street address for a person in the commonplace book system. The approach from Figure 13-1 models addresses as a series of string attributes in the Person class. Instead, consider a more complex model that represents the street address as a separate class (Figure 13-6). To fit the requirements, assume that you can use one street address in several address objects (1..* multiplicity) and that addresses can see street addresses but street addresses don't need to see addresses. (It's hard to come up with real examples that make sense with this scenario, in practice. Usually these situations wind up being composite aggregation, not freestanding objects.)

The attributes representing the street address are now in the StreetAddress class. The ODL version of the Address class now looks like this:

```
class Address (extent Addresses) {
  attribute StreetAddress Street;
  attribute string City;
  attribute string State;
  attribute string PostalCode;
  attribute string Country;
  attribute nullable_string Comment;
  string CreateLabel();
};
```

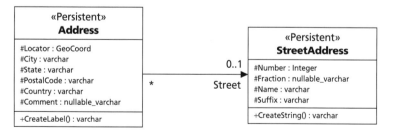

Figure 13-6   *The Address and StreetAddress Classes*

The C++ version looks like this:

```
class Address : public d_Object {
protected:
  d_Ref< StreetAddress > Street;
  d_String City;
  d_String State;
  d_String PostalCode;
  d_String Country;
  d_String Comment;
public:
  const d_String & CreateLabel(void) const;
};
```

The d_Ref template is the standard C++ representation for an OODBMS persistent reference. The template argument (StreetAddress) names the class of objects to which the reference refers.

> *Tip: The blanks between the template brackets and the class name are an emerging standard that help many compilers identify the class name properly. In this case, since the identifier is a simple name, you don't need the spaces. You may find when using complex C++ names (for example, including a name space and nesting classes or typedefs) that the spaces are necessary. Standard Template Library (STL) technology still has some complexities that can make life difficult at times.*

Directed Associations with Multiplicity Greater than 1

With a multiplicity of 0..* or * on the directed association, you are now dealing with a collection of objects rather than just a single object. Again, the directed association implies a restricted visibility for the pointing object, and the association is not a composite aggregation.

Going back to Figure 13-1, there is a many-to-many, bidirectional association between Person and Address. What if, for design reasons, you made the association directed, with the arrow pointing at the address? This would mean that you could access an address through a person, but that you could not access a person through an address. This situation, again, is rare in real-world design, but despite that the OODBMS world gives you a way to do it.

```
class Person (extent People) {
  attribute set< Address > Addresses;
  . . .
};
```

In C++:

```
class Person : public Object {
  d_Set< d_Ref< Address > > Addresses;
  . . .
};
```

You should notice two things about the C++ version. First, the set contains references to objects, not the objects themselves. That's how the C++ OODBMS maintains the objects as distinct, persistent objects outside the d_Set object. Second, you need the spaces between the > characters; otherwise, most compilers have trouble because their lexical analyzers see the >> operator rather than the template delimiters and go crazy.

If you delete an address, you'll need to go to all the people objects in the database and ask them to delete the address from their sets of addresses. That probably means adding a special operation to the Person class to handle the referential integrity updates, and you'll have to make sure to call that operation whenever you remove an address. You'll also have to make the complete set of people visible in the context where you're deleting the address.

> Tip: On balance, the added complexity of all this referential integrity management probably outweighs any encapsulation advantages you gain by using the directed link. In a regular C++ program, this structure requires the additional complexity of cache management operations, but adding in the persistence and referential integrity in the database makes it even worse. When you don't want composite aggregation semantics, it's usually best to use relationships rather than the embedded object or collection approach. That means bidirectional associations.

Bidirectional Associations with Role Multiplicity 1

The bidirectional association moves us into the world of relationships, and consequently of automatic referential integrity. First, consider the association from a class with a role multiplicity of 0..1 or 1..1 on the role attached to the other class. The class you are defining accesses (perhaps optionally) a single object of the target class. Because the association is bidirectional, there is also visibility of the association from the target class side. Finally, the target object is independent of the associating object, as the association is not an aggregation. This situation corresponds directly to the single-object relationship.

Revisiting Figure 13-6, what if the association here was not directed, with no arrowhead pointing to StreetAddress? The ODL for the Address class would look like this:

```
class Address (extent Addresses) {
  relationship StreetAddress Street inverse StreetAddress::Addresses;
  attribute string City;
  attribute string State;
  attribute string PostalCode;
  attribute string Country;
  attribute nullable_string Comment;
  string CreateLabel();
};
```

This differs from the first version of this class by replacing the attribute with a relationship, adding the inverse clause that specifies the name of the relationship on the StreetAddress side. The C++ version looks like this:

```
extern const char _addresses[]; // Address<->StreetAddress
class Address : public d_Object {
protected:
  d_String City;
  d_String State;
  d_String PostalCode;
  d_String Country;
  d_String Comment;
public:
  d_Rel_Ref< StreetAddress, _addresses > Street;
  const d_String & CreateLabel(void) const;
};
```

The standard single-object relationship d_Rel_Ref template in C++ takes two arguments, the name of the target class and a character array containing the name of the relationship in the target class (the inverse member). In this case, there will be a code (.cpp) file containing the initialization of the const character array:

```
const char _address[] = "Addresses"; // rel member of StreetAddress
```

Note: To give you an idea of the complexity behind this approach, here's a quiz. What role do you think the inverse member name parameter plays, and why don't you just put the literal string into the template argument (d_Rel_Ref< StreetAddress, "address" >)? Answer: The memory address of the variable you declare (that is, the _address character array) lets the compiler differentiate this template instance from other template instances. If you use a literal string, the address will differ each time you include the file. Then the relationship template generates many instances (once for each inclusion of the template) instead of the single one it requires [Jordan 1997, p. 123]. This is fairly typical of the complexity that

C++ imposes on the database designer (and the template designer as well).

Bidirectional Associations with Role Multiplicity Greater than 1

Now, moving to the last variation, consider the association with a role multiplicity of 0..*, 1..*, *, or *n..m*, where *n* and *m* define a multiple-object range. Again, this represents an independent object, not an aggregate. If you consider Figure 13-6 with no arrowhead again, the StreetAddress class represents this situation. In ODL, the class declaration looks like this:

```
class StreetAddress (extent StreetAddresses) {
  attribute int Number;
  attribute string Fraction;
  attribute string Name;
  attribute string Suffix;
  relationship set<Address> Addresses;
  string CreateString();
};
```

In C++:

```
extern const char _streetAddress[]; // Address<->StreetAddress
class StreetAddress : public d_Object {
  int Number;
  d_String Fraction;
  d_String Name;
  d_String Suffix;
public:
  d_Rel_Set< Address, _streetAddress >;
};
```

Figure 13-5 tells you that you have one of three choices for the collection class to use in declaring your to-many relationship: set, bag, or list. Most relationships are sets. In certain cases, you may want to be able to store the link to an object more than once. If the situation does not require ordering, you use a bag; otherwise, you use a list. Both of these collections permit duplicates. If the association requires ordering (an {ordered} tag on the role), you can use a list to specify the order. If you cannot allow duplicates, however, you must use a set, which has no ordering.

Composite Aggregations

Now let's confront the association we've been avoiding: the composite aggregation. In Figure 13-1, the Identification class relates to the Person class with a composite aggregation. The Person class owns the identification, which cannot exist without the person.

In an OODBMS, you can represent this situation in two ways: as a true composition or as a bidirectional relationship.

The composition approach lets you declare the object directly:

```
class Person (extent People) {
    . . .
    attribute set<Identification>;
};
```

In C++:

```
class Person : public Entity {
    . . .
public:
    d_Rel_Set< Identification, _person >;
};
```

The composition approach uses the attribute declaration to create the identification object set and its objects as a part of the structure of the Person class rather than as freestanding, persistent objects. When you activate the person, you activate the entire set of identification objects by value. The identification objects do not have any separate persistent object identity, so when you delete the person, you delete all of its identification objects as well.

The bidirectional approach would declare a full relationship, as the section "Bidirectional Associations with Role Multiplicity Greater than 1" discusses. The Identification objects now become first-class persistent objects with their own identity in the database, and you access them through references. The advantages of this approach include automatic referential integrity (delete an identification and the reference to it becomes null), automatic inverse relationship maintenance, automatic extent maintenance, and the ability to query the independent identification objects without reference to the person objects that contain them. The main disadvantage: you have to enforce the ownership through code instead of directly. With the true composition approach, if you delete the person, the DBMS deletes all the identification objects belonging to that person as well. With the bidirectional relationship approach, you must do this in a Delete() operation, as the DBMS will merely delete the object reference, not the object, which is independent.

> *Note: The POET OODBMS, for example, provides a feature similar to the cascading delete available with most RDBMS foreign key constraints. You can use the* depend *keyword to represent the composite aggregation and the various depth modes to control the delete propagation (PtSHALLOW versus PtDEEP gives the equivalent of NO*

ACTION versus CASCADE). These features are completely nonstandard, of course, and you can't use them with any other OODBMS.

Ternary Associations

OODBMS products do not yet support *n*-ary associations as first-class relationships, nor does the ODMG object model give you a way to declare such associations [Cattell and Barry 1997, p. 36]. You must therefore represent such relationships by creating association classes and the consequent binary relationships between the three or more related classes and that class [Jordan 1998, pp. 116–117]. For example, to represent the "plays" relationship in Figure 13-2 in ODL:

```
class Plays (extent PlaysInstances) {
  attribute interval Tenure;
  attribute date StartDate;
  attribute nullable_date EndDate;
  attribute TerminationType TerminationMethod;
  void Terminate(TerminationType method);
  relationship Person aPerson inverse Person::playsRoles;
  relationship Organization anOrganization Role
    inverse Organization::players;
  relationship Role aRole inverse Role::played;
};
```

The three binary relationships represent the three roles as to-one relationships to the association class. For abstract relationships such as "plays," you need to get fairly creative with your naming convention to specify attribute names different from the type names. On the side of the related classes, you have the appropriate collection relationships:

```
class Person (extent People) {
  . . .
  relationship set<Plays> playsRoles
    inverse Plays::aPerson;
};
class Organization (extent Organizations) {
  . . .
  relationship set<Plays> players
    inverse Plays::anOrganization;
};
class Role (extent Roles) {
  . . .
  relationship set<Plays> played
    inverse Plays::aRole;
};
```

The C++ versions of these declarations are straightforward, using the d_Rel_Set template with the types and string constants to hold the inverse names.

Disciplining Your Objects

How objects behave and how to constrain that behavior is both straightforward and very different from relational tables and object-relational types.

Behavioral Problems

The clearest difference between the direction of most RDBMS vendors and OODBMS products is the location of the behavior of the system. OODBMS products locate the behavior in the client in all but a few cases. When you define a method in a class, you are coding a program that runs in the client process rather than on the server. This makes the OODBMS slightly less flexible than the RDBMS with its stored procedures running on the database server. The job of the OODBMS is to materialize persistent objects in client memory, then let those objects do their job, coordinating through transactions, shared caches, and so on [Jordan 1998].

The advantageous consequence of this approach is the dramatic simplification of the behavioral interface. No longer do you need to worry incessantly about choosing where to execute a procedure. No longer do you need to separate your coding into C++ and stored-procedure programming languages. All you need to do is write your C++ or Java or Visual Basic program in its entirety and let 'er rip. The OODBMS, through *cache activation* (moving objects into cache memory), *pointer swizzling* (transforming references into objects in memory), *pinning* and *unpinning* (holding or freeing objects from the cache), and *concurrency management* (sharing the cache and objects in the database), provides a transparent virtual memory system that serves up objects and lets your client process all their methods.

The dark side to this approach, of course, is that you can no longer distribute behavior to all parts of the system. Simple methods that could run on the database server now cannot, but instead you must retrieve the object across the network and operate on it at the client. This restriction extends to query processing; when you run a query, you are executing behavior on the client application cache, not sending SQL to the server for execution against the shared server cache.

Object databases are thus fat-client systems. With the increasing use of application servers such as CORBA and COM systems, however, this is less of a disadvantage than it might seem. You can construct your OODBMS clients as application servers, with your truly thin clients referring to distributed objects and behavior executing on the pleasingly plump application servers.

Typically, the OODBMS will generate the appropriate factory classes or methods that the application client needs to convert the data from the database into objects with appropriate data structures. These methods should be completely transparent to the database programmer.

The constructors for the objects, on the other hand, are definitely within the realm of programming for the database programmer. The system calls the constructor when you create the object, not when you activate it (retrieve it into the application cache from the database). Constructors thus serve the same purpose for persistent objects that they serve for any object: initialization of data members, creation of nested objects, and any other initial setting up of the object.

Destructors manage memory for persistent objects just as they do for transient objects. This has nothing to do with deleting objects from the database, which you do through the delete_object method on a persistent reference or by deleting a pointer to a persistent object [Cattell and Barry 1997, pp. 140–141]. Various OODBMS implementations have interesting ways of managing locking and deactivation of objects as well as different ways to manage garbage collection of deleted objects in the database. You should definitely spend some time with your target OODBMS documentation to understand the specific relationships between object deletion, object destruction, and object deactivation.

Similarly, most OODBMS products have different ways to create and update objects. The ODMG standard calls for using the overloaded new operator with some additional arguments to support database clustering or creation in a specific database. By specifying the special database d_Database::transient_memory, you can create a persistent object in transient memory, for example. This feature again makes persistence orthogonal to type.

For updates, you need to call a special method, mark_modified(), which tells the OODBMS to lock the object and to update the persistent storage on committing the transaction. Most OODBMS products provide a way to do this automatically, so you usually don't need to worry about it. Worry about it anyway, at least until you understand precisely what your target OODBMS product(s) requires in this regard and what you need to do to be portable among multiple targets [Jordan 1998, pp. 68–69].

Setting Boundaries

Constraining behavior in the OO schema is simple. You write a program to do it. There is no such thing as a database constraint or trigger in the OO schema; it's just another behavior you attach to a class. The OO model thus transforms complex constraints into programming problems rather than database problems. As you would when writing any OO program, you identify the need for constraints in your UML model, then produce the appropriate operations and the calls from specific methods at appropriate times.

For example, if you have a UML constraint on a class that represents a class invariant constraint (a predicate that must always be true for objects of the class), you create a private or protected operation that represents the constraint, then call that operation from any class method that might cause the violation of the constraint. This will usually be a mutator method that changes the class state, or perhaps it might be a verify() method that exposes the class invariant to the clients of the class for testing purposes.

The same approach applies to primary key constraints, as the OODBMS replaces the concept with the idea of object identity. However, as the earlier section "Object Identity" points out, ODL and various OODBMS products give you specific ways to implement key constraints, both primary and candidate varieties.

More complex constraints that exist across classes in the database may require separate manager classes that enforce the constraint on the objects they own.

Objective Language

This section summarizes how you can create an object-oriented schema using the ODMG standard. The structure and language of this section mirrors the similar section in Chapter 11, "The Language of Peace." You should consult Chapter 11 for examples and details on the relational transformations and compare them to the more straightforward OO transformations here. The transformation process uses the example data model from Figures 13-1 through 13-3.

You create an object-oriented schema in two basic steps: creating classes from persistent types and creating classes for many-to-many and ternary associations. This section guides you through a complete transformation, connecting everything previously discussed into a transformational whole. You should see by the end of this chapter that the transformation from a UML design into an OO schema is much easier than for a relational or object-relational schema. Nevertheless, there is still some effort involved because of the limitations of the ODL and the programming-language-specific schema definition bindings of OODBMS products.

Persistent Classes and Interfaces

As the first transformation, create a persistent ODL or C++ class for each class in your UML data model that has the «persistent» stereotype, including association classes and classes that inherit from other classes. Name the class with the name of the UML class. From Figure 13-1, the Person subsystem, you create 10 classes: Person, Address, Identification, ExpiringID, DriverLicense, Passport, NationalID, LawEnforcementID, SocialSecurityCard, and BirthCertificate.

If there are any interfaces in your UML diagrams, create an ODL interface or C++ class for each one. If you're using the Java binding, you should transform the UML interface directly into a Java interface; otherwise, just transform it into a class.

For each attribute in the attribute section of the UML class, add an attribute to the class. As an example, for Address, add StreetNumber, StreetFraction, StreetName, StreetSuffix, Locator, City, State, PostalCode, Country, and Comment. ODL interfaces have attributes and relationships, but all this means is that you need to generate get and set methods. Interfaces do not have state and hence do not have actual data members for the attributes and relationships.

You should at this point have a transformation map that shows how to transform each data type in your data model into an ODL data type. These data types include the literal and structured types (value-based data), embedded or referenced objects (object IDs), and collections (multiple object IDs). If your UML diagram uses the ODL types, the ODMG standard provides mapping tables to the main OO programming languages [Cattell and Barry 1997]. If you have defined UML types, use the typedef and enum type declaration keywords to declare subtypes and enumerated types.

Because the C++-based OODBMS gives each persistent object identity, you don't create a primary key or candidate keys for the C++ class. Instead, you must enforce any {OID} or {alternate OID} tags as constraints using the key or unique index feature if it exists (see the "Object Identity" section) or with methods if it doesn't. You place these methods on classes that aggregate the extent of the class. If you have no such transient class, put the method on the class itself as a static member (a class-level member in UML terms). Treat the constraint as a class invariant to be checked in every method that changes objects or adds objects.

ODL uses the key specification to transform the {OID} or {alternate OID} attributes into a primary key for a class. You can also use this to define alternate (candidate) keys. BadgeNumber, for example, is an alternate key for the LawEnforcementID. You could therefore define an ODL class that specifies the key:

```
class LawEnforcementID extends Identification
    (extent LawEnforcementIDs key BadgeNumber) {
  attribute unsigned long BadgeNumber;
};
```

You can have as many keys as you like for the class.

If you are using C++, or if you choose not to use the ODL key specification, you have to enforce {OID} and {alternate OID} constraints through operations that enforce uniqueness on the extent of the class. Such an operation would be a static method in a persistent C++ declaration on the class.

```
static void CheckUniqueBadgeNumbers() const; // C++ version
```

Alternatively, if you have some kind of aggregate abstraction that represents the extent of the class, such as a cache or other collection, you can put the method on that class along with the add and remove methods that manipulate the class extent.

The end result for this stage for the Address table looks like this in a C++ POET definition:

```
persistent class Address {
  long StreetNumber;
  string StreetFraction;
  string StreetName;
  string StreetSuffix;
  string City;
  string State;
  string PostalCode;
  string Country;
  string Comment;
public:
  // Constructor
  Address();
  // Destructor
  virtual ~Address();
  // Uses memberwise copy constructor, assignment
  // Accessors
  virtual string GetStreetAddress() const; // constructs string
  virtual const string & GetCity() const;
  virtual const string & GetState() const;
  virtual const string & GetPostalCode() const;
  virtual const string & GetCountry() const;
  virtual const string & GetComment() const;
  // Mutators
  virtual void SetStreetAddress(long number,
                                const string & fraction,
                                const string & name,
                                const string & suffix);
  virtual void SetCity(const string & city);
  virtual void SetState(const string & state);
  virtual void SetPostalCode(const string & code);
  virtual void SetCountry(const string & country);
  virtual void SetComment(const string & comment);
};
```

If you did this in ODL, the appearance is slightly different:

```
class Address (extent Addresses) {
  attribute long StreetNumber;
  attribute string StreetFraction;
  attribute string StreetName;
  attribute string StreetSuffix;
  attribute string City;
  attribute string State;
  attribute string PostalCode;
  attribute string Country;
  attribute string Comment;
  // Accessors
  string GetStreetAddress(); // constructs string
  // Mutators
  void SetStreetAddress(in unsigned long number,
                        in string       fraction,
                        in string       name,
                        in string       suffix);
};
```

If there is a {nullable} tag on an attribute with an atomic literal type, and you're using ODL specifications, use the nullable versions of the types (nullable_string, for example, or nullable_long). This does not apply to enums or structured types, which cannot be null. If you're using C++, you can't represent nulls at all, since C++ doesn't have any concept of null value. If you're desperate to have nulls anyway, you can code wrappers that add null-value handling to your classes, though this increases complexity considerably.

If a class inherits from another class or set of classes, include a superclass specification in the class definition. In C++ this is usually a ": public <superclass" clause. In ODL, you use the extends keyword.

An ODL declaration for the LawEnforcementID subclass of Identification looks like this:

```
class LawEnforcementID extends Identification
    (extent LawEnforcementIDs) {
  attribute unsigned long BadgeNumber;
};
```

Alternatively, in C++ the LawEnforcementID class looks like this:

```
persistent class LawEnforcementID : public Identification {
  unsigned long BadgeNumber;
public:
  // Constructor
  BadgeNumber();
```

```
// Destructor
virtual ~BadgeNumber();
// Memberwise copy constructor and assignment operator
// Accessors
virtual unsigned long GetBadgeNumber() const;
// Mutators
virtual void SetBadgeNumber(unsigned long number);
};
```

Association classes represent associations with attributes, many-to-many associations, and *n*-ary associations that link two or more classes together. The association class contains associations to the linked classes using the appropriate collections to represent multiplicity (more on this later when you transform associations). For now, create a class that contains the association class attributes:

```
class Plays {
    attribute interval           tenure;
    attribute date               startDate;
    attribute date               endDate;
    attribute TerminationMethod termMethod;
    void terminate(in TerminationMethod method);
};
```

The actual relationships will come later, when you consider the associations to the classes.

Now add any simple class-invariant constraints to the classes and interfaces. If there are constraint boxes in the diagram, convert them into class-level (static) operations.

Now it's time to look at the binary associations. If an association has an association class, ignore the association for now. Create a relationship member for the other associations in each of the associated classes and specify the inverse clause with the name of the relationship in the other class. If the association is directed (an arrow on one side), create the relationship member only on the target class (no inverse clause on that relationship or reciprocal relationship in the other class). For the to-one side, create a simple identifier relationship. For the to-many side, create a collection-class relationship of the appropriate type. If you have a many-to-many relationship, you will have collection relationships in both classes.

> *Note: There are other possibilities, but using a bidirectional relationship is generally better. Consult the section "Associations" for a detailed discussion of all the possibilities for association transformations.*

The many-to-many association in Figure 13-1 between Address and Person looks like this in ODL (with class details suppressed for clarity):

```
class Address (extent Addresses) {
  . . .
  relationship set<Person> residents
    inverse Person::addresses;
}:
class Person (extent People) {
  . . .
  relationship set<Address> addresses
    inverse Address::residents;
};
```

For associations with association classes, treat the relationships not as direct relationships between related classes but as relationships to the association class. For example, if you added an association class to Figure 13-1 for the many-to-many association between people and addresses (PersonAddress), you would define the three classes with relationships in ODL in this way (with class details suppressed for clarity):

```
class PersonAddress (extent PeoplesAddresses) {
  attribute date startDate;
  attribute date endDate;
  relationship Person aPerson inverse Person::addresses;
  relationship Address anAddress inverse Address::residents;
};
class Address (extent Addresses) {
  . . .
  relationship set<PersonAddress> residents
    inverse PersonAddress::anAddress;
}:
class Person (extent People) {
  . . .
  relationship set<PersonAddress> addresses
    inverse PersonAddress::aPerson;
};
```

You must use this approach to represent *n*-ary associations, since you cannot directly relate more than two classes in a single relationship. The ODL for the ternary Plays association and its associated classes looks like this (with class details suppressed for clarity):

```
class Person (extent People) {
  . . .
  relationship set<Plays> playsRoles
    inverse Plays::aPerson;
};
```

```
class Organization (extent Organizations) {
  . . .
  relationship set<Plays> players
    inverse Plays::anOrganization;
};
class Role (extent roles) {
  . . .
  relationship set<Plays> played
    inverse Plays::aRole;
};
class Plays {
  attribute interval        Tenure;
  attribute date            StartDate;
  attribute date            EndDate;
  attribute TerminationType TerminationMethod;
  void terminate(in TerminationType method);
  relationship Person aPerson inverse Person::playsRoles;
  relationship Organization anOrganization Role
 inverse Organization::players;
  relationship Role aRole inverse Role::played;
};
```

For composite aggregations with only one object being aggregated, you should consider the alternative of embedding the object in the type rather than creating a relationship. If the composite aggregates multiple objects, you can represent this as a collection of child objects instead of a collection-based relationship. Using an attribute specification instead of a relationship specification expresses the strong ownership of the composite aggregation association. It does not, however, provide support for the inverse relationship.

For example, in Figure 13-1 there is a composite aggregation between Person and Identification. You can use the relationship approach, but in this case a collection attribute would be better:

```
class Person (extent People) {
  . . .
  attribute set<Identification> IDs;
};
```

The attribute does not have an inverse, so the Identification class knows nothing about its containing parent object, a Person object. If for some reason you must navigate from an Identification object to its owning Person, then use a relationship with an inverse instead of an attribute.

So much for state. What about behavior?

Operations

To represent operations in an OODBMS, create a member operation for each operation you've defined in the data model. As an example, consider the CriminalOrganization class from Figure 13-2. That class exports two operations: UpdateStatus and SetPriority, both "mutators" that change the state of a particular criminal organization object. In this case, we have two requirements: enumerated data types and updating the current object. The enumerated types are UML type classifiers that you have already transformed into ODL or C++ enum type declarations. You then need to add the operations to the ODL class and then implement the corresponding methods in the body of the class in a separate C++ file.

The ODL (or Java) interface provides a somewhat different problem. The interface is a specification of abstract behavior with no implementation or state. When you transform a UML interface into an ODL interface, you just declare the operations; there is no body file or method implementation. Instead, you add the operations to classes that realize the interface and implement them there.

You usually need to pay special attention to the constructors and destructor for each class. Ensure that the constructor sets up everything required. In the destructor, ensure that you remove any transient or persistent objects from memory. You will also find that most OODBMS products provide a set of operations on each persistent object, usually through inheritance from some root persistent object type.

Since there is no standard for creating or deleting objects from the persistent store [Cattell and Barry 1997, p. 55], each OODBMS provides its own methods for creating new objects and for deleting them when you're finished with them.

The OODBMS creates transient objects from persistent objects through special factory classes or methods that the system generates as part of the schema generation process. These factories do the translation from persistent to transient, then call your constructor to handle any transient setup required.

Removing persistent objects from memory and removing them from the database are completely separate things. Just as in a relational database, you need to decide where to put the deletion behavior and its accompanying propagation to objects that a deleted object owns. In some cases the OODBMS provides a special operation, such as delete_object in the C++ ODMG binding. You call this operation on the objects the deleted object owns, then call the operation on the object you are deleting. In other cases, this may happen automatically, as with the Java ODMG binding, which removes objects from the database when your system no

Table 13-1   *Summary of Object-Oriented Schema Transformation*

Step	Transformation
1	UML «persistent» class becomes OODBMS persistent class.
2	UML interface that a «persistent» class realizes becomes an OODBMS interface for languages that support interfaces (Java, ODL) or an abstract base class with only pure virtual members and no data members for those languages that don't have interfaces (C++, Smalltalk).
3	UML type classifier becomes enum or typedef as indicated.
4	UML attribute in class becomes attribute in OODBMS class with appropriate type transformations and restrictions.
5	Use nullable literal type (nullable_short, for example) if {nullable} tag appears and the binding you're using supports null values (ODL); otherwise, ignore it (C++, Java).
6	If UML attribute has initializer, add initialization code to constructor, either as part of the constructor method or in a C++ member initialization list.
7	For subclasses, include the superclass specification in the class declaration.
8	For association classes, create a class with the attributes of the association class.
9	For explicit object identity {oid} or candidate key {alternate oid}, specify a key declaration if your binding supports it (C++ does not, for example). If not, supply appropriate methods for checking uniqueness constraints on sets of objects.
10	Add a method to the appropriate class for each explicit constraint and ensure that the system calls that method whenever the system requires that the constraint is satisfied.
11	Create a relationship for each binary association that has no association class with the appropriate object or collection type deriving from the multiplicities of the association. Use inverse relationships unless there are explicit arrows on the association (and even then, consider it anyway).
12	Create a relationship in association classes for each role link to another class.
13	Create code or use OODBMS features to propagate deletes for any composite aggregation associations as your particular OODBMS requires.
14	Create an association class for ternary associations and create relationships from the association class to the associated classes with the appropriate data types given the multiplicities.

longer refers to them (automatic garbage collection). You usually add some kind of delete operation on the class that propagates the deletion.

Again, the OODBMS does not store or execute the operations. All behavior in an object database happens on the client, whether it is an application server, a thick-client application, or a Web browser applet.

Summary

For convenience, Table 13-1 summarizes the transformation to an OODBMS. This table is very different from Table 11-4, which describes the relational transformation, or Table 12-1, which describes the object-relational transformation. Though the basic structure is similar, the details are completely different.

Object-oriented databases give you a very different way of looking at object persistence and schema design. The design issues are the same: class structure, association structure, behavior, and constraints. You be the judge of whether the OO path for managing data is more transparent and productive than the relational or object-relational paths.

> *Tip: I've found it best to use an OODBMS for systems that either benefit dramatically from navigational, as opposed to ad hoc query, access or that are primarily object storage facilities rather than enterprise systems with many different applications in a variety of languages. For example, if your system is a C++ program that uses the database to store and retrieve objects into a shared application server, you should use an OODBMS. If your system is a large collection of Visual Basic, C++, and Developer/2000 programs with three or four different kinds of report writers and query tools, you should use an RDBMS or possibly an ORDBMS.*

You have now seen the basics of database design using UML as represented by the three major kinds of databases on the market. Your job as a database designer is to choose the right one for your needs based on the UML data models you construct. Complex or simple, the art of database design is still an art, not a science. Choose the right muse, and the database gods will smile on you.

Sherlock Holmes Story References

The following notations are used for Sherlock Holmes story references:

BLUE	The Adventure of the Blue Carbuncle
BRUC	The Adventure of the Bruce-Partington Plans
EMPT	The Adventure of the Empty House
ENGR	The Adventure of the Engineer's Thumb
FINA	The Final Problem
FIVE	The Five Orange Pips
HOUN	The Hound of the Baskervilles
IDEN	A Case of Identity
LION	The Adventure of the Lion's Mane
MISS	The Adventure of the Missing Three-Quarter
MUSG	The Musgrave Ritual
PRIO	The Adventure of the Priory School
REDC	The Adventure of the Red Circle
SCAN	A Scandal in Bohemia
SILV	Silver Blaze
STUD	A Study in Scarlet
SUSS	The Adventure of the Sussex Vampire
THOR	The Problem of Thor Bridge
TWIS	The Man with the Twisted Lip
VALL	The Valley of Fear
VEIL	The Adventure of the Veiled Lodger

Bibliography

American National Standards Institute. 1975. ANSI/X3/SPARC Study Group on Data Base Management Systems; Interim Report. *FDT (Bulletin of ACM SIGMOD)* 7:2.

American National Standards Institute. 1992. *American National Standard for Information Systems—Database Language—SQL.* ANSI X3.135–1992. New York: American National Standards Institute.

Baarns Consulting Group Inc. 1997. Frequently asked questions, DAO-ODBCDirect. *www.baarns.com/access/faq/ad_DAO.asp,* accessed on October 26, 1997.

Beizer, Boris. 1984. *Software System Testing and Quality Assurance.* New York: Van Nostrand Reinhold.

Berson, Alex. 1992. *Client/Server Architecture.* New York: McGraw-Hill.

Blaha, Michael R., William J. Premerlani, and James E. Rumbaugh. 1988. Relational database design using an object-oriented methodology. *Communications of the ACM* 31 (4): 414–427.

Blaha, Michael R., and William Premerlani. 1998. *Object-Oriented Modeling and Design for Database Applications.* Upper Saddle River, NJ: Prentice Hall.

Booch, Grady. 1994. *Object-Oriented Analysis and Design with Applications, Second Edition.* Reading, MA: Addison-Wesley.

Booch, Grady. 1996. *Object Solutions: Managing the Object-Oriented Project.* Reading, MA: Addison-Wesley.

Borges, Jorge Luis. 1962. The library of Babel. In *Labyrinths: Selected Stories and Other Writings,* edited by Donald A. Yates and James E. Irby, pp. 51–58. New York: New Directions Publishing.

Bruce, Thomas A. 1992. *Designing Quality Databases with IDEF1X Information Models.* New York: Dorset House.

Buchmann, Alejandro M., Tamer Özsu, Mark Hornick, Dimitrios Georgakopoulos, and Frank A. Manola. 1991. A transaction model for active distributed object systems. In [Elmagarmid 1991], pp. 123–158.

Cattell, R. G. G. and Douglas Barry, editors. 1997. *Object Database Standard: ODMG 2.0.* San Francisco: Morgan Kaufmann.

Chamberlin, Don. 1998. *A Complete Guide to DB2 Universal Database.* San Francisco: Morgan Kaufmann.

Chappell, David. 1996. *Understanding ActiveX and OLE: A Guide for Managers and Developers.* Redmond, WA: Microsoft Press.

Chen, Peter Pin-Shan. 1976. The entity-relationship model—Toward a unified view of data. *ACM Transactions on Database Systems* 1 (1): 9–36.

Chidamber, S. R. and C. K. Kemerer. 1993. A metrics suite for object-oriented design. Working Paper #249. Cambridge, MA: MIT Center for Information Systems Research.

Codd, E. F. 1970. A relational model of data for large shared data banks. *Communications of the ACM* 13 (6): 377–387.

Codd, E. F. 1972. Further normalization of the database relational model. In *Data Base Systems.* Englewood Cliffs, NJ: Prentice Hall.

Codd, E. F. 1990. *The Relational Model for Database Management: Version 2.* Reading, MA: Addison-Wesley.

Conference on Data Systems Languages, Data Base Task Group (CODASYL DBTG). 1971. *CODASYL DBTG April 71 Report.* New York: Association for Computing Machinery.

Date, C. J. 1977. *An Introduction to Database Systems, Second Edition.* Reading, MA: Addison-Wesley.

Date, C. J. 1983. *An Introduction to Database Systems, Volume II.* Reading, MA: Addison-Wesley.

Date, C. J. 1986. *Relational Database: Selected Writings.* Reading, MA: Addison-Wesley.

Date, C. J. 1995. *An Introduction to Database Systems, Sixth Edition.* Reading, MA: Addison-Wesley.

Date, C. J. 1997a. The normal is so . . . interesting. *Database Programming and Design* 10 (11): 23–25.

Date, C. J. 1997b. The normal is so . . . interesting (Part 2 of 2). *Database Programming and Design* 10 (12): 23–24.

Date, C. J. 1998a. The final normal form! (Part 1 of 2). *Database Programming and Design* 11 (1): 69–71.

Date, C. J. 1998b. The final normal form! (Part 2 of 2). *Database Programming and Design* 11 (2): 59–61.

Date, C. J. and Hugh Darwen. 1998. *Foundation for Object/Relational Databases: The Third Manifesto.* Reading, MA: Addison-Wesley.

Diamond, Jared. 1997. *Guns, Germs, and Steel: The Fates of Human Societies.* New York: W. W. Norton.

Dörner, Dietrich. 1996. *The Logic of Failure: Why Things Go Wrong and What We Can Do to Make Them Right.* New York: Metropolitan Books. Originally published in German in 1989.

Douglass, Bruce P. 1998. *Real-Time UML: Developing Efficient Objects for Embedded Systems.* Reading, MA: Addison-Wesley.

Dreger, J. Brian. 1989. *Function Point Analysis.* Englewood Cliffs, NJ: Prentice Hall.

Dutka, Alan F. and Howard H. Hanson. 1989. *Fundamentals of Data Normalization.* Reading, MA: Addison-Wesley.

Elmagarmid, Ahmed K., editor. 1991. *Database Transaction Models for Advanced Applications.* San Mateo, CA: Morgan Kaufmann.

Eriksson, Hans-Erik and Magnus Penker. 1997. *UML Toolkit.* New York: John Wiley and Sons.

Everest, G. C. 1986. *Database Management: Objectives, System Functions, and Administration.* New York: McGraw-Hill.

Fagin, Ronald. 1979. Normal forms and relational database operators. *Proceedings of the 1979 ACM SIGMOD International Conference on Management of Data.* May/June.

Fagin, Ronald. 1981. A normal form for relational databases that is based on domains and keys. *ACM Transactions on Database Systems* 6 (3): 387–415.

Feldman P., and D. Miller. 1986. Entity model clustering: Structuring a data model by abstraction. *Computer Journal* 29 (4): 348–360.

Fenton, Norman E. and Shari Lawrence Pfleeger. 1997. *Software Metrics: A Rigorous and Practical Approach, Second Edition.* New York: International Thompson Computer Press.

Fleming, Candace C. and Barbara von Halle. 1989. *Handbook of Relational Database Design.* Reading, MA: Addison-Wesley.

Fowler, Martin. 1997. *Analysis Patterns: Reusable Object Models.* Reading, MA: Addison-Wesley.

Fowler, Martin, Ivar Jacobson, and Scott Kendall. 1997. *UML Distilled: Applying the Standard Object Modeling Language.* Reading, MA: Addison-Wesley.

Freedman, Daniel P. and Gerald M. Weinberg. 1990. *Handbook of Walkthroughs, Inspections, and Technical Reviews: Evaluating Programs, Projects, and Products, Third Edition.* New York: Dorset House.

Fuller, Edmund, editor. 1966. *Hamlet.* New York: Dell.

Gamma, Erich, Richard Helm, Ralph Johnson, and John Vlissides. 1995. *Design Patterns: Elements of Reusable Object-Oriented Software.* Reading, MA: Addison-Wesley.

Garmus, David and David Herron. 1996. *Managing the Software Process: A Practical Guide to Functional Measurements.* Englewood Cliffs, NJ: Prentice Hall.

Gause, Donald C. and Gerald M. Weinberg. 1989. *Exploring Requirements: Quality Before Design.* New York: Doret House.

Goldberg, Adele and Kenneth S. Rubin. 1995. *Succeeding with Objects: Decision Frameworks for Project Management.* Reading, MA: Addison-Wesley.

Gray, James N. and A. Reuter. 1993. *Transaction Processing: Concepts and Techniques.* San Francisco: Morgan Kaufmann.

Grimes, Richard. 1997. *Professional DCOM Programming with CD.* Olton, Birmingham, England: Wrox Press.

Groff, James R. and Paul N. Weinberg. 1994. *LAN Times Guide to SQL.* Berkeley, CA: Osborne/McGraw-Hill.

GUIDE International. 1997. GUIDE Business Rules Project. *Final Report.* Version 1.2. October. Chicago: GUIDE International. *www.guide.org/ap/apbrules.htm* (accessed July 24, 1998).

Halpin, Terry. 1995. *Conceptual Schema and Relational Database Design.* Sydney, Australia: Prentice Hall Australia.

Harmon, Paul and Mark Watson. 1998. *Understanding UML: The Developer's Guide, with a Web-Based Application in Java.* San Francisco: Morgan Kaufmann.

Hay, David C. 1996. *Data Model Patterns: Conventions of Thought.* New York: Dorset House.

Henderson-Sellers, Brian. 1996. *Object-Oriented Metrics: Measures of Complexity.* Englewood Cliffs, NJ: Prentice Hall.

Hohmann, Luke. 1997. *Journey of the Software Professional: A Sociology of Software Development.* Englewood Cliffs, NJ: Prentice Hall.

International Function Point Users' Group (IFPUG). 1994. *Function Point Counting Practices Manual, Release 4.0.* Westerville, OH: IFPUG. *www.ifpug.org.*

International Standards Organization (ISO). 1997. *Database Language SQL—Part 2: Foundation (SQL/Foundation).* September. Accessed on May 27, 1998, at *ftp://jerry.ece.umassd.edu/isowg3/dbl/BASEdocs/public/.*

Jacobson, Ivar, Magnus Christerson, Patrik Jonsson, and Gunnar Overgaard. 1992. *Object-Oriented Software Engineering: A Use Case Driven Approach.* Reading, MA: Addison-Wesley.

Jepson, Brian. 1996. *Java Database Programming.* New York: John Wiley and Sons.

Jones, Capers. 1991. *Applied Software Measurement: Assuring Productivity and Quality.* New York: McGraw-Hill.

Jordan, David. 1997. *C++ Object Databases: Programming with the ODMG Standard.* Reading, MA: Addison-Wesley.

Karlsson, Even-André, editor. 1996. *Software Reuse: A Holistic Approach.* New York: John Wiley and Sons.

Kent, William. 1983. A simple guide to five normal forms in relational database theory. *Communications of the ACM* 26 (2): 120–125.

Koch, George and Kevin Loney. 1997. *Oracle8: The Complete Reference.* Berkeley, CA: Oracle Press/Osborne-McGraw-Hill.

Koch, George and Kevin Loney. 1998. *Oracle8: The Complete Reference.* Berkeley, CA: Oracle Press.

Kung, H. T. and J. T. Robinson. 1981. On optimistic methods for concurrency control. *ACM Transactions on Database Systems* 6 (2): 213–226.

Larman, Craig. 1997. *Applying UML and Patterns: An Introduction to Object-Oriented Analysis and Design.* Englewood Cliffs, NJ: Prentice Hall.

Lassesen, Ken. 1995. Mapping the Data Access Object: DAO 3.0. *www.eu.microsoft.com/oledev/olemap/mapdao30.htm.* October 11, 1995. Accessed on October 26, 1997.

Leach. Paul J. and Rich Salz. 1997. UUIDs and GUIDs. Internet Engineering Task Force Internet-Draft Memo. *www.camb.org/tech/dce/info/ietf-draft.txt.* February 24, 1997. Accessed on April 22, 1998.

Lee, Sing. 1997. *Professional Visual C++ ActiveX/COM Control Programming.* Olton, Birmingham, England: Wrox Press.

Lieberherr, K., I. Holland, and A. Riel. 1988. Object-oriented programming: an objective sense of style. *OOPSLA 1988 (SIGPLAN)* 23 (1): 323–334.

Logic Works, Inc. 1996. *ERwin Methods Guide.* Princeton, NJ: Logic Works.

McCabe, T. J. and C. W. Butler. 1989. Design complexity measurement and testing. *Communications of the ACM* 32 (12): 1415–1425.

McNally, John. 1997. *Informix Unleashed.* Indianapolis, IN: SAMS Publishing.

Melton, Jim and Alan R. Simon. 1993. *Understanding the New SQL: A Complete Guide.* San Francisco: Morgan Kaufmann.

Melton, Jim. 1998. SQL3 moves forward. *Database Programming and Design* 11 (6): 63–66.

Mowbray, Thomas J. and Ron Zahavi. 1995. *The Essential CORBA: Systems Integration Using Distributed Objects.* New York: John Wiley and Sons.

Muller, Pierre-Alain. 1997. *Instant UML.* Olton, Birmingham, England: Wrox Press.

Muller, Robert J. 1982. *Data Organization: The Integration of Database Management, Data Analysis, and Software Technology Applied to the National Crime Survey.* Ph.D. dissertation, Massachusetts Institute of Technology.

Muller, Robert J. 1996. Testing object-oriented software: A hierarchical approach. Paper given at the Ninth International Software Quality Week Conference in San Francisco, May 21–24. Available from the author.

Muller, Robert J., Janice Nygard, and Paula Crnkovic. 1997. Driving system testing with use cases. *Conference Proceedings of the Sixth International Conference on Software Testing, Analysis and Review.* May 5–9, San Jose, CA. Jacksonville, FL: Software Quality Engineering.

Muller, Robert J. 1998. *Productive Objects: An Applied Software Project Management Framework.* San Francisco: Morgan Kaufmann.

O'Day, Dan. 1998. This old house. *IEEE Software* 15 (2): 72–75.

Object Data Management Group. 1998. Home Page. *www.odmg.org.* Accessed on July 16, 1998.

Open Group. 1997. The Open Group Architectural Framework—Version 3. *www.opengroup.org/architecture* (accessed December 12, 1998). Cambridge, MA: The Open Group.

Oracle Corporation. 1997a. *Oracle8 Spatial Cartridge User's Guide and Reference.* Release 8.0.4. Redwood Shores, CA: Oracle Corporation.

Oracle Corporation. 1997b. *Oracle8 Visual Information Retrieval Cartridge User's Guide.* Release 1.0.1. Redwood Shores, CA: Oracle Corporation.

Oracle Corporation. 1997c. *Oracle8 Application Developer's Guide.* Release 8.0. Redwood Shores, CA: Oracle Corporation.

Oracle Corporation. 1997d. *Oracle8 SQL Reference.* Release 8.0. Redwood Shores, CA: Oracle Corporation.

Osgood, Charles E., George J. Suci, and Percy H. Tannenbaum. 1957. *The Measurement of Meaning.* Champaign, IL: University of Illinois Press.

Papadimitriou, Christos. 1986. *The Theory of Database Concurrency Control.* New York: W. H. Freeman.

POET Software. 1997a. *POET C++ SDK Programmer's Guide.* Version 5.0. San Mateo, CA: POET Software Corporation.

POET Software. 1997b. *POET ODL Compiler Reference Guide.* Hamburg, Germany: POET Software Corporation.

Quatrani, Terry. 1997. *Visual Modeling with Rational Rose and UML.* Reading, MA: Addison-Wesley.

Rational Software Corporation. 1997a. *UML Notation Guide, Version 1.1.* Santa Clara, CA: Rational Software Corporation. *www.rational.com.*

Rational Software Corporation. 1997b. *UML Semantics, Version 1.1.* Santa Clara, CA: Rational Software Corporation. *www.rational.com.*

Rational Software Corporation. 1997c. *UML Object Constraint Language Specification, Version 1.1.* Santa Clara, CA: Rational Software Corporation. *www.rational.com.*

Roberts, Fred S. 1979. *Measurement Theory with Applications to Decisionmaking, Utility, and the Social Sciences.* Encyclopedia of Mathematics and Its Applications, Volume 7. Reading, MA: Addison-Wesley.

Rumbaugh, James, Michael Blaha, William Premerlani, Frederick Eddy, and William Lorensen. 1992. *Object-Oriented Modeling and Design.* Englewood Cliffs, NJ: Prentice Hall.

Russell, Bertrand. 1956. *Portraits from Memory.* New York: Simon and Schuster. As quoted in [Weinberg and Weinberg 1988, pp. 8–9].

Schneidewind, Norman F. 1998. How to evaluate legacy system maintenance. *IEEE Software* 15 (4): 34–42.

Shlaer, Sally and Stephen Mellor. 1988. *Object-Oriented Systems Analysis: Modeling the World in Data.* Englewood Cliffs, NJ: Yourdon Press.

Siegel, Jon, editor. 1996. *CORBA Fundamentals and Programming.* New York: John Wiley and Sons.

Siegel, Shel and Robert J. Muller. 1996. *Object-Oriented Software Testing: A Hierarchical Approach.* New York: John Wiley and Sons.

Signore, Robert, John Creamer, and Michael O. Stegman. 1995. *The ODBC Solution: Open Database Connectivity in Distributed Environments.* New York: McGraw-Hill.

Silverston, Len, W. H. Inmon, and Kent Graziano. 1997. *The Data Model Resource Book: A Library of Logical Data Models and Data Warehouse Designs.* New York: John Wiley and Sons.

Simons, Robert. 1997. Control in an age of empowerment. *IEEE Engineering Management Review* 25 (2): 106–112. Reprinted from the *Harvard Business Review,* March–April, 1995.

Soley, Richard M., editor. 1992. *Object Management Architecture Guide, Second Edition.* OMG TC Document 92.11.1. Framingham, MA: Object Management Group.

Stonebraker, Michael, and Paul Brown with Dorothy Moore. 1999. *Object-Relational DBMSs: Tracking the Next Great Wave, Second Edition.* San Francisco: Morgan Kaufmann.

Teorey, Toby J. 1999. *Database Modeling and Design, Third Edition.* San Francisco: Morgan Kaufmann.

Teorey, Toby J., Dongqing Yang, and James P. Fry. 1986. A logical design methodology for relational databases using the extended entity-relationship model. *Computing Surveys* 18 (2): 198–222.

Texel, Putnam and Charles Williams. 1997. *Use Cases Combined with Booch/OMT/UML: Process and Products.* Englewood Cliffs, NJ: Prentice Hall.

Ullman, Jeffrey D. 1988. *Principles of Database and Knowledge-Based Systems, Volume I.* New York: W. H. Freeman.

Ullman, Jeffrey D. 1989. *Principles of Database and Knowledge-Based Systems, Volume II: The New Technologies.* New York: W. H. Freeman.

Vaughan-Nichols, Steven J., compiler. 1997. Microsoft COMing forward. In Executive Briefs. *Object Magazine* 7 (8): 7.

Weinberg, Gerald M. 1982. *Rethinking Systems Analysis and Design.* Boston: Little, Brown and Co.

Weinberg, Gerald M. and Daniela Weinberg. 1988. *General Principles of Systems Design.* New York: Dorset House.

Weinberg, Gerald M. 1992. *Quality Software Management, Volume 1: Systems Thinking.* New York: Dorset House.

Yourdon, Ed and Larry Constantine. 1979. *Structured Design.* Englewood Cliffs, NJ: Prentice Hall.

Index